THE QABALA TRILOGY

The Qabala Trilogy

The Cipher of Genesis
The Song of Songs
The Sepher Yetsira

Carlo Suarès

SHAMBHALA
Boston & London
1985

SHAMBHALA PUBLICATIONS, INC.
314 Dartmouth Street
Boston, Massachusetts 02116

9 8 7 6 5 4 3 2 1
First Edition
Printed in the United States of America
Distributed in the United States by Random House
and in Canada by Random House of Canada Ltd.

Library of Congress Cataloging in Publication Data
Suarès. Carlo.
    The Qabala Trilogy.
    Contents: The Cipher of Genesis — The Song of Songs
— The Sepher Yetsira.
    1. Cabala. 2. Bible. O.T. Genesis—Miscellanea.
3. Bible. O.T. Song of Solomon—Commentaries.
4. Sefer Yezirah. 5. Astrology, Jewish. I. Title.
BM525.S89 1985   296.1'6   85-8179
ISBN 0-87773-337-6 (pbk.)
ISBN 0-394-74220-6 (Random House : pbk.)

Contents

Book I: *The Cipher of Genesis*

PART THREE
THE GOSPELS

Book II: *The Song of Songs*

Book III: *The Sepher Yetsira*

PART ONE
THE PRIMARY ELEMENTS

PART TWO
THE TEXT

PART THREE
THE ZODIAC

BOOK I

The Cipher of Genesis

THE ORIGINAL CODE
OF THE QABALA
AS APPLIED TO
THE SCRIPTURES

The manuscript has been read and commented upon (in succession) by the following and has benefited by their suggestions and revisions:

Nadine Suarès, Eleanor Foster, Mary Shannon, Ferris and Iris Hartman, George Buchanan, Anne Lindbergh, Humphrey Noyes, Ernest Dale

In acknowledgment and deep gratitude, C.S.

"The heavens themselves, the planets and this centre
Observe degree, priority, and place,
Insisture, course, proportion, season, form,
Office, and custom, in all line of order."

Troilus and Cressida Act 1, Sc. iii

Foreword

CARLO SUARÈS dedicated a great part of his life to unravelling
the revelatory meanings hidden in the code of the Bible. It was,
in fact, forty years before the transcendent truths of the Bible
yielded to his patient perseverance and his unshakable conviction that the original version read in letter-numbers of the
Hebrew alphabet contained the secret of man's transfiguration.

Humphrey Noyes

Introduction

NOT VERY long ago artificial institutions and moral values were the terms for our civilization. Such definitions have gradually revealed their inadequacy in every sphere in the rapidly changing circumstances of our world, and an articulate call for the rediscovery of the sacred fount which is believed to exist in our Scriptures is heard everywhere.

Our many-sided sciences make almost daily discoveries—or inventions—of collaterals which by mere impact of observation acquire the status of distinct branches, thereby splitting further our already scattered body of knowledge. In spite of the increasing hold of mathematics on departments as far apart as optics, philology, biology or ethics, it cannot and will never discover a basic postulate befitting the simultaneous existence of a universe and of man.

Some religiously-minded people are aware of this lack of a unitary way of thought capable of including the knowledge of man and the knowledge of things. Although far too late, they are only just in time to measure, not without some perplexity, the unthought-of distance which separates them from the world as it is.

Like bewildered passengers in a ship astray on uncharted seas, whose call to Saviours is of no avail, we are told to believe in a brotherly huddle, to feed the hungry and clothe the naked as a means of atonement.

Does not the sacred thus humanized fall under Jesus' curse: *Get thee behind me, Satan: thou art an offence to me: for thou savourest not the things that be of God, but those that be of men* (Matt. XVI, 23)?

This emphasizing of "the things that be of man" stressed by

so many churches today—in an attempt to recapture their grip on human affairs—blended with a clinging to obsolete myths does not lead to the sacred fount of revelation and knowledge, but rather to an alienation from it. In order to obviate this estrangement, high authorities have asked learned personalities, priests, monks, ministers, rabbis, to co-operate in retranslating the Bible into different languages. In this connection the most ancient of ancient traditions (the Qabala) cannot but issue a severe warning to those scholars: their monumental task will not lead them any nearer the Source, not only because the Bible is untranslatable but, strange as it may seem, because it is already hopelessly mistranslated in Hebrew.

*

The twenty-two graphs which are used as letters in the Hebrew alphabet are twenty-two proper names originally used to designate different states or structures of the one cosmic energy, which is *essence* and *semblance*, of all that is. Even though they correspond to numbers, symbols and ideas, those twenty-two vastly exceed all the most exhaustive sets of classes: they cannot be distributed among things because they factually *are* that which they designate.

One has to probe very deeply into this semasiology to realize that this last statement does not exceed the limits of truth and need not be a cause of astonishment. We are approaching here a language which is not a by-product of sensorial references, but a would-be transmission from the unknown. Hence the difficulty of explaining it, because of the inability of the human mind to grasp that which is not contained in a frame of recognition.

This present essay is, however, an attempt to overcome that difficulty by suggesting a number of approaches, which, it is hoped, will gradually uncover that which is purported to be rediscovered: the secret and sacred fount lying in the hidden depths of the Bible.

A direct approach would be to introduce immediately the

code with which to decipher the Bible, and to begin with the first schemata of the Genesis: *Bereschyt Barah Elohim* . . . etc. . . . but it is doubtful whether the readers would willingly follow such a plan, without first having found a good reason for so doing. The statement that the twenty-two letters of the Hebrew alphabet are but the initials of names, the meanings of which have been lost throughout the ages, gives rise to such legitimate questions as to *how, whence,* and *why.*

The *why* is simply the fact that the Book of Genesis was originally a cabalistic script. The *whence* is lost in immemorial time, through centuries of history, proto-history, pseudo-history, myths and legends. The *how* is a secretly transmitted tradition the thread of which was never lost and which for many reasons has remained hidden. But things have come to such a point, in our present juncture of historical and psychological events, when it is necessary that it should be revealed, by bestowing its basic key: the code of those names which have been desecrated to the point of being made use of in an alphabet constituted by only their initials. (Whereas our A, B, C, and so on, are mere representations of vocal sounds, the names Aleph, Bayt, Ghimel, etc. are projections of biologically structured energies in different stages of organization.)

The decoding of Genesis and of any other cabalistic text is therefore not a mere matter of transposing from A-B-C to Aleph-Bayt-Ghimel, but a process of penetrating an unknown world by means of a manner of thinking which has to be experienced by the very use of the language which must be learned in order to understand it. However paradoxical and perhaps difficult this may appear, it stands to reason that were the Revelation a matter of ordinary words, it would be an obvious fact prone to superficial observation.

The words we use in our languages are conventional. They do not emanate from the objects which they designate. The word *house* is understood just as well as *maison* in French or *casa* in Italian: none of those words has any ontological link with the essence of the object thus specified, and their use merely helps us to recognize such objects, by means of linguistic agreements.

We come to realize that the problem of conveying the unknown could only be solved if it were possible to project the common essence of everything which is in the universe as a whole (including, of course, Man, because the essence is One). That essence in Man is according to cabalistic postulates a movement both inner and outer, which builds structures and destroys them unceasingly. Our psychological inner structures built with and upon words which never convey the things, but are our ideas of what we recognize their appearances to be, must therefore be atomized, so to speak, in order for us to partake in and commune with the cosmic unfathomable mystery of the one movement, which is life.

There will never be any explanation of why anything exists at all. The dogmas of the beginning of a Creation and a God who creates will never be anything but futile attempts to explain away the mystery which is the totality of time and space and life and, in a word: of being. On that assertion is founded the Qabala.

The Qabala—which among thousands of scripts, includes Genesis and scattered fragments of other biblical sources— stands unremittingly against every projection of thought concerning the essence of life, because projections are but images, symbols and vagrant words. Qabala existed even before Abraham and therefore does not belong to any specific tradition. It is not—as so repeatedly stated by so-called experts—a mysticism or any mysterious system of occultism. It is a way of thinking based on unitive postulates and analogical developments, of which our modern thought can well take advantage. For many centuries it has been the nutritive roots of our civilizations, hidden in the gnostic teachings and in many schools of thought. Whether deliberately ignored or criticized with blatant prejudice, whether feared or laughed at, this vital knowledge and its subdivisions of structures has always been misunderstood. The reason for such constant ostracism will appear only too clearly when this essay is subjected to the criticism of Tradition founded on ecclesiasticism. In spite, however, or *because* of the assertion that the Bible has been, for centuries, and still is being read in a sense contrary to its intent, we trust religious as well as scientific circles to respond to it with interest.

PART ONE

HA-QABALA

Ha-Qabala

FREQUENTLY, OVER the centuries, the Qabala has been lost and rediscovered. Its traces can be found in the period when, back from their captivity in Babylon, the Jews awoke to a new awareness of themselves, with Ezra, Nehemiah and others.

Looking backwards in time, we can see that the Qabala was alive with Mosheh (Moses); going back further, we find it with Abram; in still more remote ages, it disappears from the sight of enquirers, but not from the perception of those who have inherited that most ancient of ancient knowledge. All through history its transmission has been kept secret. The source of the original Qabala can, however, be grasped at any time, because it is timeless. The cabalists have always said that Abram possessed it.

Ab-Ram (the father of Ram, or according to the Semitic expression, "he who possesses" Ram) may have been an initiate of any country from Tibet to Egypt. In Tibet the name Ram expresses the universal essence, in the sense of "basis of the world", and is also sometimes a symbol of all that radiates as the sun. Ram, in ancient Egypt, was also a symbol for the basis of the world, manifested in the pyramids (in Arabic pyramid is Ahram). One of the most important persons in the Egyptian initiatic order was Ram Nak Hotep.

The name Ram is also linked to the Celtic world where, for the Druids, it was the symbol of the universal essence. It was said that those who had pierced the secret of Ram could disregard all the unessentials, retaining only the essential.

In the English sense, "ram", the animal, is found as a symbol in the esoteric teaching of the Prajna-Patis (lords of the Being);

13

it pierces through all that is not essential. Its motto is: "Let us be gods and laugh at ourselves."

According to the original Qabala, Ram expresses the "cosmic dwelling", that is, the whole perceptible extant universe in its capacity for proliferation. And Avram, or Abram, is he who, having gone through the many layers of differentiation, receives the pulsation of life which transfigures that proliferation on a level with cosmic action. In simple words, the action of an Avram in his own house has a cosmic significance.

Abraham was not a believer. He recognized the presence of life as an ally and made with it a covenant. That pact was two-fold: it included (*a*) the Qabala, that is, a direct penetration of knowledge through comprehension, examination, vision and writing, and (*b*) circumcision on the eighth day, that is, direct penetration of vital energy, transmutation of animal sexuality for the benefit of a sensitivity of the entire nervous system awakened and alert.

A few pages will later be devoted to circumcision, one of the keys to the mystery of Israel. I say that there are two keys. One is for the body, the sensory apparatus, the psyche: the circumcision on the eighth day. The other is for the mind, the contained, the human and cosmic germ of life unconditioned, which can only "be" when it is indeterminate: the Qabala.

*

Abram possessed the Qabala as knowledge and as writing. It has been said that the document whereon was inscribed the number-code of that knowledge came from Mount Ararat, where the mythical Noah's Ark had come to rest after the Deluge. Ararat, according to an ancient tradition, is the cabalistic name for a new cycle which comes into being after a long period during which the human germ has not been able to develop. Ararat means that two worlds, the timeless and the measurable (the inner and the outer) were again ready to make a fresh start. They were close together but not in any way re-

14

lated because the earlier human bodies still belonged to the
primitive female.

Noah's consciousness, absorbed by the wine which the female
earth had engendered, had sunk to a low level. The human
germ in evolution had been transferred to Shem, the eponymic
ancestor of the Semites. We must here pass over Shem's ten
symbolic generations and come to old Terahh, Abram's father.
Their marvellous story will be told in its proper place, but we
wish now to mention the place of Abram's birth: Aur Kasdeem,
translated Ur of the Chaldees. Symbolically, according to the
Qabala, it means: the light of the magicians. Aur in Hebrew
means light, and the Kasdeems are the magicians, astrologers,
diviners, who exercised great influence in those times.

The cabalists have always had a horror of the magic of the
Kasdeems. Abram is the beginning of yet another era. With
him, religion begins to free itself from the "light of the magicians", and to direct itself towards the perception of the inner
light of YHWH. In Abram's hand is a marvellous document:
the testament of a lost civilization, brought in the ark.

A few survivors had been able to preserve, in a series of
ideograms, all that men had ever known, all that men will ever
know, concerning the vocation of mankind in the presence of
the impenetrable mystery of being.

Of these survivors, Genesis says (VI, 4) that *the sons of Elohim
came in unto the daughters of men, and they bare children to them.* In
the time of Shem, they had disappeared from memory, but they
had bequeathed their knowledge orally and had entrusted their
precious document to safe hands.

According to the esoteric tradition, Abram was the first
really to understand the deep significance of their message.
The human seed had to disentangle itself from the magic of the
Kasdeem where it was being held in bondage, and had to be
thrust into the world of conflict, of uncertainty, of hope and
utter despair, of wild joy and anguish, of obstinate recon-
structions and impending disasters. Any refuge, any protecting
shelter had to be denied to it because, were it ever to remain

immobile in any peaceful surrounding, it would become static in an immature, pre-human sub-species.

That land of strife and joys and pain is called, symbolically, Canaan. Abram was sent into that land to take root and to conquer.

The biblical narrative, from there on, is a vast epic poem where all the themes of the myth reappear in a common adventure through such names as Abraham and Sarah, Isaac and Rebecca, Jacob, Leah, Rachel, Esau, etc.

The subject of that epic poem is the description of the implanting of the human seed in the symbolical Canaan, or, on another level, it shows how duality is conquered by the three-fold movement of life, in humanity-to-be.

Abram becomes Abraham, and he transmits the Qabala to his son Isaac. Isaac gives it eventually to Jacob; and Jacob, disappointed by most of his sons, chooses as the heir to that knowledge his eleventh son, Yosseph (Joseph). The way in which he makes his choice is to send him in to an ambush planned by Yosseph's brothers with the purpose of killing him.

The attempted murder of the elected one is in the purest Yahwic style. In the beginning of the myth, YHWH had become incarnate in his son Cain, and the simple presence of the timeless and indeterminate Cain had been enough to burst the bag of blood called Abel.

Of course, Cain had not killed him: Abel had fallen into the non-entity of his own conditioning, and the earth had drunk his blood. Abel cannot be reproached for being dull as are all the people who work and sweat and merely exist in their mediocrity. In him, the seed of humanity-to-be could not live.

Aware of this result, YHWH became cautious and decided to submit to a test the people he planned to utilize: he would try to kill them. If they resisted, they would be strong enough to carry the seed. Thus he commanded Abraham to kill Isaac. Elohim assaulted Jacob and wrestled with him a whole night. He deceived Moses so as to attack him unawares. (Exod. x, 1-27) YHWH says to Moses, *Go in unto Pharaoh for I have hardened*

16

his heart. (Logically he would have helped Moses had he softened Pharaoh's heart.) YHWH *hardened Pharaoh's heart and he would not let them* (the Hebrews) *go.* (Exod. IV, 19 and 24) *And YHWH said unto Moses in Midian, Go, return into Egypt, for all the men are dead which sought thy life,* . . . and when Moses is thus lulled, YHWH attempts to kill him.

In this passage (as well as in those that follow) we can see an example of the "personalization process' which inevitably occurs when these texts are read without a previous knowledge of the code which relates to their symbols. According to this manner of thinking it is, to be sure, quite evident that the cosmic vocation of Man—Adam—is to permit the two lives that make up his own double life to fecundate one another, mutually. He will thus become a new being and the actualization of the immanence, YHWH, will take place within him.

And it is of such manifestation, with its ensuing transformations, that the cabalists speak when they seem to attribute speech and action to the YHWH immanence, whose acts and words are to be found, for them, on a purely symbolic level. Further, many characters referred to in these stories (Cain, Abel, Lemekh, Noah) are mythical archetypes and should not, in any circumstances, be considered as being historical persons.

But let us return to Joseph, "sold by his brothers". That episode is a distorted description of an initiatic ceremony. Some of its elements are significant: Joseph was in a state of half-dream: he was stripped *of his coat, his coat of many colours that was on him* (Gen. XXXVII, 23-28). This is a wrong translation. His robe was the robe of spoliation (or dispossession); *he was cast into a pit: and the pit was empty, there was no water in it.* And Yehoudah (Judah) suggested, *let us* sell him, and he was sold for *20 pieces of silver.*

All these symbols are clear to those who know the Qabala.

The mythical Joseph is a dual entity. Being the eleventh son, he is both 10, which is the number of Yod, and 1, the Aleph. The Aleph allowed him to understand dreams, and the Yod gave him the capacity to purchase all the wheat of Egypt.

In very truth, Joseph's action was the very action of the myth. He was a man of the Qabala when he came to Egypt. He was a conjunction of two processes: myth and history. He was that which a few initiates in the Qabala happen to be from time to time: the historical consciousness of the myth's biological necessity. A necessity which, more often than not, has appeared under the aspect of some devastating punishment inflicted by YHWH.

Joseph brought upon his people a substantial blessing, which was immediately followed by a threat of wholesale destruction, by utter misery, by a most difficult escape, and by endless hardships. He was ambivalent. The myth is male, the earthly possessions are female.

Joseph kneaded and molded the primitive, formless substance of the human masses. He crushed them powerfully so as to compel them to react vitally.

Before his time, human Genesis was (mythically) concentrated in a family. With him was born a people, a nation.

This is how YHWH operated: there was a famine in Mitzrayim (Egypt) and in all adjoining countries. This Joseph had foreseen and he purchased for Pharaoh every grain of wheat available in the whole of Egypt. He then agreed to distribute it, but only at the price of dispossession. Thus, as a result of the operation, Pharaoh was the possessor of every acre in Egypt, and the whole people were reduced to slavery.

In the meanwhile, Joseph had asked all his family to come, and had settled them on the best land of the country so that they might multiply exceedingly.

Throughout there are two incidents which reveal to the cabalist that Joseph inherited the Qabala. In Genesis XLVII, 29, we learn that when Joseph's father, Jacob, whose real name is Israel, was about to die, he said to Joseph, *Put, I pray thee, thy hand under my thigh, and deal kindly with me.* We remember (Gen. XXXII, 25) that after having wrestled with Jacob all night, Elohim *prevailed not against him,* and wounded him in *the hollow of his thigh.*

The fact of asking Joseph to touch that consecrated wound has a very profound, symbolic meaning. An ever present mythical idea is that "he who heals must be wounded", "he who is life must have gone through death". Israel, in this episode, transfers his power to Joseph by revealing himself to him.

Another verse is Genesis XLIII, 22, in which Israel says to Joseph: *Moreover, I have given to thee one portion above thy brethren, which I took out of the hand of the Amorite with my sword and with my bow.*

The Amorite, the sword and the bow are very hard indeed to interpret! Israel never held a sword or a bow in his hands, and never fought anyone except Elohim. This is a somewhat amusing case of mistranslation, due to the rational logic of translators who, in their ignorance, could not allow themselves to believe that Israel was mentioning *the hand that had talked to him.*

The root Amer, or Homer, which is used in the original text, is a reference to speech and has become "an Amorite". A Hand that speaks is a hand that writes. The object bequeathed, about which the exegesis knows nothing, is well known esoterically. It is none other than the secret document, the trace of which is seen here.

Joseph lived a life of pomp and power. He died and was embalmed after the manner of the great of this world.

After his death, the Egyptian priests sought to find the magic object—or document—which Israel had given to his son, but they failed to do so. It had disappeared, and nobody knew where it was. Thus, many years passed by.

Then came a time when (Exod. I, 8-14) *there arose up a new king over Egypt, which knew not Joseph.* Because of the tremendous power which the throne and the hierarchy had received from Joseph, the people were more and more miserable. But also because of Joseph, *the children of Israel were fruitful and increased abundantly.* The more they were afflicted, *the more they multiplied and grew.* They became *numerous and more powerful* than the Egyptians. The harder their lives, the more bitter with bondage they became, the stronger they grew. Pharaoh decided to exterminate them. He ordered the Hebrew midwives to kill the new-born sons. They disobeyed in full agreement with Elohim; the babies were saved; and now we come to the story of Moses, and we shall rediscover the lost Qabala in an unexpected place.

The story of Moses—we prefer to use his real name Mosheh—is, in the beginning, similar to many other legends of new-born children threatened, hidden, found, saved and led towards an exalted mission.

Much has been written on Mosheh, from different points of view, but it seems to me that only the Qabala can see him in his double reality, which is both mythical and historical.

The mythical reality is the evolution throughout the ages of the relationship between human consciousness and the unfathomable mystery of existence, resulting from the laws of Moses.

We have already stated that in the perception of the fact that existence is a total mystery lies the foundation of any true religious awareness. The mystery, the realization that the fact of existence cannot be explained in words or in any other way, has always been deeply alive in the minds of the men of the Qabala.

This does not mean that their writings correspond adequately to the needs of our time.

If they said in symbols what can be set forth today clearly in words, it is because it was thus that they understood and felt. But when we want to understand and feel, we must break through those images and expressions which served them, but which no longer serve. We do not see Abraham or Mosheh as did the ancient cabalists. We see them with our own eyes and judgment. We can and must see them directly. We can penetrate their legendary existences, and so discern that they were not what they are said to have been. We can do this because the historical process functions on a certain sensorial level, whereas the mythical process concerns the psyche, and, whether yesterday or today, the Qabala is always in touch, through the psyche with the great unknown.

At certain particularly important conjunctions of this double process, the Hebrew myth becomes apparent and thrusts itself upon the objective world where it acts as a typhoon whose whirling motion draws waters from the ocean and carries them along with its own movement. The mass of waters thus captured belongs more to the cyclone than to the ocean.

Such events as those which are named Abraham, Mosheh or Jesus are thus taken over by the myth and belong to it more than they do to objective reality. Their immense importance is due to the fact that they are a conjunction of two realities. Finally, they modify the course of history in so far as they become religious phenomena.

Certain Asiatic myths carry through centuries the continuity of their religious and social structures. They can be compared to very old trees of knowledge whose fruits have dried on their branches for lack of any renewed sap. Contrarily, the Qabala has died and has resurrected many, many times amidst spectacular displays, on each occasion accomplishing and then burying its past.

If, by chance, we happen today to be in such a time, we are the very conjunction, the very timeless spark, which at one time appeared as Abraham, at another time as Mosheh, and later as Jesus. That pinpoint of recurrent eternity is the Qabala.

These considerations will be useful, we believe, now that we are about to resume our exploration of the narrative concerning Mosheh. Joseph had long been dead, and the Qabala had disappeared: both Joseph and the Qabala were completely forgotten, and the people were in utter misery.

With Mosheh springing out of the waters, a new birth on an entirely different level takes place, both identical and opposite to that which had been prepared by YHWH through Joseph.

We are compelled here, although not without some reluctance, to recall a terminology rather well known to the Qabala and to say that with Mosheh the narrative of the Emanation is now over and opens into the Creation, then into the Formation and the Action of Israel.

We said that the epoch of single men who carried the seed of human perfection has given place, with Joseph, to an epoch where that seed had to be buried in very primitive people. The tribes were 70 persons on their arrival in Egypt. But 430 years had elapsed and at the time of the Exodus, they were, according to the texts, 600,000 men, not including the children and without mentioning the women.

The problem was how to preserve the Elohimic seed, buried deep in a primitive, coarse, brutal human substance, hopelessly incapable of deconditioning itself.

The Qabala uses the word Sephiroth to express or describe different structures of the *one* cosmic energy, the Ayn-Soph. Their formulation, in the time of Mosheh, was beyond the understanding of the unevolved masses. The creative energy was bound to be deeply involved and immersed in blood.

The Sephiroth, or cosmic energies, which had operated in emanation through the myth, from Adam up to Abraham and his family, degenerated into other Sephiroth. Intelligence became Rigour, and Wisdom became Clemency, according to the Qabala.

The book of Mosheh, in fact, opens on those two key notes. This book is the book of a Creation. It is the creation of a container, of a living garment of protection for the seed of humanity-to-be, capable of not only sheltering it but also of living in symbiosis with it, of being in at-one-ment with it, until the time of the necessary ripening and ultimate destruction of the shell.

Because the times are ripe today, the entire process of birth, growth, maturity, old age and death of the myth appears to us very clearly.

The two Sephiroth, Rigour and Clemency, accompany the action of Mosheh-Aaron. The two keys to the mystery of Israel, circumcision and the knowledge of the Name, are given to Mosheh. It is a new departure and the beginning of a very long story, which lies outside the scope of the present essay. We must, however, include this story and the new expression of the Qabala as we give it in the general field of the occult tradition.

We will, therefore, give a short account of the legend of Mosheh as seen from the angle of this Qabala.

Mosheh is spelled Mem-Sheen-Hay. The Mem stands for water (as originator of existence), the Sheen symbolizes the Cosmic breath, and Hay means life. During a given liftetime, when the immense Exodus was being prepared, we can well imagine what such a revolt and such a devastating decision must have meant for the people. They had to be stirred and literally doped by miraculous messages, predictions, promises. They had to believe in something tremendous. A vigorous and active deity was needed: the need was fulfilled.

The myth, like a cyclone, fell upon them with such intensity that with the help of their heated imaginations, tremendous happenings were supposed to take place, such as the ten plagues of Egypt, when one half of any one of them would have been enough to destroy the whole country.

The most interesting part of it is the quarrel between YHWH and Pharaoh, each threatening to kill the other's first-born.* When YHWH thus threatens Pharaoh, he sets about, without wasting a minute, to try to kill his own son. (Exod. IV, 22-24) says YHWH to Mosheh: *And thou shalt say unto Pharaoh, thus saith YHWH, Israel is my son, my first-born. And I say unto thee, let my son go that he may serve me, and if thou refuse to let him go, I will slay thy son, thy first-born. And it came to pass in a place where he spent the night that YHWH met him* (Mosheh) *and sought to kill him.*

The conflict is intensified. Pharaoh oppresses the people more and more. YHWH sends all his plagues and as Pharaoh does not yield, comes to a last dramatic decision: all the new-born of Egypt are to be slaughtered.

The dispute between YHWH and the Earth (or the earthly powers) as to whose son is the first-born and what is to became of him is recurrent in the Bible, and—according to the Qabala

---

* Here, and in the following pages, we make use of the language of the Bible, which, as has already been said, personalizes YHWH, in order to render the term intelligible.

—is of vital importance for everyone of us. We shall deal with it at some length in subsequent chapters.

Another subject of dispute is "blood". This symbol has a wide range of connotations. The first plague inflicted by YHWH upon Egypt is the changing of all the water into blood. The Egyptian magicians can do it, too. Eventually Jesus will change water into wine. Blood and wine are interchangeable symbols. From Jesus' wounds it is said that the blood was mixed with water.

The night before the Exodus, the Hebrews stained their doors with blood so as to be recognized by the slaughterers and spared.

The Qabala insists on the significance of the name Adam: "dam" in Hebrew means blood. Within it is the hidden Aleph.

Another important symbol in Mosheh's story is the trans-figuration of womanhood. We shall follow this essential theme all through Genesis and as far as the Gospels. It is always through woman that every step from Emanation to Creation to Formation and to Action is achieved. In Mosheh's narrative, two midwives, in agreement with Elohim, save YHWH's first-born. Mosheh is saved a second time by two women, one of them being his sister. (The symbol "sister" will be explained at length in connection with Sarah, Rebecca and Rachel.)

One of the first episodes concerning Mosheh is when he sees an Egyptian and a Hebrew fighting. He kills the Egyptian (Harshness). He is very much afraid lest he be discovered and punished. He digs a hole in the sand and buries the body. Then he meets two Hebrews fighting and wants to intervene as he has done previously. They ask him, "Do you wish to kill us as you killed the Egyptian?" Mosheh thus realizing that his deed is known, decides to flee and save himself (Clemency).

Mosheh is therefore compelled to go to Midian, towards his destiny. The "Cohen" (priest) of Midian has 7 symbolic daughters. Mosheh meets them at a well and delivers them out of the hands of some shepherds. The daughters go to their father, whose name is Reuel (Exod. ii, 20), *and he said unto his daughters, And where is he? Why is it that you have left the man? Call him that he may eat bread.*

Mosheh eventually marries one of the 7 sisters. Her name is Zifforah.

Now begins chapter III thus: *Now Moses kept the flock of Jethro his father-in-law.* Very few readers observe that the man whose name was Reuel is now named Jethro. But the Qabala knows why this is so and how it happened.

When Israel died, his sons took his body and carried it all the way to Mamreh, to bury it. With them they carried the precious Qabala to save it from the Egyptians, and gave it in trust in Midian to some descendants of Abraham.

The mythical Reuel is clearly said to be (according to his name) Elohim's shepherd. Informed by his symbolic 7 daughters about the man who "delivered" them, he understands that, after so many years of waiting, he that was to be the inheritor of the Qabala has at last come.

The name Zifforah is again a symbol. She could be the princess Aurora of a fairy tale. Her name is the call of morning, a rising, a departure.

Reuel, having transmitted his powers to Mosheh, becomes somebody else: a sheer existence deeply immersed in its resistance to life-death. He falls, so to speak, into a coarser layer of vibrations, following the sephirotic process of incarnation. His part, as we shall soon see, will prevail in the creation of a tribal deity. So he is no longer Reuel, he now is Jethro.

Mosheh is aware of his future mission. He will serve YHWH, but so far he has not a direct revelation of what YHWH is. He is a stranger to that name, so he calls his son Gershon, which means stranger.

One day he goes with Jethro's flocks beyond the lands he usually treads. He goes into the enchanted regions of Elohim's desolate life, into the deep dwellings of existence. That region has a name: Horeb. From its terrible dryness, a spark of light flashes suddenly, an "angel", and, *behold, the bush burned with fire, and the bush was not consumed* (Exod. III, 2).

25

YHWH sees that Mosheh turns round *to see this great light*, and to wonder *why this bush is not burnt*. Then comes the revelation.

Mosheh's mission is now fully revealed to him, but he still does not know whose voice it is that speaks to him. (Exod. III, 13) *When I come unto the children of Israel . . . and they shall say to me, what is his name? what shall I say unto them?* And here come the prodigious revelation, the splendid, the dazzling truth: *"Aleph-Hay-Yod-Hay. Aleph-Sheen-Raysh. Aleph-Hay-Yod-Hay."*

All the translations of these ideograms, even in the Hebrew language, are abominable desecrations. A man skilled in the Qabala needs but to contemplate those few signs to be aware of it. If he truly is of the Qabala, the universe invades him with all that lives and all that dies, and that which exists, and that which does not exist, and that which has ever existed, and that which will be, and that which never was; though time and space are there, they dissolve into timelessness; for therein lies the prodigious mystery of all that is determined by indetermination. The sanctification is there, and a man dies to himself for being so much alive.

It is thus said: Go and say: *Aleph-Hay-Yod-Hay has sent me to you. Yes. You will say Yod-Hay-Vav-Hay has sent me to you.* Yes. Aleph-Hay-Yod-Hay. Yes. Yod-Hay-Vav-Hay. A Yod for an Aleph. A Hay for a Yod. A Vav for a Yod. A Hay for a Hay.

And that is the Qabala. It is easy to understand it when one knows the game, the game that the Aleph-life-death-life-death and the Yod-existence must play continuously; the Aleph, discontinuous pulsation, at times immanent, at times activated, and Yod permanent and continuous: Yod the perpetual loser in spite of the psyche that does not want to die. All this is easy to understand when one knows that all life is two lives and that Adam is Aleph inside the blood.

Such is the revelation granted to Mosheh of one of the two mysteries of Israel: the Qabala. The other mystery is the circumcision. It will be granted, as we all know, by Zifforah, when she will save Mosheh from YHWH's aggression (Exod. IV,

25-26): *Then Zifforah took a sharp stone and cut off the foreskin of her son and cast it at his feet, and said, Surely a bloody husband art thou to me. So he let him go: then she said, A bloody husband thou art, because of the circumcision.*

If we imagine YHWH as a tramp or a brigand at large, and fail to understand the truth underlying those symbols, this episode appears to be insane. When we know the inner, vital necessity of the myth, YHWH, Zipporah and Mosheh himself are only personifications of symbols.

The objective historical fact is that from that time on, a covenant has been established between YHWH and Israel in its flesh and life evolving towards a higher state of humanity. The movement of that life is integrated in the bodies of flesh, whether the Jews yield to it or not.

Many tentative explanations have been given of how the Hebrews crossed the Red Sea, of how Mosheh struck water out of a dry rock in Horeb, of the two columns of fire and cloud which rested on the tabernacle. Different meteorological phenomena are supposed to have happened while Mosheh was on a mountain top. Many speeches, laws, regulations, are supposed to have been delivered to the people by a so-called deity.

We will not attempt a description of the historical facts; they are so superbly invented and over-emphasized in the Bible that the whole narrative cannot be taken literally. It is, anyhow, irrelevant. Qabala can see through them.

According to the biblical tale, six hundred thousand armed men, with their wives, their children and their herds, lived forty years in a desert.

When, without any apparent reason, the deity orders a punitive expedition against the Midianites, the booty which is brought back amounts to 675,000 sheep, 720,000 oxen, 61,000 donkeys and 32,000 virgins (mentioned at the end of the enumeration).

So, approximately two million people and an equivalent number of animals are supposed to have spent forty years in a desert, moving their camp more than forty times (Num. xxxiii).

Moreover, the deity requires extraordinary offerings (Exod. xxv) of *gold and silver and brass, and blue, and purple and scarlet, and fine linen, and goat's hair and ram's skins dyed red, and badgers' skins, and shittim wood, oil for the light, spices for anointing oil, and for sweet incense, onyx stones and stones to be set in blue ephod, and in blue breastplate.* . . . And the people must build a sanctuary with a tabernacle, and instruments, and an ark, and staves, and a mercy seat, and cherubims of gold, and a table of shittim wood overlaid with gold, and dishes, and spoons, and a candlestick, and extremely elaborate curtains, and holy garments for Aaron. . . . The description of that which has to be built, wrought, inlaid and set by craftsmen of every kind, requiring every known material of that epoch, is very far indeed from the possibilities open to a huge population living in a desert—and living on manna falling from the skies!

Let us now consider the most human of all the laws which are given to those people (Exod. xx, 13): *Thou shalt not kill,* so many times quoted by so many killers.

It must be observed that the very deity that promulgates that law considers itself as being outside its own jurisdiction. When it intervenes in the history of the Hebrews, it is usually to order wholesale destruction; and Mosheh himself, the giver of the law, negates it whilst giving it.

(Exod. xxxii, 27-28) When Moses sees that because he has "delayed to come down out of the mount", the people and Aaron have fashioned a "molten calf" to worship, he becomes enraged, and he gives this order to the sons of Levi: *Thus says YHWH, the Eloh of Israel, Put every man the sword by his side, and go in and out from gate to gate throughout the camp, and slay every man his brother, and every man his companion, and every man his neighbour.*

On that day about three thousand men were killed.

It is well to remember that at the time the death penalty was inflicted for many breaches of the law which we now consider as being only minor offences. The priests had to slaughter animals every day, and the altar must have been a disgusting sight. The people were driven to a state little short of obsession by innumerable petty regulations to be rigorously observed every day, every hour, in every circumstance of life, and threatening fantastic punishments.

By what strange contrivance of the people, for what unconscious necessity, through what hypnotic influence, is this narrative to be taken at its face value and included in a "Holy" Bible?

The answer is in Exodus xxv, 21-22: ... *in the ark*, says YHWH to Mosheh, *thou shalt put the testimony that I shall give thee. And there I will meet with thee, and I will commune with thee.* . . .

The Qabala knows that that testimony was itself, the Qabala. Every possible precaution was taken by Mosheh to protect it, physically and morally, with the extreme rigour of intricate laws. He kept the people held in a magical net of authority. No armour could be too strong for the precious Revelation which was deposited in the ark. The way it came to be created can be seen in Exodus xvii, 8-16, where a mysterious Amalek fights with Israel and where Mosheh tells a mysterious Yehoushea (Joshua) to go and fight Amalek.

No explanation is given of who that Amalek might be and no exegesis, except the Qabala, has ever explained YHWH's and Mosheh's very peculiar behaviour in the circumstance: *And YHWH said to Mosheh, write this for a memorial in a book, and rehearse it in the ears of Joshua: for I will utterly put out the remembrance of Amalek from under Shamaim* (heaven). *And Mosheh built an altar, and called the name of it YHWH-nissi: For he said, Because YHWH hath sworn that YHWH will have war with Amalek from generation to generation.*

It is strange indeed to build an altar in remembrance of something that has to be utterly forgotten. And YHWH does not fight Amalek in order to gain victory: he established against him a state of perpetual warfare "from generation to generation". Who, or what, is Amalek?

Then in Exodus xviii, appears Jethro. He comes to Mosheh with his daughter Zifforah and her two sons. *And Mosheh went out to meet his father-in-law and did obeisance.* Later on, Jethro *took an offering* for Elohim, and *all the elders of Israel* ate bread with him. Finally, Jethro criticizes Mosheh and instructs him as to what he has to do. The Yahwic immanence will disappear, and the evolutionary process of Elohim will be set in motion.

Those episodes, as is always the case when something essential is said in the Bible, are not and cannot be understood by the synagogues or the churches. They have a threefold meaning (on three different levels), they describe the transformation of energy that we have mentioned above in using the term Sephiroth.

Only a careful study of the letter-numbers used in this narrative can give an adequate understanding of the (enacted) drama. We shall describe it briefly.

It begins with the fight between the children of Israel and Amalek: Aam-Lekh, on a certain level, means "that which is thine". It is an emanation of YHWH. According to YHWH's custom, it is a test intended to discover the power or resistance of Mosheh.

Were he, Amalek, an individual, he would be killed and done for, but YHWH wages an eternal battle against him. Nothing is so everlasting. YHWH is battling against a "himself" personified by Amalek.

Mosheh, in this contest, needs help. And two "principles" are within him, personified by Ahron (Aaron) and Hur. Mosheh fights thus: *When Moses held up his hand, Israel prevailed; and when he let down his hand, Amalek prevailed* (Exod. xvii, 11-12). *But Mosheh's hands were heavy: and they* (Aaron and Hur) *took a stone and put it under him, and he sat thereon; and Aaron and Hur stayed up his hands, the one on the one side, and the other on the other side.*

Thus Joshua vanquished Amalek and his people.

Mosheh then builds an altar to YHWH. We cannot, here, use any of the translations of this episode. We can only attempt to give one in accordance with the Qabala. What he says is approximately this: "YHWH has performed for me a miracle, but if the hand goes against Yod-Hay, what is the salt of it for me; but with that which is thine, I will be in the existence of two worlds."

These two worlds are Emanation and Creation. It is a certainty, according to the Qabala, that at that moment Mosheh was exactly at the junction of two worlds in apparent opposition. He realized that YHWH was staging a conflict within one single energy. The two worlds in conflict were only one world. So Mosheh could no longer fight, because which ever side he fought against was still YHWH. So he suddenly became quite still.

Now Jethro came to him. The text insists in saying that he is the Cohen of Midian, the Hhoten of Mosheh. Whenever one finds so great an emphasis, its purpose is always to attract our attention. There is something to understand which is beyond the apparent meaning of Jethro being Mosheh's father-in-law. The theme Hhoten expresses, according to its ideograms, is a state of expectancy of the primitive, undifferentiated substance. The transformation of Reuel to Jethro expresses the response of that substance to the action of YHWH upon it. The final Noun in Cohen, Midian, and Hhoten opens the way to possibility. Likewise, Joshua will be called "son of Noun".

It is said, in the translations, that Zifforah, who comes with her father, had been sent back by Mosheh. This is an erroneous interpretation of the text. Even in colloquial Hebrew, the word used is Shiloheya, which here means that Zifforah is liberated. Her second son's name is Elyezer; Elohim helps.

Jethro explains to Mosheh the point of view of the gross human substance which Elohim's process is going to mould so that it can evolve. Mosheh, who only knows YHWH's side of the question, yields entirely to his advice.

We will close this chapter with a reference to Exodus xxiv, 9-11: *Then went up Mosheh, and Ahron, Nadab, and Abihu, and seventy of the elders of Israel.* We see here four principles—or archetypes: (a) Mosheh, the cosmic breath saved from the waters; (b) Ahron, the pulsation life-death of Aleph, alive in its dwelling and acting in the game in which indetermination is at stake; (c) Nadab, the continuity of existence (and of the Qabala); and (d) Abihu, the living germ of Elohim, within that container.

Those four pseudo-persons *saw the God of Israel: and there was under his feet as it were a paved work of sapphire stone, and as it were the body of heaven in its clearness. And upon the nobles of the children of Israel he laid not his hand: also they saw God, and did eat and drink.*

This is really too crude. A God with feet, therefore a God in a body, is an idol. This passage is an exceedingly ignorant transcription of cabalistic symbols. The "sapphire stone" is the Sepher, the Book. That which is seen and acknowledged is the Qabala.

Mosheh, after this communion, does not climb a physical mountain. He ascends, so to speak in two cosmic lives, in the two lives of Yod-Hay-Vav-Hay.

Mosheh did not cross the Jordan, but the people did, ruled by Joshua, who had become the high priest of their national God.

They invaded the land of Canaan. With that expedition, the real history of the Jews begins, a history of violence, wars, destruction and massacres.

Their God never ceased to tell them, through the mouth of Joshua, that it was *He* who had fought for them, *He* who had exterminated defenceless populations. Had He not stopped the motion of the sun and thrown stones from His heaven so as the better to annihilate the victims of that invasion?

After Joshua's death, YHWH armed the sons of Judah. They attacked Jerusalem, killed its inhabitants, set fire to the town, and began to worship the Baals and the Astartes. YHWH became enraged because of this idolatry. He delivered the sons of Israel into the hands of plunderers and of all their enemies. He deprived them of every means of resistance, he drove them to a state of extreme distress and misery, and he sent Judges to rule over them.

YHWH was with the Judges and protected Israel during their lifetime, because of his compassion for the people. But at the death of each Judge, the sons of Israel became even more corrupt than their fathers had been and incurred the wrath of YHWH.

YHWH, between the extreme Harshness and Clemency, sometimes delivered the people to their enemies, sometimes allowed them to intermingle peacefully with other nations. The result was the same: the sons of Israel always relapsed into idolatry.

The traditional Qabala acknowledges the Judges. Their wisdom was of the Qabala. They were known as *Shofitim*. They acted upon the sons of Israel as a pair of bellows does on a fire which burns but feebly. They projected upon their primitive coarse substance the organic breath of cosmic life. Without this action of the Judges, the Qabala would have been lost.

But everything deteriorates eventually. The last Judges, sons of Samuel, *walked not in his ways, but turned aside after lucre, and took bribes, and perverted judgment* (I. Sam. VIII, 3-7).

Then all the elders . . . came to Samuel . . . and said . . . now make us a king to judge us like all the nations. But the thing displeased Samuel . . . and he prayed . . . and YHWH said: Hearken unto the voice of the people in all that they say unto thee; for they have not re-jected thee, but they have rejected me, that I should not reign over them.

In spite of Samuel's strong warnings, the sons of Israel or-ganized themselves into a political state, "like all the nations", and henceforth the name of Israel lost its meaning.

The entire reign of their first king, Saul, was a period of savage, cruel wars. The troubled reign of David ended, how-ever, in a more peaceful period, preparatory to Solomon's ostentatious reign.

Solomon married the daughter of Pharaoh and took her to Jerusalem, where he built his famous temple. He reigned over all Israel, made alliance with the king of Tyre, built cities, ac-cumulated great riches and died after having reigned forty years.

This highest point of kingly glory included seven hundred wives and three hundred concubines, and his reign ended with the division of the country.

Jeroboam, king of Israel, re-established the cult of idols. In this manner he wished to show his independence in the face of Judah. In the meanwhile, Jerusalem passed from a king who "did well" to a king who was *evil in the eyes of YHWH*.

The people alternately worshipped idols and submitted again to the laws of Moses: they refused to "humiliate" themselves before the prophets, then returned to their fear of them.

In the temple, the so-called cult of YHWH consisted of a repetition of formulas. The Qabala lamented, wept and cursed in anger through the prophets, but it remained unknown to the people, the kings, and even to the priests.

There was a coffer at the door of the temple where worshippers used to put coins. One day, under *the money that was brought into the house of YHWH, Hilkiah the priest found a book of the law of YHWH given by Moses* (II Chron. XXXIV, 14).

Ultimately, the movement of the pendulum between YHWH and idols came to a deadlock. It was the end of that "container", of that continuity.

The earthly adventure in Canaan had been (and still is) an error of the people. In those times, it was a necessity for the myth. Had not Jerusalem existed as the holy centre of the Mosaic Law, YHWH would not have destroyed it. Its importance lies in its destruction, not in its having been built.

For Israel in its true sense, the name Canaan is not that of a country. It has no frontiers. And YHWH in its true meaning is not a deity to be worshipped, least of all in a temple.

YHWH, then, realized that Jerusalem as a process could not evolve towards its maturity. Therefore, *he brought upon them the king of the Chaldees* (II Chron. XXXVI, 17), and Nebuchadnezzar slew all people, young or old; and he brought to Babylon all the treasures of the temple and all the treasures of the kings and princes. And the temple was burnt, and all the palaces. Jerusalem was destroyed. The few people who escaped were carried to Babylon, *to fulfil the word of YHWH . . . until the land had enjoyed her sabbaths*.

The land enjoyed 70 years of sabbaths, after which Babylon was defeated by Cyrus. YHWH *stirred up the spirit of Cyrus . . .*

and charged him to build him an house at Jerusalem (Ezra I and II), *and those which had been carried away unto Babylon . . . came again into Jerusalem.*

The fact that Nebuchadnezzar as king of the Chaldees and the symbolic 70 years of captivity are mentioned, show clearly that the sons of Israel who escaped were driven back by the ruler of their pre-natal land. They were, symbolically, thrown back inside the womb, so as to be born again. The 70 years are a sign of renewal. Under that sign, Babylon was destroyed, and Cyrus liberated the captives.

When the sons of Israel returned to Jerusalem, they were "reborn", to an extent that they had forgotten their mother tongue. They did not, however, come to realize what their universal mission was. They began to rebuild the temple, but not without great difficulties and delays.

Eventually, the temple was completed *and all the people gathered themselves together as one man into the street that was before the water gate; and they spake unto Ezra the scribe to bring the book of the law of Moses, which YHWH had commanded to Israel* (Neh. VIII, I). (Note the symbol "water gate".)

With Ezra, the knowledge of the Qabala re-emerged. It was an understanding of the primordial Revelation, combined with a submission to the laws of Moses. This double connection permitted that very small nation to survive despite the Persian domination.

According to tradition, the Book was rewritten by Ezra, who is said to have given the ideograms the shapes which we know today and to have put together the first five books, partly from oral traditions, partly from written documents.

Then came an historical period similar to many others. Hellenism influenced some of the people. As in every happy period, some Jews became assimilated, others continued to submit to the domination of ritual, and the Qabala once again disappeared from sight.

That period lasted until it was brutally interrupted by the Syrian kings, who embarked upon another period of warfare.

(The memory of Judas Maccabaeus is still alive today.) Jerusalem was captured and freed several times. Revolt succeeded revolt until the conquest of Judah by the Romans.

The history from then on is well known. We come to the destruction of Jerusalem by Titus in A.D. 70, and the ceaseless revolts of the Jews, which culminated, in A.D. 135, with the final destruction of Jerusalem by Hadrian and the Dispersion, or Diaspora.

The first three centuries of our era were a period of intense intellectual activity and of confusion of mind. Judaism was subject to ruptures of all kinds. An Hellenistic-Judaism, opposed to a talmudic rabbinism, both conflicted with a very powerful— although little-known—undercurrent of anti-sacerdotalism, which proclaimed that the universal message of Israel had been betrayed by the party of the Temple.

The author of Barukh's Apocalypse gives orders to all the priests to throw the key of the sanctuary to heaven, and to ask YHWH to preserve the House that they have not been able to hold.

The apocalyptic period did not last. Some took refuge in hope: "the Temple will be rebuilt some day". Craving for its own continuity, the synagogue settled on a few relics of ritualistic prescriptions. The Qabala became secret, occult. That germ of life hid itself in an impenetrable shell.

The outer authority was taken in charge by Instructors: the *Tanaim*. They were the custodians of the Torah, of the Law, of the prescriptions. They did not seek to proselytize. Their field of activity did not extend outside Israel. They had but one aim: the remoulding of an entity, Israel, without a State and without Jerusalem.

Their action was based on the Law and on the Commentaries (which became the part of the Talmud called the *Mishnah*), and on a life of incredible abnegation and sanctity, going as far as martyrdom. (It is enough to remember the names of Rabbi Meir and Akibah.)

It is true that some of those rabbis knew the Qabala in its

36

exoteric sense, based on the laws of Moses better than they knew
the original Revelation as it existed in a past more remote than
the times of Moses. They believed that the symbolic narrative of
Genesis was a description of actual facts, and they read those
facts upside down according to their spoken languages; they
believed in Adam's sin and the fall of Man, they worshipped a
deity which cannot but be anthropomorphized when it is
prayed to. The secret code of the Qabala was a closed book for
most, except Akibah, and perhaps a few others. But it was
necessary that it should be so, that in all their charity, in their
intense activity, they might play their part in this drama.

It was because of those meek doctors of the Law that the
Gospels were defeated in their attempts to free themselves from
the Hebrew myth.

These doctors were so obstinately adamant that the first
Christians were compelled to avail themselves of Abraham and
to find in him the origin of their creed.

Their wish was the opposite of the syncretism towards which
our time seems to direct itself. If they claimed Abraham, it was
in the hope of substituting themselves for the people who had
made a covenant with YHWH.

The Qabala knows that YHWH is not a deity but an immanence which can become alive and active when the two
vitalities in us, the container and the contained, fecundate each
other. Historically, those vitalities of Israel came into being
when the mistaken expression, material and materializing, of
the Temple and of Jerusalem, was destroyed. The Qabala, for
the time being, obeyed the Law, and reciprocally the Law held
the Qabala in great respect and honour.

Such was the truth of those times: the biological necessity of
Israel's mystery. If the first three centuries following the
destruction of Jerusalem were the most intense in the life of
Israel, it was because everything had been destroyed.

The great initiator of the Qabala in the second century was
Simeon-Bar-Yohai. Against the powerful movements called
the Talmud and the Qabala, the Christians were helpless.

They found all sorts of arguments. They said—erring profoundly—that Abraham's faith was more important than the circumcision, that Abraham is "the father of nations", that the Patriarchs obviously did not obey the Law of Moses, and that, conditioned by these laws, the Jews were only a lateral branch of the human tree.

Interpreting an important theme of Genesis in a certain fashion (which will be explained later on), the Christians proclaimed themselves to be the "eldest" because they had come "after" Israel. Had they been more mature ontologically, they would have had, perhaps, some reason for saying so. But, in fact, they were not mature.

On the Jewish side, other currents were seeking to express themselves. One thought the Law of Moses to be monolithic, and decreed that it must be obeyed in its every detail. They reasoned that, the Temple being destroyed, it was absolutely impossible to follow all the prescriptions, and that therefore it would be a sin to interpret them according to circumstances.

Others said, "Better transform than do nothing; at least, it will help to keep them in memory."

In Alexandria these developed a strong tendency not unlike that of our "reformed" synagogues.

Other Jews declared themselves to be more Jewish than all other Jews, because they were disciples of the Rabbi Jesus, in whom they saw the embodiment of the essence of Israel, which is life-death and resurrection.

We cannot have an adequate idea of the great turmoil which marked the period from approximately the third to the seventh centuries. Its centre was Alexandria. All the documentation of those centuries was stored in its library, which was burned at least three times.

One of the Ptolemys tried to launch a syncretic deity, Serapis, but his attempt did not succeed in reviving the ancient Egyptian religion. Another Ptolemy patronized the translation of the Bible into Greek. According to a legend seventy learned men made seventy absolutely identical translations of it!

Aquila, a disciple of Akibah in the time of Hadrian also made a translation into Greek. A certain Symmacus, at the end of the eighth century, made another translation which was used by a Judaeo-Christian sect.

Thus there were three different versions: the Septuagint, which was the official one in use by the church; Aquila's which was adopted by the Jews of the Diaspora; and that of Symmacus. Later on the Septuagint was accepted by the synagogues of the Diaspora who despised Aquila the proselyte.

Many other Greek versions were made. Origen who spent many years of his life in comparing them and St. Jerome who learned Hebrew for the purpose of a translation into Latin must also be mentioned.

We thus see that the widespread enthusiastic fashion for translations is not a privilege of our own times. As far back as the second century, the synagogues attempted to go towards the outer world rather than to retire into the Talmud. For that purpose, they adopted foreign languages for their liturgy.

Many Jews, however, said that when the version of the Seventy came out it was a time of great sorrow and mourning for the rabbis who knew that the text cannot be translated. They put ashes on their heads, they tore their garments, they wept and cried out that such a sacrilege had never before been committed, not even when the Golden Calf had been set up, that it would have been better not to have been born than to have witnessed the day that the Torah was translated.

Without indulging in such an excessive display of grief, it cannot but be declared that they were perfectly right. The undercurrent of their violent reaction was intensified because the Temple was no more.

The real disciple of Akibah was not Aquila, the proselyte-translator. Akibah is the very source of two parallel trends, thanks to which the Book is still alive. Akibah had two important disciples: Rabbi Meir, the master of the Talmud, and the miraculous Simeon-Bar-Yohai, the "holy lamp of Israel", to whom is attributed the origin of the Zohar, which Moses de

Leon is supposed to have written in Spain in the thirteenth century, according to certain authoritative opinions.

A note of doubt is necessary as far as the origin, dates and authors of cabalistic writings are concerned. For instance, the well known Sepher Yetzirah is known to have been written in a period preceding the birth of Islam, at any time between the sixth century B.C. and the sixth century of our era. Any scientific research within so wide a margin is hopeless.

The Sepher Yetzirah is a very short text which emerges from the thick forest of the Talmud and the Zohar. It is mentioned because it is characteristic of the way in which cabalists deliberately enrobed their knowledge in cryptic and apparently absurd utterances.

An attempted English translation of its first lines would read approximately thus: "By thirty-two mysterious paths of wisdom, Yah, the Lord of Armies, God alive ... has engraved and created His world with three Sepharim ... ten Sephiroth Belimah and twenty-letters of foundation", etc. ....

We have repeatedly stated that the letters of the Hebrew alphabet have always been, throughout the centuries, the foundation of the true tradition and the only key to the knowledge of the Hebrew Revelation.

Of course, the statement that a deity created the Universe by means of the Hebrew alphabet is literally absurd. It can be expressed differently in stating that every letter is, in fact, an ideogram which symbolizes one aspect of the cosmic energy. Thus we know where to look for meaning and purpose of the biblical text: it describes the interplay of those energies in the Universe and in Man. Thus we free our minds from all mystical imaginings. In following the text we then are subjected to an amazing mental exercise which can modify our way of thinking to the extent of uniting us with those very energies which are being described. That, and that only, is the Revelation.

At all times the rabbinical principle has held that nothing in the Genesis is there by mere chance or by mistake; nothing is useless; every repetition has its purpose; and the different grammatical mistakes according to the Hebrew language are no mistakes at all: when read according to code they reveal their meaning.

Every epoch has its own way of understanding things and of feeling them. When truth is met it is expressed differently according to the stage of mental and emotional developments of the period. In ancient times symbols, parables, metaphors, images, legends may have conveyed a meaning for the understanding. We, today, need a psychological and rational approach. Therefore it is useless—and, we venture to say, harmful—for us to dally with interpretations of interpretations of what people have supposed to be revelations put forward by Abraham, Moses or Jesus.

We have not the time to spend in the consideration of antiquated approximations to knowledge. Therefore no mere student of Qabala will ever understand the Qabala from within. Were he to read and re-read the Zohar, learn all about Simeon-Bar-Yohai, Moses of Leon, Abraham, Abulafia or Knorr von Rosenroth's *Kabbala Denudata*, he would be trying to see by looking through the wrong end of a telescope.

Nothing is important except the knowledge that the key to that Revelation is to be found in the letter-numbers. When once we grasp that, we can grope our way through them, and our very first step will already have been taken inside their cosmic life.

That Revelation is timeless and is therefore of all time. One cannot contact it if it is imagined to have happened in the past. It is of now when we accept it to be of now. Unless we are fully of our time we are seeking it in its tracks on the sands of time.

The situation of the twentieth-century man in relation to the Bible is entirely different from what it was in the second century. In those times the early Christians were trying to dissociate themselves from the Jews who had been deprived of their Church. They proclaimed that the destruction of the Temple had been a punishment and that a new Church must take the place of the old.

We have already seen some of their arguments. Their opposition to the Jews developed and intensified to the point of degenerating into a theological anti-semitism. The Jews became hated because they "had murdered God". With John Chrysostom, the Christian exegesis at its lowest level became a purely abusive oratory. According to YHWH's well-known reactions it stirred the rabbis to a still greater energy. They taught:

"Do the Christians appeal to Abraham? The Qabala dedeclares itself prior to him."

"Is Mosaic law only a lateral branch of the human tree? On the contrary, it is the protective shell of the living Revelation."

"Does faith save? Not at all. Only the Covenant with YHWH is life."

"Are the ritual prescriptions a punishment? Of course not: they prove YHWH's love for his people."

"Is Christianity the true Israel, as it attempts to say? But when, how, in what circumstance has it wrestled with Elohim and defeated him, as Jacob did when he deserved and received that name: Israel?"

From the second century until the Middle Ages the Qabala spread in every direction. Eastward, it went to Egypt, Asia Minor, Arabia, Persia and as far as India. It can be found in the Quran, and it is established that the Prophet Mohammad had been taught by Rabbis. It was carried by the Jews and Arabs into Spain, to the south of France and as far as the Anglo-Saxon world.

The end of the fourteenth century was the beginning of tragic times for the Jews. They were persecuted in Spain and expelled. They sought refuge wherever they could find it.

It was again for the Qabala a period of confusion and decline all over Europe. Although it was respected by some free minds among philosophers, alchemists and a few mystics, it degenerated into a symbolic caricature of occultism and, with the added attacks of the anti-semites, it died an ignoble death in cheap modern novels.

It had not died everywhere. By a strange historical freak, it reappeared in Egypt when Isaac Loria discovered the Zohar in Cairo. The school of Safed, which he founded, re-established the broken link between the observance of rites and the Shekinah (YHWH's exile from this earth). The school eventually degenerated into an excessive asceticism, alien to the true knowledge of the Qabala.

The state of symbiosis between Knowledge and Law had come to an end.

The last blow was given by the Jewish scholars of the nineteenth century belonging to the rational school of Judaeo-German origin. This school of thought is still in existence today, and is backed by Zionism, by the synagogues and by the official voice of International Judaism.

It considers that the cabalistical tradition in its totality is a mystical rambling which has been a poison for Israel.

This rationalism is partly responsible for the picture, common to some religions, of a YHWH reduced to an avatar of Zeus or Jupiter, sitting in a heaven. But YHWH in the true sense of its letter-code schema, cannot be corrupted by any wrong usage which is made of it. Rationalization is a corruption in itself.

The knowledge that is called Qabala must no longer be reduced to a mere subject of study for seekers of recondite mysteries. It must now come to full light and penetrate serious minds.

The synagogues can only ignore it because they have repudiated intelligence. They keep on reading and commenting on an archaic law which has no reality. The real knowledge of the Qabala recedes further and further every day because of the foolish teachings of amateur scholars who, having learned a few tricks which can be played with the letter-numbers, amuse the public with their speculations, or entertain their readers with strange stories concerning some ancient Rabbi.

The modern Rabbis have become archivists of formulas and preachers of conventional morality. We believe that most of them are quite ignorant of esoteric rabbinism, and of its many

43

interpretations, quite aside from the plain reading of the Book.

A Christian Qabala has been attempted in vain, its roots being artificial. It was intended as a substitute for the Hebrew rather than as an authentic penetration into the Scriptures.

As to the new settling of a State in the geographical Canaan, it can be understood because of the abominable slaughter ordered under the Nazi regime. From a human point of view, it corresponds to a necessity for survival and to the recurring wish expressed unto Samuel to be like unto the other nations.

It is to be hoped that to these "husbandmen" of the earth, YHWH will say what he said to Jonah: *And should I not spare Nineveh, that great city, wherein are more than six score thousand persons that cannot discern between their right hand and their left hand, and also much cattle?*

★

In brief, the Qabala today can be reborn neither in the Synagogue nor in the State that calls itself Israel. Both ignore it, so it ignores them. It has no valid motive for conforming to the very few Mosaic prescriptions which still survive and which every conforming Jew interprets according to his fancy.

It must offer itself freely to minds which are free. It is no longer mysterious and occult. On the contrary, it is intelligible and marvellously intelligent. It is the very source of the civilizations that have gravitated around the Mediterranean which are today spreading all over our planet.

It states the religious problem as it has to be stated in a time when the further the horizon recedes, the nearer we come to the Mystery.

For such minds as are no longer bounded by ancient horizons and have thus become a mystery unto themselves, the totality of life is present in action. It is the Soliloquy of the One.

ᴛhis is the true Revelation, plainly visible to all.

PART TWO

THE BOOK OF GENESIS

I

The Letter-Code

THIS WORK offers a fundamental re-reading of the text of the Bible's Book of Genesis and some of its consequences in understanding the Gospels of Matthew and John. The revolutionary meanings here presented will be of great significance, it is hoped, to those of the Christian, Hebrew and Moslem religions whose thinking has been conditioned by and rooted in the Bible. And they will be of equal importance to those non-orthodox believers and non-believers whose intelligence has so baulked at the traditionally accepted but unsatisfactory versions of the cosmic drama, to the extent that they have felt it necessary to repudiate the whole of Genesis which they are inclined to consider as being only ancient legends.

Perhaps humanity, for all these centuries, has not been ready to receive the stupendous implications arising from the true content of this book. The first point to be made is that, differing in this respect from many other so-called sacred works which, whether or not rightly understood, can at least be read in their original language, the first five chapters of Genesis have been, more than many others, open to incorrect interpretation because they are not written in words which can be translated into any ordinary language.

It may come as a surprise to many Bible readers that these five chapters were written in code and cannot be deciphered without knowledge of the code. Each letter of the Hebrew alphabet represents a specific number, the significance of which must be understood—a not too difficult process, as will be seen later on. These numbers are not to be considered in their arithmetical sense. Each one, in fact, signifies an aspect of living

47

forces at play in the Universe; and the text is intended to project these forces into our very being, thus acting as a Revelation. This process, being based in Reality, does not involve the projection of an idea. It has nothing to do with a creed; for the only principles by which it is bound are universal.

The original text deals with states of consciousness and their relationship to life as it happens now. It does not deal with anything that happened in the past. Life is *now*, and if there is anything that can be called Revelation, it cannot be an illusory explanation of what has already happened, but it is an incursion of the life process into our actual being.

The very existence of the Universe is a gigantic fact and mystery that can never be fathomed by human thought. That fact must be faced squarely, and not explained away, because so-called explanations pile mystery upon mystery and delude the mind, creating the habit of *thinking* about that which it cannot ever *conceive*.

Seen in its true light, the first verse of the Bible has an entirely different significance from that conveyed by the inadequate translation familiar to us from childhood: *In the beginning, God created the heaven and the earth.* This translation does not make sense at all, because it is unthinkable. A "beginning" of time and space is as unthinkable as is their non-beginning. Therefore, a text which proclaims the hopelessly inconceivable leads at the very start into the fictitious domains of wrong thinking. Even the word "God" is inconceivable, obviously so. The hypothesis of the existence of an unthinkable God previous to an unthinkable beginning forces the mind to confront the absurdity of a something-before-anything creating everything out of nothing.

Thus—by means of such circuitous strategems—does the psyche mesmerize the intellect so as to extort the justifications it requires in order to avoid having to face the dreaded idea of an ever-present mystery. It uses the same devious ways when shaping into symbols and images the abstract notions expressed by the original ideograms. The psyche's structure being funda-

48

mentally sensorial, its utterances in any language cannot but exteriorize its irrational longings and fears. (This fact appears when one considers that many roots of the Hebrew language have two contradictory meanings and that dynamic schemata mean for the psyche an overturning of protective structures.)

The cosmic and human drama as described in the Bible is an interplay between two partners playing against each other: *Aleph*, intermittent life-death, unfathomable, timeless mystery evading all mental grasp, and *Yod*, its projection into the time-space continuum, which is its antinomy. The winner, obviously, is always *Aleph* because all that exists must of necessity come to an end. But the psyche, dreaming of an indefinite duration—in the form of an eternal soul, for example—rejects the very notion of its own death and clings to philosophies or religions that encourage it to believe that the word "always" has a meaning.

The traditional reading of the Bible is the result of intellectual subjugation to psychological demands. The Book of Genesis when read according to custom therefore appears in the form of a story relating the facts and gestures of such people as Adam, Eve, Cain, Abel, and so forth, but whose names when read in the light of the cabalistic code reveal that they are abstract formulas of cosmic energy focused in the human psyche.

An example can illustrate this point; in the first chapter of Genesis it is repeatedly written: "and God said". There is no such word as God in the book. The schema *Elohim*, (*Aleph-Lammed-Hay-Yod-Mem*), as will be exhaustively shown later, is the process through which *Aleph* becomes *Yod* in evolutionary existence, and the schema *Yomer* (*Yod-Aleph-Mem-Raysh*) which is translated "said" is an emanation of both *Yod* and *Aleph* in a state of existence and life.

(The schema *Yod-Hay-Vav-Hay* translated "the Lord" or Jehovah, which appears in Genesis II, expresses an existence fulfilled by two lives [Hay and Hay] of psyche and body mutually fecundating one another. When this happens YHWH is alive in us.)

When decoded the letter-numbers are of such a nature as to be able to satisfy our intellect but their import can only reveal itself in the depths of our beings. They first appear in Genesis as archetypes pre-existent to any articulate language, but these gradually condense (or reduce) into allegories which in turn become constituent parts of an epic poem in which Abraham, Isaac, Jacob and their wives are the principal protagonists. This metaphysical narrative has come to be considered as being a series of episodes in the chronicles of an ancient Semitic tribe and continue to be looked upon for no apparent reason as being an important chapter in holy Scriptures of world-wide traditional beliefs.

Much later Rabbi Jesus hoped to promote a revival based on the original revelation of light in Man, which met with massive resistance originating not only in Hellenistic paganism but also on the part of the Hebrews who had forgotten the essentials of their own religion. John's gospel treats the subject of human consciousness as related to the myth of inner light.

Following these preliminaries we can now further investigate the purpose of this essay.

2

The Challenge

HEBREW writing has no numerals to indicate numbers. These are expressed by the letters of the Hebrew alphabet, each letter corresponding to a number. The origin of these numbers, so we believe, goes back to an epoch long prior to history, and ancient tradition purports to show their significance, which is that each number has a meaning in relation to cosmic forces. A similar tradition is found at the origin of the civilization of ancient Egypt. None can say whence it arose. Gradually it was lost in the course of the centuries, and the deep significance that each number was intended to convey has disappeared. Only the significance of each letter, itself composed of several alphabetical characters, has remained but in a state of degraded meaning. As an example, we have Bayt = House; but the numbers are not understood beyond their numerical meaning. The principal reason for this is that the correct reading of these numbers as they occur in word sequence is difficult, to say the least. It inflicts an unwanted exercise upon the mind crystallized by habit and inertia.

Our ordinary thinking process is concerned with descriptions of things and not with the things themselves. If we are speaking of movement we do not transmit a movement, but only the idea of movement. If we speak of music, of colour, of all that one can feel or see, we evoke in another person the images, the feelings, the symbols which have attached themselves to something similar which they remember or already know (thus producing comparison). If we say, for instance, (Gen. 1, 2) that *Darkness was upon the face of the deep*, we evoke a familiar image of night and a thought of obscure spaces. Thus what is given us is not darkness itself nor do we create a great abyss; we only call upon imagination, and each person proceeds to imagine what he wishes to imagine or what he is capable of imagining!

When communication purports to convey *the* Revelation such ambiguity can only lead to one or another of the multifarious religious interpretations which obstruct the immediate perception of the fact that the very existence of a speck of dust is in very truth the first and the last mystery. No mystery is greater than any other: the Qabala has always known it, and has therefore never raised the question as to whether God exists. For those of the Qabala, for Abraham, Moses or Jesus, the unknowable unknown is a presence. The knowing of that presence is the unknown. There is no other revelation. It is therefore and above all necessary to reject all interpretations, explanations, creeds and dogmas, all faiths and moral laws, all traditions, philosophies and theologies, so as to allow the unknown to operate directly in our minds. Then thought is free to observe the interplay of life and death and existence because it moves along with it, having shattered its fetters. The Qabala postulates that knowledge is not a formulation but a cosmic energy imparted to the mind by the letter-numbers.

Thus it is useless for the mind to try to formulate ideas about transcendence, which is totally beyond comprehension or measure. Whatever ideas of it one may think one has attained one can have only a notion of greater, better, etc. In the first place, any notion of perfection and timelessness we may form is bound to be invalidated by our inveterately dualistic mode of thought. Our whole idea of progress is based on the idea that the good is simply that which awaits us at the opposite end of a continuum which starts with the not-good. Imperfection and time do not merely enter our thoughts; they *are* our thoughts. Like any other mere tool, the mind as we use it is functionally identical with its products. The chicken and the egg of the mind produce and reproduce one another *ad infinitum, ad nauseam.*

As long as we are not in direct contact with that which transcends the human mind, the fundamental significance of life escapes us. But that primordiality invades us as soon as we decipher the first letter of the first schema of the Revelation, and the witnessing of it is the part of having it revealed, because, after all, the revelation is always there but for its being witnessed.

There is no transcendence other than our intimacy with the unknown as the unknown. Seeking it is avoiding it. It is everlastingly present in an ever present genesis. Let us therefore reread that Book, not as an archaic attempt to describe an unwitnessed creation of the world by a soliloquizing deity but as a penetration of vital energies at work in ourselves.

*

In the present book, we wish to show that the original tradition of the Book of Genesis was a correct presentation of a certain trend of thought; that this tradition was subsequently lost; that the Rabbi Yhshwh better known as Jesus, knew it; that he tried in vain to expound his truth (was it not written that his disciples understood him not?); that his teaching was submerged by paganism; that the Christian religion is but a modified form of paganism; that the Jewish religion has degenerated into a practice of prescribed ritual; that Islam, which claims to be a revival of Abraham's revelation, is rather a social and political phenomenon; and that the cabalists and the Jewish mystics have searched for and, each in his own way, have found the true primordial plan. Finally we believe that the exact meaning of the original tradition can be made apparent today. This discovery may indeed be occurring at the right time. We are at a turning-point of history. We are faced with a change of cycle calling for a renewal of man, requiring that he be bathed in the Source. Thus a many-dimensional challenge confronts us. What is first of all demanded of us is—rather than a search for absolute truth—a rooting-out of past errors, a relinquishing of long-cherished illusions.

To think erroneously regarding a subject of vital importance is to think erroneously in all domains of existence. The prime

53

objective of this Qabala is to show that all the versions of the Bible (particularly of Genesis), including the Hebrew, are in error, and that the original text is marvellously intelligible and intelligent. It has been the source of many civilizations preceding ours and it is the source out of which the future must inevitably be born.

We hope that the meaning of the biblical text will become apparent from chapter five onwards. We shall have to proceed step by step because the key of its Revelation is not to be snatched from a code but can only operate when constantly recreated by its very usage. The unceasing reading through centuries of disordered translations has made it difficult indeed to effect a new beginning in the texture of thought where religion is concerned.

After having somewhat transcribed Genesis we will in a later part of the book attempt an approach to Gnosticism and to one or two sections of the Gospels of Matthew and John, the evidences of which will, we hope, be a contribution to the understanding of essentials.

3

The Letter-Numbers

THE PRESENT writer, being obliged to use our language in order to make himself understood, cannot offer the reader the truth of Genesis, but only images of that truth. Our language is of sensuous origin. By its use, we can only understand by means of imagery. Nevertheless we shall do our best not to stray into illusory beliefs and dreams of the supernatural.

Let us now concern ourselves with the individual Hebrew letter-numbers according to the code.*

The first nine letters are the archetypes of numbers from 1 to 9.

Aleph, no. 1, is the unthinkable life-death, abstract principle of all that is and all that is not.

Bayt† (or Vayt), no. 2, is the archetype of all "dwellings", of all containers: the physical support without which nothing is.

Ghimel, no. 3, is the organic movement of every Bayt animated by Aleph.

Dallet, no. 4, is physical existence, as response to life, of all that, in nature, is organically active with Ghimel. Where the structure is inorganic Dallet is its own resistance to destruction.

Hay, no. 5, is the archetype of universal life. When it is conferred upon Dallet, it allows it to play the game of existence, in partnership with the intermittent life-death process.

Vav (or Waw), no. 6, expresses the fertilizing agent, that which impregnates. It is the direct result of Hay upon Dallet.

Zayn, no. 7, is the achievement of every vital impregnation: this number opens the field of every possible possibility.

* See chart, p. 62.
† We consider this spelling more phonetically correct than the usually adopted Beth.

THE LETTER-NUMBERS

𝔖			🐟	- - - -		🔨		
Tayt			Tsadde			final Tsadde		
9			90			900		
𝘓			𝔔	- - - -		👤		
Hhayt			Pay Phay			final Phay		
8			80			800		
𝙏			𝟕			𝟕		
Zayn			Ayn			final Noun		
7			70			700		
𝟙			𝐎			𝐎		
Vav or Waw			Sammekh			final Mem		
6			60			600		
𝘌			𝙂			𝐋		
Hay			Noun			final Khaf		
5			50			500		
𝘳			𝒬			𝘓		
Dallet			Mem			Tav		
4			40			400		
𝘯			𝐰					
Ghimel			Lammed			Seen Sheen		
3			30			300		
𝙄			𝐫					
Bayt Vayt			Kaf Khaf			Raysh		
2			20			200		
𝙻			𝒻					
Aleph			Yod			Qof		
1			10			100		

Hhayt, no. 8 is the sphere of storage of all undifferentiated energy, or unstructured substance. It expresses the most un-evolved state of energy, as opposed to its achieved freedom in Zayn.

Tayt, no. 9, as archetype of the primeval female energy, draws its life from Hhayt and builds it gradually into structures.

Such is the fundamental equation set and developed in Genesis.

The following nine letters, from Yod no. 10, to Tsadde no. 90, describe the process of the nine archetypes in their factual, conditioned existence: their projections in manifestation are always multiples of 10.

The nine multiples of 100 express the exalted archetypes in their cosmic states.

The number 1000, is written with an enlarged Aleph (Aleph, in Hebrew, actually means a thousand), but is seldom used. It expresses a supreme power, a tremendous cosmic energy, all-pervading, timeless, unthinkable.

The study of those multiples by 10 and by 100 is therefore the study of the very archetypes in their various spheres of emanation. The student will find it useful to examine them, so to say, vertically: 1.10.100-2.20.200 . . . and so on.

The choice of Kaf (20) for 500, of Mem (40) for 600, and of Noun (50) for 700 in finals of schemata means that those numbers acquire such cosmic values when they unfold in human beings. Thus: Adam is 1.4.40 when immature and achieves 1.4.600 when attaining his full maturity.

Here is a brief general view of the relationship between the archetypes and their multiples:

Aleph-Yod-Qof (1.10.100): Whereas Aleph (1) is the beat, or pulsation life-death-life-death, Yod (10) is its projection in temporal continuity. So Yod (in Hebrew: the hand), is the opposite of Aleph, its partner playing against it the game without which nothing would be. The Qof (100) is the most difficult symbol to understand. It includes Aleph exalted in its principle yet acting through its projection, against itself, and thereby being cosmically deathless. It is best seen in Qaheen (Cain) that mythical destroyer of illusions.

Bayt-Kaf-Raysh (2.20.200): Whereas Bayt (2), the archetype of all containers, has its roots in the cosmic resistance to life, Kaf (20)—in Hebrew, the hollow of the hand—is ready to receive all that comes and Raysh (200), the cosmic container of all existence, has its roots in the intense organic movement of the universe.

Ghimel-Lammed-Sheen (3.30.300): these three letter-numbers express a movement in progressive enlargement, from the uncontrolled functional action of Ghimel (3), through the controlled connecting agent Lammed (30), going as far as the universal Sheen (300), mythically considered to be the "spirit", or "breath" of God.

Dallet-Mem-Tav (4.40.400): the physical resistance of structures, Dallet (4) finds its purveyor in the maternal waters, Mem (40), where all life originates. Tav (400) is the exaltation of the entire cosmic existence in its utmost capacity to resist to life-death. The root Dallet-Mem (Dam) is "blood" in Hebrew and the root Mem-Tav (Met) is "death". Thus the two together express the complete cycle of existence.

Hay-Noun-Kaf in finals (5.50.500): the universal life, Hay (5) is condensed in individual existences as Noun (50) and is exalted cosmically as Kaf (500) in terminals.

Waw-Sammekh-Mem in finals (6.60.600): Waw (6) is the male agent of fertility, Sammekh (60) the female. Mem when in terminals (600) is the cosmic achievement of fruitfulness both in the intelligent or immaterial part of man and in the flesh. In Hebrew, Waw maintains its character grammatically as copulative or connecting agent.

Zayn-Ayn-Noun in finals (7.70.700): Zayn (7) as an opening towards all possible possibilities has its source and its vision in Ayn (70), which is the word for "eye" in Hebrew. It is exalted in Noun (700); this number expresses the very principle contended for in the interplay of energies throughout the universe:

the principle of indetermination in which life itself is at stake. Here we find Cain again.

Hhayt-Pay-Phay in finals (8.80.800): in every sphere of the emanation, from the densest to the most rarefied essence, these numbers stand for the primordial substance, the unfathomed reserve of undifferentiated, unstructured energy.

Tayt-Tsadde-Tsadde in finals (9.90.900): these ideograms express a progression ascending from the simplest and most primitive cell (or female structural energy) up to the transfigured symbols of womanhood, social and mythical.

The Book of Genesis begins with a series of letter-numbers that form a schema that is read *Bereshyt* and does not mean "in the beginning". It comprises Bayt (2), Raysh (200), Aleph (1), Sheen (300), Yod (10), Tav (400). Let us look at each one separately.

Bayt (2): Everything that exists is the conditioning of life and the life of the conditioning. Everything that is exists both internally and externally. Each germ of life has an envelope, which derives its movement from the great cosmic force of resistance to the life which is surging up from within (If the shell does not offer the right measure of resistance, the chicken will not hatch.) This whole duality of existence—and of our own thought—is conveyed by no. 2.

Raysh (200): As 2 multiplied by a hundred, *Raysh* represents the totality of the Universe, of interstellar space, of the myriads of stars and all the planets; all is conditioning of life and the life of conditioning. This is a great cosmic dwelling of life, which retains life manifested in accordance with its capacity (200). It includes the totality of nature, all existence: the myriads and myriads of water-drops, of blades of grass, of living cells, and the infinite myriads of elements living in the living elements of algae. *Raysh* (spelt *Raysh-Yod-Sheen*) gives birth to *Sheen*, the great cosmic breath that is everywhere and in everything.

Aleph (1): And behold: In this immense Dwelling, within these innumerable dwellings, everywhere there is creative immanence, spontaneous, always fresh and new; imperishable pulsation of life; recurrent sparks; life-death, life-death, death and resurrection: elusive, timeless. Its manifestation can be perceived and thought of only in this manner.

The non-thinkable has for its symbol the *Aleph* (1). The *Aleph* is always itself and never itself. It is ever recurring, though never the same. *Aleph* creates, it is creation, it is not created, yet it exists. It has no existence because all existence is continuous. It has no memory, having no past. It has no purpose, having no future. If one retains it, it remains retained. If one buries it, it remains buried. If one sets aside its obstacles, it is action. It breaks down resistances, though resistances are never broken by it. Without these, *Aleph* does not become manifest. Without *Aleph*, there would be nothing at all. Such is the image of the *Aleph*. *Aleph* itself is beyond all consciousness, human or cosmic. The image of *Aleph* is only an image, for *Aleph* belongs neither to time nor to space. *Aleph* is beyond the realm of our thought, beyond the reach of our mind.

Sheen (300): Prodigious cosmic motion. Movement of everything that exists. All organisms live through *Sheen* (300), either through or against its action, because *Sheen* is similar to a powerful breath which vivifies and carries away. Only the most extreme weakness can elude or oppose it.

Yod (10): Existence which both betrays and satisfies life. Continuity in the duration of that which duration destroys. *Yod*, projection of *Aleph*, confers reality upon all that tends to bury *Aleph* (dead or alive). Temporal *Yod* (10) is the finite which never rejoins the infinite. *Yod* is the manifested existence in time of *Aleph*, the timeless, the immeasurable.

Tav (400): *Tav* is the cosmic resistance to the life-breath which animates it. Without this resistance of *Tav* (400), life could not come into existence. This resistance to life is that which enables life to produce its prodigiously varied manifest forms.

Such is a first glimpse of the untranslatable *Bereshyt*.

*

Since the profound meaning of each letter must be grasped fully and individually before considering it in its syntax, we now suggest the following reflections concerning the very first letter of the Book of Genesis, *Bayt* (2). If we fully understand this letter-number we will not let our mind indulge in irrelevant speculation, but will resolutely face the problem of finding out whether the human mind has or has not a significance in the universe.

Both the writer and the reader of this book are, no doubt, seated somewhere and aware of their surroundings; this is the exterior aspect of no. 2. Our thought is functioning within our psyche, and also within our body—again no. 2. The psyche, crystallized as it is in self-perception, says "I am I". Our brain, encased in its skull, observes our seated body engaged in reading or writing and says, "This is I". Our own thought is the container of our consciousness. We are entities made up of many dwellings and in spite of the life which is in us we identify ourselves with those dwellings. But can we investigate them in order to uncover our life within? This is the inner search within *Bayt* (2).

But "beyond us" we are aware of a whole Universe, *Raysh* (200), cosmic container of a life that eludes all explanation. It is a fact that we cannot understand how it is that anything at all exists. After having eliminated all the secondary problems, however important—such as our sustenance—we turn to this fundamental problem of life comprehension. It is then that we discover that the only instrument at our disposal for tackling this problem is ourselves.

In order to show us what this instrument is made of, Genesis proposes a total reversal of our so-called thinking, which for thousands of years has immersed us in our dreams. This reversal may be understood by asking ourselves whether all the phenomena of our consciousness—our ideas, beliefs and opinions, our reasonings and points of view, our dislikes and preferences (belonging to a club, to a church, to a business, to the colour of a skin, to a society and a nation, etc.)—whether all these are elements contained in our mind, or if, on the contrary, they are our "containers". If all these are our containers, what about us? Where are we left? Our beings are just résumés, resultants of these dwellings.

Such are some of the quests which arise from *Bayt*, the beginning graph in Genesis, and we must here venture to lay emphasis on this first ideogram because in it is already contained the whole Revelation, if we realize that we actually are that *Bayt* and if we feel the urge to go into it in us.

The initial *Bayt* will ever be a barrier if not an opening, a protective rock if not the solvent of the definitions of ourselves which petrify the roots of our being thrust into them.

One must die while passing the threshold of *Bayt*, or, at the very least, for the reading of the Qabala to have any sense at all, one must feel in oneself the wish to go futher and more deeply into the investigation of what *Bayt* is to us, because *Bayt* is the physical support of *Aleph* without which *Aleph* has no existence.

When we understand the dwelling, the *Bayt*, we see that thinking belongs to the field of what can be seen, felt, measured. Then thought becomes very keen, very active, because it exercises itself in its proper function instead of losing all reason in trying to scale the skies: it does not go chasing after Truth with a capital T; for ordinary common sense knows that truth is re-established when one has uncovered error.

In the matter of these dwellings, our bodies, we can only learn to keep them in good condition by not identifying ourselves with bad habits. If the "I" cannot do without tobacco or drink or without artificially exciting the sexual urge, it identifies itself with sensations and pursuits which it exploits for its own psychological purposes: pleasures, ambitions, social reform, etc. The "I" forgets, or rather does not wish to know, that it *is* this sick body. The resultant illness or state of self-deception is commonly called a neurosis.

The fact of knowing that we are this *Bayt*, this container of life, this body, liberates the body and liberates us from our own selves. A fundamental truth recurrent throughout the Book of

Genesis is that life, inside as well as outside of this container, is unknowable and immeasurable. If we know its implications, we know ourselves: *Bayt* is what we are. We therefore do not possess any of the redeeming "spiritual" attributes invented by the escapist mind. Yet by knowing that which we are, we can allow that which we are not—but which is *in* us—to reveal itself through us.

There are no obscure dragons inside of us with which we must do battle; neither is there any evil that we must obliterate. Nor are the latest techniques for self-improvement or self-fulfilment, the way to liberation. All such struggle and striving, however lofty the conscious motivation, is aimed at establishing a continuity of existence and is consequently in perfidious opposition to the discontinuous life in us, which can only *be* in the newness and freshness of deaths and resurrections. This life, in the Book of Genesis, is named *Aleph.*

The code letters are not limited to a phonetic function in series which have the appearance of words or phrases, although they can be (and are) thus misread. In the instance we are considering at present, the succession *Bayt Raysh Aleph Sheen Yod Tav*—which is constantly read *Bereshyt* and translated "in the beginning"—each letter-number is the name of a cosmic energy acting both outside of us and within us, and each one of these cosmic energies is very complex. Thus the name *Bayt* includes *Yod, Tav* as its components. The name *Yod* includes *Waw, Dallet.** In *Dallet* is *Lammed, Tav.* In *Lammed* is *Mem, Dallet . . .* etc. All such analysis breaks down into letters, the components of which are repetitive (as *Mem, Noun, Vav, Tav*) or simple (as *Hay*). The combination of these residual terms reveals the meaning of the foundations, as it were, of the letters which are being analysed, or, to put it differently, the essence of the cosmic energy which they express.

Thus the language of this text is as complex as life itself, and yet the vital experience which can result from the full percep-

---

* *Waw* is the same letter of the Hebrew alphabet as *Vav*. They are used interchangeably, since the sound is somewhere between V and W.

tion of it has the simplicity and immediacy of a revelation. The difficulty for the writer will be to elucidate for his readers a text in a language which they do not know, and the difficulty for his readers will be to be compelled to enter into this language before having learned it. In fact, it is a language to be entered into and not to be learned. Its impact is direct, instantaneous and total if we meet it with a mind completely void and are willing to listen to a story which was originally intended to convey something altogether different from what we are conditioned to believe.

In the original meaning, there is no reference to a personal God; woman does not issue from a rib of Adam; she is not called Eve in the Garden of Eden; she does not disobey; there is no question of sin; the woman is not expelled from Eden; Cain does not kill Abel; he is not cursed by a divinity, but on the contrary protected; and if we jump a few hundred centuries to enter the allegory of Yhshwh, better known as Jesus, we find that the only Apostle who aided him in the fulfilment of his enterprise was called Judas. Such statements are no doubt surprising, but it is not generally realized to what extent the notions that Eve disobeyed, that Cain killed Abel and that Judas was a traitor have poisoned the mind. In a fundamental respect, these distortions are still contributing to the emotional illness and psychological disorders of the present-day world.

This and many other such misunderstandings have been brought about by an erroneous way of thinking which, since the dawn of history, it has been the general custom of mankind to follow. This way of thinking involves a usage of words whose meaning it is not possible to conceive. It gave birth to all of the early deities, as well as the latest and the most elaborate theologies. Whereas rational thought cannot but be confined within the field of time and measurement, comparison and evaluation, this erroneous thinking (as already pointed out) makes use of such exalted words as immortality, eternity, absolute, God—and innumerable other vague and emotional projections.

The language we need to use in re-reading the Book of Genesis should preclude all such errors. We shall be careful never to use a word unless its full meaning is clearly grasped. We shall hold to plain common sense and factual statements in order to keep our balance during an exploration which will cut across many deep-rooted fixations in "the thoughts of man".

4

The Thoughts of Man

IT IS the purpose of all ciphers to invest a few signs with much meaning. A peculiarity of the Book of Genesis is that it begins with a very strict and close code and gradually develops and unfolds its fifty chapters through symbols and allegories and finally through semi-historical tales.

In the severity of its beginning, in its first chapter, in its first verse, in its first sequence of letter-numbers, is the seed, and in the seed is the whole. This whole can be (and is expected to be) grasped in the *Bayt Raysh Aleph Sheen Yod Tav* of *Bereshyt*. This sequence is in the Revelation and *is* the Revelation, and those who grasp it are in the Revelation and are, in action the Revelation itself.

It is in effect a formula, or rather a fundamental equation of the interplay between *Aleph* and *Yod*. *Aleph*, timeless pulsation life-death-life-death, is shown in the first three graphs *Bayt-Raysh-Aleph* in its surging motion of creative energy, and *Yod*, the evolutionary process of existence is held, so to speak, between the hammer of cosmic metabolism, *Sheen*, and the anvil of its resistant container, *Tav*.

The complete schema goes beyond a mere formula affirming the equivalence of those two terms; its sweeps beyond every duality by amalgamating *Aleph* and *Yod* and making them one. The very formulation of that equation is therefore its solution. In spite of being introduced by means of an intellectual approach it can project in us the essential game of life and existence if we will allow it to break up our every-day linear way of thinking.

The six graphs of *Bereshyt* do not express different ideas

66

linked one to another by a logical sequence. They do not belong to any time process. They are simultaneous and can therefore be permuted so as to form different schemata, each one of them significant. But these developments cannot be considered here. It will be enough to examine the equation *Bereshyt* just as it is written.

There is no delusion in it because the Revelation is not a fantastic message from a supernatural world. Surely the fantastic thing is to be alive and yet not to know what life is. The whole mystery of life is within us, and yet we search for revelations concerning it in books. Does thinking or speaking about God give us any knowledge of what God is? Are we surprised to discover that the human mind is in a state of total contradiction? We are living in time and space, which we can measure only by sections. We can never reach the top of the ladder; for it is just as impossible for us to conceive of a beginning or an end to time and space as it is to imagine that time and space never were at all.

Thus our reasoning faculties are inadequate if we wish to express any vital truth in terms of daily language. Such vital truths are: existence, life, death, the cause of thought or the way to awaken the revelation within us. The words which our reason has concocted belong to a world where everything is measurable and contradictory (as are life and death). In fact, contradiction exists in the very thought that has coined these words. The sacred language of the letter-numbers, however, is not a product of this thought. These signs are apertures through which to glimpse the presence of the cosmic forces. What is more, they permit these forces to penetrate into our very being.

It is necessary that we understand the extraordinary dissimilarity between the language of the letter-numbers and our own language, into which the so-called translations of the Bible were made. This difference becomes strikingly evident with regard to the word *Bereshyt*, the very first sequence of letter-numbers in the Bible: 2.200.1.300.10.400. It is absurd that this should have been translated, *In the beginning (God created the heaven and the earth*). That unconceivable "beginning" abruptly thrusts the mind into the deadlock of a creed. The believer is he who dreams an unthinkable thought.

We make two fundamental errors. In the first place, our own language is an exclusive language: that is to say, if we speak the words "chair" or "yesterday" or "hot", we exclude every thought that is *not* "chair" or "yesterday" or "hot". We have thus settled our thoughts exclusively upon a certain thing or fact. But when this thing or fact is "the beginning of all things", which we cannot conceive, we do not know what we are talking about—we are simply dreaming.

The second error is to use this limiting thought in trying to perceive the totality of life; for as soon as we designate something that we do not know, we do not designate something that exists. At once, we are in the projection of our dream. We can "talk our heads off" saying words such as God, the Eternal, Supreme Being, or Universal Mind; but what we mean by those terms will never be anything more than indefinite imagery, and very mediocre and puerile at that, since it is in accordance with the limited measure of our own thought.

The result of these two mistakes is that as "believers" we tend to think of God in terms of men. We attribute to "him" thoughts, will, projects, a plan of evolution and what not. When in our thinking we relate ourselves to something which we do not know, we are, in fact, imagining something about which we are ignorant. What we need, instead of faith, is direct perception. This includes, first of all, knowledge of ourselves. Our instrument of perception being ourselves, if we do not perceive directly so as to *be* Revelation itself, why do we not "check" our instrument and detect the flaws in our functioning, instead of searching for truth with inadequate means? To discover where and what is the error: that is what truth is.

Remember, *But he turned and said unto Peter, Get thee behind me, Satan: thou art an offence unto me: for thou savourest not the things that be of God, but those that be of men* (Matt. xvi, 23). Translated into other languages, the text runs thus: *Because your thoughts are not*

the thoughts of God, but the thoughts of men (which associate themselves inseparably with continuity in existence, *Yod*).

We have often mentioned the reversal of cosmic energy from
Aleph to *Yod*. We have seen it epitomized in the historical action
of Moses. We will again witness it further on when Judas will
do what he is bidden, by becoming the instrument of *Jesus-
Aleph*'s delivery unto the world of *Yod*.

The understanding of that reversal is essential. The code of
letter-numbers will be of no avail if we do not instruct our sense-
based thought to yield to the disruptive pressure of timelessness
and to the necessity of allowing its immanence to blend with its
opposite, and still keep itself alive.

We have to remember that the only instrument of investigation that we possess is our mind. If we do not completely
understand how our mind works, this instrument will twist and
disfigure whatever of "reality" we may discover. The quality
and condition of the telescope govern the observation resulting
from its use. If there is dust on our lens, we see dark spots in the
heavens.

We have seen in the six letter-numbers of *Bereshyt* the elements
of the problem. We can now understand the *Bayt*, and *be* it
totally. But we have so far gleaned but few ideas concerning the
letter-number, *Aleph* (1)—just enough to know that we cannot
know the *Aleph*, that the *Aleph* is unknowable. If we should
pursue ideas concerning the *Aleph* following the wrong habit of
thousands of years, we shall never discover it. It is *not* a question
of finding and of understanding intellectually the creative and
timeless immanence, discontinuous and always new, having
neither past nor future, always present, in which the rhythm
of life-death is one unified whole. This *Aleph* is *in* us; but one
of the means of stifling it, of killing it, is to seek it out, to hunt
for it! There are innumerable ways of stifling and killing it. To
deny or to believe it, or to resort to alcohol or to prayers: all
these have the same disastrous effect.

Considered in its original, fundamental position, the problem is a duality—non-duality consisting of life-death *Aleph* (1),

which is intermittent, and *Bayt* (2), which is a continuing process of existence bent upon preserving its continuity. Knowing that the body is mortal, the psyche identifies itself with the continuum of existence and invents religions in order to persuade itself that it will carry on indefinitely, in the form of an immortal soul or otherwise. The psyche does not wish to understand that this belief is absurd, the "always" of duration, of time, being unthinkable.

Thus the psyche makes no distinction between what it calls the Eternal and duration. But if there is anything which transcends thought, it has nothing to do with the element of time. It is non-time. And if in that transcendence there is no time at all—nor space—then it is "happening" not only here and now, but everywhere else, no matter where or when. To project the Revelation into a morrow or into a heavenly hereafter is to imagine that, after counting to an enormous number of billions, some special number will emerge from its numerical order. Today is as good as any day, and so with a number. Piling them up will lead nowhere. To believe that Revelation took place only in the times of Abraham or of Pontius Pilate is equally mistaken.

So if, in spite of *Aleph* being within us we are in darkness and if, instead of being reborn as new beings without a past or future, we are entangled in a mediocre existence, the reason is that we prevent the *Aleph* within us from functioning. If we prevent *Aleph* from operating, then our thinking is wrong. Moreover, if we believe that the Revelation can be transmitted to us by somebody else—Abraham, Moses, Jesus or Mohammed—we are labouring under a delusion because no matter what we are told or what we have read, we shall be holding ideas about what we think someone else has experienced; these are mere projections and have nothing to do with reality.

In short, if we find what we are "looking for", it is always ourselves that we find. We must then stop searching and bring about a salutary reversal of our efforts. As a beginning, we will avoid thinking about anything that we cannot conceive of. In other words, we shall leave the mind free and simply listen to this story.

A very last reminder before going into the text: let us not build a creed upon *Aleph*. Although *Aleph* cannot be known it can be witnessed. We observe it in the fact that thought cannot think of a duration which never ends; in the fact that our everyday thought is established on a duality; and in the fact, also, that the further we investigate our own minds the deeper is the mystery of existence as such. Ultimately we come to realize that consciousness is a discontinuous phenomenon. Qabala is a training of the mind that makes it so subtle and pliable as to allow it to pass through the mysterious doorway of human genesis and enter into the sphere where life-death and existence carry on their inter-play. Jointly, on both sides, the most precious gift of life is at stake: the principle of Indetermination, which allows all that can be to become.

5

The Reading of the Text
The Creative Immanence

GENESIS CHAPTER I, I. Mistranslated, *In the beginning God created the heaven and the earth.* In the original letter-numbers this is: *Bereshyt Barah Elohim et Ha Shamaim Vay et Ha Eretz.*

Bereshyt: Containers of existences, existences in their containers. Universe containing the existences, containing its own existence. (Movement of the Universe.) Upspringing of life, intermittent pulsation invisible, not thinkable; life always new, always present, never present.

Creation! Vertiginous movement, immeasurable movement, movement that transcends all conception. In the hidden depths of movement is the secret of existence. And this movement is the custodian of all possible possibilities. Existence, projection of life, negation of existence. (Everything that exists must cease to exist.) Apparent betrayal of life. Revelation! Life-death is One. And the collision, the shock of passive resistance of the mass, the hard, the dry, the stones: blessed resistance! Without resistance there could be no birth. This is the becoming.

Thus are introduced the two partners playing against each other: *Aleph* springing from its containers, and *Yod* smitten by the "breath" of *Sheen* pressing against all that resists it so as to contain it.

Barah: Creation. Creation, violent, triumphant affirmation of the creative immanence. The surging—or revolving—action of perpetual creation gives birth to its own containers: *Bara, Bar-Aleph* means: son of *Aleph*.

Elohim: Total process through which timeless *Aleph* becomes

Yod which is of time. This process sets in motion the organic functions of living beings.

Existence is projected into the passive multitudes of resistance. These allow themselves or do not allow themselves to be fertilized after the manner of the living and the dead waters.

Et: If you are now thinking that you have understood the given elements of the problem, you are on the wrong track. You have only the *idea* of it, and the idea is not the thing. The problem, reduced to its essential equation, is: *pulsation of life and cosmic resistance.*

Ha Shamaim Vay Et Ha Eretz: The manifestation is twofold: there is the existence of that which contains and the life of that which is contained. Existence of the husks and the life of the kernels. External circumstances and interior life. The action of the gardener, of air, sun and water, and the life of the seed which will produce the plant, the flower, the fruit. The whole of existence is always in the grip of two forces which are heading towards a catastrophe that threatens, either through pressure of the life force from within or because of attack from the outside.

You can now see that the problem is unfolding: this interaction of existence and of life is like two players who agree to play against one another. If they were not thus associated, no game would be possible. If *Aleph* and *Yod* were not in that relationship, we would not be here talking about them. There would be nothing at all!

Existence is the continuing factor: vegetation and the animal kingdom. In all these existences, the pulsation of creative life—discontinuous, timeless—is so profoundly buried and hidden away that it seems to be absent. It seems to be absent everywhere: in the cosmos, in inter-stellar space, in the billions and billions of suns where we can neither perceive nor conceive of there being life, properly speaking. But in one form or another, even in no form at all, even engulfed and hidden, the creative immanence, active or inactive, is there. It is both in the movement and the beauty of the universe.

All this is said in the first verse of Genesis, and even much more. Yet all that is said there can never be totally divulged because of the unfathomable complexity of the Revelation. In this game between existence and life, the text already implies that whereas the fixed role of the vegetable and animal kingdom is existence-versus-life, the role of man is to change sides in the game: to be *Aleph* against *Yod*. From the amoeba up to man, all life is within the realm of continuity. Man, says the Book of Genesis is called upon to enter into that which transcends continuity and time. Reciprocally, when Elohim is entwined with YHWH, the process of life enters into existence. But all this is so difficult to grasp that for thousands of years people have read the Bible without really knowing what it means!

Genesis I, 2. Mistranslated, *And the earth was without form, and void: and darkness was upon the face of the deep. And the Spirit of God moved upon the face of the waters.* Let us forget this translation with its "void" earth, but let us once more review the natures of the two fundamental protagonists of the game of life versus existence: Aleph and Yod.

In order to simplify the explanation of the text in the sense of its original meaning, we shall from now on refer to the two protagonists of the game of life versus existence by their names, *Aleph* and *Yod*. We will review once more their natures, for all of this is difficult to assimilate.

(a) The name of the so-called earth, which is Eretz, begins with *Aleph*. The *Aleph* (1) is creative immanence, timeless and immeasurable, like an intermittent spark, which our thinking cannot grasp. Were we to imagine it, we should consider the *Aleph* as a succession: being, non-being, being, non-being—or life-death, life-death, life-death. The *Aleph* appears in the first verse as one of the given elements in this Revelation. But we repeat that while the *Bayt* (2) and the *Raysh* (200) are containing elements, or containers, and accessible to our thinking, the *Aleph* (1) is only an idea in the succession of *Bayt Raysh Aleph Sheen Yod Tav*, composing the first sequence in the Bible: *Bereshyt*.

Bayt and *Raysh* are understandable, but not so *Aleph*. *Aleph* is buried in Eretz. To allow it to spring forth alive in us is *the*

74

absolute function of every human being. In whomsoever the *Aleph* lives and functions is the very Revelation itself. *Aleph* is buried in all the containing elements—in the cosmic container-forms, the stars and the planets, etc., as well as in the container-forms of individuals. The word encompassing every variety of container is Eretz, which all translators have reduced to one word, earth.

What, then, is the aspect of these container-elements in which *Aleph* is buried? The life in them simply swarms, uncontrolled, in a state of (says the verse) "Tohu and Bohu", which is a jumble, a confusion, a hurly-burly, a chaos. It is a fantastic whirlpool of life, not limited to the planet earth, but cosmically including all that exists in the Universe. And, at "the face of its very self", in its very "deepness", that chaos is totally fecund, abundant, prolifically fertile. Such is the "darkness" referred to in the accepted translation. And such is the true meaning of the first part of the second verse concerning Eretz, the so-called earth; that in which *Aleph* is concealed.

(*b*) The so-called "heaven" in the first verse, the name of which is *Shamaim*, contains a *Yod* between two *Mem*. This sequence indicates the cosmic movement of *Sheen* acting against *Mayim*, the so-called waters: the two *Mem* (40) between which *Yod* is playing against its partner *Aleph* in the game of existence versus life. *Yod* is all we know and all that exists, and all that we can think about. Its mass, its space, its time are the mass, the space, the time, and the dwelling of all that exists. And it plays against its very destruction. And that which plays against it is the so-called Spirit of God, which is the tremendous vital energy of *Sheen* originated by *Aleph*. (The word God is the inadequate translation of Elohim, previously defined as a summing-up of *Aleph* in action and having nothing to do with the general idea of God, which is beyond thought.)

The process concerning the player *Yod* is obviously entirely different from that concerning *Aleph*. *Yod* is always, so to speak, between the hammer and the anvil. We mentioned that process already, giving the egg as an example. If the shell is not hard

75

enough, the germ dies for lack of adequate protection; and if it is too hard, the germ dies from too much protection. Therefore *Yod* must always be in possession of two contrasting qualities; strength and softness. *Yod* must be very earnest and single-minded and yield to the delicate hint of the weakest life within it. It must be totally still, yet quick in following the movement of all that is transient. If *Yod* insists on one of these qualities against the other, what happens is a "dead death". (This expression, *Mawt-Hamawt*, will be used in a later description of Adam in Eden.)

Thus the so-called Spirit of God acts like a steam roller every time *Yod* does not play the game properly. And that action is one of the facts of life that we know best: wars, destructions, disasters of all sorts, both in the outer world and in our own inner life; our frustrations and failures; the annihilation of our achievements; and the terrible refusal of life in response to our hopes and our projects. But from these ruins, these misfortunes, rise the triumphs of ever-fertile life. In order that the new may spring forth without ceasing, must not the old, also without ceasing, be destroyed? This destructive aspect of life is essentially the activity of *Aleph*: the action of non-temporal life against the continuity of existence, with its resulting violence and despair.

6

The Light that is Life

GENESIS I, 3-13. Verses 3 to 13 describe the activity of the cosmic forces that are indicated by the first three letters of the alphabet: *Aleph* (1), *Bayt* (2) and *Ghimel* (3). This activity is not that of the first three days of Creation, as all the exoteric traditions assert. Rightly understood, the text does not relate a Creation in a succession of six days, after which the divinity is supposed to have rested on the seventh day. This legend is too childish. A divinity who rests after his labour is too obviously a projection of the human mind. The succession of his labours is equally absurd. The creation of the planet Earth, in a totally empty universe, is contrary to all evidence. The appearance of the entire vegetable world on the third day, although the sun, the moon and the stars do not appear until the fourth, is the negation of all common sense. Only two courses are open to us; either we consider this whole story to be little more than a nursery rhyme, or else we seek for hidden meanings. For centuries, theologians have sought a solution to the problem without reaching a satisfactory interpretation.

One cannot satisfy the logic of pure reason and hold to the traditional meaning of the text, so, at the outset, let us resolutely forgo everything commonly thought about the Book of Genesis. The first step consists in rejecting the idea that a succession of events took place. On the contrary, everything happened at once, and verses 3 to 13 attempt to relate the activity of the forces *Aleph*, *Bayt* and *Ghimel*: that is to say, of the numbers 1, 2 and 3 acting simultaneously, and neither in time nor in space. Naturally, since our thinking is unable to "think" anything that is non-time and non-space, these verses

3 to 13 are symbolic and demand that the reader's comprehension extends beyond the symbols. They ask that he affect within himself the difficult reversal in the game of existence versus life, that he study what is said from the standpoint of *Aleph* and not from that of *Yod*. If for so many thousands of years this text has not been understood, except by the Qabala, the reason is that those who have read it have done so without bringing about this change within themselves.

We will now transcribe letter by letter (number by number) Genesis 1, 3 so familiar in its mistaken translation: *And God said, Let there be light and there was light.* In Hebrew it reads: *Va-Yomer Elohim Yehy Awr Ve-Yehy Awr.*

The first schema, *Va-Yomer* (Vav-Yod-Aleph-Mem-Raysh: 6.10.1.40.200), expresses an emanation (6) which projects *Yod* (10) and Aleph (1) in the basic attribute of matter, *Mem* (40) included in the universal container *Raysh* (200). *Yomer* is not a verb as part of speech attributed to *Elohim*'s predication but an action, an exertion or projection of energy, a doing. The two "players" are here said to be thrust into the sphere of appearances.

The second schema, *Elohim* (Aleph-Lammed-Hay-Yod-Mem: 1.30.5.10.40), is the process through which Aleph (1) by initiating a physiological movement (30) in life (5) comes into existence (10) and acquires the appearance of a metamorphosis (40) which offers resistance to life and therefore gives birth to living beings.

The third schema *Yehy* (Yod-Hay-Yod: 10.5.10) can only be translated "existence-life-existence". It expresses the coming into life (5) of a double existence (10 and 10) and thus describes the distinctive mark of organic life which is always a double process, inner and outer, of germ and shell or psyche and body.

The fourth schema *Awr* (Aleph-Waw-Raysh: 1.6.200) expresses the copulation of *Aleph* and of its physical support *Raysh*. As explained in the preceding schema it is a living energy, both outer and inner. The cabalists have always laid great stress on that symbol, both in its physical and in its metaphysical significance.

The fifth schema *Va-Yehy* is a repetition of the third. *Yehy-Va-Yehy* is an action in two proceedings from the one essence linked copulatively by *Waw*. It insists on the fact that *Awr*, which we call light, is essentially alive in a self-creative twofold mode of being. (The authors of this text would have had no difficulty in simply stating "Elohim made light" if it had been this that they had wished to say.)

The sixth schema repeats *Awr* and the reader must be very attentive when such repetitions occur in the Bible, because they always have a hidden purpose.

Awr and *Awr*: inner light and outer light. Whether intuition and perception, or heart and mind, or soul and body, whatever their names, when they come to mean something to us, inside us, when their joint action is fruitful, the Revelation is here.

Why has this twofold energy, deriving from the action of the universal life-force upon its cosmic container, been translated as "light"? The answer is that the Universe, considered as a space-time continuum, is set into motion at the maximum speed of which it is capable. According to a very ancient tradition, Genesis I, 3 says that that maximum speed is the speed of light. Whether this statement is absolutely correct or not, scientifically, is irrelevant. Some day it may be found that the highest speed of which the Universe is capable is not only alive but that it *is* the throbbing of life throughout the entire cosmos. This speed has a number, a measure, which defines the mass, space and time of the Universe as well as its duration.

In other words, the infinite movement of *Aleph* imprints in the mass of *Raysh* the greatest speed of which *Raysh* is capable. It can be inferred that in absolutely all components the universe yields to the mighty power of *Aleph*, or again that the universe is totally permeated by *Aleph* to the point of perpetually generating it, so that *Aleph* indefinitely becomes its own son.

To reiterate in plain and simple language, Genesis I, 3 states

79

that, as a consequence of the interplay between the pulsating *Aleph* and the continuous existence of *Yod*, *Aleph* is copulatively (*Waw*) projected into the Universe (*Raysh*). This living process is therefore expressed in the sequence *Aleph-Waw-Raysh*, which spells the word *Awr* (pronounced *Or*), which is what we call light.

We are, here, at the origin of the tradition concerning light, which the Bible mentions a hundred times or more, including the well-known words in the Gospel of John (1, 4): *and the life was the light of man.* This, however, must be put into the present tense, along with the ensuing verse, thus: *the life is the light of man. And the light* shines *in darkness: and the darkness* comprehends *it not.*

This means that it is no good our merely knowing intellectually, that the life of *Aleph* is in us. You will see, as you follow the text of Genesis, that the whole question centres upon our allowing *Aleph* to spring forth within us in total freedom. In order that this may occur, and we say this again, we must cease taking sides with *Yod* and the idea of static continuity, and play the game on the side of *Aleph*. This means, of course that we must die to every minute of every day, die to every thought, to every definition of ourselves and of our supposed relationship with a God of our projection. Far from being a suicidal process, this is on the contrary a cleaning of our "house", a letting go of the mechanism of existence to which *Yod* would have us cling. It is not possible to "believe" in a Revelation and at the same time to *be* it. Believing is an escape, a refusal of it. If there is a Revelation, it exists *now*; and that "darkness" which comprehends it is forthwith made pregnant by it. But this calls for a depth of perception and a stillness of the mind which have nothing to do with neurotic revivals and their noisy emotional overflowings. The Revelation can only "take over" in us in seriousness, simplicity and silence.

7

The Light that is Darkness

GENESIS I, 4. The beginning of this verse reads thus in Hebrew: *Veyarey Elohim Et Ha-Awr Ki-Tov.* The schemata *Et* and *Ki* having been translated in many fanciful ways according to the whims or creeds of translators, this sentence could just as well be interpreted: "and Elohim saw, because the light was good". The obviousness of such a statement would dispel the ambiguous halo of religiosity which surrounds the traditional and *God saw the light that it was good.*

The first schema *Veyarey* (*Vav-Yod-Raysh-Aleph*: 6.10.200.1) says that the impregnation (6) of the existence (10) in the universe (200) allows Aleph (1) to spring forth. Compared to *Bara* (*Bayt-Raysh-Aleph*) which in Genesis I, I means "create", *Veyarey* appears as its analytical explanation.

The second schema *Elohim* has already been explained as being the process through which *Aleph* becomes *Yod* and resurrects from that material metamorphosis. Life in its oneness moves up and down, down and up, from infinite to finite, and from duration to timelessness.

The third schema *Et* (*Aleph-Tav*: 1.400) is an equivalent to our expression: "from A to Z", *Aleph* and *Tav* being the first and last letters of the alphabet. The infinite energy *Aleph* and its container's resistance *Tav* are assembled here in a synthetic view of the fact *Awr*.

The fourth schema *Ha-Awr* adds *Hay* (5), life's archetype, to the schema *Awr* (which has been explained when dealing with the preceding verse).

The fifth schema *Ky* (*Kaf-Yod*: 20.10) says that *Awr* is only considered here in its aspect as physical support of energy. *Kaf*

81

(20) is the archetype of *Bayt*-in-existence, 2 × 10. *Yod* (10) emphasizes that existence. (The inner light will only appear in Genesis II when the birth of man will be described not from the point of view of physical evolution but through perception of its essence.)

The sixth schema *Tov* (*Tayt-Waw-Vayt*: 9.6.2) describes the female character (9) of proliferation (6) of bodies or containers (2). *Tov* is the sempiternal function of nature indefinitely repeating its prototypes. The fact that it means "good" in colloquial Hebrew reveals the deep craving of the psyche for a static state of existence.

The second part of Genesis I, 4 is always translated: *and God divided the light from the darkness*, in spite of the fact that "God" could not have previously seen the light "that it was good" had it not been already divided from darkness. In Hebrew it reads thus: *Vayavdel Elohim Beyn Ha-Awr Ve-Veyn Ha-Hhosheykh.*

The action *Yavdel* (translated divided) *Yod-Vayt-Dallet-Lammed* (10.2.4.30) introduces in the existence (10) of containers (2) the necessary resistance to life (4) which allows them to become organic (30). The schema *Beyn* or *Veyn* (2.10.700) does not mean "divide" in Hebrew, but "between" or rather "among", and according to the code it has a far greater significance. Its letter-numbers show that 2 and 10 (containers in existence) unfold a cosmic 700 which is the first and ultimate principle at stake in the universe: the freedom of indetermination. This is granted by the action *Yavdel* to both *Awr* and *Hhosheykh*.

This last schema (*Hhayt-Sheen-Khaf*: 8.300.500) when read according to the code reveals its origin and its nature. It designates the immeasurable reservoir of undifferentiated energy (8) in relationship with the cosmic metabolism (300) and the cosmic life (500). This "darkness" is swarming with all that *could* be, and its living power transcends all human thought. From it, the action of *Yavdel Veyn*, in time, order and measure, gives birth to all that *can* become and be.

The same action of *Yavdel Beyn* upon *Awr* bestows to such

elements of *Awr* as *can* be stirred into organic motion the blessed bounty of undetermined freedom.

How, when and where this liberality is taken advantage of is explained in the following chapters of Genesis and in the text-books of Qabala. What we need to know at this point of our reading is the contradictory characters, which appear in *Yavdel*, of *Dallet* (4) and *Lammed* (30). *Dallet* expresses the resistance that any given structure opposes to that which tends to destroy it. *Lammed* is the organic movement that results from the overthrowing of obsolete structures. All organic structures have a necessary quality of resistance which deteriorates into rigidity and self-preservation. Evolution, according to Qabala, is a series of simultaneous destruction-construction of resistances, the biosphere being an interplay between structures and un-structured energies (analogically *Awr* and *Hhosheikh*).

Let us look again, from that point of view, at the schema *Tov.* translated "good" in Elohim's repetitive assertion (Gen. 1, 10, 12, 18, 21, 25): *God saw that it was good*, and again (Gen. 1, 31): *And God saw everything that he had made, and, behold, it was very good*. The words translated "very good" are *Tov-Meod*: 9.6.2-40.1.4.

Not only is 9.6.2 the building of shells (or containers, or physical supports) but 40.1.4 which qualifies that process could not express more clearly the imprisonment of *Aleph* within two resistances, 40 and 4.

These assertions must therefore be understood as indicating the powerful tendency of nature to enjoy its fructification in existence by means of a repetitive process (... *every living creature ... after their kind*: Gen. 1, 21).

Let us consider by means of an example the interplay between established existence and the infinite possibilities born of life-death: as a consequence of the activity in the totality of life it so happens that in a particular place, at a particular time, a lily-of-the-valley comes into being. This flower is the maximum of life (or light) that such a place and such a time have been capable of bringing forth. So existence gloats over it and says: "Am I not beautiful? I score a point." But life answers: "Rejoice if you wish, but a lily-of-the-valley will never be anything but a lily-of-the-valley. I, life, am total and unconditioned, vast cosmic energy and movement. Out of this, anything can happen, whereas from a lily-of-the-valley, only a lily-of-the-valley can be born."

The stability of certain "living fossils" is amazing. Termites are identical with what they were during the oligocene age. Their firmly established society has indeed maintained its victory against life throughout immense geological periods. The spirit of Aleph is definitely dead in its functioning for functioning's sake. The reader of the Bible here receives a severe challenge: which of the two partners Aleph and Yod, does he wish to play for? If he associates himself with the psychological structures of his conditioning, he will build his existence (Yod) on a sense of duration and a craving for continuance—and the Revelation (Aleph) will evade him. But if he breathes the cosmic breath of life, his own "darkness" will breed the unknown which passes understanding.

Genesis 1, 5. Veiqra Elohim Le-Awr Yom Ve-Le-Hhosheykh Qara Layla (and God Called the light Day and the darkness he called Night). This translation is too infantile to be commented upon. What the verse really explains concerns the results of *Yavdel* in both *Awr* and *Hhosheykh*. *Awr* becomes *Yom*, and *Hhosheykh* becomes *Layla*.

As is always the case in the Bible, a change of name expresses a complete change of form, character and condition. *Awr* (*Aleph-Waw-Raysh*) actually becomes something different, which is called *Yom* (*Yod-Waw-Mem*), when, as has been stated so often already, *Aleph* becomes *Yod*. Yom is the projection in existence of *Awr*.

Likewise *Hhosheykh* becomes *Layla* (*Lammed-Yod-Lammed-Hay*: 30.10.30.5). When it comes into existence, this new schema, as can be seen when decoded, expresses vividly the vital quality of that obscure (unseen) existence (10) between the organic lives (30 and 30). The *Hay* (5) which completes the schema is a reassertion of life.

Thus ends the first "days", which is not a period of time but the action of *Aleph*.

Genesis I, *6-8*. These verses apparently relate the creation of *a firmament in the midst of the waters to divide the waters which were above the firmament*. And the translation goes on to say: *and God called the firmament heaven*. (In some texts; *expanse* for *firmament*.)

It is true that *Maym* (*Mem-Yod-Mem*: 40.10.40) in colloquial Hebrew means "waters". The Qabalists (and alchemists) have always considered *Maym* as a symbol of the biochemical sphere's attributes, because analogically the waters are the natural environment for epigenesis.

Let us not forget that we are dealing with a treatise on thermodynamics. We have seen in Genesis I, I a double equation of energy as *Aleph* and *Yod* (as infinite animation and as its own physical casting). *Awr* is the equation of their symbolic wedlock (*Raysh*, 200 being the symbol of the entire cosmic physical support). We have then seen *Yavdel* as the biosphere's process which originates two trends of structures in each of the two aspects of energy, *Awr* and *Hhosheykh*. In Genesis I, 6-8, which we are now considering this entire process is seen as from the point of view of *Bayt* (2), so-called the second "day"; *Bayt* being the symbol of all containers. The protagonists, *Raysh* and *Aleph* must be expressed now as they appear in existence. But we know that *Aleph* does not possess the quality of existence in duration. Therefore its symbol must perforce be *Qof* (100) because, as we have already stated, *Qof* is symbol of cosmic *Aleph* in existence, both *Aleph* and *Yod*, blending the opposites, timelessness and time. *Raysh* and *Qof* assert their existence *Yod*. But what is the result of this wedlock? It obviously is *Ayn* (70), the principle of indetermination, which is the common stake of both parties. The equation thus formed, *Raysh-Qof-Yod-Ayn* (200.100.10.70): reads *Raquiy*, and is an energy which, not being fixed in extent, has the intrinsic quality of expansion. Energy in expansion: that is the definition of space according to Qabala. It is in expansion because, as its own container, energy cannot cope with itself. It cannot but be perpetually its own overflowing.

We are very far indeed from the "firmament" which is supposed to translate *Raquiy*, and further still from its other name "heaven" of the canonical text.

Shamaym (the schema which is translated "heaven") is simply the impact of *Sheen* (300), the cosmic metabolism, upon *Maym*. The elements of *Maym* that bear the impact are stirred by the *Ayn* (70) of *Raquiy* and they set into motion their own metabolism *Lammed* (30). The schema thus obtained is *Mem-Ayn-Lammed* which is read *Me-aal* (40.70.30) and is translated "from above", or "which were above", according to the traditional English version. The elements of *Maym* that do not bear the impact become unavailable for conversion into functional work and in that state of entropy, they return to *Tav* (400) in which the undifferentiated *Hhayt* (8) restores the resistance of *Tav* (400). The schema of that part of *Mem* is therefore: *Mem-Tav-Hhayt-Tav* (40.400.8.400). It is read *Metahhat* and is translated "from under" or "which were under".

Thus is seen the separation of the "living waters" and of the "dead waters", from the viewpoint of *Bayt* (2), said to be the "second day". It is an explanation of the mechanism by which, in Genesis I, I, *Shamaym* is formed.

Genesis I, 9-10. We can now come to the explanation of how *Eretz* is formed. The English version is: *And God said, Let the waters under the heaven be gathered together unto one place, and let the dry land appear; and it was so. And God called the dry land Earth; and the gathering of the waters called he Seas; and God saw that it was good.* We have dealt enough with the saying, the naming and the self-congratulation of that deity. These verses explain how the energy which, through entropy, having returned to the cosmic reservoir of amorphousness, re-enters into the general cycle of life.

If we keep in mind the trajectories of *Aleph* and *Yod*, we already know that we are now going to witness *Aleph's* burial, that is, its factual deposition under earth.

The preceding verse has shown *Yod* in existence, plainly visible in *Maym* (40.10.40), held in between two biological resistances thrust into motion by Sheen (*300*) as expressed by the schema *Shamaym*. Those were the waters "above", or the biosphere.

Next we come to examine the inorganic waters "below". The Hebrew text says that they *Iqaoo* (*Yod-Qof-Waw-Waw*: 10.100. 6.6) *El Maqom Ehhad*. *Iqaoo* is the most rational and intelligent schema that can be constructed in the circumstance. Let us imagine symbolically the energy called *Aleph* falling into a *Yod* far below the organized life of the biosphere and yet proceeding along in a loop, upwards. The junction between *Yod* and *Aleph* is *Qof*, as already stated. So *Qof* is called for, appears, and with it the double *Waw* which will eventually be doubly fruitful. The second schema *El* (*Aleph-Lammed*: 1.30) need hardly be explained: *Aleph* is born again here bearing its active quality, *Lammed* (30). With the next schema *Maqom* (*Mem-Qof-Waw-Mem*: 40.100.6.40) we see *Qof* alive and fruitful taking the place of the dead *Yod* of *Maym* (100.6. in the place of 10). The last schema *Ehhad* (*Aleph-Hhayt-Dallet*: 1.8.4) means "one". It is the name of no. 1 and it expresses in a stupendous way the metaphysical disappearance from our sight of Aleph, as it actually is projected into 8 and 4.

We must add that the root of *Maqom* in Hebrew is *Qom*, to rise, to stand up, to arise. The scribes and translators, unaware of the text's meaning, could not imagine the so-called waters arising in one single upright flow of energy! In consequence, the following schemata are inverted in meaning. The schemata for *and let the dry land appear* are only two: *Vetrayeh Hayabasha*.

Vetrayeh (*Vav-Tav-Raysh-Aleph-Hay*: 6.400.200.1.5) and *Hayabasha* (*Hay-Yod-Bayt-Sheen-Hay*: 5.10.2.300.5) say that *Tav* and *Raysh* fertilized by *Vav* give birth to *Aleph* alive, and that the life *Hay* in existence *Yod* of containers *Bayt* create the very cosmic breath, *Sheen*, which is life, *Hay*.

Thus is completed the round-about journey of living energy. The beauty of its being buried in *Eretz* (*Aleph-Raysh-Tsadde*:

1.200.900) which we call earth, and which is the substance of our bodies, is its perpetual potential resurrection in us. Final *Tsadde* of *Eretz* (900) stands for beauty.

Genesis I, *11-27*. These verses further relate the facts pertaining to *Yom Shlyshy* (*Sheen-Lammed-Yod-Sheen-Yod*: 300.30.10. 300.10) translated "third day". The schema for "third": *Shlyshy*, with its two *Sheen* and two *Yod* is significant. We have seen so far the cosmic metabolism burying itself in itself in the shape (*Eretz*) of its own container. We will now see its resurrection. Genesis I, 11: . . . *let the earth bring forth grass . . . herb . . . fruit. . . whose seed is in itself*. . . . And Genesis I, 12: . . . *the earth brought forth grass . . . herb . . . fruit . . . whose seed was in itself . . .* etc. . . .

In spite of the lame translation, the two *Sheen* and two *Yod* appear here: one life is mentioned as universally bestowed, and another is endogenous. The schemata for "let the earth bring forth" are *Tadshey Ha-aretz* and the schemata for "and the earth brought forth" are *Va-Totsey Ha-aretz*.

The fundamental difference between *Tadshey* and *Totsey* has been overlooked by the translators. *Tadshey* (*Tav-Dallet-Sheen-Aleph*: 400.4.300.1) is the universal call of *Tav* (400) to the archetype of resistance *Dallet* (4), and hence the universal organic process *Sheen* (300) gives birth to *Aleph*. But *Totsey* (*Tav-Waw-Tsadde-Aleph*: 400.6.90.1) as the response of *Eretz*, manifests a 6 instead of a 4 and a 90 instead of a 300. In this difference the whole of the myth is included.

Nature's innate quality is a non-resistance, a yielding in the absolute meaning of that word: a bringing forth fruit. Therefore the Dallet of resistance is eliminated in exchange for *Waw*, and the *Sheen* is ignored for *Tsadde*.

Tsadde is not only an archetype for beauty. It also expresses the construction of forms, the building of structures, beginning with the cell, upwards. *Aleph* in *Totsey* is reborn, but either stunned or asleep or very young indeed. It will have to transcend the vegetable and the animal kingdom of *Tov*, the perpetual yielding to repetitive prototypes, until Adam learns with

Raa, traditionally said to be "evil", how constantly to destroy and rebuild his world.

Genesis I, 14-26. The creation of the sun and moon on the "fourth day" with all the vegetation on earth developing on the "third day" clearly demonstrates that the "days" are not a succession in time.

The schema for "fourth day" is *Yom Raby-y* (*Raysh-Bayt-Yod-Ayn-Yod*: 200.2.10.70.10) in which the response of the physical supports 200 and 2 to the impetus of life reveals its adequacy (the 70 in between two *Yod* means that the germ of indeterminate freedom is held inside the double existence of organic life).

We must keep in mind that *Yom* is a coming into visible existence of *Awr*. Number 4 always expresses a resistance. We therefore understand that the sun and the moon, introduced here as luminaries, have their exact illustration in electric light bulbs utilized as resistances in a circuit in such fashion as to obtain light.

Just as *Yom* fourth brings about a resistance projected into the creation (*Awr*) of *Yom* first, the fifth begets birds and fish as living beings into the waters (above and below) of *Yom* second, and the sixth introduces all the beasts of the earth and *Adam* (male and female) into the creation of *Yom* third. There is a direct correspondence between 1 and 4, between 2 and 5 and between 3 and 6.

Cabalists must ever consider that the physical, sensorial world is an inverted symbolical projection of reality. The earth and waters, the vegetation, the fish and fowl, the animals and man, all these must be decoded so as to reveal what they actually stand for as structured living energy in multi-term analogical series.

8

An Adam and a Sabbath

WE MUST revert to certain developments in Genesis I, which had to be overlooked in a first panoramic view.

Genesis I, 22. In this verse *Elohim* blesses the "great whales", all the creatures that move in the waters and every "winged fowl". The blessing is *Yebarekh* (*Yod-Bayt-Raysh-Kaf*: 10.2.200. 500). The whales are *Tanynym* (*Tav-Noun-Yod-Noun-Mem*: 400.50.10.50.40) and the pleonastic winged birds are *Oof-Kanaf* (*Ayn-Waw-Phay—Kaf-Noun-Phay*: 70.6.800-20.50.800).

That blessing is the bestowal of cosmic life (500) to all that lives in the waters. The particular spelling of the schema *Tanynym* expresses a double life (50 and 50) born out of 400, and *Oof-Kanaf* (literally the bird-wing) expresses a fleeting uncertainty born out of 800, and alive in 800. And thus ends that which is accomplished by *Yom* fifth, the no. 5 being that of life.

Genesis I, 24. *Eretz*, the earth, is mentioned in this verse, as the third Element, after air and water (fire, *Esh* will appear much later, in Genesis II, with *Esha*, the woman, its feminine).

Genesis I, 26. In this verse is the creation of man. Its serial number, 26 is that of *YHWH*, sometimes called *Yahveh*, sometimes Jehovah, and, in the English Bible "The Lord". We will deal later with that schema. It is spelt *Yod-Hay-Waw-Hay* $(10+5+6+5=26)$, and its first appearance will occur in Genesis II. The creation of man in a verse bearing the number 26 is a prefiguration of the *YHWH*, which has hitherto not been mentioned. Man does not appear here as the exclusive product of the earth, but as proceeding from the *Elohim* which, as we know, is the vital process of the *Aleph* in action. The text which has been translated, *Let us make man in our own image, after our likeness*, actually reads approximately thus (we will not follow it here letter-number by letter-number): From the living process of *Aleph* in its cosmic body-container springs forth a factual life upsetting the mechanical repetitions of nature (where every pattern is a fixed prototype). Here an Adam is created who is in contact with the powerful movement of the Universe, and in whom every possibility is latent.

"Adam" is *Aleph immersed in blood*, but this blood is not "all-absorbing"; it can become "cosmically fruitful", which means that the human body can come to radiate cosmic energy. The schema for man (*Adam*) is *Aleph* (1), *Dallet* (4), *Mem* (40 or 600). The fact that *Mem* final can be 40 (i.e. resistance) and can leap to 600 (i.e. cosmic fertility) indicates the vast range of possibilities in man. The true vocation of mankind is this transfiguration of 40 into 600. The text goes on to say that Adam can be considered as a living shadow, or image, of the Elohim: given the potential of greater power of resistance than any other being, he can become the receptacle of the greatest intensity of life on this planet. (In a certain respect, we can see this illustrated today wherever men are being trained to withstand the strain of living in rockets, beyond gravitation, on the floor of the oceans, in the antarctic icefields, or to test their physical and psychological resistance in all kinds of competitions.)

Genesis I, 27 says that *Adam* is created male and female; *Zakar* and *Neqivah*. In the letter-numbers which express this fact, *Zakar* (7.20.200) and *Neqivah* (30.100.2.5) we can see a relationship between the sexes which can well come as a surprise for the reader. Whereas *Zakar* does not possess the capacity by which all possible possibles can come into existence, in *Neqivah* the cosmic *Aleph* is active. This theme is so important in the development of the allegory that it must be explained at once.

The letter-numbers which designate the male (*Zakar*) are 7 constricted by containers that are both factual (20) and cosmic (200). The number seven is familiar to us being that of a state of transition: the seventh note of a scale is constantly tending towards a new octave; a seventh chord in music is a means of modulation into a new key. The number 7 is potentially open to anything which may happen to alter a previously established pattern. *Eretz*, as we have seen in the third "day" of Genesis I, 11-12, responds with a yielding of the cosmic life and produces beauty and an infinite variety of vegetation though each species is limited to the capacity of its own seed.

Whereas *Eretz* is thus enclosed in its natural repetitive process, *Adam's* blood is open to every transfiguration. For over and beyond *everything that creepeth upon the earth*, which can only develop *after his kind* (Gen. I, 25), *Adam*—as mankind, both male and female—is given a special "blessing". This blessing receives a different response from man and woman. The man (7.20.200) is constantly being upset by and upsetting history, driven unconsciously by his inner 7 towards an ideal cosmic 200; whereas the woman (50.100.2.5) is forever reshaping the 50 and 100 with the aim of safeguarding the home (2.5).

In order that *Aleph* should be born into human society, the passive female side of *Adam*, obviously, must transform itself and rise above the female "containing element" (the body). Until this has happened, the activity of the male will only be chaotic agitation. The theme of the necessary transformation of the feminine is very important in the Bible. We shall meet it again in the feminine types of *Esha*, Hhevah, Sarah, Rebecca and Rachel, etc., ... up to Mary, mother of Jesus. All these are symbolical personifications of what women must learn to become. It is unfortunate that inadequate translations have prevented women from grasping the truth concerning themselves as it is set forth in the Book of Genesis. Thus women allow themselves to be misled into allowing the male—in such fatuous roles as a high priest of racism waving the Bible, or some head of state invoking divine vengeance in a "holy war"—to exert every possible pressure to persuade all humankind that "God" is a "He", with "his" code of morals, "his" wars, etc., etc.

The Bible, from beginning to end, in every instance where

the transformation of woman is stated and taught, will never be truly understood until the transformation has become a reality alive and active in humanity. If popular thinking has been content that one woman should have been transformed in such fashion as to have become the "Mother-of-God", it is an evasion, a fantasy, a flight from reality. The lesson to be learned from the text we have just considered is far more profound and is to be lived in the here and now.

Genesis II, *1-3*. We read in the translations of these verses that thus creation is finished, that on the seventh day Elohim ended the work which he had made and rested on the seventh day, and that he blessed and sanctified that day because he rested from his work.

Of the many complex schemata of these verses we will only examine the following:

Yshbot (*Yod-Sheen-Bayt-Tav*: 10.300.2.400) translated "he rested".

Yom-Hashby-y (*Yod-Waw-Mem—Hay-Sheen-Bayt-Yod-Ayn-Yod*: 10.6.40-5.300.2.10.70.10) translated "day seventh".

Ybrakh (*Yod-Bayt-Raysh-Khaf*: 10.2.200.500) translated "blessed".

Yqdesh (*Yod-Qof-Dallet-Sheen*: 10.100.4.300) translated "sanctified".

According to the code, we see that the "resting" is a deep penetration of 300 into 400; the schema for seventh, shows that the life (5) of 300, in its physical support (2) is at rest because the 70 by which its influence is brought to bear is seen to exist in 10.70.10. According to these numbers, the "blessing" and the "sanctifying" express the fact that the universe is autonomous and free. The schemata concerning no. 7 says that the universal life is satisfied in that which exists (the infinite is satisfied in the numbers that support it physically), because 7 in existence (70) is satisfied by the very existence of all that is. In 70 is a motion which maintains every possible possibility of unfoldment.

So we are not in the least obeying a biblical precept when we think that we have to be bored on Sundays or Sabbath and do nothing. The "blessing" of no. 7 is meant to liberate in us some potential hidden faculty. We can use a day of leisure to find out whether some quality exists in us or not. If we can use it to discover a latent talent or a useful hobby, to explore nature, or in any way to expand our inner or outer horizons, then we will have a Sunday or a Sabbath in the true spirit of the Bible. Churches, synagogues, temples or mosques, their ceremonies and their prayers, have nothing to do with the true Sunday or the true Sabbath.

The "blessing" and the "sanctifying" of the number 7 also have a definite meaning. Both words, in their original letter-numbers, signify joyfulness, a sense of extraordinary freedom, a life open to anything that may come to it. And the blessing which is granted is the sanctification of freedom. This is the immeasurable joy of yielding, of letting be, of not imposing any psychological structure upon anyone. From that point of view, we can receive the "blessing" and "sanctifying" of life every day in the week.

A SUMMARY OF THE SEVEN DAYS

The first and foremost thing to keep in mind is that the "days" of creation describe a simultaneous, perpetual, and ever-present action of the 3 archetypes *Aleph*, *Bayt* and *Ghimel*, of their corresponding *Dallet*, *Hay*, *Waw* and of *Zayn* the seventh. They describe the autonomous life and movement of the universe.

Awr (*Aleph-Waw-Raysh*) is symbolically the copulation of the discontinuous and unthinkable *Aleph* and of its cosmic container *Raysh*. Its result is the greatest speed of which the universe is capable. It is identified with light.

Yehy Awr Va-Yehy Awr ("let there be light and there was light") when read letter by letter is actually: "the life of all existence (double), consequence of *Aleph* in copulation with the universe"

Awr is *Tov*, i.e. conditioned and repetitive. It is a structured energy distinct from *Hhosheykh*, which is the life of undifferentiated primordial energy.

Awr coming into existence becomes *Yom*. *Hhosheykh* becomes *Layla*.

The verb *Yqra* must not be translated "said". There is no divinity using a vocabulary. *Yqra* is an emanation of the two partners in the cosmic game of life-death and existence: *Aleph* and *Yod*.

Aleph is in everything and everything is in *Aleph*. *Bayt* (physical support) is with everything and everything is with *Bayt*. *Ghimel* (movement) is energy and all energy is *Ghimel*.

The container *Eretz* engenders nature in its beauty according to what it is but not according to what the cosmic breath is.

Visible reality is an inverted symbol of an invisible reality.

Yom seventh is the autonomy of the universe. It is autonomous because it has the capacity of allowing *Aleph*'s resurrection. Had it not that capacity, it would not exist.

ADDENDUM

The words (Gen. 1, 5, 8, 13, 19, 23, 31) *And the evening and the morning were the* (first, second, third, etc. . . . .) day contradict my assertion that those days are simultaneous and not consecutive.

The schemata concerning those passages are: *Ve-Yehy Ayrev Ve Yehi Voqer. Yom (Ehhad,* etc. . . .).

The schema *Yehy* is the one that is translated "let there be" (light) and "there was" (light); it is here translated "were". Such variations indicate that the necessities of a rational grammar must not be considered. That schema cannot be translated: it propounds synthetically the concepts Existence-Life-Existence and suggests the springing forth into existence of something alive.

The schemata *Ayrev* and *Voqer (Ayn-Raysh-Vayt—Vayt-Qof-Raysh)* when read in succession 70.200.2 - 2.100.200 (and if it is remembered that *Yom* is *Awr* appearing into existence) clearly reveal a rhythm, an alternation, a circuit which from the indeter-

THE CIPHER OF GENESIS

minate 70 in the cosmos (200) affects the individual 2 and from 2 returns to 200 through the mediatory *Qof* (100).

This, which we should venture to call an umbilical rhythm, pertains to the first six letter-numbers and not to no. 7. It is apparent in the order of the world, in nature and its seasons and in everything which is only *Tov*. In mankind groping in strife and blood towards its indistinct maturity it does not exist. He, however, who would live that rhythm in accordance with the cosmic breath of life would be highly benefited by it. Let us read the text as it is written, however mistranslated: "and the evening and the morning" (are a day). The day is meant to begin in the evening. When night begins to fall, he (Adam) retires and purifies his body and soul. During the day he has met many difficulties; many problems, many uncertainties have assailed him. Now he collects his thoughts, he stills his passions, he communes with himself and with the essence of life, and as *Hhosheykh* comes upon him and in him, the impersonal creative powers can gradually unfold. That is *Ayrev*, the 70.200.2. Then, in the morning, the *Voqer* 2.100.200 can set out again from the house, the *Bayt*, and refreshed by *Qof*, again meet and renew the challenge of *Raysh*.

He who, in the evening of his life, would find the freshness of newly lived morning, that man would be a man of *Qabala*.

9

An Arising

GENESIS II, 4-6: *Here are the generations of Shamain and of Eretz, created the Yom that YHWH Elohim made them. And the plants of the fields were not yet on Eretz and the herbs of the fields had not yet grown because Yod-Yod-Elohim had not caused it to rain on Eretz and there was no Adam to cultivate. But Ad arose from Eretz and watered the whole face of Adamah.**

Because it is prescribed in the Jewish religion never to pronounce YHWH, this schema is sometimes reduced to Yod-Yod and always uttered *Adonaï* (The Lord). Thus, in order to avoid desecrating whatever the formula YHWH stands for, it is interpreted as designating an anthropomorphous deity: in English, the Lord God.

YHWH: 10.5.6.5, Existence-Life-Copulation-Life, expresses in existence the two lives (that of the container or shell or physical support, and that of the contained or germ or inner life) that fertilize each other. This double impregnation can only occur in Man and as long as it does not occur YHWH is immanent but unborn. We will often refer to this schema. For the time being, in Genesis II, 5-6, Adam has not yet appeared. We will see him created in verse 7 before all the animals.

The impulse to his creation is given (Gen. I, 6) when *Ad* is born of *Eretz* and waters *Adamah* (translated "there went up a mist from the earth . . ."). This fact symbolizes the endogenous quality acquired by *Eretz* on *Yom* seventh.

The point of view of Genesis II is here already apparent. It does not belong to a Yahvic tradition different from and in-

---

* The whole meaning of those verses is in the schemata according to code. I therefore refrain from quoting the traditional English text.

consistent with the Elohimic tradition of Genesis I (as has been stated by scholars). It describes the universal life-energy as seen from inside, from its essence, and no longer through its evolutionary aspect. The essence is included in the appearance, the beginning is in the end and the end is in the beginning.

Hence the schema *Ad* (*Aleph* and a resistance, *Dallet*). *Aleph* immersed in the non-resistant Eretz springs forth with a resistance that does not belong to the limited response of *Eretz* to the cosmic breath, and it "waters" (fertilizes) that *Eretz* and transfigures it in such fashion as to give it the status of *Adamah*, (translated "ground") the feminine of Adam.

This is a good example of how, in literal Hebrew and in its translations, the text loses its meaning. There is no contradiction between Genesis I where *Adam* is born at the final stage of an evolutionary process and Genesis II where he is born previous to all other living beings.

The essential conclusion of Genesis I, 5 (YHWH-Elohim "had not caused it to rain") is that the planet Earth is expected to have in itself the capacity of transmuting its substance. Genesis I, 6 (the going up of *Ad* as the creation of *Adamah*) proves that it has indeed that capacity. Hence, in Genesis I, 7, man *can* be created because it is ascertained that the substance of which he is made (*Aafar*: 70.80.200 translated "dust", of *Adama*) sets into indeterminate motion (70) the lowest strata of energy (80) in the cosmos (200).

This so-called "dust" (symbolic of crumbled rocklike rigidity) leads us by means of its letter-numbers to the realization that *Eretz* is not only the Earth. This schema stands for all cosmic bodies and for every aspect of their components, from their simplest chemical elements up to their highest biological aggregates.

10

The Adam and the Garden of Eden

GENESIS II, 7. *YHWH-Elohim* forms *Adam* of the "dust" of *Adamah* and breathes the breath of life into his nostrils.

When all these schemata are read according to the code we see that the letter *Pay* or *Phay* (80) appears in "dust", "breathes", "nostrils" and that *Sheen* (300) appears in "breath". The result of the operation is *Adam* becoming a living *Nefesh* (50.80.300). No. 80 stands for all the undeveloped strata of energy. It is given life in *Adam* by *Sheen* (300), the cosmic metabolism. Here the text leaves us in doubt as to whether this Adam, this allegorical personage, created without any connection with evolution and indeed without any past, personifies an individual or the whole human race.

The truth is that this Genesis, this creation of a complete Adam, has not yet taken place—although it may now be in process of becoming. We can begin to understand this allegory when—rather than imagining it as a mere myth of our remote past—we see that, potentially, the complete Adam can come into being within us *now*. Adam is seeking birth, but we stifle it every day in its womb. Now that we know that the mature Adam does not yet exist, let us see what happens in the Garden of Eden, so often referred to with such childish imagery.

Genesis II, 8-9. These two verses describe the Garden of Eden. Verses 10 to 14, in which are mentioned four rivers, are not as important as the rest. In verse 15 *Adam* is put into Eden. These verses raise three fundamental questions.

First: Why in this chapter is Adam created before the animals, while in chapter 1 he was created, logically, at the top of the evolutionary scale?

Second: To what cosmic forces, to what aspect of life, does the famous Garden of Eden correspond, and where is it located?

Third: Why is it said in Genesis II, 8, *and there* (in the Garden) *he put the man whom he had formed,* and later, in Genesis II, 15, (he) *took the man and put him into the Garden of Eden . . .?* Is this repetition simply a copyist's error?

The replies to these questions concern each and every one of us. Of all the beings living on this planet, man is the only one who, according to the Book of Genesis, must not be defined. We are here at the very core of Genesis: the birth of our pre-natal humanity. Imagine a primal germ of life which, throughout a lengthy series of evolutions, has developed functions of perception, of assimilation and of action. It has passed through successive mutations and given birth to more and more highly evolved species.

We can consider each animal species as being a fixation within physiological limits. This fixation, this halt in development, is an accumulation of experience that is called instinct. Instinct is an indefinite repetition of the same gesture, with a reduced margin of possible modifications. All the animal species of the Book of Genesis are considered as being the lateral branches of the tree of life, of which man occupies the innermost part, the core, in an upward surging motion of the very heart of the trunk.

Genesis is quite clear in saying that man did not descend from anything, not even a monkey. Everything which did not become Adam, whether monkey, flea, fish, or elephant, came to a halt at one level or another of evolution and shot out a branch which ends where it began. Consequently, each species is compelled to exist in a milieu which varies only to a slight extent. If the milieu alters beyond the species' capacity of adaptation, then the species dies. None of the animal species is capable of radically modifying its milieu. Each species carries on indefinitely within its limited means of survival; and when these means become inadequate, the disappearance of the species seems to leave Nature totally indifferent. For the genus *Homo*, however, the situation is completely different. Man is motivated by extraordinary violence. Our century alone, with its two overwhelming world wars, the folly of which is evident, has seen the disappearance of more empires than history ever recorded and has traced millions of miles of new frontiers which have no chance of permanent survival. Yet even this wholesale destruction and change has had a lesser impact upon the human psyche than the relentless onslaught of science upon our notions about the universe, the constitution of matter, and the nature of our own faculties. Our shocked and bewildered minds seek refuge in a permanent truth, but the how and where of the search elude us. The Book of Genesis suggests a threefold approach to this quest: a vision of the interior world (which will answer my first question); a perception of the exterior world (which will answer my second question); and the understanding of the world, which deals with the structure of the psyche, which will answer my third question.

Concerning the first question, note that Genesis II differs from Genesis I in that it is the interior vision of what Genesis I describes from an exterior viewpoint. This vision is interior because, as we have already said, YHWH is the vital process of Elohim, which has plunged into the interior of existence (seen as continuity): into its temporal and spatial life. This incarnation has set human destiny in motion. This incarnation is *a germ which does not halt at any point of evolution.* This germ is, then, anterior in origin to all the latest branches. Adam is the firstborn, which means that he is never allowed to be "born" in the sense that the birth of a pattern is a fixity in a fixed setting.

The second question is: Just what is the Garden of Eden? It can be seen by reading, one by one, all the letter-numbers which describe it, that this is one of the most dangerous places in the whole world: *Gan-Eden*: *Ghimel-Noun—Ayn-Dallet-Noun*: 3.700-70.4.700. The numbers 70 and 700 are those of the destruction of obsolete structures. In fact, life—understood totally—is, in Genesis, repeatedly said to be life-death. The life to which

Adam is called is a series of destructions and new beginnings. Allegorically, life is "saying" all the time that this "germ" of humanity must always be prevented from achieving perfect protection and shelter. If ever it should find a fixed refuge, a comfortable stability, it would settle down lazily into a sub-human species; it would become one of these side-shoots on the tree of life. Reflect for a moment how certain tribes have remained undeveloped on account of a too pleasant or a too severe climate, or even from physiological or psychological causes. Thus, as they have become fixed in their mode of living, their faculty of adaptation has ceased to function and they are totally overwhelmed if they come into contact with the maelstrom of life in the twentieth century.

Let us consider now the phrase (in Genesis II, verse 9), *the tree of knowledge of Tov and Raa,* translated good and evil. All the Hebrew words relating to this tree (such as *gan, beeden, meqaddam*) convey intense movement. In fact, it is a whirlwind destroying all that is obsolete, as well as all accumulations, which must constantly be swept away by the totality of life that is creative and always new. This concept becomes clear to us when we realize that, in reading the Bible as we know it, the word *Tov* according to its letter-numbers (*Tav-Vav-Vayt*: 400.6.2) expresses the continuity of existence to which we cling as "good", and the word *Raa* (*Raysh-Ayn*: 200.70) that which upsets our static habits of living is translated "bad".

In spite of ourselves, the meaning of our true name of Adam is safeguarded. It is preserved in all that abolishes rigid, exclusive habits of thought and identification, as in nationalism, sectarianism and racism, etc. All this crystallization of thought and attitude courts disaster because it is the wrong way to play the game of living. So here is the answer to my third question: Genesis II, 8 is not read correctly. In this verse it is not *Adam* but the name *Adam* that is put in Eden so as to safeguard it.

The psychological structure of society teaches us to play against life, on the side of fixed continuity of existence, as if it did not wish the floods of life to reach us. And yet what *life* continually proposes is that we ride the waves, swift and over-whelming as they are.

Naturally, in order to play the game fully, we have to die and to be reborn every instant. That is, we have to accept the death of a Rabbi called Jesus in accordance with its original intended meaning—as a symbol for the way of life-death, and not as a substitute for our yielding to this intermittent pulsation in our own daily lives.

11

The Adam within the Gan Eden

THE ALLEGORY of this Adam in this "garden" Eden, *Ayn-Dallet-Noun*: 70.4.700, is very complex and difficult to understand. One must examine it very carefully and patiently and not advance until one has assimilated it step by step. The garden east of Eden is: *gan beeden meqaddam* (Mem-Qof-Dallet-Mem: 40.100.4.40 or 600), and its letter-numbers give such precise information concerning it that no doubt is possible. This purely symbolic garden is ahead of and beyond us, in anticipation of Adam. It is characterized by the greatest instability imaginable. The "germ" Adam is to be thrown into a state of great activity, a whirlwind which will never give him time to "fossilize" or to stay fixed in any time or circumstance.

The substance of this garden is named Adamah and life (YHWH-Elohim) causes this substance to bring forth, symbolically, everything that can stimulate the senses and awaken the appetite of Adam: *every tree that is pleasant to the sight, and good for food* (Gen. II, 9) and, in the middle, the two famous trees—of life, and of "good and evil". The significance of this symbolism is quite logical. As stated above, what is placed in this garden is the germ, the essence, of the human being as formulated in this book. The germ of humanity can never totally come to rest, never completely become static. This germ is an essence, a movement, a dynamism constantly projected ahead of itself— which, so to speak, never overtakes itself. Thus, although this germ is neither masculine nor feminine, here in the "garden" it possesses all the masculine characteristics and none of the feminine. The feminine of the life-germ is Adamah, from whom spring the remarkable trees in question.*

Thus, symbolically, the essence of Adam in Eden is masculine in character, and the feminine element within him is the substance of Adamah from which arises everything that is capable of developing man sensorially. You will see that this fact is important. In the midst of this sensorial development in Adam, in the very heart of it, are the two "trees" similar in appearance: for the tree of "life" is that of life-death, the non-continuous pulsation of life; and the tree of "good and evil", on another level, is the tree of *Tov-Raa, Tov-Raa*, the tree of fixation-destruction, fixation-destruction. The latter dominates every phase of this Adam's life and every aspect of the institutions and societies man has created. In short, the tree of life is that state in which the full pulsation of life can be attained at Adam's maturity. The other tree is that state in which Adam, not yet mature, not yet really born (the condition of Humanity at present), is caught in a continuous series of catastrophes. Everything that Adam wishes to build, whether in himself or outside of himself, crumbles to pieces.

Since Adam, at this stage of the allegory, is in a pre-natal state, the tree of life is not yet accessible to him. It is equally evident that if this human embryonic form, merely a potentiality and without substance other than that of Adamah, should set into motion the whole mechanism of *Tov-Raa*, with its chain of destruction, he would die, instantly crushed by what he had provoked. He would die, says the text, *Mawt Hamawt:* a *dead* death (without resurrection).

The allegory now shows life in its attempt to define the femininity in Adam's nature, to discover a womanliness different from the animal-female quality. Here, as usual, the text is mistranslated and misunderstood. First of all, notice the succession of ideas: if you eat of this tree, you will be annihilated.

* Notice how the symbols are sometimes interchangeable in the Bible. But we also frequently see them classed in the categories of masculine and feminine: as, for instance, fire, blood, wine (masculine) and water, earth, bread (feminine).

Tov is missing as long as Adam is alone: this volatile germ must be given flesh and continuity or, in other words, this embryo that is to develop must become incarnate. For this to come about, Adam must have a partner *against* him. This is the exact meaning of the text. Here again, we find the notion of a partner *against*; for man must learn to play his role and woman hers, in this partnership of life-existence against (and for) each other!

Adam now must pass a test to prove himself deserving of this partner. He must demonstrate that he has advanced far enough in the evolutionary scale to merit human incarnation. This is the test: YHWH-Elohim creates all the animals and shows them to Adam, *to see what he would call them* (Gen. II, 19). Adam looks at them, one species after another, and names them all. Each species is exactly what Adam calls it. Just what does all this mean, the "naming" and this being named? The reply is illuminating: Adam recognized each species as being an off-shoot from his own central trajectory. We know now that this is true, embryologically. The human foetus passes through all the phases of evolution in the course of its development. Adam, in placing the various species sees his own embryonic past and declares: I see nothing which is altogether like me. Thus, Adam has passed his test; for he no longer identifies himself with the animal phase of his evolution. Consequently, he is ready for incarnation.

This coming to birth takes place in Genesis II, 21-22. Unfortunately, our translations relate the childish story of Adam's sleep and of a woman being formed from one of his ribs. Is the extraordinary popularity of this interpretation through so many centuries due to its stupidity, or have its symbols a psychological attraction that could be explained through analysis? In the text, as we learn to read it, there is no "sleep" and no "rib". The germ Adam is immersed in *Tardamah*, which is an incarnation in its cosmic sense (Adamah being its living reality as human flesh); and the absurd rib is *Tsalaa*: namely, the womanliness of that incarnation, animated by a dynamic movement.

In other words, these two symbolic beings, man and woman,

are supposed to be free of their animal past, accumulated in the course of previous evolution. They are supposed to be free from instinctual, repetitive automatisms. This past is no longer active within them. This is what *Adam* says in Genesis I, 23. The name of this woman (spelled *Aleph-Sheen-Hay*) is pronounced *Esha*: *Esha* is the feminine element of cosmic fire, inasmuch as she springs from *Esh* (*Aleph-Sheen*) fire. Notice the spelling of *Eesh* for man: (*Aleph-Yod-Sheen*). *Adam* discovers this, his new name. (The addition of *Yod* to the name of fire indicates that this "fire" comes into existence in man.) A remarkable feature of these ideograms is that *Esha* does not really exist although she is alive (she has no *Yod* but has the *Hay* of life). The fire, *Esh*, from which she proceeds, has neither life nor existence. It is a pure archetype *Aleph-Sheen*. As to *Eesh*, the man, he has the *Yod* of existence but no *Hay*: he is not really alive. When we deeply investigate the notions, existence and life, we can discover that those schemata are an excellent and well-observed description of what our humanity actually is.

Verses 21 and 22 of Genesis II show how Esha is formed.

(*a*) The so-called sleep of Adam is a marvellous event, the reflected action of which is seen in the sleep of the newborn child. Compared to every other species where the newborn animal is automatically set into motion by an accumulated knowledge, the human being is born to learn; and his *not-knowing** is in proportion to his evolutionary development and tends to create the greatest possible intensity of life.

(*b*) Adam's consciousness is now freed. It leaves him and plunges into *Tardamah* (deep sleep). This schema is *Tav-Raysh* (400.200) and *Damah*, the feminine of blood. *Tav* (400) is the total resistance of life's physical support (the universe) and *Raysh* is the total organic process of universal life. We can translate that "deep sleep" symbolically by saying that in it Adam's blood is mated with the highest power of cosmic energy. Then, into this now pregnant flesh a double life is projected. The

---

* i.e. freedom from the animal instinct and influence of the accumulation of the past.

THE CIPHER OF GENESIS

extraction of a rib has no connection with the cabalistic meaning of the text. The schema for rib is a shadow to which is added 70: it is the opening of all possible possibilities for man.

(c) Next YHWH-Elohim "builds" (*Yod-Vayt-Noun* final: 10.2.700) that fragment, that is, relates it to the tremendous cosmic 700. It results in a separation as if two rooms were separated by a partition or in the manner of one cell that divides and makes two; but the two parts are motivated by the same movement!

(d) The concluding phase of the operation consists in the closing of the reservoir from which the new life was taken.

Adam coming to himself, whoever and wherever he is today, and whatever his name, knows neither *Eesh* nor *Esha*, the archetypes of an *Adam* in whom Dam (the blood) is transmuted from 4.40 to 4.600.

We wonder if one must of necessity be a cabalist to understand this language or if it has a chance of being heard more widely. We will again endeavour to describe the mutation of Dam from 4.40 to 4.600.

We know that Adam is a schema for the human being. It indicates that *Aleph*, the pulsating creativeness of life-death, is within him, struggling so as not to drown in the absorption of Dam, 4.40. The earth, as *Adamah*, claims that blood as belonging to it. It says, mythically: I, Adamah, am your mother and spouse; you, my husbandman, are kin to me: you are earth.

If we accept this proposition and live accordingly, the *Aleph* in us suffers death by suffocation, just as it is buried in *Eretz* where nature continuously repeats its prototypes, each according to its species.

But the Hebraic myth states that YHWH-Elohim has breathed in man the *Sheen* (300) which is the organic movement of the whole universe (Gen. II, 7). This develops into the well-known dispute between YHWH and the earth as to whom the blood belongs.

YHWH's point contended for in argument is founded on a basic postulate of Qabala: the unity of energy and of its contradictory aspects as spirit and matter, good and evil, high and low, etc. They coalesce in the synthetic formula *Yod-Hay-Waw-Hay* where their two lives fertilize each other.

What has just been described is seen as from within cosmic forces in their relationship one with another. It is not by any means the description of a caveman descended from a pre-anthropoid type. This is a story at once abstract yet concrete, allegorical yet real, inspired yet rational. If one really wishes to comprehend it, one must receive it at the highest level of intelligence. Immaturity becomes little short of criminal when it persists in devitalizing the mighty sweep and content of the Book of Genesis, and when its comprehension inflicts unjustifiable dogmas in the name of religion.

Genesis II, 24 is so little understood that certain exegetists maintain that it is an interpolation: *Therefore shall a man leave his father and mother, and shall cleave unto his wife: and they shall be one flesh.* We can set aside this translation which debases this verse in subservience to certain social interferences in conjugality (such as alleging divorces to be against the will of "God", etc.). After having said that Adam and Esha are bound towards a new life, this verse does not in any way say that they are "one flesh", but that they join in the common action in favour of a containing element, psychological and physiological, which must express the cosmic movement of life as well as the resistance to it.

Verse 25 goes on to say *not* that they are naked and unashamed, but that Adam (he is not mentioned as Eesh) and his Esha both incorporate the number 70, which is the realization of all the possible possibilities. The letter-numbers go on to explain that this no. 70, which is the source of all that lives, is enclosed, submerged, in the "waters" (for, as you remember, all existing life begins in the water element). The end of this verse 25 states that Adam and his Esha, being enclosed as they are now in an envelope of great resistance, seem to have lost their cosmic life. We will presently see that Nahhash, the serpent, gives life back to Esha.

In concluding here this brief reading of chapter II, it is of interest to infer from it that it contains a description of the vital biological process through which life comes into existence. It also shows the primordial importance of the role the woman must play in the engendering of the human being.

But we all have, in varying degrees, both masculine and feminine elements in us. Whether we be men or women, we must all be Adam; and we should all learn to know what is the feminine—especially psychologically—within us. As long as the static, conserving element within us does not yield to the up-springing of cosmic fire that burns away the past and its false revelations, we shall maim the life within us and continue to go begging at the doors of religion for a knowledge which will escape us.

12

What is God?

WITH THE eating of the apple, we are reaching the story which, for centuries, has been one of the world's best-known tales. Ever since the Christian religion incorporated this narrative from the archives of an ancient Semitic people, long after its original significance had been lost, the story has always produced a sensation. No fairy tale has ever been able to compete with the talking serpent, or the enchanted garden, or the moral tree with its apples of good and evil—far more evil than good, according to the exoteric traditional interpretation, in which we delude ourselves into seeing good as evil, and evil as good.

In the preceding chapter we did not wish to enter into the incongruities that appear in the translation of this text, for we wished to deal first with what is most meaningful in the Garden of Eden. It has extraordinary import. In this present epoch (we write in the nineteen-sixties), we are approaching a turning-point of history at such speed that the full content of this message must be understood, and lived, if there are to be "new" men and women such as these of which the world is desperately in need. The Book of Genesis (Genesis means "birth") indicates what we must do to be born afresh, to be "new".

Each one of us has a choice to make and may do so freely. The choice is this: we can, if we wish, live after the manner of the animal species, which ceased to advance in the scale of evolution and continued to live within the limits of their conditionings, and the accumulation of their inherited automatisms, confined to strictly limited forms. Most of the time, we limit our conception of what we are by the patterns with which we fill our minds: *our* culture, *our* way of life, *our* traditions, *our* morals, *our* imitations, *our* ways of thinking inherited from the past, which we seek to carry into the future. By maintaining all these attitudes—with the help of our environment, our churches and our schools—we are actually stifling and killing the human-being-to-be which waits within us.

We are apparently trying to settle down into a prehuman sub-species. One thing is sure: we are not Adam, neither are we Eesh and Esha. We are rejecting the Revelation. Our right-eousness and religiosity are hypocrisy. This is one choice, the easy one. In that choice, men will go on debasing womanhood, strip-teasing them for the purpose of sexual gratification, denying them equality, exploiting them or subjugating them, and imposing an exclusively male government on the world. Reciprocally, by devious means, women will take their revenge by exploiting man's ambitions and vanity. And they will *grab*. This state of affairs is *pre-* or rather *sub-*human.

The other choice means breaking with all this because one sees that it is already obsolete. One must then reject all the psychological conditioning which is forced upon us by society, by tradition, by a projection from the past. Such a choice is not easy. It is difficult to understand, let alone to live. Yet only this choice can transmute the Revelation of the Bible into living reality.

Let us now consider some of the incongruities in the accepted narratives concerning the Garden of Eden. Why did the so-called God need to plant a tree giving the knowledge of "good and evil", in a garden whose only inhabitants were forbidden to eat of it? For whom, then, did he plant that tree? He planted all the trees for the nourishment of man. Yet we read: *We may eat of the fruit of the trees of the garden: But of the fruit of the tree which is in the midst of the Garden, God hath said. Ye shall not eat of it* (Gen. III, 2-3). We know from Genesis II, 9, that *the tree of life is in the midst of the garden*. Now just think for a moment: not only did this perfidious "God" set a trap for his creatures, but he deliberately caused a misunderstanding. For both of these trees were in the middle of the garden, and they were surely just alike. How could anyone know which was which? Esha in good faith had no idea of disobeying. Moreover (and here is another incongruity in imputing a fault to Esha), *she could not disobey* because the interdiction had been placed *only upon Adam.* Look at the situation again. Not only was there no prohibition laid upon Esha, but was not Esha herself created expressly so that Adam, in case he should eat of this fruit, would not "die a dead death" as would have been the case had he been left alone!

As to the creation of Adam and Esha, we hope you have admired the manner in which this deity complicated the operation. For him who had merely to speak the word to make the whole universe appear in the shortest possible time, why should it have been necessary, before creating man and woman, to reduce himself to human proportions? (Perhaps like Alice in Wonderland he drank of a bottle labelled "drink me" and became very small indeed.) He must have been no larger than human because otherwise he would not have been able to gather dust in order to make Adam, then blow into his nose, and later give him anaesthetics, extract a rib, go *walking in the garden in the cool of the day* (Gen. III, 8) and finally, in a true Victorian spirit of propriety, *make coats of skins* and clothe both man and woman (Gen. III, 21).

We shall not waste time on these puerilities. The attentive reader can find quite a number of them should he be so inclined. All we wish to emphasize is that serious-minded individuals, unable to accept certain parts of the text, simply pass over the most troublesome passages, placing them, in fact, outside the Revelation properly speaking. Such persons think they have shown broad-minded indulgence in overlooking numerous foolish details of ancient folklore which they regard as being due to the ignorance of copyists. But strangely enough, these very passages, re-read in their original letter-numbers, often reveal meanings which we can least afford to disregard. We have already said that it is not possible to reconcile the two readings, the familiar translation and the direct reading of the letter-numbers in the original Hebrew text. If we wish to read a text prepared for adults, we should abandon the mistranslations that have been current for so long.

Two questions arise: why is this story always read "upside down", and why does this version enjoy such great popularity? The answer springs from a profound psychological truth. The story, in its veritable nature, is frightening. But how can one be afraid of it if one has not understood it? The answer is that the psyche knows unconsciously that the story is dangerously upsetting. It creates a religious taboo to protect itself. The teaching that results from this translation is that mankind must remain in an infantile state and obey those who speak in the name of a "father" located in heaven. The dogma of original sin as disobedience is maintained to prevent disconcerting discoveries concerning that deity. For instance, an obvious ambiguity is created by YHWH with the two trees. Then, having created two adults who from the outset knew how to talk, why could not "he" or "it" have told them how to discriminate between a green and a red light (or how to recognize any other signal as being a danger zone, had there been one)? The truth is that this story is a magical snare where fear sees birth as sin, freedom as disobedience, nobleness as ruin. It is not the serpent who is the tempter. The deceiver is the so-called God, YHWH, and the deceived is the reader. Does this appear ridiculous? The scandal is the world-wide picture of a good old father seated in the heavens, benignly observing us.

If one reads the Bible correctly, one will see that the character of YHWH is always ambiguous. For instance, when Moses, who is afraid to go and meet Pharaoh, asks for advice in Midian (Exod. iv, 19), YHWH replies: *Go, return into Egypt: for all the men are dead which sought thy life.* This is equivalent to an ambush, for we are later told that *it came to pass by the way in the inn, that the Lord met him, and sought to kill him* (Exod. iv, 24). From the standpoint of this "God", Moses is a unique and invaluable collaborator. Without Moses, one may ask whether there would ever have been any Revelation at all. Then why should there be that treacherous move to lull Moses into a sense of false security, the better to assault him unawares? A man of weaker character and stamina, whose resistance was inadequate to the tasks that lay ahead, would have been killed. A deeper investigation into the matter reveals an aspect concerning the symbolic wife in whose house Moses came to rest. She had to undergo a test for maturity and awareness. Had she not been equal to the situation the human adventure undertaken by Moses would not have proceeded further.

Here is another example. It is in the story of Jacob's struggles against the angel. Long before Moses, Jacob is a most important figure in this ancient human history. We will discuss his story in detail later on. For the present, we read from the English translation of Genesis xxxix, 24-29 and find that *there wrestled a man with him* does not explain that the assailant is really Eesh, or YHWH. Jacob wrestles with him *until the break of day*. He clasps Eesh so closely that eventually Eesh cries out, *Let me go*; and he answers *I will not let thee go except thou bless me*. And when Eesh blesses him, he gives him his new name, Israel, signifying (according to the Hebrew as we read it): You have exerted your lordly power upon Elohim and Anashim (men as descendants), and you have consumed them. Eesh is no other than a personification of Elohim; and Israel knows very well what has happened, for he says: *I have seen Elohim face to face.*

Eesh, the archetype of Adam-Elohim is therefore none other than the total process of mankind.

The crux of the matter is this: whoever wrestles with Elohim and defeats him, is rewarded with his blessing; the blessing of course of life itself, and not of an absurd deity. In brief, Jacob, becoming Israel, reabsorbs the totality of duration, past and future. In many instances YHWH-Elohim appears thus as being life itself, unpredictable, unknowable, challenging. It remains for us to become alive to its intensity.

13

The Old Man of the Mothers

So FAR, we have expounded the significance of the Garden, the Trees, Adam, Esha and YHWH-Elohim. Only Nahhash, the serpent, remains to be studied, after which we will be in possession of all the clues concerning this allegory. The serpent plays an important part in many ancient myths. He appears in several cosmogonies as being present at the origin of creation, and at times as encompassing the earth. He has multiple meanings dealing with the general evolution of life, as well as with that of the individual in both body and psyche. In certain theosophies his name is *Kundalini*, and he springs from the genitals and ascends the spine. His "fire" is initiatory and becomes knowledge through transmutation of sex into creative intelligence. Factually, the serpent is phallic and nakedly so. (Genesis III, 1 ought not to read, *now the serpent was more subtle than any beast*, but "more naked".)

Hidden and coiled inside hollows and cavities of the earth, he suddenly darts out with swift swinging blows. He is therefore considered mythically as being the son of Earth, the male energy born into the primordial Mothers. Is he not that Phallus, the very resurrection of *Aleph* from its earthly entombment? Is he not the best possible resurrection of *Aleph*, according to Eretz's capacity at the time?

Somewhere in the background of our ancestral memory we have a fossilized stratum recalling that the earth put forth great and successive efforts in order to engender beings that could stand upright. The biblical serpent who appears upright is the symbolic descendant of the great saurians of early geological epochs, creatures that occupied the planet for millions of years prior to man's appearance. This serpent is then the symbol of the most alive creature that earth was able to produce until a certain epoch.

Now there are Adam and Esha, symbolizing an absolutely new era. Who are they: she the spouse of fire (or the feminine fire), he no longer knowing whether he is Adam or Eesh? It is as if they were not wholly there, as if they were just emerging from oblivion. Adam, especially, is almost entirely asleep. Does he not resemble a newborn child? While the animal species respond to life with a series of automatic reflexes suited to their needs, this Adam will have to learn about everything without recourse to animal instinct. Just here at the extreme limit of a passing era appears the old, the very old serpent who originally symbolized the "male" begotten by Adamah.

Nahhash, the carrier of all the memories of time, of all forgotten wisdom, now has the mission of transmitting duration to these two new beings; for until they possess the totality of time, they will not be wholly incarnate. They cannot exist unless this last link is provided. They must consume the past and be its fruition. Within them, as they are presented in this story, there already exists the intermittent pulsation of life-death—life-death. They must become the whole game of life, not only this discontinuous element but the continuous as well. The mission of Nahhash, the serpent, is to plunge them into what one can, in a sense, call evolution. He must transmit his life to them; he must join the "earth" fire to their fire from "heaven".

He cannot transmit this to Adam who is as unstable as if he had been knocked on the head. But the serpent tentatively addresses Esha: "Has Elohim really said: You shall not eat of every tree?" The answer should have been: "No, it was YHWH-Elohim, not Elohim, who said some such thing—not to me, but to Adam. And he said it because at that time Adam was alone and if he had eaten of that tree, he would not have survived a single instant. That is why YHWH-Elohim created me—so that Adam could eat of that tree without dying." Had Esha thus responded with the true facts, this story would never have become so widely accepted as it is. Why? If we are not afraid, we can find the answer to that question.

14

Are We Afraid of the Bible?

WE WANT the psychological security of a protecting deity, whereas we can become *as gods, knowing good and evil* (Gen. III, 5), just as the serpent said. This statement, which really means that we can be the whole process "Elohim", is confirmed by YHWH-Elohim: *the man is become as one of us* (Gen. III, 22). Rabbi Yhshwh, better known as Jesus, is supposed to have quoted that assertion; but, of course, he who referred to himself as Ben-Adam (mistranslated as "Son of man") knew the meaning of the letter-numbers. Not even his disciples understood that sacred language, as they themselves said. This understanding is not easy, but it is one thing to make a serious attempt to understand a somewhat difficult code, and it is quite another to run away from it and to dream that the mystery of life-death and existence can reveal itself by means of a few legends.

The fact (which one can verify for oneself) is that the copyists, priests, rabbis and theologians have systematically discarded every statement in the Bible that destroys man's sense of security in a steady continuity of existence. But the Bible is a Revelation only in so far as it includes death in life, thereby disrupting every psychological certainty. Vested authority throughout the ages, however, has reversed and betrayed this biblical message of life-including-death and has promised existence-after-death, which is not the same thing at all. Death is actually here, as a vital aspect of our everyday life, at every moment. When we come to see that we are constantly waging a battle (psychologically) for the continuity of our existence against the life-death within us, and when we come to learn (from the Book of Genesis) that that combat must cease by our becoming that very life-death, a disruption occurs in our thought process and in our psychical armour, which liberates us into life. And this is precisely the thing, the life-stimulating thing, that we are afraid of.

It is important to learn that our urge towards static permanence goes very deep. Constantly, we shy away from something that might upset us. This we automatically classify as "harmful". For instance, look again at the tree which, so the translations state, is "the tree of knowledge of good and evil". The schema *Tov*, translated "good", expresses the static, materializing, carnal action of the primitive female (symbolically considered under all its aspects). That action nourishes and strengthens the *Bayt*, the "house", the shell.

The schema *Raa* ("evil") leads all structured energy towards the indetermination of 70; it cannot therefore but tend to destroy all that is static, determinant, conditioning.

Any static factor in our minds eventually jeopardizes the flow of newness, of freshness, which is the specific quality of human genesis. The cause of fear is easy to see: one does not want to be disturbed; therefore one calls good anything which is the mind's container, and calls evil everything which will endanger the maintenance of one's armour of certainties. And the translators, by supporting this reversal, have seen to it that we should be conditioned to a view of life that mocks all true values. When one reflects that *Tov* (translated "good") really means limited in its material proliferation and that the process *Raa* (translated "evil") is really a loosening of our bonds, a thawing out, an awakening or quickening of the life force, one can understand that the action of *Raa*, far from being in any sense evil, is something designed to save our life.

The misunderstandings with which we have grown up are too numerous to be dealt with in one small volume. Here, however, is another vital example. We have seen with the episode of Jacob wrestling with Elohim that the process of evolution in time is satisfied only when overcome and "conquered". Thus Esha, in plucking the apple, understands and integrates the

Elohimic process and it is satisfied. An extraordinary thing then happens to Esha. When she is questioned concerning this event, she does not—as the translations assert—reply, *The serpent beguiled me* (Gen. III, 13). What the true reading gives is far more significant. The Hebrew phrase, *Hanahhash Hashayiny*, as is so often true in the most beautiful passages, is impossible to translate in two or three words. It has to do with the action of the letter *Sheen* which we met with after Adam's so-called sleep. *Sheen* (300), it is remembered, stands for the cosmic breath of life, and we have seen that the true meaning is not that they were "naked" and "not-ashamed" (which has nothing to do with the letter-numbers of the text), but that they were left without the *Sheen*. Now *Hanahhash Hashayiny* simply means that Nahhash, the serpent, *"Sheens"* her: that is, he blends his earthly fire with her lost heavenly fire, which thus comes to life again. Some traditions have identified this *Sheen* (300) with the mythical "Spirit of God".

But we are afraid to pluck the fruit; and because we wish to rationalize our "sins" of omission, we invent a prohibition and carefully project the allegory into the past, when in fact the fruit is ready for us to harvest here and now. Esha did not live centuries ago, and we wonder if she is even born yet.

The psychological process by which a revelatory and profoundly challenging book is consistently and forever misread is, after all, quite easy to understand. The reason that the tale of the talking serpent and the magic apple outlives every other fairy story is that we are afraid of it.

15

A General View of the Issues Involved

ESHA, STIRRED by the whirl of life transmitted to her by the serpent, awakens. The fruit she has eaten develops her sensorial faculties, as well as those of Adam. This is the birth of *Homo sapiens*. Psychic energy (what the psychologists call libido) invades her body. The sexual urge is dominated and sublimated through a new sensibility. This sensibility is generated in Esha by the eating of a fresh and perfect fruit, the life of which antedates all animal evolution. This life is transmuted directly into Esha, without the least connection with the intervening phases of evolution, represented by the serpent.

The dialogues between YHWH-Elohim, Adam, Esha and Nahhash must be read from the original letter-numbers in order to savour their real meaning to the full. The familiar words and phrases, "afraid", "naked", "I hid myself", "woman", "beguiled", "cursed", "enmity between serpent and woman", "in sorrow thou shall bring forth children", "cursed is the ground for thy sake", "dust thou art", etc., are all corruptions. We cannot read chapter titles in the English Bible, such as *The serpent deceives Eve* or *The punishment of mankind*, without feeling— as we see the incredible results of fear—a surge of both anger and compassion. It blocks even one's capacity to read. Eve does not even exist at this point in Eden. Esha is not Eve: Hhevah, who is Eve, comes later (Gen. III, 20). And for God's sake (or for man's) why should the earth be cursed? The neurotic idea that a divinity can curse is crude, primitive, prehistoric. This idea of a curse is born out of fear. Can "God" be afraid?

Misinterpreted for centuries, the Bible has been a fatal cancer in the mind. Its vitalizing beauty still awaits discovery. The symbolic ejection of Adam from the womb (called Eden) is an allegory of a birth. Do you see that to call this birth a curse is to refuse it? Do you see that ideas of punishment and a fall based upon this false premise retard the genesis of all human beings? And what happens if a birth is unduly delayed? The foetus dies.

The end of Genesis, chapter III, 24 by comparison with the original text seen through its letter-numbers, is madness. If our deity is Life, why did "he" place *at the east of the garden of Eden the Cherubim, and a flaming sword which turned every way to keep the way of the tree of life?* Can Life put an obstacle to life? Unless we understand that—psychically—the angel has to be assaulted, overcome and literally consumed and that the flaming sword and even the tree of life itself have to be eaten up, digested and absorbed, we shall continue to cling to the miserable, cramped and frightened existence we call life; and the fear of "evil" (good) and "death" (life) by which we deceive ourselves into projecting the so-called religious standards of morality will ensure our continued exploitation.

Before we proceed into Genesis IV, where all the personages are archetypes, let us recapitulate the contents of Genesis I, II and III, as read from their letter-numbers.

Genesis I: The anatomy of the process of intermittent energy "associated-against" a continuum of space-time. The interiorization of that energy within the continuum. The continuum becomes autonomous.

Genesis II: Consequences of the autonomy of the continuum (self-induction). This process as seen from the interior. The appearance of YHWH and of the germ in which unconditioned energy can and must rise again. Neither life in its character of discontinuous, pulsating, immeasurable energy nor life in its character of the continuum-existence would be anything, one without the other; nor could either even exist if they were not playing each against the other.

Genesis III: The anatomy of the human germ in which this interplay between existence and life takes place. The incarnation of this germ. In man is centrifugal energy, buried, dormant in his very blood. This energy only expresses itself by unco, ordinated outbursts of activity. The real issue—the resurrection of organic, creative energy—depends upon woman; the female in her, being by nature the protectress of the continuum, existence, must transform itself. Esha takes the decisive step and brings about a transformation of the animal erotic-sensorial faculties; the eating of the fruit is an allegorical representation of the blending of existence and life within the human kind of the two players.

As we shall see, Genesis IV deals with the implanting of this whole process in the human psyche by means of personifications of the cosmic interplay of energy and mass, both within and without ourselves.

16

Genesis IV: The Archetypes

ADAM HAS now emerged from the womb, but he remains until Genesis x (Noah's posterity) a mythical, symbolic being. He is still merely a legend and rightly so. He is, as yet, far too immature for his presence to be felt in the world of existence. In simple terms, Adam expelled from Eden means that this myth declares mankind to be born. The text says that only Adam is expelled, not *Esha*. When Adam names his wife *Hheva* he extracts her from the archetype *Esha*. We must not forget that in the Bible a new name given to a person indicates a mutation. *Esha*, abstract schema, spouse of the cosmic fire, remains inside Eden, whereas a different personification, Hheva, accompanies Adam in his earthly adventure.

But in this embryology a (declared) birth is a fixation in a pre-human state. Therefore historical man must constantly revise his notions of what is really human, whilst historical woman must unfold the inner *Hheva*, symbol of accomplished womanhood, of transcendent femininity, that has yet to come into being.

Since she appears at the beginning of this phase of the story, she must be understood. From the outset, she represents in womanhood everything which, much later on, Yhshwh (known as Jesus) represents in manhood. This is evident from her letter-numbers *Hhayt-Waw-Hay*, which are a projection of YHWH. If it is understood that Hheva thus embodies in her very nature the supreme archetype of womanhood, it will be seen that there is no need to deify any woman, virgin or otherwise. Hheva being a materialized counterpart of YHWH, this archetype is shown to be at the very core of life-in-existence

Esha, still in the womb of Eden, is the inexhaustible flame, always alive. Hheva is that flame in existence: the complete archetype. In fact, all the personages in Genesis IV are archetypes.

The human psyche—yours and that of everyone born since the appearance of *Homo sapiens*—is enclosed within itself, much as if it were a chrysalis enclosed within its self-spun cocoon. Or again, human consciousness encased in the ego, is similar to a traveller who has taken shelter from imminent danger in a securely locked cabin. In the midst of the surrounding human and cosmic violence, the voices of initiates—those who have perceived the essentials—describe the interplay of existence and of the non-temporal. But the projections of the archetypes here involved (Adam, Eve, Cain, Abel, etc.) strike the protective shell of the psyche and cause reactions that distort it and are often the very opposite of what the archetypes represent. The psyches enclosed in their cells of refuge perceive in the message of the archetypes nothing but the voice of the big bad wolf who, so they think, is trying to demolish their dwellings, their *Bayt*—as in fact he is, though with motives they cannot evaluate.

But these archetypes, personifying as they do the cosmic interplay of energy and mass, inner as well as outer, are the framework upon which our psyches build themselves. The archetypes, Adam (static) and Eve (dynamic), are in us prior even to the formation of our psyches. Whatever their names, they exist in every human being. In some parts of the world they may be called Vishnu and Shiva, or Yin and Yang, or otherwise. Since the constant reaction of the psyches is that of self-protection, these archetypes are perceived as being positive when they are negative, and static when in fact they are dynamic. Though we may glimpse traces of reality within the essence of our nature we cannot fathom this essence as long as, in the interplay between life and existence, we identify ourselves with existence, duration, and a past which we project into the future.

In other words, we are forever placing ourselves in opposition to, and in conflict with, the vital action of the archetypes, at the very origin of our psyches; and in so doing, we continually propel ourselves into a contradiction that becomes more and more intense. We are the containing elements of the archetypes, as well as the resistance to what they contain. We are at the same time life and that which encompasses life, providing the resistance enabling life to manifest itself. Whenever this resistance becomes too strong, the life force cannot get through to us.

We see the approach of this phenomenon when we become obsessed with the acquisition of multitudes of "things"—automobiles, television sets, gadgets of all sorts, enormous bank accounts, etc.—and when we begin to consider such things as being indispensable to life. When these or other materialistic and mechanistic pursuits absorb our attention and energies, we are headed for a salutary, though drastic and at times painful lesson. Sometimes such a crisis—particularly where we fail to comprehend its significance—can be deadly in its effect.

We have already mentioned the destruction of Jerusalem, its people, its temples and palaces by YHWH. It is only one example of the persistent destruction of "containers" by life-death.

It is essential for us to understand that if we, existence-in-life, are contemptuously oblivious of the livingness in which we have our being, then life-in-existence reasserts itself in no uncertain terms. In our daily living we are seldom aware of being in the grip of these complementary forces, but they are everywhere discernible once our eyes are opened. Our world of today is perilously unbalanced, reflecting our inner states of chronic disorder. Either we execute an about-face within our psyche or we drift into stagnant waters, or worse. We must change places in the game and so liberate the quality of life which Nahhash, the serpent, brought forth in Hheva.

Returning to Genesis IV, 1, and the birth of Qaheen* (not to be pronounced Cain), we see that after he is born Hhevah says, *Qaneetee* *Eesh Et YHWH*, which does not at all mean: *I have begotten a man with the aid of the Lord.*

We have already stated that the schema *Et* (*Aleph-Tav*) is a combination of the first and last letters and corresponds to our expression "from A to Z". The translators have totally neglected it in the first verse of Genesis (the creation of *Et Ha-Shamaim* and *Et Ha-Eretz*). This *Et*, every time that it is used, indicates that the schemata referred to are equations in the form of blunt formulas which include (from A to Z) the premises and the conclusions of given processes. They are, therefore, if we understand their unfoldment, both the summing up of the problems and their solutions.

So when Hheva says: I have "acquired" (we can keep that translation for the time being) *Eesh Et YHWH*, she actually says that she has "acquired" the archetype *Eesh* which "from A to Z" is *YHWH*.

The consecrated version: "I have acquired a man from the Lord" is an unforgivable betrayal of the text. It weighed and still weighs heavily upon the minds of millions. Its responsibility in our human misfortunes is beyond evaluation.

We begin here to understand why, according to Qabala, the archetype *Hheva* is so important. It is the first time that YHWH is mentioned alone, without Elohim, and it is mentioned by the woman *Hheva*, in a flash that pierces through the entire process of duration.

Considering the exceptional importance of that passage and the historically disastrous interpretations concerning *Qaheen*, we must briefly analyse the schema *Qaneetee* (*Qof-Noun-Yod-Tav-Yod*: 100.50.10.400.10). It includes the very name of Qaheen (Cain) with the permutation of *Noun-Yod* instead of *Yod-Noun*, so arranged as to block 400 in between two *Yod*. Those two *Yod* are the sign of a double existence and can be interpreted as

---

* The use of "Q" for the "K" sound is unavoidable, since Q (100) and K (20) are not interchangeable, meaning-wise.

expressing the objective and the subjective spheres. The 400 is the resistance (as of a chalice) of the Creation to the cosmic *Aleph* (*Qof*:100) that is in it (and yet overflowing).

It is not by mere chance that the schemata *Qaneetee* and *Qaheen* begin with the *Qof* of Qabala.

When eventually Hheva gives birth to Hevel (not to be pronounced Abel), it is not even said that Adam "knew his wife again". But later on, after the disappearance of Hevel, it *is* said: *And Adam knew his wife again: and she bore a son, and called his name Seth: For God, said she, hath appointed me another seed instead of Abel, whom Cain slew* (Gen. IV, 25). Here we must read Elohim for God, Hevel for Abel, and Qaheen for Cain; thus the final phrase becomes: Hevel whom Qaheen has shattered. We will presently explain the difference between the "shattering" and the "slaying" of the traditional version.

For the moment, notice the difference between these three births: (*a*) In the case of Qaheen, Hheva entirely overlooks the role of Adam; this corresponds to the obliteration of Joseph, spouse of Mary, by the Church. Hheva declares and affirms: I have acquired Eesh, the living cosmic fire, which is YHWH (the process of life-in-existence). In other words, she is defining the terminal omega of the allegory: the resurrection through womanhood of the immeasurable energy incarnate in existence. No passage in Genesis is clearer than this, or as total and absolute. The ending of the allegory is fully implied in its beginning. Qaheen is YHWH incarnate. Any other interpretation is psychological murder. (*b*) Hevel is nothing more than the carnal proliferation of the female in Hheva. This son has nothing of Adam, or rather he has from Adam solely the *dam* (blood in Hebrew: the blood which Adamah drinks). (*c*) With the birth of Set, who takes the place of Hevel, Hheva recognizes that it is Elohim who is there. Elohim, it will be recalled, is the evolutionary process within the duration of existence. It is this Set who will become the mythical ancestor of the human race.

It cannot be overemphasized that the ecclesiastical traditions, giving as they do the words "God" for Elohim and "the Lord" for YHWH, bar the road to the understanding of the Bible. It is important to remember the real significance of these two schemas at the outset of any study concerning Qaheen. Elohim (*Aleph-Lammed-Hay-Yod-Mem*), read according to code (1.30.5.10.40), expresses the fact that the timeless discontinuous pulsation which is *Aleph* (1) underlies the functional movement of organisms (30), their life (5), and all existence (10) with their resistance to life (40). Thus Elohim is both an unique and a plural process. This process of life-death-in-existence is the only active agent in Genesis I. It can only put into motion the repetitive production of prototypes, until the "blessing" and "sanctifying" of no. 7 in Genesis II, 3, which opens the way to all indeterminate possibilities.

YHWH is an altogether different sphere of life. Its schema 10.5.6.5 can only be actualized when the copulation (6) really takes place between 5 and 5, and that can only happen in mankind, between body and psyche. Obviously it cannot happen between a nutshell and its nut, nor between an eggshell and its germ, and no animal can ever decide to take control over its own body.

The key to this we already know: it resides in the mutually fertile relationship—5.6.5—of the two aspects of life with which we have been dealing all along: the existence and the immanence, the temporal and the timeless, the finite and the transcendent, the outer and the inner, the container and the contained, the objective and the subjective, etc. All this, of course, has nothing to do with any "lord" or "God" to be worshipped. It has to do with a relationship of inter-fertilization that can happen at the moment of our "seeing" it. And we can only see it when we strip off our Abel skin and understand and become Cain, fully alive and responsive.

★

The allegory of Qaheen, though short, is so full of detail that we can only give the essentials of it. Does Qaheen—a bit stunned in the capacity of YHWH incarnate—"till the ground"? No. He establishes his dominion over Adamah (see letter-numbers). And Hevel establishes his dominion over the flesh of the herds. In the process of time (after the passing of an era) Qaheen establishes a relationship between YHWH and himself. Hevel then imitates him and produces offerings to YHWH. There is nothing wrong with Hevel; since he cannot help being a specimen of ordinary, petty, toiling humanity. YHWH accepts his offerings. But Qaheen, being YHWH itself, incarnate but in a state of amnesia, worships an image of himself, which he projects, thereby creating a distance between himself and himself. Since this form of worship reflects a lack of self-knowledge, it is rejected.

This drama is at the core of human experience. We are told that Christ is within, or that there is an Atman, immortal soul or essence within us. Instead of plunging into that living life, what do we do? We worship a picture of what we suppose it is, which cannot be but a projection of its shell or container.

The dialogue which results from these rejected offerings, if correctly read, is one of great beauty. In fact, it is a soliloquy within YHWH the archetype and YHWH incarnate. The few verses which follow (until Genesis IV, 16) are one of the summits of the archives of humanity. If we enter into this soliloquy, if it comes alive in our hearts and minds, we penetrate into all the suffering in the world; the suffering of love, of death. And beyond and above it, incorruptible life can come into being.

We must allow our mind to be still, then ask ourselves sincerely whether we can make head or tail of the following little speech: *If thou doest well, shalt thou not be accepted? and if thou doest not well, sin lieth at the door. And unto thee shall be his desire, and thou shalt rule over him* (Gen. IV, 7). Somehow Qaheen comes to understand the riddle in the original form of the verse—which (fortunately for him) is not expressed in the existing translation. YHWH has no need to explain it. Its key, hidden in its letter-numbers, can be discovered and lived in freedom. It is the key of life. Were it a teaching or a commandment, Qaheen would obey it, thereby losing his and his brother's freedom by becoming his "brother's keeper".

The Hebrew text of this verse, when read in current language, is not correct grammatically. It mixes the masculine and feminine of certain words. But there is no logic in judging a text according to the grammatical rules of a different language. We must therefore discover whether the apparent mistakes make sense when we read them, according to the code, as they are.

The text begins with a schema which is approximately read "Hello". It is not translated in the English version, and in some other versions it is supposed to be an interjection meaning more or less "Isn't it?". Its letter-numbers are *Hay-Lammed-Vav-Aleph*: 5.30.6.1; and as is the case in several other important verses we are here dealing with an "opening statement" in the form of an equation which this verse is meant to solve. When 5.30.6.1. is solved in action within us, the revelation is there; Qaheen will understand it and act accordingly. His mission— mythically, that of God in exile—is to give life (5), organic movement (30) and fertility (6) to Aleph (1).

The following schema is *Aleph-Mem—Tav-Yod-Tayt-Yod-Vayt*: 1.40—400.10.9.10.2. It describes what happens when *Aleph* cannot overcome the resistance of *Mem* (40): it becomes buried in cosmic resistance (400) in which the original female archetype (9) is solidly encased in between two *Yod* (10.9.10) for the benefit of its personal dwelling (2). This schema is read *Teeteev*, which, as a word in the ordinary language, is derived from *Tov* and means "Thou doest well". This unfortunate "doing well" leads to the following schema, *Sh-et*: 300.1000.400, in which we witness the cosmic organic life (300) of the most exalted *Aleph* (1000) desperately hurling itself against the obstinate resistance of 400. The ecclesiastical interpretation, has it thus: "Shalt thou not be accepted?"

Such is the alternative for *Aleph*. From then on the schemata, till the end of the verse, are an analysis of the other alternative, Aleph's resurrection and its action upon any individual. It begins by negating the Teeteev thus: *Vayim Lo Teeteev* and *Vayim Lo* is: 6.1000.600—30.1000. Some texts emphasize the cosmic nature of these numbers, *Aleph* as 1000 and *Mem* as 600, by enlarging them graphically (as an echo of the original code?). This considerable reinforcement of *Aleph* and *Mem* makes a tremendous impact on *Teeteev* and upsets it.

We thus see in the next schema an organic movement (30) grafted, so to speak, on the undifferentiated reservoir of life (80) and the cosmic resistances—existence yielding to this life as archetype (8). This schema, therefore, is 30.80.400.8. It is pronounced, as a word, *Lepetahh* and is meant to be, in its translations, "at the door". However, even in colloquial Hebrew, *Petahh* (or *Fetahh*) is meant to be any opening. We have here, an example of the debasing of the ontological language into a sensorial, image-making idiom. The opening truly exists: it is in the organic motion (30) granted to the primal life, non-identified, non-evolved, from which the original female draws its life.

We now come upon the drama which is so often described symbolically in the Book of Genesis: the reaction of the female. The following schema is *Hhatat*: 8.9.1.400. The sequence is obvious; let us look at it again: 30.80.400.8—8.9.1.400. We see that the action upon 80 and 8 was aiming at the female (9). And now, in spite of the 400 still waging a rear-guard defence, *Aleph* has been introduced in close contact to 9 (this action expressed by 8.9.1.400 is strangely enough translated "sin").

The result of this penetration is an inner turmoil in the female (or the unconscious, in the psyche); and this new vibration is an extraordinary peace and flowering, a cosmic transfiguration of the feminine, a dialogue being born between the deep layers of the unconscious and the outer consciousness.

This flowering is expressed in the schema which follows: *Robetz* (*Raysh-Bayt-Tsadde*: 200.2.900). Now the "house" (2) is cognizant of its cosmic appurtenance (200), and the feminine is totally transfigured (900). As often happens in current Hebrew, this schema, read as a word (*Robetz*) has two contrasting meanings: to lie down and brood, and to sprinkle or spread knowledge, Ontologically, both meanings are correct and not at all contradictory.

We now come to the schema which, in Hebrew and in every translation, is supposed to mean "and unto thee": *Weyilekh* (6.1.30.10.500). It expresses the productive (6) drive of *Aleph* (1) imparting functional movement (30) to its eternal "partner-against" (10). Here they at last meet and the result is 500: cosmic life in existence!

The following schema depicts the game, the interplay which results from this happy meeting. It is read, more or less, *Teshooq-too*. The root *Shooq* is the oriental bazaar, where all goods are exchanged. The schema is 400.300.6.100.400.6. We see the 6 in it twice, one being in between two 400s and one outside. This schema opens an infinite vista to our meditation. It shows, in action, the cosmic "breath" (300) constantly in fertile symbiosis with the cosmic *Aleph*, happily alive in the cosmos. The final 6 leads us in the spirit of hope to the last three schemata, the concluding two being linked with a hyphen *Ve-ata Timshal-Bo*: 6.1.400.5—400.40.300.30—2.6. This conclusion of verse 7 (note this number again) of chapter iv (note this number, too), opens an inexhaustible field for meditation and knowledge: the drastic cleavage between 400.40 and 300.30.

In résumé, we have learned from this verse that if and when the cosmic *Aleph* is alive and active in us, it permeates directly the unconscious and silences it, after which an exalted, scintillating stillness permeates our being in fruitful commerce and consummation, beyond time and beyond evolution. The inner dialogue is instantaneous in its effect. Qaheen understands its message. He becomes the container of timeless life; and, as such, he goes toward Hevel—man conditioned according to his time and location—and speaks to him, although their separation has already taken place. But Hevel cannot understand; he cannot even hear Qaheen's parable, and he dissolves into what he essentially is: a bladder of blood. This blood is drunk by the female, Earth. The text does not say that Qaheen slays Hevel:

it says that he *is* *Yaqam,* meaning elevated, raised, exalted above Hevel.

So YHWH and Qaheen look for Hevel and do not find him. There is only that pool of blood which Adamah, the enormous female-to-be-conquered, is drinking. And it is the curse of this female which is upon Qaheen. It is preposterous to think that he is cursed by "God". On the contrary, it is written: *Therefore whosoever slayeth Cain, vengeance (of YHWH) shall be taken on him sevenfold* (Gen. IV, 15). Qaheen will always re-emerge seven times more strongly: his number is 7: *Qof-Yod-Noun* terminal (100.10.700). It is an intense life, terrifying to whoever curses it. Qaheen, as life-death, life-death, is the ceaseless, intermittent pulsation that will always triumph over the female element of resistance forged with blood. He is here, now, present, as he was present always, although more often than not unidentified.

All this is, as well as it can be put, the literal meaning of the Scriptures. The historical reaction to it is the sanguinary, cruel and frightful history of man throughout the ages. In these thousands of years, more and more worse and worse wars have succeeded one another. We have wholesale murder, racial hatred, hatred between peoples of different coloured skins, different nationalities, different religious or economic creeds— each individual killing in order to "protect" himself (as if in killing, one were not killing oneself) whilst Cain is "righteously" disgraced and ostracized.

During all this time, while "Cain" (misinterpreted) is forever cursed by mankind's unending fratricide, Qaheen, who cannot prevent Hevel being killed by his own conditioning, is in deepest mourning *in the land of Nod* (Nod means sorrow.) This land is *east of Eden,* there where the tree of life is. This "land of Nod" is none other than the Land of *Yod,* where the Y is brought to life in N (50): *Noun-Vav-Dallet* instead *Yod-Vav-Dallet.*

The verse (Gen. IV, 16) dealing with Qaheen's "going out from the presence of the Lord" describes an action concerning Qaheen in relation to an aspect (or projection) of YHWH in the world of time and evolution where Qaheen must live—or, to put it differently, where YHWH must become incarnate. The verse begins thus: *Veyotse Qaheen Melafne YHWH.* The action *Veyotse* (6.10.90.1) states the equation that the verse must solve: Qaheen's mission will be to apply fecundity (6) to the existence of Yod (10) so to elevate the female to its power (90) and thus liberate *Aleph* (1). He will do it *Melafne YHWH*— which, in numbers is 40.30.80.50.10—YHWH. We see that every one of these numbers is a multiple of 10, i.e. existential. Through 40, the 30 acts upon 80 and the 50 upon 10. This signifies that in (or by) the resistance of existence (40) the movement (organic) of 30 is given to the reservoir of primordial existence (80) and that life-in-existence (50) is given to Yod (10). This action is, in a nutshell, the definition of YHWH (10.5.6.5). One of the fives of YHWH acts as 30 upon 80, the other as 50 upon 10. Thus are interpreted the two lives with which we have been concerned all along, the 30 affecting the contained (germ of life-to-be), the 50 its container (*Yod*).

The last two schemata of this verse, *Qedmat-Eden,* translated "east of Eden", are: 100.4.40.400—70.4.700. They are like a thunderbolt, a fantastic *coup de théâtre,* for anyone who would doubt the meaning of this code. They show *Qof* acting as a spear and piercing through and through every layer of resistance (4.40.400), every crystallization of the mind, every established certainty, and projecting the archetype (4) of such resistance into the actualization of all possible possibilities (70) and its cosmic significance (700). This action, this preservation of every possibility, obviously destroys every prototype, everything which is fixed, established, or built to endure.

It is not surprising that for the conditioned mind Cain is a killer, whereas he is the very action of YHWH.

17

Intermezzo

GENESIS IV, 17-26 is very interesting, but we are afraid it would confuse the issue were we to go into it even briefly. The same holds true of Genesis V, in spite of its great importance. This chapter deals with the two lines of descent that originated with Adam. The first line, by YHWH, is continued through Qaheen. The other, by Elohim, is transmitted by way of Set.

Both of these descents are, of course, purely symbolic. They are however, intimately interrelated since that of Qaheen constantly reacts upon the pseudo-historical descent of Set.

We are dealing here with an astonishing poem in code, respecting that interplay of cosmic energies which has, from the very beginning, been the constant subject-matter of the Book of Genesis: the immanent energy of Qaheen is projected from the interior, or the "inner light", and is in no way subject to time. That of Set is concerned with the evolution of the "containers" and with their special and particular forms or shapes. As we have already learned, the ultimate purpose of this interplay is Indetermination.

In Genesis IV and V every name has a meaning: Enoch and Enos, Mehujael and Mahalalel, etc, as well as the phrases introducing each name, whether it is or is not said that so and so "lived and begat", whether their days are eight hundred and ninety-five or only sixty-five, whether Lamekh takes two wives and avenges Qaheen seventy and sevenfold, or whether Enoch "walks with God", or whether there is a relation between the seven generations through Qaheen and the ten through Set. All this calls for a rather complicated analysis of the relationship between numerous archetypes and historical humanity. It clearly shows the significance of Qaheen and his action upon the generations of Set. Meaningful as these interrelationships are, for the time being their further development must be put aside, because of their great number and complexity. Were we to attempt a transcription coupled with constant explanations of the code we would soon be lost in a maze. That chapter must be read directly with full knowledge of the graphs and code.

Likewise, we will not go at length into the story of the Deluge, although the origins of this legend reveal certain elements of the conflict between the different symbols which we have been examining. The incoherence in the behaviour of a divinity who decides to suppress all life because his creation has gone sour, and who in this drastic operation carefully preserves a sample of each of his created species so that he can keep alive what he intends to destroy, is a stepping-down to the folklore level of some of the contradictions with which we are now familiar. And the picturesque Odyssey of Noahh and his Ark furnishes amusing decorations for nurseries.

The Deluge, no doubt, was really a cataclysm that was apparently the end of a world and, for those to whom it happened, the end of *the* world. Then came the surprising discovery that everything was beginning again. The Semitic genius grafted some interesting symbols onto these archaic memories, such as the Ark itself, the raven, the dove, and of course, all the numbers involved: one hundred and fifty days of water, the grounding of the Ark on the seventeenth day in the seventh month, the decreasing of the waters until the tenth month, the name Ararat, etc. Each episode of this legend merits careful study, but we shall keep to its broad lines.

After the Deluge, we leave the archetypes and enter into another domain. Here the archetypes, the framework on which the psyche builds itself, engender categories of symbols. One can follow these until the fiftieth and last chapter of Genesis which concludes with Joseph's death at the symbolic age of a hundred and ten years. Then one can trace the development of these symbols right through into the Gospels of Matthew and John.

We have already shown the keys to the understanding of these stories. The general tenor of them is as follows: the principal themes are the allegories of (*a*) *Aleph* in the blood and *Aleph*'s inevitable resurrection; (*b*) the earth (soil) as Adamah— the female of Adam—and Adam as being mankind; (*c*) Elohim seen as the life-process of *Aleph* and *Aleph* as pulsating discontinuity life-death, Elohim being its movement and its projection into the continuity of existence; (*d*) the story of Esha and Eesh, being archetypes of "fiery" womanhood and manhood; (*e*) the nature of YHWH as being the double life (inner and outer) of all lives which can only come into being in mankind where the two lives fertilize each other; (*f*) the interplay between life and existence (life as life-death—life-death operating upon the existence of all that exists); (*g*) the perpetual delaying of the birth of the human germ, always prevented from settling down into any fixed or permanent conditioning as is the case for the germs of life in the animal kingdom; (*h*) the wrestling between Elohim and YHWH; (*i*) the conflict between YHWH and Adamah, hence the conflict of their so-called "sons"—in other words, between the offspring of YHWH through Adam and the offspring of the Mothers (Adamah); (*j*) finally, and most important to full understanding, the process of womanhood's sublimation.

In spite of their seeming complexity, were they alive within us through one single act of understanding, all these themes would sow the seed of Revelation in our being. Let us now pass on to a consideration of some of the major landmarks which high-point the extraordinary unity in the line of thought which acts upon us, from the myth of Adam to the myth of Jesus.

18

Noahh and his Sons

GENESIS IX, 5. Here is another unfortunate example of the in-adequacy of the translations. After blessing Noahh and giving him instructions, "God" says to him: *And surely the blood of your lives will I require; at the hand of every beast will I require it, and at the hand of man; at the hand of every man's brother will I require the life of man.*

We submit that this makes no sense at all. In its correct reading, this verse refers to the conflict between YHWH and Adamah, who disputes the blood of Adam. YHWH does not "require" it (Noah's, i.e. Adam's, blood); the letter-numbers state, rather, that he confers upon it a cosmic significance and the cosmic energy of *Sheen*.

It is surprising that among the different meanings of the root Hhai the one selected by the translators is "beast". We know that when leaving Eden Adam *called the name of his wife Hheva because she was the mother of Kol Hhai*: "all living" (Gen. III, 20). The conflict between *YHWH* and *Adamah* is now taken over by the evolutionary process *Elohim-Noahh*.

You remember that Adamah (earth), "opening her mouth", drank Hevel's *dam* (blood), poor Hevel being no more than that. The *dam* of Adam must sublimate itself—the *Mem* of its name must jump from its lower value 40 to its exalted value 600, and the letter-numbers explain that Adam must become the "brother" of Eesh; we now understand that this mutation is to be brought about through blending man as a product of the earth with man endowed with celestial fire.

Genesis IX, 13. The appearance of the rainbow as a covenant is, of course, a resurrection of light (*Awr*, whose letters are

Aleph-Waw-Raysh) above the "waters" (the carriers of life).

Genesis IX, *20.* Noahh becomes a "husbandman" and plants a vineyard, say the English translators. It is interesting to note that the word husbandman for farmer is literally correct. Noahh transmutes downwards his "Eesh" quality of fire by becoming Eesh (husband) to Adamah (the earth). The earth reproduces this fire as wine (the wine as symbol expresses that fact, as the Qabala well knows).

Genesis IX, *21.* The strange fruit of the nuptials between Eesh (as man-fire) and Adamah is Yeen (*Yod-Yod-Noun*) a double existence in number 700. (Notice that 700 is also the key-number to Qaheen.) This *Yeen* is a sort of tornado in which anything can happen. The English word wine is the Hebrew word scarcely modified; so also is the Latin. (Incidentally, it is not generally realized how many of our words derive from, or are, the Hebrew ones.)

This verse exemplifies the fact that the symbols of blood and wine belong to the same category. Having drunk, Noahh—as is expected if his name, *Noun-Hhayt,* is understood—loses his adamic quality and sinks into an unevolved state. The relationship between him and Adamah is all to Adamah's advantage. Noahh's consciousness now lapses into the unconsciousness of undifferentiated cosmic life and "uncovers" the true significance of this Noahh whose numbers reveal that he is a life not yet entered into the process of evolution (he falls asleep with his genitals uncovered).

Genesis IX, *22-25.* Hham unexpectedly sees the nudity of his father. He calls his two brothers to come and cover their father, but Noahh curses one of Hham's sons, Canaan, who had never been near him. As is so frequently the case throughout the Bible, the stories of Genesis which appear to be most absurd when traditionally misread turn out when correctly interpreted, to be full of the richest meanings; and this one is no exception. It scarcely needs to be pointed out that if we read the story of Noahh, with the idea that it has to do with real people, it becomes a monstrosity. Here we have a father whose lack of self-respect is such that, being drunk, he lies quite naked. One son, seeing this, is seized with fright and dares not look at his father long enough to cover him. He calls his two brothers who approach backwards, bearing a blanket. The drunkard now regains his senses and launches a malediction. Upon whom? Upon Hham who saw his father's nakedness? Not at all, Noahh curses Canaan, the fourth son of Hham.

No commentator—except in the Qabala—has ever explained this. Thus the story is twisted; and most of its readers think it is Hham who was cursed, which after all would be bad enough. As the letter-numbers give it, the truth of this story is fairly complex. After the Deluge, there is another Genesis: in other words, evolution has ceased because of world destruction and must start again out of a state of primordial life. Noahh, the human germ, symbolically plunged into non-differentiated life, is therefore obliged to re-cover the ground it lost in the Deluge. Notice that this process is strikingly true of life, psychologically speaking. It often happens that although we seem to have evolved towards a true understanding of essentials, we suddenly find ourselves faced with the question on a new and higher level, where we discover that we have really understood nothing at all and consequently have to begin all over again.

Another biological concept that Genesis often presents is that the human "germ" must be constantly prevented from stabilizing itself in a static form of conditioning. Thus it appears that the first-born are the youngest from the standpoint of evolution, because they are the least mature; and conversely, it is the latest born who are endowed with the greatest maturity.* If we assimilate this point of view, we will cease to think of our ancestors as pillars of wisdom and maturity. We will think of them, instead, as representing a younger, more primitive humanity than ours; and we will bestir ourselves to make valid our own more mature vantage point and begin to search for Revelation in ourselves.

* We must keep in mind that the notion is in reference to the general evolution and not to individuals.

We read in the text that Noahh's sons are mentioned in the following order: Sem, Hham and Japhet (Sem and Japhet are the biblical versions). Yet it is clearly stated several times that Japhet, the last named, is big, great. Understanding this and Noahh's state of involution, we can see why Japhet, the "enlarged one", is relegated to the last place; for the exalted one in earthly values is thus the youngest in point of evolution. But Sem, whose *Elohi* is YHWH, is the eldest in point of evolution and therefore inherits the highest rank in the human germ's evolutionary process. The text is very insistent upon the fact that Japhet's is the greatest, though the youngest in maturity. As for Hham, the youngest, he is the second named. In these allegories, the impersonations of no. 2 are always in a dangerous position, the 2 symbolizing the static condition, enclosed in the dwelling of *Bayt* (2). We have seen Hevel dying of it. In this case, Hham (*Hhayt-Mem*), corresponding to the numbers 8.40, is the "son", the exact extension prolongation of Noahh (*Noun-Hhayt*). The process of Noahh Hham is *Noun-Hhayt-Mem*, which is read Nahham, a root which, as often happens in Hebrew, means different things. It can be translated as repentance, pity, consolation or vengeance. It is in any case a fall, a negative movement. When Sem and Japhet arrive, walking backwards, they face evolution and cover the originative, unevolved "father" whose state of being has been defeated and confounded by the great "female", Adamah, because of his having drunk of her "blood", her wine.

When this correct backward direction is taken, Noahh does not really "curse" Canaan (the fourth son of Hham). The word *Arawr*, which has always been translated as "curse", is an extra *Raysh* projected upon *Awr*, the word for light. The reinforced resistance is a multiple of *Raysh*'s already resistant 2. It is the number 4. Noahh projects this onto Hham's fourth son, Canaan, who (symbolically) is thus destined to become the "territory" where Sem must develop.

Mount Ararat, where Noahh's legendary Ark is said to have landed, also has two *Raysh*, meaning two worlds: the temporal and the invisible. In *Arawr* they are copulatively related. It is in this double world, so complex and difficult to grasp (with its doubled resistance) that the human seed entrusted to Sem is sown and must evolve. It implies many deaths but also many stubborn resurrections, many disastrous errors but a tenacious survival.

This biological law is always apparent in the so-called curses of the Bible. It is important to recognize this because once we have freed our mind from the fear of a cursing deity, life stands a chance of being understood.*

It must be added that, according to the code, Canaan is not really supposed to become *a servant of servants to his brethren* (Gen. IX, 25). The schema *Aabd* (70.2.4) indicates a state of conflict between the dauntless 70 and the combined boundaries of 2.4. (*Aabd* was translated "slave" when qualifying Qaheen's relationship with *Adamah*, but slavery always breeds revolt. In Qaheen's case it did; in Canaan's case it also does.)

So the *Arawr* of the repentant Noahh falls upon Canaan whose letter-numbers are 20.50.70.700. They project the seed of life, 50, into the tremendous uncertainty of Qaheen's 7 exalted to the hundreds, that is, into a world that will never afford it any restful shelter. Such has been the blessing of YHWH, all through history on its people. The precision of the symbolic text is such that in Genesis IX, 27, it is said: *Elohim shall enlarge Japhet and he shall dwell in the tents of Sem.* According to the Qabala, Sem, being symbolically the human germ that does not cease its evolution, will assimilate and encompass all the humanisms of our heritage.

We cannot reject the Scriptures, which represent a valid part of this heritage. We must, rather, turn upon them the search-light of impartial investigation, thereby recovering the vital meanings lost in the debacle of mistranslation. As one philoso-

---

* When the "curse" *Arawr*—1.200.6.200—comes into existence, its *Aleph* (1) becomes 10 and Raysh (200) is alive with Hay (5); thus the Schema becomes 10.5.6.5.: *YHWH*. This identity of a so-called curse and a so-called deity is revealing of the state of psychological fear which underlies the ecclesiastical traditions.

pher puts it, man is "condemned to meaning". We cannot
escape the real truths of the Bible, although we have ignored
them for so many centuries. To rediscover them now we must,
in a way, "walk backwards". We cannot escape because these
truths and our own nature are inseparably one.

Genesis xi, *1-8—Babel.* The praiseworthy attempt to become
one people and to have one language is shattered (in the translation) by a so-called God who shamelessly declares the malice
of his venture. *Let us go down,* says he, *and there confound their
language, that they may not understand one another's speech* (Gen. xi, 7).

This shattering of Babel is a direct reference to the necessary
hindering of mankind's premature birth, a principle which has
been set forth in our preceding chapters. We can therefore
assume that Babel is Bible. The original meaning of it had to be
confounded and distorted because mankind was not yet suffi-
ciently evolved—not yet ready for the rebirth, or mutation,
which the Bible describes as our potential. Does the renaissance
of ontological insight in the present-day world indicate an
emergent readiness?

19

A Preamble to Genesis XI and XII

THESE CHAPTERS contain a list of Sem's descendants, as far as Abram. From here on, until the close of the fiftieth and last chapter, Genesis becomes a vast epic poem whose meaning has hardly begun to be grasped.

Like a majestic space ship, originating in archetypal spheres, this saga comes down to geographical earth and links itself with history. It embodies all the vital elements, all the archetypes, all the symbols which were described in the preceding chapters. Its extraordinary message is not given in terms of an historical chronicle. In fact, its historical aspects derive from the ontological significance of such names as Abraham, Sarah, Isaac, Rebecca, Jacob and Rachel, as well as such geographic names as Sichem, Moreh, Bethel, Beer-Sheba, Sodom and Gomorrah.

The myth is pre-existent to recorded history. This myth is the condensation in our human societies (pre-human, we prefer to say) of cosmic forces unnoticed by man. We are each one of us a focal point at which energies that pass our understanding meet and function. Due to erroneous self-perception, we struggle perpetually among the contradictions that we engender, attributing to ourselves a false reality.

Were we to follow, step by step, this long saga of Abraham, Isaac and Jacob, it would fill a large volume; and even then it would be useful only to those who have assimilated the ancient code-language of the letter-numbers, of which only the rudiments are given in this book. We shall therefore limit ourselves to a few of the most significant passages.

As a guide for the journey, the symbolic meaning of the

numbers 1, 2 and 3 must be kept firmly in mind. *Number 1*, Abraham, symbolizes the arising or upsurge of the unconditioned germ on its way towards its totally realized human maturity. *Number 2*, his son Isaac, symbolizes the rooting of this germ in a conditioning which if allowed to act, would cause it to come to birth prematurely. *Number 3*, Isaac's son, Jacob, symbolizes the moving forward, biologically, of the germ. In the 1, 2, 3 sequence of this forward movement, the number 2 of the germ, Isaac, is in a very dangerous position! We must grasp this symbolism if we intend to have a notion of what this epic poem conveys. Also, we must remember all the themes which have been expounded from the very outset of this allegory.

The theme of this vast epic poem is the implanting of the human seed, of which the eponymic ancestor is Sem, in the mythical land of Canaan. When YHWH became, through Moses, a tribal deity and the Hebrews forgot the original Revelation, they mistook Canaan for an actual country and waged ruthless wars to conquer it. This is one of the countless examples of the perils inherent in local-temporal interpretation of Scriptures that are universal and timeless in their original import.

20

Abram and Sarai

GENESIS XI. Among the innumerable messages that can be decoded from the Bible's "calculator" the story of Abram is so important that the three so-called "monotheistic" religions dutifully consider this personage to be their ancestor. Sem, the eponymic ancestor of the Semites, is said to have begotten a son at the age of one hundred (the number symbolizing the perfection of manhood). The time was two years after the Deluge, number 2 signifying the "dwelling" or container that the new seed must build for itself. After the enumeration of Sem's descendants, we come to old Terahh, Abram's father, who was of the ninth generation that issued from Sem.

Terahh, with his family and his flocks, lived in "Ur of the Chaldees", and it was in this land that Abram was born. Special importance attaches to the name of Abram's birthplace. This is because the word Ur is, essentially, *Awr*. As you will remember, *Awr* means light; and the Chaldeans (Kasdeem) were magicians. So it was in a place that the Bible qualifies as "light of Magicians" that Abram grew up. The ancient light of magic handed down from primitive civilizations had come to a point where it could give birth to a bearer of the inner light. So far, the light was still uncertain. It did not prove strong enough for the immediate birth of Elohim's Light. So it was inevitable that Abram, who was to receive this new Light, should be removed from Ur.

The epic poem which relates this odyssey is filled with meaning when read according to the numerical-code. Even in the résumé which follows, this will be apparent. Once upon a time, in the Land that dwells in the light of Magicians, the seed of humanity under this magic light emphasized the number 70: the safeguard of every unconditioned human possibility. Seventy then brought forth the number 3 (Terahh begat three sons "at the age of 70"), three roots by which the seed sought to take form. But since in the "light of the Magicians" the third seed could not mature, it died. (Gen. xi, 28: And Haran died before his father Terahh in the land of his nativity, in Ur of the Chaldees.) Seed number 2 (Nahhor) went its own way. Seed number 1 (Abram) had to be saved—that is to say, rescued from the static subhuman order of things, where magic overpowered the bodies and ruled the minds.

So the impersonation of no. 70 took this one root which was left and saved it by leaving Ur of the Chaldees with its static light of magic and moved towards the land of strife and pain and joy and great uncertainty and total insecurity, where the seed of humanity must take root if it is to survive and come to maturity: Canaan.

They never went beyond *Hharan* and old *Terahh* died there at the age of two hundred and five. Or, to be more accurate, I should say that the schema *Terahh* consumes itself in the schema *Hharan* as can be seen by comparing the cogent numbers: 400.200.8—8.200.700.

It is interesting to compare the name of *Haran* who *died before his father Terahh in the land of his nativity, in Ur of the Chaldees* (Gen. xi, 28) with the name of *Hharan* of the place where Terahh died. It is of extreme interest to study the story of *Lot*, son of that *Haran* who died where he was born, and the story of *Sodom* and *Gomorrah*. The words ascribed to YHWH when assigning his mission to Abram, *Lekh-Lekha*, have also great significance. Those narratives are inexhaustible in meaningful details.

Abram having gone back to *Ur* leaves at last definitely, with his wife Sarai and his nephew *Lot and the souls that they had gotten* (Gen. xii, 5) and they reach Canaan. The name of that symbolic earth is the equation, the solution of which Abram has the mission to bring about. It is the land of all the conflicts of the

149

world, of all violences, of all impediments to freedom. And it is in the midst of it that Abram is committed to sow the seed of the human-to-be.

That germ will have to take root in Canaan and, paradoxically, will have to avoid remaining fixed in it. It will have, under the sign of no. 3, to conquer the duality symbolized by that earth. In the midst of cruel battles it will have to learn how not to battle, because taking part with one or other of the contestants would prevent its ripening.

Thus begin the adventures of Abram the initiate. It is the story of the greatest conquest that mankind must achieve.

In Canaan Abram starts on his mission with the action of no. 3: he builds three altars to YHWH: two upon his arrival, one later on. The first altar is mentioned in verse no. 7. *Abram* builds it *unto the plain of Moreh* (*Mem-Waw-Raysh-Hay*: 40.6, 200.5). He builds the second between *Beth-El* (the house of Elohim) and *Aai* (*Ayn-Yod*: 70.10).

Under the impact of these first intrusions into its passivity, Canaan reacts and resists: there is a famine.

Abram and Sarai are obliged to "go down" into Egypt, the name of which is Mitsraim, symbolizing (as shown by its letter-numbers) the fat, female earth with its rich, physiological substance. Now we come to Abram's apparently insane statement that Sarai is his sister. She is kidnapped by Pharaoh; and when Pharaoh learns that she is Abram's wife, he gives her back to him and exclaims (paraphrased): "Why did you say she is your sister and not your wife? I would have left her alone! Now take her, and go away, both of you!"

Here again we see that it is in the most absurd passages that we may find the most important lessons. Abram wishes to elevate woman to the free rank of a "sister"; he wishes her status to equal his, so that she can become his companion, fully collaborating with him. He does not wish woman to remain merely at the level of a concubine in a harem. Sarai, however, does not understand; and in the land of carnal appetites, she yields in the manner of a mere creature of the flesh.

Genesis XIII. Through this adventure—resulting from the woman's lack of maturity—Abram's terrestial wealth increases (we can meditate upon, and verify this fact every day). In Canaan, however, work awaits him. Abram returns to the place where he had built his second altar. This is between *Bayt-El* and a place whose numbers are 70.10: *Aai* (you remember the significance of 70). This is the place where Lot and Abram separate. Lot is attracted by what the numbers describe as a well-watered plain, and he goes towards Sodom and Gomorrah.

The difference between the name *Sodom* and the name *Adam* lies in the fact that Sodom has in it no *Aleph*; this is replaced by *Sammekh*, with the numerical significance of 60. Thus the blood of Sodom—unlike that of Adam, which is *"Aleph"* in the blood—is incapable of sublimation. Gomorrah is synonymous with slavery.

Abram, failing to vitalize Lot, is now free and can retire into *Mamre, which is in Hebron* (these names need not be explained here), where he builds the third altar to YHWH.

In fact he inserts the no. 3 (Gen. XIII, 18). He fertilizes the two *Mem* of *Mamre* (*Mem-Mem-Raysh-Aleph*) by enlarging them to the cosmic level Raysh, whereby Aleph springs forth. Hebron, or rather Hhevron (8.2.200.6.700) is a primordial state of energy elevated to the highest cosmic exponent 700.

Genesis XIV. The story of the war between the four kings is too long to tell here. But it is a phase necessary to the fulfilment of Abram's mission.

Genesis XV. The symbolic episode of cutting the carcasses of different animals in halves and the burning fire which passes between them is also too long to relate. It is a test, which Abram passes successfully. YHWH then makes a covenant with Abram and "gives" him, or rather says that he gives him, all the land between Egypt and the Euphrates.

The myth, at this point, tends more and more to materialize into geographical realities and its language accompanies it, so to speak, in making this "landing". The original schemata become real persons and the cosmic energy, designated as YHWH, becomes a divinity.*

Genesis XVI. Sarai now brings her servant woman, Hagar, to Abram; and this Egyptian handmaid becomes pregnant. She despises Sarai and taunts her with being a barren wife. Sarai is angry. This servant has no intelligence; she is just an animal, passive and subjugated as are all the Egyptian women Sarai has seen. Sarai discharges her, and Hagar is greatly afflicted.

YHWH comforts her and tells her the exact opposite of what is related in our translations, where he is supposed to say to *Hagar* (Gen. XVI, 12) that *Ishmael*, her son (eponymous ancestor of the Arabs), *will be a wild man; his hand will be against everyman and every man's hand against him,* whereas he actually says that *Ishmael will be a prolific Adam, his hand with all and the hands of all with him.*

This utterance to a prolific woman is logical. But Sarai is fore-ordained to a different destiny: she must develop her intelligence and give birth to a germ that will for ever continue its growth. It will not yield to any conditionings inviting it to become a lateral branch of the tree of life. Through cruel pains and sorrows it will have to learn how to become indeterminate even to its own perception.

* The cabalists have never anthropomorphized YHWH or Elohim. Their symbolical language has led the non-initiates astray. According to the fundamental textbook of Qabala, *Sepher Yetsira*, Abram owes his revelation to his intelligent study of the structure of energy.

21

Circumcision
(Genesis XVII, 10-15)

THUS SARAI attains the perfection that is required of her. She reaches it at an age symbolizing the perfection of woman: 90 years. At the same time Abram reaches the symbolic age of perfection in man: 100 years. YHWH then reveals to Abram his mission, and Elohim confers upon him a new life. This is symbolized by a new syllable in his name: *Thy name shall be Abraham* (Gen. XVII, 5). Immediately, there follows, clearly and explicitly stated, the covenant of circumcision.

It appears as a covenant not between YHWH and Abraham, but between Elohim and Abraham, and it is only after its establishment that Sarai's name is changed to Sarah.

Circumcision at eight days is generally considered a hygienic measure, though actually something far more important is involved: the transformation of the human body. The rationale is the need to sever manhood (as typified by Adam) from the purely animal heritage through a process of sublimation and transformation.

In the biblical allegory, we have seen Esha in the Garden of Eden taking the initiative in man's sensorial and cerebral development. As we shall see later on—with Sarah, Rebecca, Rachel and Mary-mother-of-Jesus—the human germ develops into manhood if the woman is able to sublimate the primordial female within herself. But the fact of circumcision in the human male actually makes a profound contribution to the development of woman. It affects both sexes, physiologically and psychologically.

This shock is deeply felt by the individual. Undergone eight days after birth, as it is among the Jews, its effects are so decisive within the structure of the unconscious and the vital centres that it is justifiable to find in circumcision a factor of the exceptional history of the Jews. We may well suppose that those who instituted this practice did so with a specific goal in view. Circumcision intensifies the development of the sensorial apparatus through an effective co-ordination of sensory activity; it awakens the intellectual faculties; the sexual energy is utilized by the body prior to the awakening of sex.

The result is a freer self which transforms and assimilates the elements of its environment according to the needs of its own individual development. At the same time this self is carried along by the inner movement which engenders that faculty of assimilation. The individual is in perfect harmony with the rapid changes of the world.

These remarks may give insight into the manner in which the vital and contradictory movement set up in the human process by the circumcision is considered, in mythical terms, as a "pact" with Elohim (which is this process). This pact causes the movement of the universe to penetrate into the very flesh of the body, and into the mind as well. In fact, it has "conquered the flesh" by obliging it to transmute, to transfigure, itself.

This is a theme already familiar to us; the transmutation of what is fixed and static (in this case, the flesh, the blood, the "dam" of Adam), so that it can eventually allow the life of *Aleph* to be resuscitated.*

* For further elaboration upon the subject, see Note 2, "Circumcision," p. 221.

22

From Sarah to Rebecca

GENESIS XVIII, 12. *Sarah laughed to herself, saying, After I am grown old shall I have pleasure, my Lord being old also?* The Hebrew text states later on that Isaac, her future son, is *Yitzhhaq*: he who laughs. And we shall see that his life is, for the most part, a comedy.

We can pass over the sordid story of *Lot*, remembering chiefly that this schema (*Lammed-Waw-Tav*: 50.6.400) is foredoomed. His wife does not even have a name. Looking *back from behind him* (Gen. XIX, 26) she becomes *a pillar of salt*. His two daughters who sleep with him when he is drunk are symbolic. The ignominious decline of *Lot* as an archetype is a consequence of his weakness.

Genesis XX, *1*. Abraham sojourns between *Qadesh* and *Shur* (between 100.4.300 and 300.6.200). These numbers show a balancing or rhythm, from the cosmic *Aleph* (100) to its metabolism (300) and back to the universal "container", 200.

We now come upon a second episode dealing with a kidnapped woman: *And Abraham said of Sarah his wife, She is my sister: and Abimelekh King of Gerar sent and took Sarah* (Gen. XX, 2).

But womanhood has progressed and, in contrast to her experience with Pharaoh, *Sarah* successfully passes the test. *Abimelekh* has a dream in which *Elohim* says to him: *Thou art but a dead man, for the woman which thou hast taken: for she is a man's wife.* So he does not come near her.

Genesis XX, *12*. *Abraham* reveals, or suggests, that *Sarah* is his sister because they both have the same "father". But—adds *Abraham*—she is not *Imi*'s daughter. In a restricted sense, *Imi* means "my mother". *Abram* however, according to Qabala, declares himself here, *Ben-Adam*, son of Adam, just as Jesus did, at a much later date. And the very important fact is that he includes *Sarah* in that denomination, thereby acknowledging her spiritual elevation.

Genesis xx, *16*. *Abimelekh* makes atonement to *Abraham* with a *thousand pieces of silver*. One thousand is the most exalted state of *Aleph* (the word Aleph actually means one thousand in Hebrew). Symbolically this means that *Abraham's* undertaking is successful.

Genesis xxi, *1. And the Lord visited Sarah as he had said, and the Lord did unto Sarah as he had spoken.* Can it be said more clearly that it was YHWH (mistranslated "the Lord") who engendered *Isaac*, *Sarah's* son?

All dogmatic faith being laid aside, this verse must be understood as it is written. Is it necessary to state that the "mystery of Incarnation" through Mary-mother-of-Jesus is neither unique nor even original?

This point is so important that one of Qabala's most fundamental postulates must here be insisted on: YHWH is not a deity. We have often said that, according to Qabala, the real mystery which it is totally impossible to understand is, simply, existence. Any deistic notion serves to remove from the mind, by means of fallacious explanations, the disturbing realization of that all-invading immediacy.

The natural supports of these devices are omnipotent deities, because in fairy tales magic wands are their own explanations: magic is magic and God is almighty, and for many that is enough.

This verse does not claim a priority for Sarah's pregnancy through "the Lord". When YHWH ceases to be anthropomorphized, *Sarah* and *Yitzhhaq*, and for that matter *Abraham*, must solely be a set of schemata, or formulas, expressing different states of energy. They must abandon the human shapes that the psyches have kept alive, as complexes, through many centuries, with the obstinate—and unconscious—purpose of not wishing to understand them.

Between YHWH as a "Lord" and *Sarah* as a woman, the "doing unto her as he had spoken" loses its meaning. The text actually reads: *Ve-YHWH Paqad Et Sarah*. The schema *Paqad* (80.100.4) shows that in the primordial unstructured energy (80) the cosmic *Aleph* (100) creates a resistance (4) that sets it in biological motion. In terms of psychology it can be said that this is an awakening of the subconscious and unconscious strata. It is given to that part of symbolic womanhood which is in everyone of us, whether female or male.

Let us now consider the schemata *Abram* and *Abraham*, *Sarai* and *Sarah*. In *Genesis* xvii, *5* (5 is *Hay*) *Abram* had been given an extra life *Hay* (5) when a covenant was established between him and YHWH. This means that the *Aleph-Bayt* (Ab) of *Ab-Ram*, representing the entire Alphabet of that initiate's knowledge, became creative. Its action upon Ram became alive as shown by the *Hay* (5) being introduced between *Raysh* and *Mem*. So whereas *Abram* is 1.2.200.40, *Abraham* is 1.2.200.5.40, thus allowing the final *Mem* to become 600. The perfect *Abraham* is therefore 1.2.200.5.600.

In *Genesis* xvii, *15* (3 × 5) *Sarai* became *Sarah*. The schema *Sarai*: 300.200.10 was transformed into 300.200.5 which means that the existential *Yod* (10) of *Sarai* is, in *Sarah*, the *Hay* (5) of life.

Genesis xxi, *2* to *Genesis* xxv, *20* contains so much significant detail that it should be read attentively. Briefly, here are some of the episodes it relates: the second expulsion of *Hagar*; the well of *Beer-sheba* (the word *Sheba* means seven); the long discussion between *Abraham* and *Abimelekh* concerning a *well of water*; *Abraham*'s gift to *Abimelekh* of *seven ewe lambs* as token of his good faith (as always, the number 7 is associated with *Abraham*'s actions); the so-called sacrifice of *Isaac*, which finally was not required (it was another instance of YHWH's testing, as happened in the case of *Jacob*, and of *Moses*); the *four hundred shekels of silver* paid for *Sarah*'s place of burial by *Abraham*; the hesitations as to the land where the human seed, *Isaac*, should be given in custody; the choice of the woman who, next, should carry forward the lineage of exalted womanhood; *Rebekah* drawing water plentifully from the well; and the proof that *Rebekah* had reached the stage of feminine transfiguration required of her before she could become *Isaac*'s wife (Gen. xxiv, 29: *And Rebekah had a brother*, meaning that she had attained the "rank" of sister). Then another long description of *Rebekah* drawing water at the well; and finally, the significant statement when *Rebekah*'s mother and brother joins her father at the moment of *Rebekah*'s departure: *And they sent away Rebekah, their sister. . . . And they blessed Rebekah, and said unto her: Thou art our sister* (Gen. xxiv, 59-60).

Genesis xxiv, 67 relates an incident which, considered psychoanalytically, shows a regressive tendency in the character of *Isaac* (he being the number 2 of the lineage *Abraham, Isaac, Jacob*). *And Isaac brought her into his mother Sarah's tent, and took Rebekah, and she became his wife: and he loved her: and Isaac was comforted after his mother's death.* Love for the mother here appears as a symptom of regression.

This transference is well known today and was certainly understood by the authors of Genesis because nothing could better describe *Isaac* being no. 2. The schemata, ideograms, numbers, symbols in this text confer on the myth a psychological meaning parallel to its factual narration. When discovered in the depth of our beings, it can well strike us as being a revelation.

Genesis can thus be read at four different levels: the anecdote, the symbol, the ontology and finally at a level which transcends speech and cannot be communicated.

We will later quote and comment upon *Genesis* xxv relating *Abraham*'s death, *Ishmael*'s posterity and *Isaac*'s two sons. First an important event must be mentioned: *Isaac*'s dwelling in *Gerar*. It is one of the important parts in Genesis, where the revelation most deeply resides. We will only consider the first twelve verses of that chapter.

Genesis xxvi, *1-12: the anecdote.* There is a famine and YHWH appears unto *Isaac*, forbids him to go to Egypt, and promises a blessing if he remains in the land. *Isaac* obeys and dwells in

Gerar. And the men of the place asked him about his wife and he said she is my sister, for he feared to say she is my wife lest the men of the place should kill me on account of Rebekah (verse 7).

However, *Abimelekh*, through his window, sees *Isaac* and *Rebekah* talking and joking together. He calls *Isaac* and says to him: *Certainly she is thy wife, and how hast thou said: She is my sister?*

Isaac answers: *Because I said: Lest I die on account of her.* And *Abimelekh* says: *What is this thou hast done unto us? Almost had one of the people* copulated with her (I must forgo the prudish "married" of my English Bible).

Such is the hopelessly absurd anecdote. Once already, when in Egypt, *Abram* had said of *Sarai*: she is my sister, and Pharaoh had slept with her. Then, realizing the truth, he had angrily returned her to *Abram*. A second time, *Abraham*, in *Gerar*, had said of *Sarah*: She is my sister, and *Abimelekh*, warned in a dream, averted just in time the widespread calamity which would have fallen upon his kingdom had he taken *Sarah*.

And now, in the same *Gerar*, *Isaac* repeats to the same *Abimelekh*—who has not forgotten his former narrow escape—the same old insane story. But this time, *Abimelekh*, looking out of his window, actually sees that *Isaac* and *Rebekah* are man and wife, and the danger thus avoided is such that he orders: *He that touches this man and his wife shall be put to death.*

The very inconsistency of those stories solicits our attention. Were *Isaac*'s fears simply unjustified, there would perhaps be some sense in declaring *Rebekah* his sister, but his utterances clearly appear as a diabolical trap set for the purpose of destroying *Abimelekh*'s entire kingdom.

It has already been said, concerning the *Abram* and *Abraham* episodes, that in the second one *Sarah* is not taken, which means that the symbolical woman, typified by her, has evolved. In the third adventure, *Rebekah* openly, in public, conversing pleasantly with *Isaac*, declares herself to be fully adult and free. She is on a level with her husband, a companion, a "sister" to him. We have now to examine the symbols.

Genesis XXVI, *1-12: the symbols. Isaac's* sojourn in *Gerar* cannot be understood symbolically unless examined in the general context of the myth. We must therefore summarize the symbols concerning that narrative from *Abram* on.

Awr-Kasdeem (1.6.200—20.300.4.10.40): the light of magicians.

Terahh (400.200.8): *Abram's* father. Just as *Noahh* (50.8) this schema is symbolic of the ending of a cycle. The cosmic resistance 400.200 that has animated it returns to no. 8, the reservoir of undifferentiated energy.

Abram (1.2.200.40) becoming *Abraham* (1.2.200.5.600): the initiate propelled by a renewal of energy 1.2 and acting upon the cosmic "house" 200, conferring upon it a new life, 5.

Nahhor (50.8.6.200) *Abram's* "brother", his counterpart. This schema symbolizes a life in existence (50) reverted to its primordial state (8) and fertilizing the 200 from within. The direction of that flow of life is opposite to that of *Abraham*.

Haran (5.200.700) is a premature birth having no viability. Its 5 is lost in 200 and is projected in 700 without having matured. It "dies" in the presence of its father, in its place of birth.

Remember that *Terahh* "aged 70" gives birth to no. 3 (three sons). But the "Light of Magicians" is not enough. It cannot guide the human seed towards the light that it carries within itself.

Canaan (20.50.70.700) is the place (20) full of existential life (50) where all the uncertainties, all the creations and dissolutions, all the discoveries, inventions, buildings and shattering disruptions of structures must perforce happen (70 and 700). It is in the midst of that turmoil that the human seed can and must evolve and grow. It must never allow itself to rest because if it is not active it regresses. The symbol *Canaan* is over the whole planet in every conflict, in every tragic error as in every beautiful and transient achievement. In it, mankind must come to understand its cosmic significance.

We cannot, in this essay, go into the vast epic poem of that spiritual conquest, symbolized in the deeds of *Abraham, Isaac* and *Jacob*. Its decoding would take far more space than could be devoted to it in this book. Every name of person or place, every action, contention, truce or covenant has its inner meaning and should be examined with care.

Abraham and *Sarah* at the respective ages of 100 and 90 symbolize with those numbers perfect manhood and perfect womanhood. The extra *Hay* (5) granted to *Abram* and *Sarai* is the proof of it.

Abimelekh (1.2.10.40.30.500). Literally: "my father King" is the symbol of temporal sovereignty. He has the knowledge of *Aleph-Bayt* and the power of unchallenged rulers. Those rulers can bestow their grace at the call of YHWH whose servants they are. They can also at his call throw their might into the balance and annihilate the people, as had *Neb-u-khad-nez-zar* in Jerusalem by the *wrath* of YHWH (Chr. II, 16-17).

Yitzhhaq (10.90.8.100) the no. 2 of the *Abraham-Isaac-Jacob* triad. This schema is a paradox. Essentially it belongs to a triune movement. In its physical disposition it is twofold, and has to be so, as a link between the conqueror 3 and the conquered 2 (duality as symbolized by *Canaan*). Its structure is ingenious. Its 8, between 90 and 100, is almost farcical. No wonder that Yitzhhaq means "he laughs".

But the 3 in disguise, the comedy, the laughter are playing a deadly serious game, at its most critical stage. *Isaac* must give birth to *Israel*. In his schema is the seed of man-made-perfect, but in such a condition as to have no possibility of action. *Yitzhhaq* is a paradoxical balance of a pre-evolved 8 and a totally evolved (female and male) 90 and 100. In this schema the beginning is included in the end: the entire evolutionary process is out of its range. So *Yitzhhaq* is in a state of paralysis: *his eyes were dim* says the text (Gen. XXVII, 1) but we are not compelled to believe it. His blindness is the pretence of a helpless man. His helplessness however is dramatically true. Anybody acting from out of the current trend of existence can give a shattering blow to this strange state of neutrality between a pre-structured energy (8) and a total maturity (90.100). And *Isaac* in *Gerar* knows it. Any man, in whatever condition, can destroy him by simply touching him. He also knows that the human-to-be is entirely in the care of womanhood. If *Rebekah* is not, symbolically, his "sister", his companion, and if she does not take upon herself the task of rescuing the precious seed within Jacob, the evolution of man is doomed.

Abimelekh is aware. He knows. Hence his drastic order: not only *Rebekah*, but also *Isaac* must not be touched!

Genesis xxvi, *1-12: the ontological meaning.* The key to this "sisterhood" is in the schema *Ehhot* (*Aleph-Hhayt-Tav*: 1.8.400) which means "sister", although in the Hebrew language, sister is spelt *Aleph-Hhayt-Waw-Tav* (1.8.6.400). This addition of *Waw* converts the schema into a purely physical classification.

Ehhot is a simple formula. Its 8, between *Aleph* and *Tav* is everything that *Aleph* must impregnate. We must keep in mind *Aleph* in fullness (*Aleph-Lammed-Phay*: 1.30.80). Its action is the biosphere's metabolism. It is the creation of living beings following cosmic nuptials, always referred to by Qabala either as *Awr* (light) in physical appearance, or otherwise.

In the metaphysical sphere of our present narrative, we use a direct relationship between the 10.90.8.100 of *Yitzhhaq* and the 1.8.400 of *Ehhot*, and we have come to understand that ontologically *Ehhot* is not a sister, but *Aleph*'s spouse. *Aleph* is timeless, *Ehhot* is of time. To become spiritually pregnant means, for her, initiative, action, freedom, self-reliance. The centrifugal male energy can sow the seed of illumination; its structure depends on the centripetal energy building it in its right direction. Then the "spouse" is "sister".

Yitzhhaq is supposed to fear *lest the man of the place should kill* (him) *for Rebekah* (Gem. xxvi, 7). What he says in fact is: *Pen Yehregouni Anshi Hamaqom Aal Rivqah.* In numbers: 80.700—10.5.200.3.50.10—1.50.300.10—5.40.100.6.40—70.30—200.2. 100.5.

By which he means: my unformulated (80) energy is lost in the (700) cosmic indetermination. The existent (10) life (5) of the universe (200) must be organic (3) so as to be realized (50) in existence (10). This must be done by *Aleph* (1) alive (50) acting through the breath of *Elohim* (300) so as to come into existence (10). Then, and then only can life (5) act upon matter (40) so as to allow the cosmic *Aleph* (100) to impregnate (6) matter (40), which means conferring the sanctified 70 to organic energy (30). This would be a projection of the universal 200 into the individual 2 and the individual would emit (put forth) the cosmic Aleph (100) alive (5)!

This last schema 200.2.100.5 is none other than *Rivqah* (*Rebekah*). Its utterance in six words is a complete metaphysical *exposé*.

Lastly there is the pseudo-window through which *Abimelekh* sees the couple. This symbolic king typifying all temporal sovereigns looks *Beaad Hahhalon* (2.70.4—5.8.30.6.700), translated "from the window". It is true that *Aad* can mean "from", but it also means "eternity"; and *Hhalon* can mean "window" but the same root *Hhiloni* means "secular". Cabalists have almost constantly resorted to such double meanings. We must understand here that Abimelekh, symbol of worldly power, looks upon the couple that symbolizes the totality of universal life from his "secular eternity". Through him and her, talking pleasantly together, he has the vision of what she really is: spouse, not sister when men and women are considered as projections of cosmic energy.

The text says: *Yitzhhaq Metzahheq Et Rivqah Ishtou*: he laughs, he jests with her. There is in that description a sense of relaxation, a communion in a happy state of achievement that no translation can render truly. Abimelekh's clear awareness of it is an extraordinary blending of eternal structured energy as time and duration, and of eternal timelessness.

Genesis XXVI, *1-12: the ineffable.* The direct understanding in one single act of perception of the above three spheres can clarify to the reader what the Revelation really is.

Genesis XXV, *21-23: Yitzhhaq* addresses a prayer to *YHWH* because *Rivqah* is barren. The prayer is listened to favourably.

Rivqah conceives twins who struggle together within her. She says: *If so, why this my desire?* And she questions YHWH.

Rivqah is barren and YHWH intervenes, as *Sarah* was barren and YHWH intervened. *Rachel* will have to wait 7 years and 7 again. This insistently deferred action illustrates not only the necessary procrastination of Genesis where the human germ is concerned but also its intimate relationship to YHWH.

In answer to *Rivqah's* question, YHWH reveals to her that two *Goim* (nations) are within her (the narrative is thus clearly in the sphere of phylogenesis) and that *the elder shall serve the younger.*

This is a reference to a recurrent theme: in the genealogical tree of mankind extending through many centuries, the first born are the least evolved, because they are the youngest, the furthest from maturity.

We know that *Rivqah's* first-born is *Yissav* (Esau). He will therefore have to submit to the second-born, the elder *Yaaqov* (Jacob). *Rivqah* understands the message as we also must learn to understand it.

The schemata of the two brothers identifies them completely. *Yissav* (70.300.6) is all possibles (70) acting through the cosmic metabolism (300) genetically (6). *Yaaqov* (10.70.100.2) is essentially different. His 70 is the result of a rooting in existence (10). It brings forth a cosmic *Aleph* (100) and projects it in *Bayt* (2), the individual "container".

These schemata may be a surprise to those who remember the description of *Esau*, heavy, hairy, earthly, and of *Jacob*, weak and meditative, but it must not be forgotten that at this point in the narrative one of the two brothers must personify no. 3 and thrust roots into *Canaan*: *Canaan* being the world at large with its miseries, its exploitations, and its struggles for freedom. The seed of the human-to-be must not and cannot establish itself in any given condition. It must be adaptable and unadapted; it must be in this world and above it, as swift as the flow of contingencies so as neither to rot in dead waters nor be overrun.

Yissav's possibilities (70) are carried away, blown around in the uncertainties of the universal flow of life (300). He is too primitive, too raw to find in himself enough strength to build a resistance to life. He will be prolific (6) and that is all that is to be said for him at the moment.

Yaakov's 70, on the contrary, is fully existent in between 10 and 100. All his energy is concentrated in 2, his *Bayt*: the building of a strong individuality. The text says that his is *Tam* (400.40). This is a remarkable schema. It expresses the greatest possible resistance to life, both in a cosmic sense (400) and existentially (40). Only a great intensity of life can be in need of such a resistance. The word *Tam* in Hebrew means innocence, simplicity, sincerity, integrity, and it is said (Gen. xxv, 27) that *Jacob* is a simple man, living in his tent, whereas *Esau* is a great hunter and a worker in the fields.

Before coming to the contentious "dish of lentils", the "selling" of *Esau's* birthright, and the lives of the two brothers a few words must be added concerning their parents.

Rivqah (200.2.100.5). As we have seen her she is accomplished, transfigured. She will be ordained YHWH's agent of a sacred transmission through *Jacob*, which will deprive him of all his father's earthly possessions in favour of *Esau*. It must be noted that *Rivqah* is the only one to converse with YHWH.

The traditional well-known story is as follows: *Isaac* is prepared to give his blessing to *Esau* but *Rivqah* disguises *Jacob*, sends him to his old and blind father so as to deceive him, and *Isaac* blesses *Jacob* believing that it is *Esau*.

What is less known is that *Isaac* is acting a part: he is not deceived, he is a willing accomplice. Let us read the details of that blessing.

Yitzhhaq calls "his son" *Yissav* and tells him: *I am old, I know not the day of my death* (Gen. xxvii, 2). He sends him out to hunt and asks him to cook a savoury dish of venison, *that my soul may bless thee before I die.*

And Rebecca heard when Isaac spake to Esau his son. . . . And Rebecca spake unto Jacob her son. . . . The text insists on saying that

Esau is *Isaac*'s son whereas Jacob is *Rebecca*'s son. She informs *Jacob* of what *Isaac* has said to *Esau* and tells him to fetch *two good kids*. She will *make them into a savoury meat* that *Jacob* will bring to *Isaac*, so as to receive the blessing intended for *Esau*.

Jacob answers that his brother is *Sayir* (hairy) (300.70.10.200) whereas he is *Hhalaq* (8.30.100) (Gen. xxvii, 11). These schemata have a double meaning: *Sayir* also means that *Esau* is carried away as by a tempest—and in analysing his name we have seen that it is so: he cannot take root in *Canaan*. *Hhalaq* besides meaning *I am a smooth man*, expresses the fact the *Yaakov* is helpless: he has no means of action.

And *Jacob* goes on to say: *My father peradventure will feel me and I shall seem to him as a deceiver; and I shall bring a curse upon me and not a blessing*. But answers *Rebecca*: *Upon me be the curse, my son*. . . .

The schema translated "curse" is *Qlalah* (100.30.30.5). The root *Qof-Lammed-Lammed* is another example of ambiguity in the Hebrew language. In colloquial Hebrew it means (pronounced *Qilel*) "curse", but its double *Lammed* following *Qof* expresses a double organic movement issuing from the cosmic *Aleph*, so swift and dynamic that we can well understand its impact being felt as a "curse" by the psyche. The schema *Barakah*, translated "blessing", is exactly *Qlalah*'s opposite. Its numbers 2.200.20.5 describe a happy and completely static life in which the psyche can rest and slumber.

Rivqah's utterance, when decoded, reveals itself to be in the core of the myth and of *Yaaqov*'s action in it: "I take upon me", she says, "your *Qof* (cosmic *Aleph*) and its dual functional energy."

It is to be noted that *Yitzhhaq*, *Rivqah* and *Yaaqov*, all three have the *Qof* (100). According to the cabalistic rationalization, one *Qof* is enough, two would propel anyone beyond our tangible universe. So *Rivqah* must take *Yaaqov*'s *Qof* upon herself, she must denude her son, send him deprived of what he essentially is. He must be totally empty so as to be in disguise and receive his *Barakah*.

When we really consider the words "upon me be the curse",

we see that they have no meaning, because there is no curse. When we consider *Qlalah* according to code, and do not read *Qilel* (the Hebrew for curse), we can meditate upon the deep general meaning of that narrative and discover its beauty.

And here is the comedy: *Rivqah* dresses up *Yaaqov* in *Yissav's* best clothes and covers his hands and neck with the skin of the kids. And when thus attired *Jacob* presents a dish to his father. *Isaac* asks him who he is (why ask if he thinks he knows it is *Esau*?). *Jacob* answers that he is *Esau* and that this is the venison. Isaac asks *How is it that thou hast found it so quickly? Jacob* answers that it was given by YHWH-*Elohim. Isaac* feels him so (he says) as to be sure that it is Esau. He actually feels the hands covered with kid skin and says: *The voice is Jacob's voice, but the hands are the hands of Esau* (Gen. XXVII, 22).

What an incredible statement! *Isaac* has recognized *Jacob's* voice and blind or not he cannot possibly have mistaken a piece of lamb's skin hastily put upon a hand for a hand, however hairy.

Not only is he not deceived but his declaration is so obviously a make-believe that there must be a powerful psychological reason for the persistence of the belief in this deception.

We hope to uncover gradually the reason in the next chapter. We can state it as being our conclusion: *Jacob*, whose real name, *Israel*, will be revealed, has inspired fear in the hearts of millions.

When *Esau* returns from his hunting he cries out bitterly because *Jacob* has received the blessing of the first-born of YHWH. *Bless me, even me also O my father*, says he. And *Isaac* gives him the blessing that will bestow on him all the richness of the earth (Gen. XXVII, 39-40).

Behold, thy dwelling shall be the fatness of the earth and the dew of heaven from above. And by the sword shalt thou live and shalt serve thy brother: and it shall come to pass when thou shalt have the dominion, that thou shalt break his yoke from off thy neck.

And because *Esau* inherits all the riches and all the power on earth, he hates *Jacob* and plans to kill him. When summoned by his mother, *Jacob* prepares to escape. He then again meets *Isaac*, undisguised this time, and *Isaac*, suddenly not too old to understand nor too blind to see (he will live many more years) instructs him clearly and in detail as to where he must go and as to what he must do, and he endows him with great authority as *Abraham's* successor.

23

Jacob and Esau

THE QUESTION as to who is legally the elder of twins has often been discussed. To my knowledge many judgments have considered it to be the second to emerge from the womb.

But the strife between *Jacob* and *Esau* has nothing to do with genetics. It is on an ontological level. Its far-reaching drama so vividly portrayed is a projection, on the psychological and pseudo-historical level, of one of the most important themes of Genesis: the conflict between YHWH and the earth as to who is the bearer of the evolutionary human seed: YHWH's son or the earth's son?

Those two symbolical descendants are perpetually battling in the individual and collective subconscious—alas too often the winner emerges as *Esau*.

In the narrative the conflict is centred upon the schema *Adam: Aleph-Dallet-Mem*: or *Aleph* in *Dam* (blood). In which of the two brothers is the seed of *Aleph*'s resurrection?

As in every one of its essential points the significance of this narrative is hidden in words having a double meaning. *Adam* means red and presently we shall even see it translated as "pottage"!

In Genesis xxv, 25, *Esau* is thus described: *The first came out red all over like an hairy garment*. In Hebrew: *We-Yotsey Harishon Admoni Kelou Kiaderet Saar*.

We have already met the root *Yotsey* when, on the "third day", the earth *Totsey* (produces) its vegetation in its limited response to the cosmic flow of unlimited energy *Tadshey*. We said that this reponse is a non-resistance, a yielding, a bringing fruit in which the *Dallet* of human resistance to life is eliminated in exchange for the proliferating *Waw*. The schema *Yotsey* clearly qualifies *Esau* as being a product of the earth.

The schema *Admoni*, translated "red", is *Adam* with the addition of *Waw-Noun-Yod* (6.50.10) which confirms humanity as being prolific flesh in existence. As to the schema *Saar* (300.70.200) we have already said that it expresses a kind of tempest, sweeping *Esau* away in the cosmic metabolism.

Esau's rough appearance and his rustic pursuits seem to contradict the idea of his being carried away in the cosmos, but suggests rather that his taking root in the land contradicts the human necessity of taking a firm hold upon the swiftly moving world in the process of which lies his own gestation. *Esau*, in the primitive state of humanity intimately involved in nature, is obviously related to the cosmic metabolism, but as a product of the earth he "yields", whereas the true *Adam* "resists" and develops his individuality.

So *Yissav* is an *Adam* produced by the earth. As such his appearance is "adamic" meaning simply "red".

It is an exhilarating experience to enter into this dramatic confrontation, to live it in one's own self. *Isaac* in the guise of an earthly father, receives from the earth (*Adamah*) a son. He is the best and only *Adam* she can produce, but he is spurious as compared to the real archetype.

Is it simply a comedy? Or, rather, are we not called upon here to be witnesses of a blending, a symbiosis between two vital currents of the one living energy manifesting itself in opposite directions so as to assert itself by its own negation?

Esau smells wholly of good earth. His *is as the smell of a field which YHWH has blessed* (Gen. xxvii, 27). He is powerful, violent and he knows how to hate. *Esau* is repeatedly said to be *Edom* (1.4.6.40): an *Adam* in which is introduced the copulative *Waw* of proliferation. And who is *Edom*? Genesis xxxvi gives the generations of *Esau who is Edom: their riches were more than that they might dwell together*. They were leaders and mighty kings, and do we not know the famous descendant *Herod* who swore to murder all the newborn males so as not to miss murdering Jesus?

As to *Yaaqov* all that need be added here to his description concerns the root *Aaqov* (70.100.2), which has as many meanings in Hebrew as *Jacob* has ways and means of avoiding being imprisoned in any one definition. The root 70.100.2 means heel —and we remember that Jacob is born holding his brother's heel: a clear symbol of this other meaning: "to hold back". The root 70.100.2 stands also for "deceitful, a deep deceit, a provocation", and this meaning obviously has its origin in the biblical narrative. It also stands for "consistent" and "logical", which, after all, is perhaps *Jacob*'s best description.

Genesis xxv, *28-34*. We can now describe the famous meeting of the two brothers. We will not quote the text: *Esau*'s selling his birthright for a mess of pottage is famous in proportion to its absurdity.

The words: *And Isaac loved Esau because he did eat of his venison but Rebekah loved Jacob* (in verse 28) are a key to what follows. We must remember *Rebekah*'s communion with YHWH and therefore her *Yahvic* love for *Jacob*. The text cannot more clearly show a contrast between *Isaac* and *Esau*'s material food and *Rebekah* and *Jacob*'s spiritual nourishment.

Therefore, when we read *Jacob sod pottage* we are bidden to understand those words as symbols. The text (xxv, 29) is: *Ve-Yazed Yaaqov Nazeed*. This is what he does: 6.10.7.4— 50.7.10.4. The 10 and 7 and alternately the 7 and 10 come to a head in the resistance (4) of *Dallet*. We have often insisted on the importance of *Dallet* (the central letter of Adam) as being the backbone of man's resistance to life, and we have seen *Esau*'s deficiency in that respect. The so-called pottage which *Jacob* is said to be cooking is the elaboration of *Israel*'s remarkable perennial striving towards a mature *Adam*.

And Esau came from the field and he was faint. And Yissav said to Yaaqov: Feed me with this Adam, with this very Adam for I am faint: because his name was Edom. Following our previous explanations, this passage is now clear enough when we discard the word pottage which has been arbitrarily added and when we leave the word *Adam* as *Adam*. What *Esau* actually wants, according to the text is: *Min Ha-Adam, Ha-Adam Hazeh*: "of this *Adam*, the *Adam* this one, because his name is *Edom*".

And said *Yaaqov: Mikrah Kayom Et Bekoratekh*. The root *Mikrah* has different meanings and as is generally the case, the tradition has seized upon the wrong one. It can mean "sell", but it also means "to recognize, to know". This is far more correct even grammatically, because there is no "me". The sell "me" is a distortion. "Sell as today" would raise the question "to whom"? And again *Bekoratekh* does not at all mean "your birthright" but "your being the first-born".

So *Yaaqov's* utterance means: "recognize as today, from beginning to end (*Et*) (or: in its total significance) what is meant by your being the first-born (or your being the early fruit)".

And *Yissav* said: *Behold I am dying. What is it to me to be the* (Being) *first-born?*

We know that he cannot be hungry or if he is hungry that he can go to his tent and eat the meal that is surely, as usual, prepared for him when he comes from the fields. He is not hungry but *Edom* facing *Adam* is stricken to death. And we remember the conditioned "son of woman" *Abel*, being annihilated by the mere rising of *Cain*-YHWH in front of him. These were the archetypes in the beginning of the myth. But here, where the archetypes are brought down to the level of symbolical human beings, the story is different: *Swear it, said Yaaqov. He swore and acknowledged Yaaqov as elder. And Yaaqov gave Yissav bread and Nazeed Aadasheem and he ate and drank and rose up and did not care who was the elder.*

The schema *Aadasheem* has degenerated into being lentils. In Qabala it is read in several ways. *Aad-Dassa* is symbol of an eternally fructifying vegetation. As to the bread (*Lehhem*) it has been throughout the ages a symbol of communion.

Thus Jacob bestows to his earthly brother the nourishment best fitted to his nature, and this ends one of the most beautiful and most misinterpreted episodes of Genesis.

Esau's acceptance of not being the first-born is necessary to *Jacob's* incarnation as *Aleph*. It reminds us of *John* 1, 5: *And the light shineth in darkness and the darkness comprehended it not.* *Esau's* spiritual submission will allow the myth to be carried by its own impetus towards its symbolical completion. It is to be hoped that when better understood it will hasten towards its actualization.

★

To follow *Jacob* throughout his struggles and adventures would need another book. He seeks safety in flight when *Esau* sets out to kill him, and in exile lends himself as servant to *Laban*. It is a strange, profound and constant unconscious element in history that the *Adams* and the *Edoms*, the dispossessed and the wealthy contend for the colour red. Dressed in purple-red, kings have proclaimed their rights as inheritors of the earth, even as today the disinherited, in pursuit of the same claim, gather around red flags. Red is *Adam*, red is *Edom* and red is the blood.

So goes Jacob, carrying with him nothing more than a blessing. Then we read of his dream, a double ladder where angels descend from heaven to earth and ascend from earth to heaven (symbol of the one living energy) and the appearance of YHWH to him and that place being named *Bayt-El*: house of *Elohim*.

Then *Jacob* in *Hharan*, in the home of *Laban*, son of *Nahhor*; his seven years toil for *Rachel*, and it is *Leah* "whose eyes are weak" that he finds in his bed; and his other seven years for *Rachel* (2×7 is a clear symbol); and the servants given to him as wives; and all his children, and his cunning deeds, thanks to which he is able to feed his family and to free himself from *Laban;* and the flight, with *Rachel* riding a camel and sitting on the idols of her father.

Jacob is neither a saint nor a hero. He is no Siegfried, no shining St George fighting dragons. He is *Tam*, simple, hard-working and ingenious enough to gather riches in spite of being exploited and cheated by *Laban*. And when at last he has his freedom, he is old and exhausted.

Genesis XXXII: After having made an agreement with *Laban*, *Yaaqov* is blessed by him. On his return journey, after a whole life in exile, in vision he meets *Elohim*'s angels and he sends messengers to his brother, and he tells them: *Thus shall ye speak unto my lord Esau: Thy servant Jacob saith thus: I have sojourned with Laban and stayed there until now: and I have oxen, and asses, flocks and menservants, and womenservants; and I have sent to tell my Lord, that I may find grace in thy sight.*

The messengers return with the dreadful news that *Esau* is on his way at the head of 400 armed men (note no. 400).

Yaaqov is very much afraid and in distress. He divides his people and his flocks, herds and camels into two camps, thinking that if *Esau* destroys one, the other can perhaps escape, and he prays: *Elohi Ab Avraham Va-Elohi Abi Yitzhhaq. YHWH which saidst unto me: Return into thy country and to thy kindred and I will do thee good! I am too small for all thy mercy and all thy truth which thou hast bestowed upon thy servant and his people. I have passed over the Jordan and now I am become two camps. Deliver me, I pray, from the hand of Esau for I fear him, lest he should come towards me and towards the women and the children; and thou saidst: I will surely do thee good and make thy seed as the sand of the sea, which cannot be numbered (for multitude).*

He settles down for the night in that place and sends to *Esau* a considerable amount of livestock. He then fords a stream with his wives and children. The place is called *Yaboq* (10.2.100). And in great anguish he remains alone in the stillness of the night. Alone and helpless in the dark: what better conditions for *Elohim* to answer his prayer by trying to kill him?

Let us see this clearly: *Yaaqov* is attacked by *Iysh: Aleph-Yod-Sheen,* that is: by the full might of cosmic energy: *Aleph* and *Yod* as the two contradictory aspects of that one energy and *Sheen* as their joint action, *Iysh* is a tremendous concentration of vital energy, and its impact upon *Yaaqov* is a supreme test: the climax in *Jacob*'s life. If he resists he truly is the carrier of the human seed.

And Iysh wrestles with him until the breaking of the day, and sees that he cannot prevail against him and touches the hollow of his thigh and the hollow of the thigh is out of joint as he (Iysh) wrestles with him. And he (Iysh) says: Let me go, for the day breaketh. And he (Yaaqov) says: I will not let thee go except thou bless me. And he (Iysh) says: What is thy name? And he (Yaaqov) says: Yaaqov. And he (Iysh) says: not Yaaqov shall be henceforth thy name, but Israel (Yod-Seen-Raysh-Aleph-Lammed: 10.300.200.1.30) for thou hast fought Elohim and the generations of men and hast prevailed.

And Yaaqov asks and says: Tell me, I pray, thy name. And he (Iysh) says: Why is it thou ask my name? And he blesses him there.

And Yaaqov calls the name of the place Peniel (Pay-Noun-Yod-Aleph-Lammed: 80.50.10.1.30) because I have seen Elohim face to face and my breath has been preserved.

And the sun rises and he passes over Peniel and he is lame.

Genesis XXXIII. Soothed by *Yaaqov*'s most generous gifts and by his respectful behaviour, *Yissav* kisses him and they both shed tears, not however before *Yaaqov* had bowed down seven times and declared *Yissav* as the sun to him.

Following lengthy compliments on both sides, *Esau* invites *Jacob* to his place of residence in *Seir*. Answers *Jacob*: *My lord knows that my children are young and that my flocks cannot go fast. Let my lord go ahead of me. I will follow him unto Seir.*

Esau therefore goes back to *Seir* and, turning in a different direction, *Jacob* goes towards *Succot*.

Genesis ends with the story of *Joseph* which has been mentioned in the first part of this book. As to the twelve tribes they cannot be considered in this volume.

★

Note 1. The question as to whom belongs by right the colour red appears in *Genesis* XXXVIII, *28-29*: *Tamar*, pregnant by *Judah*, has twins. One of them puts out his hand and the midwife binds upon it a scarlet thread. He draws back his hand and the other child emerges. It is interesting to note that that other one is *Pharez*, supposed to be Jesus' ancestor (through his father Joseph).

Note 2. Matthew II, *18*, quoting Jeremiah when relating Herod's tentative murder of the newborn children says: *In Rama was there a voice heard—And weeping and great mourning—Rachel weeping for the children—and would not be comforted—because they are not.*

PART THREE

THE GOSPELS

I

The Essential Theme

THE ESSENTIAL theme in the myth of Jesus is death and resurrection. This allegory has been introduced with such pageantry that its protagonist has been deified; the brilliance of the drama has obscured its meaning.

But certain clues, especially in Matthew and John, lead us to understand that the Rabbi who gave rise to his own legend knew quite well the original meaning and the cosmic significance of the *Aleph-Bayt*. In other words, we have every reason to believe that he was a highly initiated Cabalist.

He certainly tried to explain these things to his disciples, but, by their own admission, they did not understand him. We cannot be surprised: Qabala is difficult, even for minds trained in psychology and in philosophy. The churches have either ignored it or attempted to refute it (see Hippolytus), or condemned it when it appeared in what is known as gnosticism (see *Pistis Sophia*).

Jesus—or *Yhshwh* as his name was, according to Qabala—insisted on the essential theme that runs as a visible-invisible thread throughout the Bible: the constant psychological death and resurrection which is the real cosmic call to the human being. Only through that intermittent psychic pulsation of *Aleph* can the creative life manifest itself.

That life is always new. It has therefore neither past nor future. It is not dependent on time or space. It is not "conscious" in the sense we give to that word, because consciousness implies memory. Therefore it is not we who resurrect, but life impersonal. And because our thought is always a process of continuity in duration, that resurrection is nothing that we can "think".

179

The process of life eludes our comprehension but we must not allow our intelligence to elude the process of life.

A creed is a system meant to represent that which cannot be represented. It is therefore always a portrayal of images. These images are either, externally, those of beings or objects, or, in the mind, thoughts, intuitions, feelings, sensations.

We can hardly imagine Rabbi *Jesus* resorting to such crude deceptions. It is reasonable to suppose that he was in direct contact with the creative cosmic energies or, in other words, that the Revelation was with him. In that case he could not possibly have conceived a mythology to explain away the mystery that he personified. And it is most improbable that he came to save that which must be destroyed by life, those foci of static, fossilized energy which so often think themselves to be human.

But he did mention the life that can be saved when one "loses" one's life. We will not, however, comment upon his teaching, nor upon the guilt complex that has crystallized around him to the point of relegating him to a far-away heaven and weeping endless tears over his dead body. If we can only explore deeply enough the strange worship of crucified life we can surely discover many of the secret recesses of the human mind.

Hidden behind its unconscious motivations, the psyche, fearful of the unknown, remains dormant in the interpretations of its own myths.

In the next chapters we will deal with two such interpretations: we will see in *Matthew* XVI, *13-25* an episode concerning Peter, and in *John* XIII, 18-32 the narrative of the Last Supper, which especially concerns *Judas*.

Peter, or Jesus Rejected

MATTHEW XVI, 13-25. In those days Caesarea was a new city. It was founded by Philippi as a result of a Hellenistic revival centred around a miraculous grotto dedicated to the god Pan. The city was built in the Greek style. If the Rabbi *Yhshwh* went there, it was in the hope of introducing his own revival in place of that of an ancient religion which had lost its vitality.

In conformity with the letter-numbers of the original Revelation, the Rabbi designated himself as *Ben-Adam*. The Rabbi affirmed something of great importance. We have only to examine carefully what the letter-numbers of these words convey. First, let us consider *Ben*. The Hebrew letters involved (*Bayt-Noun*) speak to us by means of their numbers (2.700). "Two" means a dwelling, a receptacle. "Seven hundred" means all the possible possibilities open to man (7), raised to the hundreds and thus to cosmic importance. Now, *Adam* (1.4.600, which are the numbers of *Aleph-Dallet-Mem*) gives us, as you may remember, the pulsating, uncreated and creative life within the very blood of man. It is within our capacity either to drown this *Aleph* in our blood or to allow it to resuscitate. (This meaning of *Ben-Adam* as "son of man" evades us.)

Thus *Ben-Adam*, decoded from its numbers, means: "I am the receptacle of everything that can result from the resurrection within me of the living *Aleph*." The Rabbi thus affirms that *Aleph* in its purity springs forth from his own flesh and blood and that his acts are the expression of all that can come forth from *Aleph*, the unknowable, the immeasurable: they do not operate in the world of established structures.

This affirmation places the Rabbi intelligibly as well as intelligently. We can sense his existence at the very heart of the cosmic pulsation: that creative force designated by the *Aleph*, with its letter-number 1. There is no need to graft onto this any anthropomorphic mystery. On the contrary any adjunct whatsoever could only weaken the affirmation made by this integrated man. His affirmation, if properly understood, suffices to destroy all paganism, all idolatries.

In Caesarea, however, it was not understood. And yet the population, little satisfied with the promised "new look" of the old god Pan, was groping for something new. Jesus became the object of this search, as Matthew recorded. When *Yhshwh* asks, *Who do men say that I*, Ben-Adam, *am?* the answer is: *Some say that thou art John the Baptist: some Elias: and others, Jeremiah, or one of the other prophets* (Matt. xvi, 14). It is obvious that no one has understood. Turning then to his disciples, the Rabbi asks, *But who say ye that I am?*

We have only Greek versions of their answer. It is even probable that the first texts of the gospels were in the Hellenistic language. However, certain clues, especially in Matthew, lead us to believe that the Rabbi taught in Hebrew. We can infer from them that Jesus tried to oppose the Hellenistic revival by revealing the deep sense of the original Revelation. But the minds of his contemporaries were not ready to understand the *Aleph-Bayt*.

The Hellenistic answer, attributed to Simon, "Thou art Khristos", is preposterous. The very idea of being called Khristos—or Christ, the Anointed, in modern language—so horrified the Rabbi that he later on *charged . . . his disciples that they should tell no man that he was Jesus Christ* (Matt. xvi, 20). And WHAT HE MEANT COULD NOT HAVE BEEN OTHER THAN WHAT HE SAID.

In Hebrew, Simon probably said: "Thou art *Ben-YHWH-Elohim*" (or *Ben-YHWH*), thus emphasizing the Rabbi's statement. And this answer would have been in accordance with the profound original theme of Genesis, which, ever since the appearance of YHWH, proclaims the primacy of his symbolic offspring over the earth's (*Adamah's*) offspring of flesh and blood. We remember *Qaheen*, son of this primal cosmic energy, rising above his brother *Hevel*, and *Hevel* thereby being reduced to a mere pool of blood. We have learned, through all the allegories, of the struggle between the *Aleph*, which wills to spring forth, and the blood which tends to stifle it.

In conformity with this process, the Rabbi probably answered Simon in terms of which Matthew still shows some visible signs: *Blessed art thou, Simon Bar-Yona: for flesh and blood hath not revealed it unto thee, but my father which is in heaven* (Matt. xvi, 17).

We know that the "father" is YHWH. As to "heaven", *Shamaim*, we have seen that it is the action of *Sheen* (a cosmic breath) upon the symbolic "waters" (*Maim*) of life as existence, and we also know that it is the action of timeless YHWH permanently pervading the Universe. We can thus compare *Shamaim* and YHWH:

Shamaim: *Sheen-Mem-Yod-Mem*: 300.40.10.40
YHWH: *Yod-Hay-Waw-Hay*: 10. 5. 6. 5

This comparison of the two schemata reveals that the schema YHWH (as "father") truly is included in *Shamaim*: no. 10 corresponding to 300 shows it in existence, no. 5 and 5 corresponding to 40 and 40 shows them alive, and no. 6 corresponding to no. 10 shows it to be fruitful.

By declaring himself *Ben*-YHWH Jesus identified himself with *Israel*: *And thou shalt say unto Pharaoh, thus saith YHWH, Israel is my son, my first-born* (Exod. iv, 22), and we do not see any reason for not accepting that statement. An interesting fact is Jesus qualifying Simon *Bar-Yona*: son of *Yona*, the dove. It is not generally known that the dove personifying the Holy Spirit has been, since time immemorial, the symbol of Israel.

Let us follow the scene, step by step. *Yhshwh* says, "I am Ben-Adam." Simon must have replied, "I know that you are *Ben*-YHWH." In this reply, the Rabbi sees that Simon understands the origin and ultimate purpose of human evolution.

We do not know to what extent it is possible to unearth a truth buried under centuries of intentional misinterpretations. Apparently it cannot be done by means of exegesis. But the truth included in both Testaments can certainly be discovered when one identifies oneself with the word Israel, whose full meaning is: a continuous and winning battle against *Elohim*. *Israel* is timeless. *Elohim* is temporal.

The Rabbi wishes to establish a human brotherhood. He wishes to condense all human evolution, all duration into one single point. Simon, in a flash of perception, sees that point in the Rabbi because the Rabbi is the transcendence of that which he claims he is. That one single point is the *Aleph* alive, the pulsating timeless life-death-life-death.

Between the Rabbi and Simon, between Simon and the Rabbi a sudden flash of truth explodes, as it will explode for centuries in the minds of millions: it blasts the Hebrew *Yod* and replaces it by *Aleph*.

Yod (10) is the very basis of the religion, as set forth by Moses. This religion knows only the *Yod*: ten males belonging to this religion have the power to perform the authorized religious service. Ten males "unite in heaven" that which they "unite on earth". In a wider sense, the mosaic religion links those who belong to it in an existential, historical *Yod*.

The springing forth of *Aleph* is, on the contrary, a personal event. For a very brief instant Simon, facing Jesus, actually sees *Aleph* in the Rabbi. Seeing it is enough: it is a Revelation. And the Rabbi also sees it in Simon. As soon as it is seen, *Aleph* disappears, slips away because it has, in fact, no existence.

So alas, the second part of the episode is an anticlimax: Simon hears Jesus state the fact: *thou art Ab-ben* (Matt. xvi, 18) *and on Ab-ben I will build.*

The name Peter is derived from the Greek *Petros* which means stone (hence our word "petrify"). It is highly improbable that a Rabbi taught his disciples in Greek. In Hebrew, the word *Aben* (*Aleph-Bayt-Noun*) means stone. According to Qabala "thou art stone", and the building on that petrification conveys the very opposite of what the Rabbi wished to say and do. His essence (the essence of the Hebrew revelation) is life, energy, perpetual movement. In conformity with the cabalistic tradition, Jesus must have used an expression having several different depths of meaning. *Ab-Ben* combines *Ab*: father, and *Ben*: son. It expresses an origin and an end. (It has finally come to serve as name for the philosophers' stone, the supreme object of alchemy, supposed to change base metals into gold.)

Simon, his flash of perception having already passed, and with his limited knowledge and understanding, took upon himself the mission of becoming Peter, thereby of becoming "Satan".

Matthew XVI, 21: *From that time forth began Jesus to shew unto his disciples, how that he must go unto Jerusalem, and suffer many things of the elders and chief priests and scribes, and be killed and be raised again the third day.*

Verse 22: *Then Peter took him, and began to rebuke him, saying, Be it far from thee, Lord: this shall not be unto thee.*

Verse 23: *But he turned, and said unto Peter, Get thee behind me, Satan: thou art an offence unto me: for thou savourest not the things that be of God, but those that be of men.* It is worth noting that this violent condemnation of Peter (in verse 23) follows closely upon verse 19, in which Peter is given *the keys of the kingdom of heaven.*

Satan is a Hebrew word (*Seen-Tayt-Noun*: 300.9.700). In colloquial Hebrew it means the adversary, the accuser, and also Satan, as we know it in English. According to code, we see that the elemental female (9) is held as between pincers by the cosmic breath 300 and the indetermination at stake, 700. It resists both impacts, as it is in its nature to do. Its essence is continuity, its function is proliferation of elementary units.

When *Tayt* prevails it is as a queen-bee or a church, the adversary of the Aleph, of infinite cosmic life-death. In other words *Satan* is a continuity in existence which resists its own necessary destruction. Psychologically, it is a confinement in structures that hinders the flow of life-death in the mind.

The Rabbi was so well aware of this meaning of the word

Satan that immediately after having rejected Peter as head of a church, he told his disciples (Matt, XVI, 24-25): *If any man will come after me, let him deny himself and take up his cross and follow me. For whosoever will save his life shall lose it: and whosoever will lose his life for my sake shall find it.*

The rest is a confusion of doubtful symbols that we need not examine: the essential theme of Qabala has made itself apparent in *spite* of . . . *Satan!*

3

Judas, or Jesus Accepted

THE AUTHOR of John's Gospel, whoever he may have been, was familiar with *Aleph-Bayt*. We shall probably never know how any of the Gospels came to be written. It is possible that the original texts were already in the Hellenistic language currently spoken at that time. And perhaps the opening words of John's Gospel, *In the beginning was the Word, and the Word was with God, and the Word was God*, were an attempt to translate *Bereshyt Bara Elohim* for a public who, in any case, could not have understood the ontological meaning of the letter-numbers (or the simple fact that in *Bereshyt* are the elements which create Elohim, and not the reverse). Strangely enough, in their attempt, throughout the centuries, to simplify this difficult language for the understanding of all, the authorities have rendered it incomprehensible. The simpler the text, the less (in this case) its meaning.

In the beginning of this book, it was stated that the composite *Elohim* expresses the life and action of *Aleph*. It was also pointed out that no letter-number—whether *Aleph*, *Bayt*, or any other—has its full meaning except in its relationship to others. This is because each letter-number is a symbol for one aspect of life's totality. Likewise, every colour in the rainbow is *of* and *in* the light.

In revealing the ontological meanings of the letter-numbers and of their schemata (including *Elohim*) the Qabala permits us to grasp intellectually that which John's Gospel, in any ordinary language, projects under vague symbols.

The original theme developed by John is: *the light shineth in darkness and the darkness comprehended it not* (or received it not)

187

(John I, 5). That image can be and *has been* interpreted in a thousand ways. We feel justified in thinking that that darkness is the *Hhosheykh*, mentioned in Genesis as opposed to *Awr* (light). It is the cosmic receptacle of undifferentiated energy which comes to life when it is fertilized. In the psyche *Hhosheykh* is an energy that has not yet been structured.

Only when the psyche becomes cognizant of its structured elements can it die to the perception of itself as continuity. It can then free itelf from that which appeared as being "contained" in its sphere of consciousness, but was in fact its "container". It can open itself to the unutterable reality of *Aleph*. Then, the marvellous pulsation of life-death can permeate it and the individual is called upon to partake of the universal life.

John the gnostic was cognizant of that truth and he also knew that it was necessary to strike and wound and transpierce the slumbering minds of his time. He, undoubtedly, was one of the two disciples who contributed to the enacting of the tremendous drama of death and resurrection, the other disciple being Judas.

Peter's incomprehension, coming after the lightning flash of intuition which he had earlier had as Simon, left *Yhshwh* no hope of making himself understood except by one or two of his disciples. But how to "stage" so grandiose a symbol? We do not intend to try to fathom what could have gone on in the mind of Jesus. We only wish to point to the fact that aside from the outwardly observed historical events, the collective psyche pursues its own mythological course. This may well be a determining factor as regards the reality of our world as history records it. At certain times of great psychological crisis and of transformation of human consciousness, the collective myth can even project its images with such violence that they materialize into all sorts of manifestations, termed occult—such as parapsychical phenomena, magical apparitions, and mysterious historical (or hysterical) happenings.

It is likely that such events occurred around the person called Jesus, whether he really lived during the time of Pontius

Pilate or whether he lived, as many people suppose, about a hundred years previously in the person of a Master of Wisdom among the Essenes. Even taking into account the extravagance of popular imagination concerning his miracles, it is highly probable that this personage did have exceptional powers. These powers, as well as his teachings, have profoundly influenced the human psyche. People find themselves in the impossible situation of "believing" what he taught and at the same time being unable to put these teachings into effect. Who among his believers ceases to worry about tomorrow, either in this world or in the next? Who amongst them relinquishes his possessions, either here or in the hereafter? Or accepts still more blows from an enemy who has already struck him once? Or loves his enemy, etc., etc.? Nothing of all this teaching influences our stubborn desire for self-perpetuation.

Thus, while a great many seek, few find. And from the inner conflict arise our hypocritical morals and all the self-justifications invented by a guilt complex which has been festering for two thousand years. The Rabbi saw that, in his time, the direct comprehension of his teaching was impossible. Thus he was compelled to revert to a symbol.

Whether the characters of this drama actually existed or not is irrelevant: they will live and act in the psyche as long as it is not understood that that myth belongs to mythology.

If the name Judas, burdened with twenty centuries of hatred, is synonym of traitor, it is because it stirs up reactions such as Peter's *This shall not be*, modified after the event into: "Woe, it has been!" and ending in utter confusion. The grief is inconsistent with the facts that the event occurred according to the Father's will; that the will was a sacrifice; that the sacrifice was a redemption; that had it not happened the believers would not have been redeemed from sin; and so on, and so on. . . .

The psyche entangled in its contradictions knows deeply in itself and does not want to know that if "it had not been" life would be peacefully lived in ignorance of its ill-defined culpability.

Of course the psyche does not want to "deny itself" and "lose its life", but craves for continuity. The real culprit, the offender, is none other than Jesus for having stated his necessity as being everyone's necessity. So Jesus is eliminated and sent to an imaginary heaven—and the scapegoat is Judas. As to Peter's church, it rests upon an intricate system of self-preservation originally established in opposition to Jesus' essence: Israel. That was the beginning of theological anti-semitism.

Judas the "traitor" became identified with the "deicides", the Jews. Peter's successors declared themselves to be what they actually were, princes of this world; and the Devil was invented in order to allow the real Satan to operate undisturbed.

These remarks lead us to the deep, vast, sorrowful, cruel drama enacted by mankind. It is difficult to see it in its innermost structure. If it could be thus seen—not only by the few—it would mean a sudden ripening of our state of being.

Let us examine it through John's central symbol: the light, impersonated by Jesus, shines in darkness and the darkness personified by Satan and its princedom (mankind) does not receive it. Obviously, Jesus' purpose is to be received.

Now let us translate this in terms of Qabala: the Rabbi having declared himself *Ben-Adam* is for the time being the personification of the timeless Israel. He is the beginning in the end and the end in the beginning. He does not belong to the time-process. But he wishes to and must "die" in his contact with the historical process, which is of time. He whose name is *YH-Sheen-WH*, that is YHWH in action (Sheen), wants to and must descend deeply into the world (the legend says that he descended so deeply as to go as far as Hell, where he spent three days). By doing so he wishes to and must be in a fleeting duration-non-duration, an actualization of YHWH in the sphere of existence.

The first time, in Caesarea of Philippi he—or the *Aleph* in him—had been recognized but not acknowledged by Peter-Satan. John's Gospel, in the narration of the Last Supper, now shows us, as we read it, that Judas-Satan acknowledged him and obeyed him.

JUDAS, OR JESUS ACCEPTED

The schemata of Jesus and Judas are most revealing:

(Jesus) *Yhshwh*: *Yod-Hay-Sheen-Waw-Hay*: 10.5.300.6.5
(Judas) *Yehouda*: *Yod-Hay-Waw-Dallet-Hay*: 10.5. 6. 4.5

The *Sheen* in YHWH, for Jesus, and the *Dallet* in YHWH, for Judas, are remarkably placed, in inverse order, preceding and following *Waw* (6).

It is to be noticed that Yehoudi in Hebrew means Jew. Its spelling *Yod-Hay-Waw-Dallet-Yod* where the final *Hay* of YHWH is replaced by *Dallet-Yod* means that one of YHWH's *Hay* (life) becomes, with the Jews, an existential resistance to YHWH in *coniuncto oppositorium*, without which YHWH would only be an abstraction.

These oppositions are perfect illustrations of the double contradictory movement so constantly expressed in the Hebrew myth. This movement of life and existence can be compared to a belt that joins two rotating wheels, one above the other. Seen on one side the belt appears to have an ascending motion, seen on the other, it seems to descend. When the movement is very swift, superficial observers do not see it. Thus the revelation appears to them to be fixed, established, by an Abraham, a Moses or a Jesus.

We must now quote the translation of John XIII, 2: *And supper being ended, the devil having now put into the heart of Judas Iscariot Simon's son, to betray him* . . . and we ask: What—or who, in that archaic belief—is the devil?

The origin of this word is to be found in the resistance set by the letter *Dallet*, as we have just seen it (devil, demon, diable, daimon all with a D).

In Jesus-*Yhshwh*, the *Sheen* is a cosmic action. The Hebrew root *Sheen-Dallet* (*Shed*) means violence, ruin, and ultimately, devil. This is one of the many evidences of the forgotten cabalistic origin of the Hebrew language.

The necessary resistance to life, without which life cannot evolve its structures, has become, by the ever-static will of the

191

psyche, a "traitor". In fact, that which gives Judas his impulse is none other than Jesus' Daimon: his active principle.

The Rabbi was very observant of the cabalistic way of thinking. Having identified himself with *Aleph*, he compelled himself to play his part. He knew that *Aleph* is helpless and cannot act, but is acted upon. *Aleph* is buried in *Eretz*, immersed in Adam's blood, murdered when the primordial female prevails, spent when darkness does not "comprehend" it. . . .

Jesus repeatedly, but in vain, tried to have himself arrested. He openly challenged the other rabbis: he attracted enormous crowds; he violated the Sabbath; he raised a scandal in the synagogue; he was socially subversive; and all having been of no avail, he chose to set the Last Supper in the habitual place where he always met his disciples, instead of escaping as he was begged to do.

Are we really supposed to believe that the officers and men did not know that place? That they had not had many better opportunities of arresting Jesus? That they had to be led in the night by Judas? Or course not! Judas and the darkness are more in accord with the myth than with what can have happened, if it ever happened at all.

Jesus has come to fulfil the Scriptures, which means that he must bring them to consummation. They must come to their mythical end. Mythologically, the light (or *Aleph*) is neither accepted by darkness nor can it give itself, and we are to understand that that situation has been in that deadlock ever since the beginning of time.

Any event pertaining to the myth must be perceived in its general context. The one single purpose of the myth is to reveal the possibility of YHWH's penetration into the human race (YHWH being considered in the sense given by the code).

In the beginning *Cain*, personifying "his father" YHWH, annihilated *Abel*, the conditioned man, by his mere presence. Later, in an epic metaphysical poem, the no. 2 of the *Abraham-Isaac-Jacob* triad had to appear in disguise so as to insert what he actually represented (no. 3) into Canaan. He succeeded, but

Esau facing no. 3 (*Jacob*), felt that he was dying. Later still *Jacob* fought during a whole "night" (integrating the total darkness of the mind) to avoid being killed by *Elohim*, but he was wounded by him in *Kaf-Yerekh*: 20.800—10.200.500 (translated: *the socket of his hip*), which means that in his "container" (20) the totality of undifferentiated cosmic energy—or unconscious darkness—(800) came into existence (10) and became cosmically (200) alive (500). Thus wounded, Jacob "limped", the schema being 90.30.70.

That was *Elohim*'s penetration in the body, an event pertaining to evolution in time. Another vital penetration had to occur in the psyche, in the inner life lying in darkness, and that had to transcend time: it had to be YHWH's. But that which is timeless is not in existence in time. It is not in existence: this means that it must die in it. Life must die when plunged into existence.

Jesus came to play the part of *Aleph*. He revealed himself at the symbolic age of 30, was delivered to darkness and acknowledged with the payment of 30 pieces of silver, dying at the age of 33. None of those numbers has any historical foundation, but they are mathematically correct in the myth: Jesus is twice in 30 and dies in twice 3.

We are here in a deep mystery which can be solved as a mathematical equation, but only apprehended through Qabala.

Jesus is the 2nd Person of a Trinity. He is in the same situation as was Isaac: the events are beyond his control, but can they be taken in hand by someone else? Yes and no. The person who will be able to carry on will have to be clearly designated by Jesus (as Jacob was designated by Isaac) and will have to receive his formal investiture.

Isaac had not the power to act but had the power to transfer his power to *Jacob*, and *Jacob* became *Isaac*'s fulfilment.

Likewise, in mathematical cabalistical logic, the Rabbi *Yod-Hay-Sheen-Waw-Hay* had not the power to act but had the power to transfer his power to a chosen disciple, so as to fulfil through him the purpose that the myth had been pursuing *even before the world was* (John XVII, 5).

We have read the story of the Last Supper a thousand times in the four Gospels; and the more we thought about it, the more incomprehensible it seemed. We could not find where or how there was any betrayal in it. *Verily, verily, I say unto you that one of you shall betray me* never rang true; for nothing, either in the beginning or in the end of this narrative, corresponds to what would have happened if a man—or a god—had been betrayed in the execution of his plans. On the contrary, the details of the narrative appeared more absurd in proportion as our conviction grew that they had to do not with an historical fact, but with a psychic reality.

We felt that this narrative was a turning-point in the evolution of the human psyche and that the projection into the narrative of the idea of betrayal was an artifice, *in extremis*, of the psyche, to save itself from any shadow of co-operation in the drama. Here, it was felt was the account of the last game between the two players we had come to know so well: the "mythified" son of heaven and the "mythified" son of earth. And we became convinced that the narrative, whether or not it had been tampered with in the course of the ages by translators, interpreters, priests or *vox populi*, was a libellous record.

Not having the authentic record of this important incident (just where are such accounts to be found?), we could not enquire—as one could in the Book of Genesis—into each letter-number, to discover its true meaning. For no sacred number-language exists in Greek or Latin. The only hope there was of finding a clue lay in the study of other translations to see whether they had been less dishonest than the English version and whether, if so, they could put us on the track of something.

By good luck, the well-known French translation by Louis Segond, Doctor of Theology, gave a clue. Here it is: *En vérité, en vérité, je vous le dis, l'un de vous me livrera* (John XII, 21). The concluding phrase, here, means: One of you will hand me over —or *deliver* me. All of a sudden we had the thrill of discovering something fantastic: the true story of Judas. And the traitor, we saw, is not Judas; the traitor (or rather one of them) is none other than the interpreter who in any one of the false versions has misread the text. As you remember, Jesus is there reported as having said, "One of you shall betray me."

Let us look carefully at the text of John, and notice how the author attempts to make us understand the true picture. If we suppose that Jesus had announced in the presence of the apostles that one of them would be a traitor, what would have happened? Just imagine these men surrounding their beloved Master. Imagine yourself in the situation of the Master telling you, "There is a traitor among us." You, knowing that you were not a traitor, would have jumped to your feet and seized any kind of weapon you could lay your hands on. There would have been eleven of you. And the twelfth would have been quickly overcome and made captive. This is so evident that the very fact of it never having been put forward is just one more proof of how colossal is the psychic barrier, the taboo which humanity has raised against this narrative of Judas for two thousand years. It hardly seems credible, but one must concede that it is so.

John's text is so important that it must be quoted in full.

John XIII, 18-19: *I speak not of you all: I know whom I have chosen: but that the scripture may be fulfilled. He that eateth bread with me hath lifted up his heel against me. Now I tell you before it comes that when it is come to pass ye may believe that I am he.*

In the light of Qabala these verses could hardly be clearer: Jesus is not speaking of all the apostles, but of Judas whom they may think he has chosen by mistake. However, he knows that he has chosen him to fulfil the Scriptures concerning *Ben-Adam.* According to Genesis xxv, 26, the human-to-be seed, *Jacob-Ben-Adam,* was in the womb holding *Esau-Edom*'s heel, lifted against him. Eventually, *Esau*-son-of-the-earth was compelled to confess that *Jacob*-son-of-YHWH was indeed the carrier of the seed, and *Jacob* gave him bread as a token of communion. *Esau* lived, but there was no truce.

However, the fulfilment of the myth and of man must necessarily be an integration in one single individual of the two aspects of vital energy first symbolized by *Cain* and *Abel*, then by *Jacob* and *Esau*, and now by *Jesus* and *Judas*. This is exactly what Jesus says: "now I tell you, before it happens, so that you may believe that I am he". He, meaning obviously Judas if we simply read the text as it is, considering that the "he" mentioned two lines ahead is him.

John XIII, *20-27*. Notwithstanding the clarity of these statements Jesus insists: *Verily, verily I say unto you: He that receiveth whomsoever I send receiveth me, and he that receiveth me receiveth him that sent me.* He will send Judas and Judas will be his *alter ego*.

Then: *When Jesus had thus said he was troubled in spirit.* Why was he troubled in spirit? What could have thus perturbed him? In uttering those words he must have suddenly realized in absolute fact that he, Son-of-YHWH, had actually become incarnate. He had become also son-of-the-earth. It must have been a terrific experience.

We now come to the dramatic *dénouement* and in quoting it I will substitute a more adequate expression for the deadly, the destructive word, "betray".

. . . *and (Jesus) testified, and said, Verily, verily, I say unto you, that one of you shall* HAND ME OVER (OR, DELIVER ME). *Then the disciples looked one on another, doubting of whom he spake. Now there was leaning on Jesus' bosom one of his disciples whom Jesus loved. Simon-Peter therefore beckoned to him, that he should ask who it should be of whom he spake. He then lying on Jesus' breast saith unto him, Lord, who is it? Jesus answered, He it is, to whom I shall give a sop, when I have dipped it. And when he had dipped the sop, he gave it to Judas Iscariot, the son of Simon. And after the sop Satan entered into him. Then said Jesus unto him, That thou doest, do quickly.*

Here again the text is so clear that it cannot be misunderstood if we do not interpret it wilfully in such fashion as to infer from it the opposite of what it says.

In spite of two thousand years of theology, the only one with whom Jesus communes is Judas, and however bewildering for the minds that can only function one way, the direct effect of that communion is that Jesus introduces Satan into Judas.

And now, having materialized Satan, Jesus speaks to him as a master to his dependant: *That thou doest, do quickly!*

John XIII, *28-30: Now no man at the table knew with what intent he spake unto him. For some of them thought, because Judas had the purse, that Jesus had said unto him, Buy those things that we have need of against the feast; or that he should give something to the poor. He then having received the sop went immediately out: and it was night.*

None of the eleven were aware of what was happening. We know that they were half asleep, or mesmerized, or probably overwhelmed by the tremendous outpouring of energy that was to shatter forever the foundations of the human mind.

The most decisive words of any myth in any time had been uttered. And now had come the moment of suspense.

And those words, for some of those men, so deeply slumbering, have meant "go and buy cakes" . . . Moreover it was night: what a time for such errands!

But John is now aware. He, so near his Master, as actually to be touching him, must feel the tremendous vibrations. What is it that he sees? How does he know? Many years later when dictating his Gospel to his disciples, he stated that *Satan* entered into *Judas*. Was it a conclusion? A knowledge acquired at the end of his life?

We cannot answer these questions, and they are not relevant. Our real question is: this suspense is not of time, therefore it is now, here, facing us and in us. Do we see it? Do we feel it? Do we understand it?

Here are, in us, standing face to face, Jesus and *Judas*. Who are they? What are they? And we hear Jesus giving his order: What you are to do, do it quickly, and John has just told us that this order is given to Satan who has taken possession of Judas.

Have we emptied our minds of all the infantile ideas and pictures of the "devil"? Have we deeply integrated every myth and mythology? Are we actually inside the inexplicable mystery of all that exists? If so, we can understand and rejoice: *John* XIII, *31-32.*

Therefore when he was gone out, Jesus said Now is the son of man glorified and God is glorified in him. If God be glorified in him, God shall also glorify him in himself and shall straightway glorify him.

We can no longer be deterred by the real meaning expressed in such a symbolic and archaic way: the fact has been stated already: he that receives the one that Jesus sends receives Jesus and receives the one that sent Jesus. It is clear that Jesus sends Satan. So he who receives Satan receives Jesus, hence he receives God.

In terms of traditional religion this statement, in spite of it being so clearly written in John's Gospel is monstrous and frightening.

In terms of gnosis it is the statement of a simple fact: there is only One energy, only One life, only One movement. All is one and one is in all. The One is the one game of life and existence, of energy as energy and of energy as its own physical support, which is its own resistance to itself, without which nothing would be.

4

Epilogue

THIS NARRATIVE has neither beginning nor end. It has to do with the drama of the human mind, enclosed in its psychical egg shell. It deals with the tragedy of timeless life imprisoned therein, life which more often than not is extinguished by the hardening of the shell.

We have tried to elucidate what the unfortunate Hellenization of the ancient Hebrew Revelation has termed Logos or Word. The entire Revelation is contained in the meaning of *Aleph, Bayt, Ghimei, Dallet,* and the rest of the letter-numbers of the sacred language. Far more than a mere series of letters, they represent an anatomy of the cosmic interplay of energies and resistances of which each of us is but a transient condensation. Now the Door is opened, or rather we have a key to it. For the time being, let us go no further. Anyone who so desires can move into the vitalizing study and dig—not too long in the Book itself, but in his own mind, going on indefinitely making his own discoveries.

It is possible to bring down the working of the cosmic principles, so to speak, to a point where we can see them functioning in our daily life. Thus it is in our everyday behaviour and in the working of our mind that Genesis and Yhshwh's teachings can be fruitful. We can be a point of consciousness to which the Revelation comes. But this we cannot be if we cling to traditional belief, ritual and authority founded upon the misunderstanding and negation of the essential truths of these teachings. All such philosophies, theologies, creeds or worship—whether spiritualistic or materialistic, individual or social—are but static projections of the psyche: of a shell.

The potential effect of the "Word", as we perceive it through the living significance of *Aleph-Bayt*, is not just a sterile reaction against organized religions that have grown around it. On the contrary, meeting the tremendous challenge of this re-reading can be as fruitful as the emergence of a germ of life when, at its proper stage of maturity, it shatters the shell that encloses it. The protection afforded by its dwelling, the *Bayt*, is necessary during growth; but carried into maturity, it suffocates the *Aleph* within.

Once more let it be emphasized that what we have tried to convey in this book has to do with the germ, the inner core of humanity as seen from within, from the very essence of it. Our time calls for maturity. This is what we are called upon to attain. We need but to stand receptive in the way of the blessing of maturation, which is the breaking of the shell that bars us from interaction with the universal life-force.

Human history has been the record of a monstrous massacre For centuries it has recounted stories of wholesale slaughter in wars, decapitations, mutilations, and death by fire and torture. Our epoch, far from eliminating these barbarities, girds itself for even more monstrous destruction with computers for "perfecting" the means to this end. No less brutal is the fact that the greater part of humanity suffers from poverty, ill health and hunger.

Considering the appalling martyrdom of hundreds of millions of human beings, it is strange that one single death, unrecorded in its time and hence of uncertain occurrence—the death of Jesus on the cross—has generally assumed such magnitude in human consciousness as to overshadow virtually all the others. The reason lies in the fact that the psyche lives its own history in parallel with recorded history. Psychological events, being lived directly, are often far more stirring than concrete facts. There is no better illustration of this than the Crucifixion itself, casting as it does its tremendous shadow over the world.

The psyche may not be aware of the historical conditions which, at the time of Pontius Pilate, transformed the pleasant

Hellenistic mythology into a tragedy. The symbols typified by Zeus and his half-heavenly, half-human offspring were shifted to a new aspect of the pagan Father and his son, thus obliterating the Hebrew revelation and all that the Rabbi Yhshwh did and said according to that ancient tradition. Therefore, his teaching of love has persisted in the realm of the thoughts of men—which are "of Satan"—and has been disconnected from the source, which is timeless, ever fresh and new, beyond all measure and transcending all thought.

The Light that was Crucified

THROUGHOUT THIS essay, from Adam to Jesus, we have introduced vibrations that should, up to a point, help certain psyches to overcome a passive stage of development that fixes them as chrysalids in a condition in which they are in danger of dying whilst dreaming their myths.

For fear of facing the uncertainties of real space, these psyches wither in imaginary celestial regions, all the more deceptive in that they are linked to historical events.

The reversing of values, thanks to which the psyche anaesthetizes itself, transforms at all costs a myth into an historical reality whose existence is violently denied by those who believe in a contradictory myth. These opposing views sometimes lead to the most fantastic inventions, as for example, the narrative linked to the talmudic tradition called *Toledot Yeschou*, in which Jesus is said to have been the illegitimate son of a woman hairdresser and of a certain *Pandera*.

The passionate arguments between the early Church Fathers and the Rabbis concerning the origins of their respective revelations have unfortunately engulfed the fundamental religious problem in a morass of historical interpretations. The opposing parties pursued their arguments with fierce tenacity on subjects such as the crossing of the Red Sea by the Hebrews, or the question of who were the witnesses of Jesus' empty sepulchre. It was of prime importance to them that things should have happened in a certain way and not otherwise.

Such discussions about Moses, Jesus or the Buddha have always been and still are based upon a dualistic conception: the existence of two different worlds (this one and the one above or beyond) and upon the idea that one or other of the exalted founders of these religions has opened a line of communication between this world and the other. The resulting creeds are therefore based upon ritual, prayers and other forms of worship that are claimed to lead to the unknown.

The essential point of each creed is to prove that its founder has actually opened the said line of communication. The evidences brought forth are usually miracles, apparitions, voices calling, meteorological phenomena, which infer that to prove its existence the other world must upset this one.

We have often said that the primary purpose of all established religions is to prevent, to remove from the mind, the perception of the immediate all-pervading mystery: the fact that the mere existence of anything at all cannot and never will be explained.

We think that justice has been done to Moses in ignoring his miracles and in stating that his religion was the building of a protective shell for a profound truth: a shell that has no longer any purpose.

Likewise, we must do justice to Jesus in eliminating his miraculous aspects that have nothing to do with the truth which can be discovered in the original Hebraic myth: the game of indetermination played by *Aleph* and *Yod*.

When that game is truly perceived by us, YHWH springs alive and the *spirit of truth* (*John* xiv, *16-17*), foretold by Jesus, dwells within us.

The important point of contact between Hebraism and early Christianity can only be shown in the almost unknown link between the original Qabala and Gnosticism, against which the Church built its defences. We will point out some of its elements, without which this essay would not be complete.

According to *Matthew* xxviii, Mary Magdalene and the other Mary go to the sepulchre, there is an earthquake, an angel descends from heaven like a bolt of lightning, the keepers almost die of fright, the angel says that Jesus has been resurrected, the women depart, Jesus meets them, they fall at his feet and worship him. Later on, the disciples (except *Judas*) see Jesus on a mountain in Galilee, they worship him *but some doubted.*

According to *Mark* xvi, Mary Magdalene, Mary the mother of James and Salome go to the sepulchre, they see there a stone that has been rolled away and a young man dressed in white; they are very much afraid, the young man tells them to notify *his disciples and Peter* (note the obvious interpolation). They run away. *After that he appeared in another form unto two* disciples. He later appeared to the eleven and then *he was received into Heaven and sat on the right hand of the Lord.* (Note this last mythological touch, coming straight from Olympus.)

According to *Luke* xxiv unnamed women go to the sepulchre with spices, two men are standing there *in shining garments*; they say that Jesus has risen according to his promise. That same day two disciples, one of them named *Cleophas* and the other unnamed are on the road to *Emmaus.* Jesus meets them on the way, *but their eyes were holden that they should not know him.* They walk and spend the whole day together, Jesus speaking at length. In the evening *their eyes were opened and they knew him and he vanished from their sight. And they said one to another: Did not our heart burn within us while he talked with us by the way, and while he made plain to us the scriptures?*

According to *John* xx, Mary Magdalene alone goes to the sepulchre, sees it empty, runs and tells Peter and John. The two go with her to the sepulchre and see the linen shroud lying on the floor. Mary weeps and sees *two angels in white, sitting.* They ask: why do you weep? She says: *because they have taken away my Lord* ... Then ... *she turned and saw Jesus standing and knew not that it was Jesus* (v. 14). He speaks to her but she *supposes him to be the gardener* (v. 15). Then he calls her "Mary" and she says *Rabboni, which is to say Master* (v. 16), but he tells her not to touch him.

That same day Jesus appears to the disciples *when the doors were shut* (v. 19). Having thus appeared, he shows his hands and his side so as to be recognized, and speaks briefly to them. Thomas is not there. When the others tell him about the appearance, he does not believe them. He says that unless he touches Jesus he will not believe that he came in the flesh. Eight days later the disciples are again together, Thomas included. Jesus appears again, *the doors being shut* (v. 26). He tells Thomas to reach out his hand and to touch him, and adds: *be not faithless but believing* (v. 27) and Thomas believes *without touching him.*

The strangest narration concerning these apparitions is in *John* xxi.

Seven disciples are on the shore of Lake Tiberias. Simon-Peter says: *I go a-fishing. They say unto him, we also go with thee.* That night they do not catch anything. *But when the morning was now come, Jesus stood on the shore: but the disciples knew not that it was Jesus.* He tells them to *cast the net on the right side of the ship* and they cannot draw it in because it is so full of fish. Then John says: *it is the Lord* and Simon-Peter who was naked puts on his coat and plunges into the lake(!) The others come in a little boat, dragging the net full of fish.

When the discrepancies are eliminated from all these narratives, the constant factors are the presence of Mary Magdalene, the absence of Mary the mother, and above all the fact that when Jesus appears he is not recognized and that when eventually he is recognized, he does not allow anybody to touch him.

According to *Matthew*, some of the disciples "doubt". According to *Mark*, he appears "in another form". *Luke* resorts to an euphemism: "their eyes were holden that they could not see", but he finally states that after a whole day Jesus is at last recognized because of what he said, which is a most strange way of recognizing a person with whom one has lived until three days before that particular meeting.

John the Gnostic is the clearest of all. He knows that the most successful way to hide a secret is to say it openly but casually. It was very astonishing when it was discovered that, in the narration concerning Thomas, Jesus appears when the doors are shut. In relating this story John carefully repeated that statement for fear that it should be overlooked. When the form of Jesus appears the second time and meets Thomas, Thomas is persuaded that faith is better than knowledge. Once before it did not allow Mary Magdalene to touch it.

Concerning the apparition on the shore of Tiberias, John quotes himself as having said: It is the Lord, when he was told where the fish were: poor evidence indeed. Simon-Peter's behaviour is farcical as the story goes, but not in symbol; he puts on his coat and jumps into the lake, instead of meeting his Master on the shore.

This passage and the following concerning Peter were written in order to be understood by cabalists and gnostics. Their meaning was eventually lost. It is not our purpose to examine them in detail, but it must be shown in which direction one must look.

Simon-Peter puts on his coat and does not forget to tighten his belt (*he girt his fisher's coat*, says the text); he then goes into the water. This is exactly the opposite of what is known to be the ritual of certain initiations. We recall Joseph being stripped naked by his brothers and thrown into a dry well, and we said that the episode is the distorted narrative of a ceremony of initiation. John, for those who know how to read, says that Peter is in a regressive stage. His further dialogue with the form of Jesus is revealing. Jesus would never have offered his love to the highest bidder: in verses 15, 16 and 17 the apparition asks three times of the man who had three times denied Jesus if he loves it more than the others do. Peter says he does. Then three times it says: *Feed my sheep.*

These words, according to Qabala, are the best evidence that this apparition behaved as *Satan*, because to be the sheep of anyone, even the sheep of Almighty God, if such a being exists, is an abomination to *Ben-Adam*.

In brief, when all those narratives concerning the resurrection are considered, there can be no doubt as to the correct view of docetism concerning it. According to that early doctrine, Jesus never appeared in the flesh, but in an "astral" body, as theosophists would call it today. The apparitions were not denied by docetism, nor do we see any reason not to consider them as metapsychical phenomena such as have often been observed and studied.

The early fathers of the Church fiercely refuted docetism but with very unconvincing arguments, except where simple faith in resurrection of the flesh is called for. Our contention, however, is that the entire question is irrelevant and immaterial. It only detracts from the essential, which is our psychical maturity and our impregnation by cosmic energies capable of recreating us anew from moment to moment.

One of the most important Gnostic archetypes is Mary Magdalene. Of its many names we will only mention *Myriam M'Gadola*. The root *Mareh* (*Mem-Raysh-Aleph-Hay*) in Hebrew means image, appearance, vision, mirror (whence derives the English word: mirror). *Iam* is always a reference, to the sea or to a still water acting as a mirror. *G'dola* means big.

The Mary Magdalene out of whom Jesus *had cast seven devils* (*Mark* xvi, *9*) is the female element transfigured by this "casting out" of no. 7. This archetype is visionary in a real sense; it is, in its symbolical form, the woman exorcized by her cosmic spouse and sanctified by the expulsion of the seven resistances to the sacred no. 7 of indetermination. She is the necessary witness, the only possible witness to the resurrection of *Aleph*. She is the eternal prostitute, eternally redeemed and regenerated: the human psyche. Mary Magdalene is symbolically—and alas only symbolically—the final act of a drama that the mind dreams for fear of losing itself in its completion.

With *Myriam M'Gadola* or Magdalene we are at the very centre of the essential elements of the myth, in the deepest symbols of Qabala, of Gnosis, of alchemy, and of many other expressions of what is often included in the words "occult" or "esoteric".

As we read this schema we see it to be similar to a peaceful mirror of still waters. It reflects the vision that the living light projects upon the world. It is the vision that the world projects upon the world. It is the vision that the world projects upon light. It is the substance purified: the structured energy as it appears to itself in its own evolution. It is the perpetual gnostic throbbing of energy in a symbiosis of pregnancy and virginity.

Myriam M'Gadola emerges from the vast primordial mass of waters, from the perpetual undifferentiated energy constantly expanding in its apparent evolution. Energy, in spite of building its own container, cannot resist itself to the point of containing itself.

Through the entire myth we have now seen how energy is structured, from the undifferentiated stage to the indeterminate stage, by the interplay of the four symbolical elements.

Water mixed with earth must pass through fire's formative power to gather resistance, and air is the transmitting element. Those elements are primitive and archaic for the non-initiate, who only consider them in their objective reality, but in truth it is very difficult to follow them symbolically and psychologically through the evolution of the myth.

Fire and Air are male. Earth and Water are female. Light (*Awr*) is, as we have seen, the copulation of *Aleph* represented by Fire and Air and of its cosmic container, *Raysh* represented by Earth and Water. The results of their union is an evolution of the Female: inorganic exterior light becomes organic and inner, through a process of differentiation which culminates (for our planet) in man.

One of the aspects of this myth is the birth of a deity and the virginity of its mother. This theme is far from being specifically Christian: it existed in many ancient civilizations. When it is taken literally and considered to be an historical event the belief in that objectivity is a subjective matter. The stronger the objectivity, the deeper the subjectivity: the psyche seeks in it a refuge, a fixation, and thereby stifles the *Aleph* and its eternal life.

It may well be that the greatest error of the Christian dogma is the assertion that the Holy Ghost engendered an infant only once, and at a certain date. It is irrational to think that the timeless, unthinkable, infinite immanence is not in all times and in all places in intimate copulation (symbolically speaking) with the world since it constantly bears fresh and unexpected fruits.

The real feminine archetype in this myth is the perpetual lover, Mary Magdalene, and not Mary-Mother-of-Jesus who belongs to the past and is therefore in a state of regression. When the archetypes are thus understood, the fact that Jesus rejects his mother, and repeatedly refuses her advances, far from appearing strange and abnormal strikes us as being in perfect accordance with the myth.

Having identified Myriam as the psyche we can understand how the human mind, when it is really in love with the infinite cosmic energy, can always be impregnated by it, thereby becoming perpetually fresh, new, virgin. It may give its fruit but it never is its "mother". It can progress on the path of understanding so far as to emit the spark of *Aleph*. The spark dies and resurrects intermittently and does not acknowledge its mother.

We are never justified in approaching the problem of knowledge by reversing its symbols. These images are but projections of the individual and the collective unconscious. They are regressive, they belong to the past, whereas knowledge is the immediacy of our own maturity.

The crucifixion then, assumes its proper meaning: far from being a torture and a death it appears to be a relaxation, a rest: it is both the separation and the union of the invisible *Aleph* and of the material *Yod*. It is a life so intense as to appear motionless, its vibration being too swift to be perceived.

The real cross is alive. It is nowhere as clearly depicted as in the shape of *Aleph*. Its diagonal line expresses the primordial element of life, and I believe that biologists have indeed discovered that organic life begins when an element in crystallization is thus set. On the upper right hand side of *Aleph* a sign in the shape of a hammer suggests the hammering of the invisible world, and on the lower left hand side a sign in the shape of a leg suggests the march of time.

However eloquent, that figure is only a symbol. We must

never forget that any description of *Aleph* fails to describe it: *Aleph* transcends thought. This assertion is fundamental in Qabala and in Gnosticism.

Cabalists, it can be said, in brief, explored the structure of energy, outer and inner. Gnostics have emphasized the inner life. Both have rejected the canonical teaching according to which the inner life can be lived vicariously by means of an objectified myth.

According to Gnosis, therefore, the crucifixion exists and yet does not exist; it happened and yet it did not happen; it is of time and yet it is not in the process of time.

As an example of those mystic texts, here is a quotation from part of the Gnostic Acts, known as the Leucian Acts of John, taken from an English translation of this by G. R. S. Mead, published as far back as 1907.* They purport to date from very early times, before the Gnostics came to be considered heretical, that is to say prior to A.D. 150—say about A.D. 130. To our mind, it is enough that such things have been thought and lived. In the myth, which is the true history of the psyche, there is greater revelation of truth than in any chronicle of the time. These inspired writings deserve to be widely known.

The first of the passages which we wish to quote from these Acts of John is a Mystery Play, danced and sung by Jesus, whilst his disciples move in a circle around him, responding with "Amen" at the end of each verse:

We praise thee, O Father;
We give thanks to thee, O Light;
In whom darkness dwells not.

· · · · · ·

I would be saved and I would save
I would be loosed and I would loose
I would be wounded and I would wound
I would be dissolved and I would dissolve
I would be begotten and I would beget

* *The Hymn of Jesus* and *The Gnostic Crucifixion* (Stuart & Watkins).

I would eat and I would be eaten
I would hear and I would be heard
I would understand and I would be all understanding

. . . . . .

I would flee and I would stay

. . . . . .

I would be atoned and I would atone
I have no dwelling and I have dwellings
I have no place and I have places
I have no temple and I have temples
I am a lamp to thee who seest me
I am a mirror to thee who understandest me
I am a door to thee who knockest at me
I am a way to thee a wayfarer.

. . . . . .

Now, answer to my dancing. See thyself in me who speak and seeing what I do, keep silence on my mysteries.

Understand by dancing what I do, for thine is the Passion of man that I am to suffer.

Thou couldst not at all be conscious of what thou dost suffer were I not sent as thy word by the Father.

Seeing what I suffer, thou sawest me as suffering; and seeing, thou didst not stand, but wast moved wholly, moved to be wise.

Thou hast me for a couch: rest thou upon me; but who I am thou shalt not know when I depart; what now I am seen to be, that I am not. But what I am thou shalt see when thou comest.

If thou hadst known how to suffer, thou wouldst have power not to suffer. Know then how to suffer and thou hast power not to suffer.

. . . . . .

As for me, if thou wouldst know what I was: in a word, I am the Word who did dance all things . . .

'Twas I who leapt and danced.

(And here John himself takes up the narrative.)

(1) And having danced these things with us, Beloved, the

Lord went out. And we, as though beside ourselves, or wakened out of sleep, fled each our several ways.

(2) I, however, though I saw the beginning of his passion could not stay to the end, but fled to the Mount of Olives, weeping over that which had befallen.

(3) And when he was hung on the tree of the cross, at the sixth hour of the day, darkness came over the whole earth. And my Lord stood in the midst of the cave, and filled it with light and said:

(4) John! To the multitude below in Jerusalem, (it appears that) I am being crucified and pierced with spears; and reeds and vinegar and gall are being given to me to drink. To thee now I speak, and give ear to what I say, 'Twas I who put it in thy heart to ascend this mount, that thou mightest hear what a disciple should learn from master and man from God.

(5) And having thus spoken he showed me a cross of light set up, and around the cross a vast multitude, and therein one form and a similar appearance, and in the cross another multitude not having form.

(6) And I beheld the Lord Himself above the cross. He had, however, no shape, but only as it were a voice—not, however, this voice to which we were accustomed, but one of its own kind and beneficent and truly of God—saying unto me:

(7) John, one there needst must be to hear these things from me; for I long for one who will hear.

(8) This cross of light is called by me for your sake sometimes Mind, sometimes Jesus, sometimes Christ, sometimes Door, sometimes Way, sometimes Bread, sometimes Seed, sometimes Resurrection, sometimes Son, sometimes Father, sometimes Spirit, sometimes Life, sometimes Truth, sometimes Faith, sometimes Grace.

(9) Now, those things it is called as towards men; but as to what it is, in truth, itself, in its own meaning to itself and declared unto us, it is the defining and limitation of all things, both the firm necessity of things fixed from things unstable and the harmony of wisdom.

(10) And as it is wisdom in harmony, there are those on the right and those on the left—powers, authorities, principalities and daemons, energies, threats, powers of wrath, slandering— and the lower Root from which have come forth the things in Genesis.

(11) This then is the Cross which by the Word has been the means of "cross-beaming" all things, at the same time separating off the things that proceed from Genesis and those below it, from those above, and also compacting them all into one.

(12) But this is not the cross of wood which thou shalt see when thou descendest hence; nor am I here that is upon the cross, I whom now thou seest not, but only hearest a voice.

(13) I was held to be what I am not, not being what I was to many others; nay, they will call me something else, abject and not worthy of me. As, then, the place of rest is neither seen nor spoken of, much more shall I, the Lord of it, be neither seen nor spoken of.

(14) Now, the multitude of one appearance round the cross is the lower nature. And as to those whom thou seest on the cross, if they have not also one form, it is because the whole race of him who descended hath not yet been gathered together.

(15) But when the upper nature, yea, the race that is coming unto me in obedience to my voice, is taken up, then thou who now harkenest to me, shalt become it, and it shall no longer be what it is now, but above them, as I am now.

(16) For so long as thou callest not thyself mine, I am not what I am. But if thou harkenest unto me, hearing, thou too shalt be as I am, and I shall be what I am when thou art with thyself, as I am with myself; for from this, thou art.

(17) Pay no attention, then, to the many; and them that are without the mystery, think little of: for know that I am wholly with the Father and the Father with me.

(18) Nothing, then, of the things which they will say of me have I suffered; nay, that Passion as well, which I showed unto thee and the rest by dancing it, I will that it be called a mystery.

(19) What thou art, thou seest; this did I show unto thee. But what I am, this I alone know, and no one else.

(20) What then is mine, suffer me to keep; but what is thine, see thou through me. To see me as I really am I said is not possible, but only what thou art able to recognize as being kin to me.

(21) Thou hearest that I suffer, yet I did not suffer; that I suffered not, yet I did suffer; that I was pierced, yet I was not smitten; that I was hanged, yet I was not hanged; that blood flowed from me, yet it did not flow; and in a word, the things they say about me I had not, and the things they do not say, those I suffered. Now what they are I will riddle for thee; for I know that thou wilt understand.

(22) Understand, therefore, in me, the slaying of a Verb, the piercing of a Verb, the blood of a Verb, the hanging of a Verb, the passion of a Verb, the nailing of a Verb, the death of a Verb.

(23) And thus I speak, separating off the man. First, then, understand the Verb, then shalt thou understand the Lord and in the third place only, the man and what he suffered.

(24) And having said these things to me and others, which I know not how to say as he himself would have it, he was taken up, no one of the multitude beholding him.

(25) And when I descended I laughed at them all, when they told me what they did concerning him, firmly possessed in myself of this only, that the Lord contrived all things symbolically and according to dispensation for the conversion and salvation of man.

214

Circumcision

WE BELIEVE that circumcision is an important factor in the Genesis of man (or resurrection of *Aleph*). We therefore offer here a tentative introduction to the study of its physiological and psychological consequences.

The foreskin, in enveloping the gland, shelters it from all contact. Because of this protection the non-circumcised child lives until the age of puberty as if that organ, as a sexual organ, did not exist—except in those momentary states of excitation to which, as everyone knows, the child is subject. At such times the mucous lining, which is very sensitive, causes a strongly localized pleasure in the sexual organ. It is not until puberty that the gland undergoes exterior contacts sufficient to establish an active transmission throughout the whole sexual system. Until that time, the system can be compared to a dead-end street, without traffic, without exchange, inasmuch as the fixation of the centre of interest is blocked at the entrance.

The practice of circumcision on the young child results in (1) a physiological shock, accompanied by (2) a partial desensitizing of the gland (which makes, later on, for a lack of violently concentrated sensation) and followed by (3) an indefinite prolongation of the sexual shock in the whole organism because of the uncovering of the gland. From that time on, the gland will continually undergo contacts which will be transmitted to nerve centres, to an entire apparatus still in the original stage and incapable of any impulse towards sexual functioning. We know that the sexual instrument is not isolated. It is in contact with the sensorial functioning of all the senses. (This is evident when an erotic state transforms the five senses, conferring upon them an erotic character and focusing them for its own use.)

This awakening in the child obviously cannot bring forth in him capacities which he does not possess. However, with equal opportunity, his faculties will be better organized and exploited.

This is not the only aspect of the question, nor is it, perhaps, the most important. Circumcision in the extremely young child creates a shock around which the psyche builds itself. It is true that an important shock has already taken place: the birth trauma, recorded in the crystallization of a "snowball" of reactions which will become the self. But the trauma of circumcision immediately introduces within that psyche a mobile element; it is not buried as soon as it is produced, but is prolonged indefinitely and radiates within the vital centres during their formative periods.

Thus, in the non-circumcised, the psyche is crystallized around a birth trauma, which is slowly but surely interred by the child's reactions to his environment. The younger the child, the more malleable he is, so that these reactions act upon him like a mold.

This procedure is violently troubled by circumcision at eight days, because it introduces a purely individual shock, a moving traumatism that concerns the very fibres of his being. Instead of a slow condensation of fluctuating elements determined by the surroundings, we find an active, awakened, vital centre in full process of organization, capable of transforming its reactions to the environment into purely individual elements. Not only does the individual consciousness—the "I"—construct itself more rapidly, but its foundations are laid in a living, flexible element constantly related to the development of the individual.

But how is a woman affected by all this? And is the social attitude of the Jew influenced by circumcision? The Jewish woman is, indeed, transformed by the fact of the man's having been circumcised. This practice, having existed for many centuries, has brought about certain hereditary modifications in both male and female: these include a great nervous sensibility due to an especially complex nervous system, always on the *qui vive*, always mobile and on the watch, ready to shift balance, even to lose balance; a precocious, sometimes excessive intellectuality; and a mind which, though strongly determined, is nevertheless mobile and pliable.

Besides the hereditary transmission of qualities such as these, there exists a Jewish mode of behaviour, on the part of man which necessarily reacts upon woman, and also a particular state of consciousness that expresses itself socially. (It is dangerous to venture into generalizations. Besides, "the circumcision of the hearts" which was mentioned some two thousand years ago, would be, if understood, the quickest and most revolutionary way towards human fulfilment.)

Sex is obviously a determining factor in every society. Being a projection of cosmic energies, it can well be translated in terms of *Aleph* versus *Yod*. At the bottom of the scale, in one of the most primitive manifestations, we see the male bee dying in the sexual act. In such societies, the female organizes an immutable functional order, in which the *Aleph* is constantly murdered. On a higher animal level, the sexual activity is dependent on recurrent needs, and both males and females are conditioned by seasonal rhythms. The species cannot evolve; they remain within the framework of *Tov*, which is continuity in time.

The human condition is a state of conflict, a struggle, symbolically between YHWH, who aims at freeing the *Aleph*, and Eretz (the earth) who, as we have seen, "drinks the blood" of Hevel, his Adam bereaved of *Aleph* (dam meaning blood).

Let us now consider the three following cases: (*a*) non-circumcision; (*b*) circumcision at puberty: that of Ishmael, son of Hagar, the enslaved woman; (*c*) circumcision at eight days: that of Isaac, son of Sarah.

The uncircumcised. For the uncircumcised, the eruption at puberty of a centrifugal force generally leads to an upheaval. At that age, a deep sexual disturbance may be felt by an unprepared organism. New, unexpected sensations upset the static balance prevailing hitherto (or, alas, not upsetting it, leave it static). An outburst takes place, as after the bursting of a dam. Naturally, these cases are extreme; and once again, one cannot generalize, for one can easily find cases of sexual development which invalidate these remarks in one way or another. But one thing is certain: cases of sexual "revelation", of disturbance of masculine vitality, of interior realization, or of reorganization of spiritual life due to coitus, are not the case of Israel. It is equally certain that the search for union by identification of two beings in the sexual act and the desire to plunge into the sexual abyss in order to be identified with the great "vital currents" of nature (as sung or described by writers and vaunted as being the source of spiritual, artistic and passionate ideals) are an abomination in the eyes of Israel, circumcised at eight days and carrying in his flesh the pact with Elohim.

Circumcision at puberty. Quite different is the result of circumcision when it takes place at the age of thirteen (the boy's age of puberty), as is the case among followers of the Moslem faith. With the violent sexual shock, at the prodrome of puberty, the sensorial perceptions suddenly become purely sexual. This drains the masculine energy towards sex, maintaining it there in a continually erotic state. As a consequence of this practice, a stoppage of the intellectual faculties and even a regression due to sexual excess may be produced.

Circumcision at eight days. A manner of confronting the paradoxical double movement of which we are made is presented by circumcision at eight days (*Aleph* versus *Yod*). It not only polarizes the subconscious around an awakening vital energy and constructs within a mobile psyche, but the contributary elements are, themselves, mobile.

When, at the age of two or three months, the intelligent coordination of movement begins to occur, there is already, in the circumcised child, a subconscious "nucleus" around the sensorial activity which engendered it. The psychophysical exchanges become intense. The young self, attached to its vital centres, gradually eliminates the elements imposed by its environment, and, because of this, finds itself carried away by a permanent contradictory movement within itself. The developing self is in a state similar to that of a chicken which, during its life in the egg, devours its own substance (the white of the egg). Later on, when the male centrifugal force assumes its sexual character, it finds that its "enemy" (the psyche), grown strong because of having fed upon its substance (sexual), has proclaimed itself master of the house. What takes place psychologically is clear enough. The sensibility of the sexual organ has been dulled—whereas eroticism is, on the contrary, highly branched and subtle. Thus sensuality becomes imaginative but does not disrupt the individual's consciousness. Erotically, the man is more like a valley watered by innumerable streams than like a deep gorge where an overwhelming torrent rushes along. Instead of the man being carried away, his mind rules. Sensuality and imagination are at work, but the individual remains "himself". He does not lose consciousness of himself. He cannot possibly lose this awareness during the act of coitus.

Thus we see that man, endowed with his self (which, though static by nature, shelters living seed) must struggle against and overcome the centrifugal sexual movement which tends to lead him into the abyss of the female. Circumcision at eight days helps him powerfully. It gives him the additional dynamism necessary to ensure his escape from the "queen bee" aspect of woman.

Woman. Whereas through all the symbols, allegories and legends concerning YHWH in the Book of Genesis, emphasis is laid on the sublimation of womanhood as a determining factor in human evolution, the covenant between YHWH and Abraham in view of this may well appear as a contradiction; for it aims to dissociate man from the animal species by an operation upon man's flesh only.

It may, however, be noted that, the human psyche being of the same centripetal nature as the feminine sexual function, two contrasting energies to be readjusted do not exist, in womanhood. So woman's problems can and must, psychologically, be dealt with directly. In this field she cannot but respond to Abram's deep and constant wish: "Woman, thou art my sister, my companion." In the truest Hebrew tradition, where the male cannot possibly sink into the primordial female abyss, a psychological and physiological relationship comes into being, thanks to which the woman is given every chance to become supremely intelligent. This is far more real than the projection (in an imaginary heaven) of a mere symbol of the feminine archetype to be worshipped, such as, for instance, Mary, Mother of Jesus.

Social. Centrifugal boys and centripetal girls have different centres of emotional and mental activity, and this well before puberty. Puberty is the result of a slow process of development which has, over a period, been leading the boy outwards and the girl inwards. In this sense it can be said that the emotional and mental life of the child is of the same nature as his sex.

While the development of the self (which is cumulative) finds no opposition in the maturing sexual process of the girl, whose elements are primarily static, with the boy the case is different: there is conflict. As soon as a centrifugal vitality develops in him, it tends to carry the self along with it. Here we see the circumcised and the uncircumcised behaving in opposite ways (with innumerable exceptions). The former does not succeed in ridding himself of the self-consciousness which is well trained to gallop without faltering over moving elements; on the contrary, the latter (the uncircumcised) has the greatest difficulty in not letting himself be carried away by the collective torrent in which his individuality is drowned. He is centrifugal at a moment when his individuation is not assured; and because of that, he risks losing it. It is difficult for him to free himself from his environment and to achieve maturity, because his faculties are conditioned by collective automatisms. He may even go so far as to let himself be swept into some sort of a turbulent current.

We need seek no further for an explanation of the bands of turbulent youths which nowadays are to be found in all countries. Carried away by centrifugal, erotic passion that has drained their emotions as well as their reason, these young people, in love with those who impose themselves on them, carrying emblems, repeating slogans and waving flags, undergo a heroic exaltation which only tears them away from individual egocentricity to topple them into the collective self, which is as functional and "female" as any hive of bees. Their immature freedom breeds a conformity of a kind that tends to regress to a would-be sub-species, where the individual would be in danger of getting lost in a feeling of "belonging".

YHWH is absent from manifestations such as these.

BOOK II

The Song of Songs

THE CANONICAL
SONG OF SOLOMON
DECIPHERED ACCORDING
TO THE ORIGINAL
CODE OF THE QABALA

Introduction

THE BOOK of poems which in Hebrew is called *Sheer Ha-Sheereem*, in Latin *Canticum Canticorum*, and likewise in different languages, such as French, *Le Cantique des Cantiques*, appears in the English Bibles (the King James' and the Revised Standard Version) under the title of *The Song of Solomon* for no reason that we know of.

The word *Shalomoh* is mentioned in the first verse but in no way means Solomon. When this pompous king is introduced in the third person (III, 6-11) he is described with such scorn and such a sense of ridicule that he becomes a comical figure. Not so for our canonical translators who, following their own interpretation, modified the original text so as to adapt it to their belief.

Another reason for King Solomon not being the author of this book is that he was not a cabalist; whereas here we are in the very heart of Qabala, even more so than in the two other great cabalistic writings: *Genesis* and the *Sepher Yetsira*.

It was through the authority of Rabbi Aqivah that *The Song of Songs* (as we must name it) was accepted as being one of the canonical scriptures.

Aqivah, born in 40, was executed in 135, having spent many years in prison as a supporter of Bar Kokhba's revolt. His intense political activity and his subsequent martyrdom are recorded as only one aspect of his outstanding personality. His interpretation of the Scriptures has again a twofold character. Finding the basis of the Oral Law in every letter, every peculiarity, and even in every supposed grammatical mistake of the Scriptures, he is credited with being the "father" both of

225

the Mishnah and of the Qabala, Rabbi Meir and Simeon-bar-
Yohai having been his disciples.

Aqivah was strongly opposed to those of his contemporaries,
such as Rabbi Ishmael, who declared that the Scriptures "speak
the language of men". In his mind, Abraham's Revelation and
the law of Moses were both blended in the Torah, where
nothing is form only, but everything is essence.

When, during that first century, many discussions arose as to
which books should be accepted as sacred and which did not
have that qualification, the canonicity of the Song of Songs was
hotly disputed.

In its popularized tradition, that book was attributed to
King Solomon. The glamour of its supposed author was, however, all but convincing as a proof of its having a sacred
character. The majority of the Rabbis declared that these very
profane love poems (as they were and still are read) had to be
eliminated. But Aqivah intervened with the powerful authority
that he alone had, in such words as to force the issue: "the
whole universe is not worth the day that book has been given
to Israel," he declared "because all the *Ketoubim* (Scriptures)
are holy, but the Song of Songs is the most holy".

With such an extraordinary statement Aqivah was asserting
with no ambiguity that those poems have an inner mysterious
meaning, unknown even to the Rabbis. Some of them, therefore, thought it advisable to "hide" that book, that is to label it,
not profane but secret. But Aqivah prevailed, the book was
declared canonical, and its meaning became guess-work
resulting in many strange interpretations.

It was thought that a holy book on love must necessarily deal
with the love of God interpreted allegorically. That opinion
came to be widely accepted by the Jewish and Christian
Exegesis. The Jews were taught that this text was a description
of Yahveh's love for his People, with references to Exodus. Its
reading therefore has become ritualistic on the eighth day of
Passover. But the Christians were taught that it was a song of
the love of Christ for his Church, or of his love for the Christian

souls, or even for the Virgin Mary. Others discovered in it a description of the love of the God-Sun for the Goddess-Moon; others a political allegory; others a dialogue between Isis and Osiris; others declared that it pictured the myth of Adonis. Those controversies were at times very violent.

In his History of Hebraic and Jewish literature, Mr. A. Lods mentions the case of Theodore of Mopsueste, condemned by the Council of Constantinople (553) for having seen in the Song the story of Solomon's wedding with an Egyptian girl, the case of Castellion who had fled from Geneva and the case of Louis of Léon who was thrown into the prisons of the Inquisition for the same reason.

The interpretation of the Churches is no different, even today, from what it has always been. For the sake of propriety the lovers are said to be a married couple, and their love a conjugal allegory of the love of God for Israel and of Israel for its God. All the Prophets, from Isaiah to Ezekiel, are quoted by the Synagogue to prove that point, whereas the Christian Churches have but to alter the names of God and Israel to prove that here is expressed the love of Christ for the Church and the Church for Christ. Some ecclesiastical authors believe that the text can also be a dialogue between the Soul and the Mystical Body of Christ. Saint John of the Cross, Saint Teresa of Avila, and others, are sometimes referred to as having expressed the real meaning of the Song.

However, it is difficult to imagine Yehovah addressing Israel, or Christ the Church, with such words as*: *O that you would kiss me with the kisses of your mouth . . . O fair among women . . . I compare you, my love, to a mare of Pharaoh's chariots . . . Your cheeks are comely with ornaments . . . Your neck with strings of jewels . . . Your eyes are doves behind your veil, your hair is like a flock of goats . . . Your lips are like a scarlet thread, and your mouth is lovely . . . Your cheeks are like halves of a pomegranate . . . Your neck is like the tower of David . . . Your navel is a rounded ball . . . Your two breasts are like two fawns* . . . and, likewise, it is difficult to imagine the Syna-

---

* We quote, here, as in the rest of this volume, the Revised Standard Version.

gogue or the Church saying of Yahweh or Christ: *his head is the finest gold . . . his cheeks are like beds of spices . . . his lips are lilies . . . his body is ivory work . . .* or saying to a deity: *O that you were like a brother to me . . . if I met you outside I would kiss you . . .* etc.

Because the Song is included in the Bible, the ecclesiastics thought it their duty to compare it with the mystical adventures of John of the Cross or Teresa of Avila. It is a well-known fact that those Saints ill-treated their bodies and strained them to the point of torture, whereas the Song has an essentially sensuous quality: *While the King was on his couch, my nard gave forth its fragrance . . . My beloved is to me a cluster of henna blossoms . . . our couch is green . . . I am a rose of Sharon, a lily of the valleys . . . with great delight his fruit was sweet to my taste . . .* All the exquisite spices, nard, saffron, calamus, cinnamon, myrrh, aloes, are brought in to excite the senses: *your lips distil nectar . . . the scent of your garments is like the scent of Lebanon . . .* and the young lovers, in their enjoyment call upon the whole of nature to partake in their fruition: *the flowers appear on the earth, the time of singing has come, and the voice of the turtledove is heard in our land. The fig tree puts forth its figs, and the vines are in blossom, they give forth fragrance.*

All is spring, all is young, fresh, gay, sunny, bright. By what strange distortions of the mind has "the dark night of the soul" ever been mentioned here, with no sign of reason? The non-clerical commentators have generally adopted a naturalistic matter of fact version: this is, they say, a simple poem describing the love of a beautiful dark girl and a fair boy. But this thesis does not solve the mystery of Aqivah's emphatic statement that of all the Holy Scriptures this one is the Holiest, or why the ancient Rabbis and the Fathers of the Church have been compelled to declare it canonical. In aggravation of its profane character, not once does it even hint at the existence of a God. Is it in spite of or because of that omission that it was so sacred in Aqivah's mind?

The ancient and extremely profound science of Qabala, has suffered different fates. Genesis is not known as its oldest treatise, and is mistranslated so as to say, more often that not, the opposite of what it means.* Another fundamental treatise of Qabala is the *Sepher Yetsira*, a textbook that has baffled the cabalists throughout the centuries, because it was written for those who already knew its secret code.

There are several other books of Qabala, unacknowledged as cabalistic, such as Ecclesiastes and Jonah, but the *chef-d'œuvre* is the Song of Songs, because by means of an astoundingly clever wording, it is true throughout all the levels of manifestation as they interblend and intertwine in our human minds. It is truly the song of the two young lively lovers, it is true allegorically, true symbolically, and true inasmuch as it expressed most vividly the science of Qabala. It is a book of joy and a book of learning, a book of delight and a book of Revelation. It is Knowledge as all Qabala is, but at its highest and deepest level.

In this volume our purpose is to introduce that Knowledge. We deem it our duty to state, before any other development, that the views of the modern Jewish authorities on Qabala are erroneous. Whilst constantly introducing it in the history of Jewish mysticism, they produce lengthy learned data on Jewish cabalists, never on Qabala itself, for the obvious reason that they do not know it. Qabala, originally, was neither Jewish nor mysticism: it declared itself as a tradition issued from Abraham, who was an ancient Chaldean belonging to a much older period than Moses', and it asserted that Abraham's Revelation was direct Knowledge, devoid of mysticism.

The two traditions, Abraham's and Moses', gradually diverged. The laws of Moses established the frame for Jewish survival by means of a codified way of life, customs, habits, and a distinct manner of thinking, vividly apparent in the Talmud. Abraham's Knowledge (the Qabala) declined because the cipher was lost. It sank to such a low pitch as to symbolize an obscure, occult, unintelligible blurb, to be scoffed at.

The responsibility for the loss rests foremost with those Rabbis who, knowing the code, hid it so artfully in the letters

---

* See our previous volume *The Cipher of Genesis* (Stuart & Watkins, London and Shambala, Berkeley, California).

of the Hebrew alphabet as to deceive the readers. This skill is mostly apparent in the Song of Songs, where the keywords are chosen so as to tell two or three different stories, almost consistent, except in a few passages openly admitted to be obscure. When all is read and deeply understood according to the cipher, it is not difficult to guess why the Rabbis such as Aqivah so carefully disguised their words: they had no other way of safeguarding both the Revelation that they had in trust and the safety of their own lives, against the traditional beliefs and uncompromising rigour of the Synagogue.

In order to guide our readers through the stupendous depths of the Song of Songs, we have inserted in this volume:

A chart of the Hebraic signs that are used as an alphabet; we designate them as *Autiot* because this word, meaning generally "signs", outspreads their specific function as constituents of an alphabet. Moreover, it is a well-known fact that the Hebraic script has no special signs for numbers, and for that purpose uses those of the alphabet. So we indicate in our chart the numbers corresponding to every sign.

A simplified explanation of the meaning of the signs, and of their interrelationship in terms of numbers, between units, tens and hundreds (1.10.100 and so on).

A spelling of the *Autiot* according to our judgement. (The spelling varies, depending on different schools; for instance Hay (5) is, by some, spelt Hay-Aleph, by others Hay-Yod, whereas we have good reasons for writing it without any adjuncts.) Our phonetic spelling is not always in accordance with the one that is most widely known (thus Bayt for Beth) because we have established it in conformity with the pronunciation in the Middle East. It is, however, impossible to differentiate, with our alphabet, Kaf of Qof, Samekh of Seen, Tayt of Tav, or to hint as to how Ayn (70) must be pronounced. (We must insist on the fact that our explanation of the cipher is reduced to a skeleton. Were we to develop the *Autiot* we would raise complexities in which the non-specialized readers would be lost. For instance, Aleph is spelt Aleph, Lammed, Phay:

Lammed is spelt Lammed, Mem, Dallet: Dallet is spelt Dallet, Lammed, Tav . . . and so on. . . . Every one of those signs is an equation which includes other equations, and their relationship reveals the process of the structured energy in its innumerable expressions.)

Our version of the Song, not as a translation of the canonical, but as a *Midrash*, that is, an exposition based upon its inner cabalistic meaning.)

Our commentaries verse by verse, including every time: the Hebraic text; a phonetic transcription; the text quoted from the Revised Standard Version of the Bible; a repetition of the verse according to our *Midrash*; and finally an explanation, more or less developed according to the necessity of the verse.

The Autiot

Letter	Name	Value	Letter	Name	Value	Letter	Name	Value
🌣	Aleph	1	𝆑	Yod	10	𝂃	Qof	100
𝆑	Bayt Vayt	2	𝆑	Kaf Khaf	20	𝆑	Raysh	200
𝆑	Ghimel	3	𝆑	Lammed	30	𝆑	Seen Sheen	300
𝆑	Dallet	4	𝆑	Mem	40	𝆑	Tav	400
𝆑	Hay	5	𝆑	Noun	50	𝆑	final Khaf	500
𝆑	Vav or Waw	6	𝆑	Sammekh	60	𝆑	final Mem	600
𝆑	Zayn	7	𝆑	Ayn	70	𝆑	final Noun	700
𝆑	Hhayt	8	𝆑	Pay Phay	80	𝆑	final Phay	800
𝆑	Tayt	9	𝆑	Tsadde	90	𝆑	final Tsadde	900

An Explanation

THE PRESENT writer, obliged to use our language in order to make himself understood, cannot offer the reader the truth of Genesis, but only images of that truth. Our language is of sensuous origin. Through it, we can only understand by means of imagery. But we shall do our best not to wander off into illusory beliefs and dreams of the supernatural.

Let us now concern ourselves with the individual Hebrew letter-numbers according to the code.*

The first nine letters are the archetypes of numbers from 1 to 9.

Aleph, no. 1, is the unthinkable life-death, abstract principle of all that is and all that is not.

Bayt† (or Vayt), no. 2, is the archetype of all "dwellings", of all containers: the physical support without which nothing is.

Ghimel, no. 3, is the organic movement of every Bayt animated by Aleph.

Dallet, no. 4, is the physical existence, as response to life, of all that, in nature, is organically active with Ghimel. Where the structure is inorganic, Dallet is its own resistance to destruction.

Hay, no. 5, is the archetype of universal life. When it is conferred upon Dallet, it allows it to play the game of existence, in partnership with the intermittent life-death process.

Vav (or Waw), no. 6, expresses the fertilizing agent, that which impregnates. It is the direct result of Hay upon Dallet.

Zayn, no. 7, is the achievement of every vital impregnation: this number opens the field of every possible possibility.

* See chart, p. 14.
† We consider this spelling more phonetically correct than the usually adopted Beth.

Hhayt, no. 8 is the sphere of storage of all undifferentiated energy, or unstructured substance. It expresses the most un-evolved state of energy, as opposed to its achieved freedom in Zayn.

Tayt, no. 9 as archetype of the primeval female energy, draws its life from Hhayt and builds it gradually into structures.

Such is the fundamental equation set and developed in Genesis.

The following nine letters, from Yod, no. 10 to Tsadde no. 90, describe the process of the nine archetypes in their factual, conditioned existence: their projections in manifestation are always multiples of 10.

The nine multiples of 100 express the exalted archetypes in their cosmic states.

The number 1000, is written with an enlarged Aleph (Aleph, in Hebrew, actually means a thousand), but is seldom used. It expresses a supreme power, a tremendous cosmic energy, all-pervading, timeless, unthinkable.

The study of those multiples by 10 and by 100 is therefore the study of the very archetypes in their various spheres of emanation. The student will find it useful to examine them, so to say, vertically: 1.10.100-2.20.200 . . . and so on.

The choice of Kaf (20) for 500, of Mem (40) for 600, and of Noun (50) for 700 in finals of schemata means that those numbers acquire such cosmic values when they unfold in human beings. Thus: Adam is 1.4.40 when immature, and achieves 1.4.600 when attaining his full maturity.

Here is a brief general view of the relationship between the archetypes and their multiples:

Aleph-Yod-Qof (1.10.100): Whereas Aleph (1) is the beat, or pulsation, life-death-life-death, Yod (10) is its projection in temporal continuity. So Yod (in Hebrew: the hand), is the opposite of Aleph, its partner playing against it the game with-out which nothing would be. The Qof (100) is the most diffi-cult symbol to understand. It includes Aleph exalted in its principle yet acting through its projection, against itself, and thereby being cosmically deathless. It is best seen in Qaheen (Cain) that mythical destroyer of illusions.

Bayt-Kaf-Raysh (2.20.200): Whereas Bayt (2), the archetype of all containers, has its roots in the cosmic resistance to life, Kaf (20)—in Hebrew, the hollow of the hand—is ready to receive all that comes and Raysh (200), the cosmic container of all existence, has its roots in the intense organic movement of the universe.

Ghimel-Lammed-Sheen (3.30.300): these three letter-numbers express a movement in progressive enlargement, from the uncontrolled functional action of Ghimel (3), through the controlled connecting agent Lammed (30), going as far as the universal Sheen (300), mythically considered to be the "spirit", or "breath" of God.

Dallet-Mem-Tav (4.40.400): the physical resistance of structures, Dallet (4) finds its purveyor in the maternal waters, Mem (40), where all life originates. Tav (400) is the exaltation of the entire cosmic existence in its utmost capacity to resist to life-death. The root Dallet-Mem (Dam) is "blood" in Hebrew and the root Mem-Tav (Met) is "death". Thus the two together express the complete cycle of existence.

Hay-Noun-Kaf in finals (5.50.500): the universal life, Hay (5) is condensed in individual existences as Noun (50) and is exalted cosmically as Kaf (500) in terminals.

Waw-Sammekh-Mem in finals (6.60.600): Waw (6) is the male agent of fertility, Sammekh (60) the female. Mem when in terminals (600) is the cosmic achievement of fruitfulness both in the intelligent or immaterial part of man and in the flesh. In Hebrew, Waw maintains its character grammatically as copulative or connecting agent.

Zayn-Ayn-Noun in finals (7.70.700): Zayn (7) as an opening towards all possible possibilities has its source and its vision in Ayn (70), which is the word for "eye" in Hebrew. It is exalted in Noun (700); this number expresses the very principle contended for in the interplay of energies throughout the universe: the principle of indetermination in which life itself is at stake. Here we find Cain again.

Hhayt-Pay-Phay in finals (8.80.800): in every sphere of the emanation, from the densest to the most rarefied essence, these numbers stand for the primordial substance, the unfathomed reserve of undifferentiated, unstructured energy.

Tayt-Tsadde-Tsadde in finals (9.90.900): these ideograms express a progression ascending from the simplest and most primitive cell (or female structural energy) up to the transfigured symbols of womanhood, social and mythical.

A spelling of the *Autiot*.

1	Aleph	Aleph-Lammed-Phay (1.30.80)
2	Bayt (Vayt)	Bayt-Yod-Tav (2.10.400)
3	Ghimel	Ghimel-Mem-Lammed (3.40.30)
4	Dallet	Dallet-Lammed-Tav (4.30.400)
5	Hay	Hay (5)
6	Waw (Vav)	Waw-Waw (6.6)
7	Zayn	Zayn-Yod-Noun (7.10.50)
8	Hhayt	Hhayt-Yod-Tav (8.10.400)
9	Tayt	Tayt-Yod-Tav (9.10.400)
10	Yod	Yod-Waw-Dallet (10.6.4)
20	Kaf (Khaf)	Kaf-Phay (20.80)
30	Lammed	Lammed-Mem-Dallet (30.40.4)
40	Mem	Mem-Mem (40.40)
50	Noun	Noun-Waw-Noun (50.6.50)
60	Sammekh	Sammekh-Mem-Khaf (60.40.20)
70	Ayn	Ayn-Yod-Noun (70.10.50)
80	Phay (Pay)	Phay-Hay (80.5)
90	Tsadde	Tsadde-Dallet-Yod (90.4.10)
100	Qof	Qof-Waw-Phay (100.6.80)
200	Raysh	Raysh-Yod-Sheen (200.10.300)
300	Sheen	Sheen-Yod-Noun (300.10.50)
400	Tav	Tav-Waw (400.6)

The Midrash of the Song of Songs

The so-called SONG OF SOLOMON

A Version by George Buchanan
from Carlo Suarès' French text

THE TITLE ACCORDING TO QABALA

The Residue of Residues OR Quintessence of Quintessences

I

1 Poet
The Residue of Residues is the witness of her Peace.

2 Psyche (thinking of Breath)
Let his fire set me aflame.

Breath
Two resistances call to me from you. For in Earth, my Fire makes nothing but wine.

3 Psyche
You are in your Name, generous giver. You cause the Immanence to well in the depths. Therefore you are loved by her who seeks your impregnation.

4 Breath
Let me be lodged within you. The knowledge of kings is tempting me but cannot contain me. Only in the joy of loving you can I find my depth.

5 Psyche
Breath, you take me from the daylight. Already I am not what I was. New life starts in my inmost being. Girls who live in quiet cities, see, uncertainty is my peace!

237

6 Blackness of the sun puts conflict into me. The sons of Earth despoiled in me what was lush. I didn't want my vine any more.

7 Woman
No question of my hiding from the world. Show me your place of work, your place of leisure. I want to be along with you in the open.

8 Breath
If you don't know where I am, most lovely woman, let time-lessness come alive for you: bring into duration two lives and two existences as one.

9 I see you are still under the spell of those with worldly prestige.

10 But I shall fertilize your duality. In you will be the whirling of opposites.

11 Which will transmute love into gold. But your silver desire will transmute that gold into love.

12 Psyche
I am not any more under the seeming eternity of the strong. My sharply awakened senses drive me into the universal Unknown.

13 Because you are in me I am the Holy Apostasy. Breath from the lower depths, over against Breath from on high.

14 From contact with my resistances you turn again into yourself in an endless resurrection to new life, which is my Knowledge.

15 Breath
How lovely you are, my friend, how lovely! This rising Spring in you speaks for Israel.

16 Psyche
What beauty, my loved one! We delight in our newness.

17 The place where we rest together cannot be destroyed.

II

1 Breath

I am in your body, depth of the upper Breath, Breath of the depth, double Emanation.

2 Lover (to woman)

And you are these two Breaths, in existence and life, among unshaped substance.

3 Woman

I see you as you appear to me. I was full of joy, inhabiting my body, and there you sprang to life from your tabernacle of glorified dust.

4 You carried me to an intoxication where consciousness must stop or lose itself. But your new life in me is a response to love.

5 Oh that I could be strong enough to take your seed into my body! And be living Breath in its living support!

6 His left hand conveys the sacred Name. His right hand is about me and makes me breathe it.

7 Girls of the city! I send you the Heavenly Company. Do not shut away the universal splendour inside your frozen institutions. Don't dispute it; it *is* the Emanation.

6 See, Breath rushes through Space towards me, violently breaks into my strength, rays out inside me.

9 And this radiation is a new birth, original, organic, developing in me.

10 Saying "Enter your own organic movement, then go into the world's, towards yourself".

11 For the sake of shared pleasure, my feminine sex opened the way to Breath. I have gone beyond myself and come to my Essence.

12 Now I have knowledge of universal impregnation. Constructive energy works in the two lives of nature. Breath is conceived in the flower buds, is welcomed by the songs of time.

13 Lover
Everything is made vibrant by Breath, even the fig tree in the dry sands. Get up, beautiful friend, move towards your selfhood.

14 Breath
I am reborn. Immanence rises from your depths, having passed through a cycle in primordial stuff. Developed forms conceal the living drive within them. Guard against the spell of their rhythm, since you are true perception, mysterious presence of uprightness, symbol of Israel. You voice my name.

15 Guide the new life which is growing in you. The young foxes ravage the flowering vines. But your vine, need you abandon it?

16 Psyche
Breath is mine. I am his. Let him stir and guide me. Two Breaths as one.

17 Before the day leads you to an irreversible event, be, my love, the indeterminate freshness of your universal home.

III

1 Person
I heard him, he came into me, but I am still looking for him. His breath and my body are united, yet I do not know where this union took place. His presence in me was radiance; so bright—how could I catch hold of it?

2 I set out to look for him among the items of my work. Contradictory, they turned me round and round upon myself, and I did not find him.

3 Their energies swirled in self-protection, closing in, pressing upon me as I went on asking: where is my love?

4 Psyche
They emptied me out. Then I found him who was being born, found him in the cell that was engendering me: a union of two who were because they were not yet.

5 Women
Daughters of the false styles of peace! I send the Heavenly
Hosts against you. Love which is not a source is only unsatisfied
desire.

6/11 Poet
At a certain distance from the false styles of peace I see another
false peace: of passiveness. What smoke rises from that desert?
King Solomon, whose name is pretended Peace, for whom the
quintessence is what perfumers make, burns day and night
those scented extracts, a pretended residue. He puts himself, as
it were, in a box, a stately conveyance. War-men to the number
of 60 (the number of the female sex), the bravest of Israel,
watch over his night fears, for he does not resist life with suppleness; rigidly he resists death. His passiveness holds Emanation
in check. When Breath enters into him, he will burst. The shell
concealing him depends on the stuff of female submission. They
are busy about his inertia. Pretended royalty is on his head.
Crowned by his mother on his wedding day, this Solomon, this
pseudo-king, is the female queen!

IV

1 Lover
How beautiful you are, my friend, how beautiful! Through the
veil of appearance your eyes are the fountain of Israel. You are
the vision where time and timelessness meet, to be prized as a
multitude that springs from eternity.

2 Poet
Such is the dominance of your femininity. The second or female
aspect of your energy I have seen represented by a pompous
and nervous actor wearing a crown, who lay on a scented cloud.
His hands are full of wealth but he carefully washes them.
Compare him to a flock of sheep, dead though not dead,
without understanding.

3 This second aspect of your femininity is dullness, like a sin, separating you from yourself, a flaw behind the smooth exterior.

4 You are different from that, supple and strong, for your two resistances fructify one another. They build a stronghold for Aleph, the defender of those that rest in Him, the All-Powerful.

5 In and through your two resistances the Breath of Life and the Breath of Existence are at the same time taken in and given out.

6 Breath
Before the dull day takes from me what is possible and makes it irreversible, I give life to your two aspects. One is your holy uncertainty, the other will go back to unshaped substance.

7 You, my dear one, are the beautiful transfigured sanctuary of my indetermination.

8 Come with me, come and contemplate our common origin. Your person is double and so is your lunar symbol. I bury myself in you and I come out from you: one act in two opposite directions.

9 Sister of Breath, your organic life redoubles my unity. You are able to build me and still be one with me.

10 Companion of Breath, my Fire in the Earth is only wine, but you breathe me out and this breathing surpasses the whole content of the skies.

11 Companion of Breath, blessedness of the perceived Incarnation, you sustain organic movement and are that movement itself. You are, from depth of your origin to depth of your presence now, an endless movement of contraries. You are the peace of that movement.

12 To look at what exists is to look at absolute Mystery. To look at you is to open oneself to the mysterious metabolism of Emanation, for your presence creates it.

13 You are the apple of the tree and the sensuous taste of it. You are the fragrance of fruit and of stimulating drugs.

14 In you are the fruits of the earth that go back into the elements. In you are the Principles of the waters animated by Breath: in you also is the intelligence which conceives those Principles.

15 The double movement of the waters rises in the wells and comes down from the hills.

16 Person
May the depth of depths free the depths of Indetermination! May my twofold organic resistance enter the organic life of Breath! And Breath live its own life!

V

1 Breath
I have gone into my bodily support. In response to your call I have gathered in you what is mine. I have gathered my exchange money—30 pieces—which you kept inside my name. I have used up what wildness still remained in you. I have founded the unity of my work. The beginning and the end are one. You who hear me, be happy!

2 Person
Though I am asleep in Duration I perceive my heartbeats and the world's heartbeats in identical discontinuity: that of living and dying Breath. He lives and dies: lives dying, dies living. He says: "Open yourself for me, from you I am being born".

3 He says: "I am stripped of the symbols that disguised me. I have no appearance, for any form would exclude others. But your form is purified by the emptiness which begat me. Therefore you can evolve in duration and yet be clean."

4 Woman
My love makes him resilient. As soon as he appears in the richness of my body he disappears in the empty places of my mind.

A contradictory movement! He goes inversely to his coming, yet the cave of my being is quickened by his vibration.

5 I was set going by his Breath, so that I should give birth to something without blemish. But his seed is impaired by his being fixated on me: everything I touch is of the past.

6 I am open to my love, Breath has gone back to its origin, has disappeared. Through hearing his Word I found that origin. There, among the creative Forces, I invoked our Union, and two lives spoke to me.

7 The Powers-that-be who in buying Breath build their cities send their agents against me: strip me of my latest form. See me now naked and free. The veil of my appearance is lifted, showing the visible One to be twofold.

8 Girls of the misleading peace of cities, if you meet him I love, tell him that what I built in myself has disappeared. My love for him is no more than the rhythm of a holy dance.

9 *Girls of the cities* (*singing*)
Mah-Dodekh Midod,
Ha-Yafah, Benashim,
Mah-Dodekh Midod,
Schekakhq, Hishbaatanou.
To this incantation she dances rhythm 3.2.3.3-3.2.3.5. (She dances the interrogation of the girls, as follows).
Who is your lover among lovers, most beautiful among us?
Who is your lover among lovers, that you so cry out to us?

10 *Feminine Sex*
From the pinnacle of my depths, I see my Love. Edom, son of Earth, of royal birth. He is the cell united with mine, to elaborate earthly strength. He and I are two bodies in one.

11 *Phylum*
The Principle of Breath, Fire in Matter, is Adam, of perfect red and pure gold. But as soon as he penetrates the formative

energy he is Edom. Woman, his emanation shoots spirally in the shadows of the womb.

12 Poet

The brilliance of his eyes is as wet mud which he washes in milk so as to appear purified. He makes his home among the shape-less human mass.

13 He revives his life with ointment and drugs, as one might give new scent to the petals of withering flowers which are losing their smell.

14 Woman

With a turn of his hand he changes love to gold and the Sepher to Sapphirs, for in him are two Breaths. What would become of the upper Breath if the Tabernacle of Edom had not the lower Breath to resist it?

15 Poet

I see him, a marble idol on a golden plinth.

In truth his legs go in opposite directions, one from back to front, the other from front to back, he pivots continually on himself.

Woman

If I did not see him as an idol I would not see him: if he did not modify Breath I would not hear him. But he speaks and arouses my desire. Such is my love, such is my Shepherd, daughters of the cities.

VI

1 Poet

Where has he gone, beautiful woman? You called him, visited him, and you have seen only an idol that turned love to gold. Answer my cry! What has become of Breath?

2 Psyche

He has gone down into himself in the organic sphere. There he nourishes the human herd with pure sap and takes hold of two

Breaths that exist and live together. True, I dreamed an idol, but beyond that idol I recognized him.

3 *Woman*

I have found unity again: the intemporal and the temporal are two Breaths in one.

4 *Lover*

My dear one, you are as beautiful as the solution of a difficulty. Your life as lived creates Breath, like peace descending; and Breath creates you, an intense proliferation.

5 Let me sink in your stream of energy. You offer all that's possible, all the possibilities opened by your two resistances to life: your biological existence and your Breath breathing with mine.

6 *Breath*

The female that underlies your femininity is like a flock of sheep, a biological magma, unfertilized by me. Among the sheep, some will go back into primal substance, others into the evolutionary flow, being innocent and pure.

7 But you, pure like them, fertilized by me, safeguard indeterminancy, strong because you are the residue of successive forms.

8 *Lover*

There are 60 queens: the female sex figure; there are 80 concubines: the figure of undeveloped substance.

9 But you are unique, in you is the ever virginal beginning. To me you are the ideal of a pure woman.

10 *Poet*

What is this dark unearthly light? It is energy going down into the female and rising in the male. Between them is uncertainty.

11 *Psyche*

I am this uncertainty. Who am I in whom the two poles of life meet? I have sunk into my biological sphere to see if the Principle which bore me has endowed me with its rising sap.

In the Father's vineyard I have seen Breath put under the ground, there meeting with its universal Tabernacle, its bounding through the whole Creation, its reburial, its setting-out again, and I knew that that very pulsation was the life of all nature.

12 In my dream I did not know it. I was still under the spell of those with worldly prestige.

VII

1 Poet

Return, return, but to lived reality, you whose name chimes with Peace. Return, return . . . I have made you speak and your voice came now from one sphere, now another. It is time you came to earth, so that we could see you, and that Breath restores me to my exact self. Why did I see you like a hesitation between two Breaths? I want to sing my love:

2 Noble girl: how beautiful has been your evolution, as your looks show! The curves of your hips seem to torment themselves as if they wished to be independent even of what made them.

3 You rule over the borderline of the lunar crescent in its shrinking phase, you rule over the lunar energy which fills the bellies of women: you control births according to your wisdom. Your anger is that of Sarah face to face with the woman-slave Agar.

4 Your divinity is in you. It forms two free Emanations, from four Elements.

5 Your head is Fire. The Air, through your neck, nourishes the temporal part in your body made of Earth and Water. The length of your neck is a measure of Time. Your eyes flash with the essence of intemporal Fire. They give benediction. Your bright thought waits for the iron bars to open behind which are the rabbis. Your anger is as a great whiteness facing the spilt blood.

6 Earthly fire is active in your fertile body. The fire of your thought transmutes the blood in a way unknown to kings.

7 The blending of Breath and its vessel, how actively organic it is; blending in you, girl of delight!

8 You grow straight upwards as if your blood were transfigured, omnipotent as if the Fire of Knowledge burned in you.

9 I said to myself: "Rise to this high condition, take this two-fold fullness, that it may become Omnipotence for you, where all branches of knowledge meet. Let the one of the beginning be as the many of the End."

10 My love, your desire is wine to me ... *Woman* ... wine that goes towards the one I love. Its utter rightness makes words come from our sleeping lips.

11 I am his. But his desire weighs upon me.

12 It depends on you, my love, whether our union can reconcile the contraries.

13 Come with me, let us go and see if the spring is yet here. I shall reveal the names of things as they are renewed, and you will learn who you are.

14 The flowers of earthly love give off their scent. Everything exquisite is at our doors. But my love for you is not in these aspects of Duration.

VIII

1 *Woman*

Who will teach you to be for me like a newborn brother not yet depraved by time? I would quench your thirst in the realms of Space and, moreover, do so as a free woman.

2 I would unite your incessant beginnings beyond time with my inheritance through the generations. Living together, we would mingle these two streams ...

3 But his left hand brings me the Sacred Name while his right hand embraces me: one hand does not know what the other hand is doing.

4 By the living Seven, girls of false peace, why in your cities, in your fortified cities, do you well up love in a non-stop state of desire?

5 Voice
Who is this woman who stands up in a place where there are no cities, in a desert quite different from the desert where Solomon lies in his palanquin? She is by herself, sustained by her only love.
Woman
Breath, through my love I woke you under the tree where pure juice rises, where your mother Earth kept you in holy sleep till I came.

6 Breath
Let me be as a seal in the centre of your being, a seal on the arm of your doing. Love is powerful as death, absolute as the grave, excluding what is unreal. Its heat is that of the Fire, the Fire of the daughter of Yah.

7 Lover
This love cannot be extinguished by water, even rivers of water could not put it out. A man who tried to get it with heaps of money would be met with contempt.

8 Woman
Our sister, a woman-child not yet awakened by Breath, what will we do about her when she receives Breath?

9 Breath
If she is only organic matter, she will be shut away in her desires. If she is responsive, circumstances will help me to shape her.

10 Woman

I am organic matter, but I am all powerful and give answer to Breath. In this twofold existence, as far as concerns Breath, lies the origin of his Peace.

11 Among his other riches Solomon had a vine. He had its fruit pressed by country workers. Each gave a thousand coins for his share of the grapes.

12 My vine is organic Breath in my organic life. Yours, Solomon, the thousand coins, and two hundred coins for those who keep the fruit.

13 Breath

Woman symbol of all life and you who listened to my call, hear me . . .

14 Person

He is gone! . . . Go out, my love! Be like the Armies of Breath who transcend the Heavenly Hosts.

Commentaries

THE TITLE: שִׁיר הַשִּׁירִים

Phonetically, according to the canonistical tradition: *Sheer Ha-Sheereem.*
According to the Revised Standard Version: *The Song of Solomon.*
According to Qabala: *Shiar Ha-Shiareem.*

In Hebrew, song is *Sheer* or *Sheerah.* The word *Sheer* (plural *Sheereem*) means poem, song, and also residue, remainder, in which case it is pronounced *Shiar* and *Shiareem.* Both interpretations are correct, but the second is known only to Qabala. The deepest meaning of the title is therefore:

THE RESIDUE OF RESIDUES

OR

QUINTESSENCE OF QUINTESSENCES

We will explain it while commenting upon the first verse.

251

שִׁיר הַשִּׁירִים אֲשֶׁר לִשְׁלֹמֹה׃

PHONETICALLY: *Sheer* (or *Shiar*) *Ha-Sheereem* (or *Ha-Shiareem*)
Esher Leshalomoh.
RSV: *The Song of Songs that is Solomon's.*
QABALA: Poet: *The Residue of Residues is the witness of her Peace.*
Or (the) Residue of Residues confirms (or praises)
(for or because of) her Peace.

Why all those Sheens? One for Schiar, one for Shiareem, one
for Esher, one for Shalomoh? Why is the title Shiar Ha-
Shiareem repeated in the verse? In what way is it the witness of
her Peace? And who is she, whose Peace is it?

As the tree is in the seed, so is the meaning of the Song of
Songs included in its title. The first verse is a further clue to the
whole text, when the significance of its signs (*Autiot*), especially
of the signs Sheen and Raysh, is understood.

Sheen (300) is a well-known equivalent for *Rouahh Elohim*
(translated Breath of God) whose letter-numbers add up to 300.
The letter Raysh, 21st in the alphabet, is spelt Raysh-Yod-
Sheen, and thus introduces Sheen before its actual appearance,
22nd in line of order. This, according to a secret cabalistic
tradition, means that the cosmic Breath of Life (300) is self-
generated by the existent universe, or physical container (200)
of the One, the all-pervading Life.

In the word *Sheer* the alphabetical order of the letters Sheen
and Raysh is reversed. The study of the alphabet from Aleph to
Tav, and again from Tav to Aleph, is a very serious matter:
the sequence beginning with Aleph is a metaphysical study of
Timeless Energy as it flows towards its temporal Sanctuary,
Tav; and the sequence beginning with Tav illustrates the same
flow as it bounces from and is generated by that Sanctuary.
This vision of a double flow (or Breath) as one (or of a one
Breath in two simultaneous and equally active energies) is

fundamental in Qabala. It precludes all priority attributed either to the finite or to the infinite. Our minds, kneaded into Time and Space, will never know how either one or the other exists at all. No theology will solve that Mystery, but we can commune with it by perceiving directly the One twofold Breath in its innumerable structures.

In a first mental perception, we can read the three last letters of the alphabet in their order: Raysh, Sheen, Tav and understand how Sheen is engendered through a long process starting from Aleph. Then we can begin by Tav and, reading Tav-Sheen-Raysh, see how Sheen is born from Tav.

We can thus understand this fundamental statement of Qabala: The Beginning is in the End, the End is in the Beginning. The significance of the schema Sheer (or Shiar) now appears: Sheer is Sheen-Yod-Raysh, and Raysh is Raysh-Yod-Sheen:

Sheer: Sheen-Yod-Raysh: 300.10.200.
Raysh: Raysh-Yod-Sheen: 200.10.300

Sheer, with Raysh written in full (300.10.200.10.300) shows one Breath (300) in existence (10) acting upon the Cosmic Container (200) and, from this 200, an existence (10) giving birth to a second Breath (300). This second Breath is none other that the first, just as 300 is none other that 300.

This One in Two (or these Two in One) has (or have) appearance and speech with the two protagonists of the Song. "He" symbolizes the Breath from Aleph, and "She" the Breath from Tav. "They" meet (or "It" meets Itself: "It", the Unnamable) and with great joy they discover each other's beauty in an ecstasy that rapidly vanishes. Their meeting was but a fleeting recurrent instant, never to be captured in duration. The Song teaches us that the two are in us, their dialogue a soliloquy of the mind eternally evading certainty.

Such is the very holy theme of the Song of Songs, as it is epitomized by its first Schema: *Sheer*. The whole text is perfect from beginning to end. Every one of its *Autiot* is relevant and meaningful, every one of its verses is an opening on unfathomable beauty and love. Its reading is a perpetual discovery, a constant deepening of Abraham's Revelation. We will limit elucidations to such points as will be apt to guide our readers towards the Sacred Fount.

The reading is truly beneficent when the passage from the essential meaning of the *Autiot* to their factual meaning is understood and experienced.

Thus, after having cast a light on the root *Sheer*, we can and must project the meaning of that abstract quality into the world of existing forms and actions. *Sheer*, when lived, appears as a response (or Breath: Sheen) to the Universe (Raysh). It is a canticle, a hymn of supreme delight, a Revelation of the human and universal Reality, a double emanation, a double creative tide: in very truth, a Breath.

The plural *Sheereem* is not rhetorical. It asserts that these poems are the core, the essence of the achievement of all the love poems, of all the love songs that have or will ever be written or sung. Is that the reason why they are anonymous? Has Aqivah worded the title? Had he, himself, with his exceptional insight, written out, assembled and perfected a collection of ancient poems that had been transmitted orally? The fact remains that we do not know their author or authors, and that, of all people, it could not have been the inflated King Solomon.

Following *Sheer Ha-Sheereem* is the extraordinary schema *Esher*. It had appeared (Ex. III, 14) when Life-Death (Aleph) and Existence (Yod)—the two partners "against" each other whose "game" is all that was, is and will be—revealed themselves to Moses as being both alive. That Revelation was condensed in the equations *Ehieh-Esher-Ehieh* (Aleph-Hay-Yod-Hay-Aleph-Sheen-Raysh Aleph-Hay-Yod-Hay). Hay being 5, the sign for Life, the equations 1.5.10.5-1.300.200-1.5.10.5 means:

(a) The Energy that is beyond all thought (Aleph) is alive, and the Energy in Existence (Yod) is alive;

254

(*b*) Esher explains how it is so: both are alive through the Breath (Sheen) from Aleph, as it operates in its Cosmic "Dwelling" (Raysh);

(*c*) (that is why) the Energy that is beyond all thought is alive and the Energy in Existence is alive.

Not only is that Revelation very different from the famous *I am who I am* (or, according to other versions: *I will be that I will be*), it contradicts it by stating that Aleph and Yod are alive because of and through their impact.

Esher, coming after *Sheer Ha-Sheereen*, develops its explanation with reference to the two Sheens and the three Yods included in those schemata. Yod written three times is a very alive partner to the so far unmentioned Aleph. *Esher* introduces it and shows its action upon Raysh, thus explaining how Yod came to life, and completing the picture. But we are not yet told by what process the two lives, of Yod and Aleph, have generated, and this is revealed in the last schema of the verse: *Leshalomoh* (30.300.30.40.5), where we see two organic animations (30 and 40: one for Aleph one for Yod) encompassing a Sheen that has recovered its unity. Their joint action in the biosphere (Mem) is alive with Hay.

We can now transpose *Leshalomoh* into the idiomatic "for her Peace" and live that Peace in the feminine (or container) quality of our being: in our psyche, our mind, our body. We can indefinitely meditate upon the splendour of this first verse, in its completeness. We can feel the vibrations of that hymn of joy and love, and open ourselves to the inner cabalistic meaning of *Sheer Ha-Sheereen*: *Shiar Ha-Shiareem*: the Residue of Residues.

The word Residue, in alchemy, was a substitute for Quintessence. It specified what was thought to be a last substratum apart from the four elements, latent in all things, a refined extract of the purest and most essential part of any substance. In logic, the method of Residues consists in the study of any phenomenon by way of eliminating successively the effects from known causes, so as to reduce it to the essential.

It will be seen in our following pages that both meanings are
perfectly adapted to those poems, whose ultimate title, is
therefore *The Residue of Residues.*

I

2   יִשָּׁקֵנִי מִנְּשִׁיקוֹת פִּיהוּ כִּי־טוֹבִים דֹּדֶיךָ מִיָּיִן׃

PHONETICALLY: *Yishoqani Minshiqot Peehou Ki-Toveem Dodeykha
Myayeen.*

RSV: *O that you would kiss me with the kisses of your mouth! For your
love is better than wine.*

QABALA: Psyche (thinking of Breath): *Let His Fire set me aflame.*
         Breath: *Two Resistances call to me from you. For in Earth
         my Fire makes nothing but wine.*
         Or: (She): Let him inflame me with the flames he
         produces. (He): Your nipples are better than wine.

In the first part of this verse the Psyche invokes an exalted
Power that she does not see; in the second part the answer
comes with the explanation of why it is given: "He" sees "Her"
and is attracted by her inherent quality.

Yishoqani: the root *Nishaq* means to be kindled, set afire. It is
described by its *Autiot:* Noun-Sheen-Qof (50.300.100). The
canonical "kiss me" is but a very weak metaphor of its intensity.
The schema *Yishoqani* (10.300.100.50.10) is an appeal to the
organic Sheen of the cosmic Aleph, Qôf. This appeal is
subsequent to the episode of the woman's awakening in the
Garden of Eden by the serpent *Nahhash* bearer of the Earthly
Sheen. When questioned, she answered: *Ha-Nahhash-Hashiani:*
he "Sheened" her, so to speak, with his Sheen born of the
Earth, and awakened her sensorial faculties. Now, in the Song
the schema *Yishoqani* shows that the called-for Sheen-Qof is
factually alive with Noun and that it is inserted between two
Yods, two existences.

COMMENTARIES

In *Minshiqot* we see the preceding schema projected upon Tav. The three last letters, Qof-Waw-Tav illustrate the flow of cosmic Energy (Qof) as it fertilizes (Waw) its Container (Tav), after having penetrated all the layers of its structures.

The action of Tav is the next schema *Peehou*. Idiomatically it means "his mouth", but according to *Sepher Yetsira* the human mouth is made and shaped by Tav. So *Peehou* is the result of the preceding verse. *Peehou* begins with Pay (or Phay: 80) that represents the undifferentiated Energy. The following Yod-Hay-Waw says that this 80 is alive and fertile; *Ki-* (because) *Toveem Dodeykha Myayeen.*

Toveem is the plural of *Tov.* We have seen this word in Genesis* repeatedly translated as "good", whereas it expresses the vibrations of physical supports set in motion by the Breath. *Dodeykha* means "your nipples" but we translate it "your two resistances": two Dallet. In *Myayeen* (wine) are two Yods, as in *Yishoqani.* We know that Yod-Yod means "God" in the canonical tradition, and we must keep in mind the essential leitmotiv of the Song: the inner quest for the mythical divine Incarnation of Breath as Fire (*Esh*: Aleph-Sheen). When in earth, it is only reborn as wine (wine, fire, blood belong to the same category of symbols). Wine, spelt Yod-Yod-Noun (10.10.700) projects Yod-Yod in the cosmic indetermination (700) (Final Noun) of a mind deeply asleep, as is shown in Noah's allegory. The earth cannot structurize Aleph's Fire: it drinks it, as it drinks Abel's blood; or it reduces it to wine; or it acts as a sieve and it becomes "hell's fire", in a mythical "below". In a word: it cannot "resist" Yod-Yod.

But the woman's nipples are two "resistances", two responses to Yod-Yod: they come alive with her sexual awakening and with her second awakening through motherhood.

In the Song, two Dallets, two Sheens, two Tayts, two Samekhs, two Yods will often describe the inner process of the double folded Single Energy.

* *The Cipher of Genesis.*

257

I

3

לְרֵ֙יחַ֙ שְׁמָנֶ֨יךָ טוֹבִ֔ים שֶׁ֖מֶן תּוּרַ֣ק שְׁמֶ֑ךָ עַל־כֵּ֖ן
עֲלָמ֥וֹת אֲהֵב֖וּךָ׃

PHONETICALLY: *Le-Rayhha Shemenekha Toveem Shemen-Tooraq Shemaykha Aal-Ken Aalamot Ehevokha.*

RSV: *Your anointing oils are fragrant, your name is oil poured out; therefore the maidens love you.*

QABALA: *You are in your Name, generous giver. You cause the Immanence to well up in the depths. Therefore you are loved by her who seeks your impregnation.*

In the preceding verse, "He" was considered apart from the concrete, and had no name. Now "She" names "Him", in compliance with the ontological tradition where every new step in the evolution of human mind is consecrated by womanhood.

This naming is a complex matter and a hopeless endeavour unless one delves deeply into the Sacred Language, where, unlike all known idioms, *the word is the thing, and the thing contains its own name.*

Breath, in English, is only a symbol for the Timeless Energy that has neither shape nor substance. How can we "name" It unless we "see" It, and how can we "see" It if It has no perceptible substance? But if we do not find Its name, we do not know It, and the Song will only be a poetical fiction. This third verse is crucial. It compels us to learn instantaneously the sacred way of thinking, depending on the sacred language.

The entire process of learning, understanding, discovering, opening and entering, is condensed in three equations, the first three schemata of this verse; idiomatically *Le-Rayhha* means "because the perfume"; *Shemenekha*: (of) "your fats"; *Toveem*: "are good". We have already seen this last schema in the preceding verse.

Le-Rayhha (Lamed-Raysh Yod Hhayt: 30-200.10.8) is an organic factual process (30) active in the universe (200) whose

258

existence (10) generates the archetype (8) of undifferentiated energy. In other words, it is the disintegration of organic substance. For instance, an essence of flowers disappears into nothingness when it has exhausted all its perfume.

In the Jewish idiom, *Rayhha* is only an equivalent for fragrance, scent or perfume: words, words, without any inner meaning. But when we read, with full knowledge of the cipher, *Le-Rayhha* addressed to Breath, we understand the inner process of perfumes, and, analogically, we enter into the secret relationship of Breath and Substance. We then discover a fount of endless meditations that can carry us to the greatest depths.

Shemenekha (Sheen Mem Noun Yod Khaf: 300.40.50.10.500) is an example of the use of words with different meanings. *Shemen* is "fat", "richness of substance" (as in the expression "the fat of the land") and includes *Shem* (name). This schema declares that *the name is in the substance*. But how can we perceive the substance of Breath, evanescent as a fragrance? The analysis of *Shemenekha* shows the Breath (300) in the biosphere (40) alive and existent (50.10) and projected in the cosmic life (500). Breath, after having dived into the concrete, has disappeared in the unseen abstract Life.

The answer is in the third schema: *Toveem*. (Tayt Waw Vayt Yod Mem: 9.6.2.10.600). Tayt is the cell, the origin of any living process, Waw is copulative, Vayt is a physical support, Yod is an appearance, final Mem is cosmically copulative. So *Toveem* is the cosmic response of the living cell to the action of Breath. In other words: "I, Psyche, discover your name-substance through your action".

This is corroborated by the following schemata: (therefore) *Shemen Tooraq Shemaykha*: (therefore) the name-substance of *Tooraq* is your name.

The key-word *Tooraq* (Tav Waw Raysh Qof: 400.6.200.100) is the response of Tav to Qof. It concludes the mental process that began when "She", knowing herself to be generated by Tav invoked Qof. It is indeed a Revelation: Qof is discovered in Tav's response to it. The Psyche understands that the "naming" of its own substance (the knowledge of its structure) is the very naming of Breath! The Breath from below and the Breath from above are One.

The reader can now decipher the last schemata and fully understand this verse according to our *Midrash*.

I

4   מָשְׁכֵנִי אַחֲרֶיךָ נָּרוּצָה הֶבִיאַנִי הַמֶּלֶךְ חֲדָרָיו

נָגִילָה וְנִשְׂמְחָה בָּךְ נַזְכִּירָה דֹדֶיךָ מִיַּיִן מֵישָׁרִים אֲהֵבוּךָ׃

PHONETICALLY: *Mashkani Ahharaykha Narootsah Havyani Hamelekh Hhedarav Naghelah Venishmayhhah Bakh Nazkirah Dodeykha Myayeen Meyshareem Ahebokha.*

RSV: *Draw me after you, let us make haste. The King has brought me into his chambers. We will exult and rejoice in you; we will extol your love more than wine, rightly do they love you.*

QABALA: Breath: *Let me be lodged within you. The knowledge of kings is tempting me but cannot contain me. Only in the joy of loving you can I find my depth.*

Or: ("He"): Introduce me into the process of your structure; the king has invited me to study in his religious school; but we praise your nipples more than wine, and more than the austere people who love you.

"She" has named "Him". His name was hidden in the structure of her own substance. Now, she is aware of that structure: it is fashioned by the One Energy, flowing from Aleph (or Qof) to Tav and from Tav to Aleph. "He", being now named, has become a living entity, and the poem will unfold a dialogue between two symbols, through which the reader will be in touch with the factual cosmic life.

In his answer, "He" asks her to receive him in that structure that she has seen as being herself: the three first schemata are:

Mashkani (Mem Sheen Kaf Noun Yod: 40.300.20.50.10.): (in your) biological process (40) (emitting) the Breath (300) (through your) body (20) alive in existence (50.10) *Ahharaykha* (Aleph Hhayt Raysh Yod Khaf: 1.8.200.10.500) (allow the) Aleph (to act upon) the undifferentiated energy (8) (in the) universe (200) (of) appearances (10) (which is) cosmically alive (500). *Narootsah* (Noun Raysh Waw Tsadde Hay: 50.200.6.90.5) (So that) your conditioned life (50) (in relation with) the universe (200) (be) connected (6) (with) the creating of structures (90) alive (5).

The letter Tsadde, seen in *Narootsah*, always refers to the formation of structures. It appears in *Atsilot*, the cabalistic Sphere of Formation; in *Yetsira*: the book of structures, etc. . . .

The rest of this verse needs no further explanations. It is said by "Him", not by "Her" as the canonical versions assert. The *Hheder* where the King invites him is, idiomatically, a religious school.

I

5 שְׁחוֹרָה אֲנִי וְנָאוָה בְּנוֹת יְרוּשָׁלָ͏ִם כְּאָהֳלֵי קֵדָר
כִּירִיעוֹת שְׁלֹמֹה׃

PHONETICALLY: *Shehhorah Ani Ve-Nawah Benot Yaro-Shalom Ke-Aheley Qedar Ki-Riyot Sholomoh.*

RSV: *I am very dark, but comely, O daughters of Jerusalem, like the tents of Kedar, like the curtains of Solomon.*

QABALA: Psyche: *Breath, you take me from the daylight. Already I am not what I was. New life starts in my inmost being. Girls who live in quiet cities! See: uncertainty is my peace!*

Or: "She": The Sheen has carried me into the undifferentiated Energy. A new life is born in me. Daughters of those who dwell in peace! I dwell in *Elohi*, and my peace is Uncertainty.

The first schema *Shehhorah* (Sheen Hhayt Waw Raysh Hay 300.8.6.200.5) shows the Breath (300) blowing upon the undifferentiated Energy (8). This energy thus becomes copulative (6) in relationship with the Universe (200), and gives it life (5).

This flow of Energy operates in opposite direction to the flow from Aleph, through *Elohim*, mentioned in Genesis, I, 3 (the appearance of light). Light, *Awr*, (Aleph Waw Raysh)* is the direct conjunction of Aleph and Raysh. *Shehhorah* is its antithesis. It expresses the Breath (Sheen) born of the root *Shahh* ("to sink, bow down") and of *Shahhor* (blackness). This qualifies adequately the undifferentiated energy.

The second schema *Ani* (Aleph Noun Yod), idiomatically means "I, me, myself". It shows an entity, Noun, living between the two contrasting energies that act "against" one another: the timeless Aleph and the temporal Yod. The ego is both their battle and their battlefield. When Yod is the stronger, Aleph is silenced, and definitely so, in cases of extreme self assertion. When Aleph's presence is deeply felt, Breath carries the individual beyond the ego.

The third schema *Ve-Nawah* (Waw Noun Aleph Waw Hay: 6.50.16.5) means far more than the idiomatic "and nice, pretty, comely". It shows a conversion of the ego, with Aleph settled in the core of the individual. Yod has disappeared and the copulative 6 appears twice: once for the existential life, 50, corresponding to Yod, and once for life as archetype, 5, corresponding to Aleph.

In résumé, *Shehhorah Ani Ve-Nawah* means "the Sheen has stirred in me a life that I had smothered in darkness; now my inner structure is modified".

"She" now addresses *Benot Yaro-Shalom*: the girls who "see" the peace. *Yaroshalom* in one word, and with inappropriate signs for vowels, has always been translated Jerusalem, in spite of the fact that its spelling lacks the Yod of *Yeroshalaïm*, the real name of that city.

* See *The Cipher of Genesis.*

One of the essential Keys to the Song is the play of words: Yaro-Shalom (the peace that is visualized), purposely meant to be mistaken for Jerusalem, and *Shalomoh* meaning at times "her peace" and at times Solomon.

In this verse, I, 5, "She" gives a first glimpse of what "her" peace is as opposed to the general meaning of that word. She says to the girls (following her thought): (I am) *Ke-Aheley Qedar*, idiomatically: as (the) tabernacle (of) the action of being dark.

In *Ke-Aheley* (Kaf Aleph Hay Lammed Yod) we see Aleph alive and active. In *Qedar* (Qof Dallet Raysh) we see Qof (the cosmic Aleph) acting upon "her" innermost resistance, Dallet, with an opening upon the Universe, Raysh. (Dallet) (4) is the archetype of Tav (400).

We are dealing here with a subtle and complex thought expressed with mathematical precision. Every sign adds its meaning to the whole, the meaning of which is included in every part, at a depth that cannot be fathomed. When looking carefully at the schema *Aheley*, we see that it is a permutation of *Elohi* (the Energy that is worshipped under the name "God")

> Aheley: Aleph.Hay.Lammed.Yod.
> Elohi: Aleph.Lammed.Hay.Yod.

thus stating that there is no substantial difference between the two.

The verse ends with the statement: (and I am as) *Ki-Riyot Sholomoh*. Here, *Sholomoh* is Solomon. His *Riyot* to which "She" compares herself have nothing in common with the curtains of the canonical version (curtain is *Rilon*). This misinterpretation is an example of the way the Scriptures have been distorted: when the translators could not find any idiomatic meaning to a word, they resorted to approximations, which were not always convincing.

The root of *Riyot* (Raysh Yod Ayn Waw Tav: 200.10.70.6.400) is *Raa*, (Raysh Ayn: 200.70). We have explained this word at length when dealing with the "Tree of good and evil" of the Garden of Eden.* "Good" stands for *Tov* (repetition of prototypes) and "Evil" for *Raa* (destruction of obsolete structures) Ayn (70) being the archetype of all possibilities, i.e. uncertainty.

By comparing herself to Solomon's *Riyot*, "She" challenges that king's rigid structures, with her sense of freedom in uncertainty.

I

6

אַל־תִּרְאֻנִי שֶׁאֲנִי שְׁחַרְחֹרֶת שֶׁשְּׁזָפַתְנִי הַשָּׁמֶשׁ בְּנֵי אִמִּי נִחֲרוּ־בִי שָׂמֻנִי נֹטֵרָה אֶת־הַכְּרָמִים כַּרְמִי שֶׁלִּי לֹא נָטָרְתִּי׃

PHONETICALLY: *Al-Tirooni She'ani Sh'hharhhoret Sh'shzafatni Ha'shamesh Bni Imi Nihherou Bi Shamooni Noterah et Hakiramim Karmi Sheli La Natarti.*

RSV: *Do not gaze at me because I am swarthy, because the sun has scorched me, they made me keeper of the vineyards: but, my own vineyard I have not kept!*

QABALA: Psyche: *Blackness of the sun puts conflict into me. The sons of Earth despoiled in me what was lush. I didn't want my vine any more.*

The first schema *Al* does not necessarily mean "Do not". We are free to read it *El*. In this text, as in all the ancient scriptures, the vowel signs have been added at later periods according to their canonical interpretation. Even the separation of the letters into words is arbitrary. Originally all the letters followed each other without any interval: they were meant to be read and understood one by one, and their interrelationship had to be discovered and recreated by the cabalists.

Let us read the first schema, Aleph-Lamed, *El* instead of *Al*. It can mean "to, towards, at, near", or "God", "deity,

* See *The Cipher of Genesis.*

264

COMMENTARIES

strength, power", and let us link it with the following letter,
Tav, separated from *Tirooni*. The sequence Aleph, Lammed,
Tav is the essential equation and theme of the Song. Its numbers,
1.30.400, show an organic action set in motion by Aleph,
towards Tav. We can compare *Rouni* and the following
schema *Sh'ani* thus:

Rooni Raysh Aleph Noun Yod or: Raysh-Ani
She'ani Sheen Aleph Noun Yod or: Sheen-Ani

We have previously analysed Ani, the "me", the "self".
Through the action of Aleph upon Tav, we see it here emerging
from Raysh (200) and acquiring the Sheen (300).

In the Garden of Eden, the human psyche is "sheened" by
the Serpent born of the Earth, and it is a fact that the human
kind is at pains to transcend that condition. Here, the psyche
does not seek any escape. It knows itself to be *Rooni* (born of the
cosmic container, Raysh), but it also receives the Sheen from
Aleph, because it has discovered that Aleph and Tav are one.
The song, from now on, will describe the Sacred game of the
two flows of Sheen. We see them already at play in this verse,
with three Aleph, three Tav, and six Sheen: one Sheen for
every Aleph and one for every Tav.

It is a fascinating game, easy to follow in the Song because its
description is so accurate, not so easy to disclose in ourselves,
but unexpectedly vitalizing when we do.

In the following schema, *Sh'hharhhoret* (Sheen Hhayt Raysh
Hhayt Raysh Tav: 300.8.200.8.200.400) we are back to the
interplay between Raysh and Sheen and we can observe the
reaction of the bestowed Sheen upon Raysh: it kindles in
the individual, both the physiological "container" and the
psychological "contained". (Hhayt Raysh Hhayt Raysh,
pronounced idiomatically *Hhirhher*, means "to kindle, to
provoke a strife".)

The two following schemata, *Sh'shzafatni Ha'shamesh*, mean
idiomatically "the sun has coated me with pitch". The root
Zafat meaning pitch is written Zayn Phay Tav (7.80.400). It

265

shows the sign, 7, of all possibilities—hence of uncertainty—
thrust into the unstructured 80, and projected towards 400. In
the preceding verse the psyche had declared: "it is uncertainty
that is my peace". But when that uncertainty actually penetrates
into the hidden unstructured realms of the individual, it
generates a conflict between mind and body. After having seen
the light of Aleph, the psyche feels itself symbolically smeared
with pitch.

This darkness is due to the "Sun", *Shemesh*. Here again, with
Sheen Mem Sheen, we see the two flows of energy in inverted
directions. One Sheen activates the biosphere (or water) Mem;
and the other is generated by the biosphere. The astrological
name for the Sun is *Hhamah* (Hhayt Mem Hay).* It shows the
two contrasting effects of the sun: in the absence of Mem
(water) it destroys; with it, it gives life.

The rest of the verse is symbolically clear. The vine (*Kerem*:
20.200.40/600) is a well-known symbol of richness and life.
The "Father's vineyard" will be mentioned, verse VI, 11.

I

7   הַגִּ֣ידָה לִּ֗י שֶׁאָהֲבָה֙ נַפְשִׁ֔י אֵיכָ֣ה תִרְעֶ֔ה אֵיכָ֖ה
תַרְבִּ֣יץ בַּֽצָּהֳרָ֑יִם שַׁלָּמָ֤ה אֶֽהְיֶה֙ כְּעֹ֣טְיָ֔ה עַ֖ל עֶדְרֵ֥י
חֲבֵרֶֽיךָ׃

PHONETICALLY: *Haghidah Li Sh'ahavah Nafshi Eikhah Tir'ah
Eikhah Tarbeets Betsaharayeem Shalamah Ehieh Kioteyah Aal Eedrey
Hhabereykha.*

RSV: *Tell me, you whom my soul loves, where you pasture your flock,
where you make it lie down at noon; for why should I be like one who
wanders beside the flocks of your companions?*

QABALA: Woman: *No question of my hiding from the world. Show
me your place of work, your place of leisure. I want to be
along with you in the open.*

---

* See *Sepher Yetsira*. (Les Editions du Mont-Blanc, Geneva).

The cabalistic *Midrash* of this verse is deliberately concise. It abstains from mentioning the pastures, flocks, rests at noon, wanderings and companions of the canonical texts. This is a very holy scripture, not a bucolic poem in the style of Virgil.

The two key-words of this verse are: *Ahavah* and *Ehieh*. *Ahavah*: Aleph Hay Waw Hay, or Aleph alive, Vayt alive, is the word for love in the Jewish language. *Ehieh*: Aleph Hay Yod Hay, or Aleph alive, Yod alive, is the schema, the meaning of which was revealed to Moses in the hopelessly untranslatable utterance *Ehieh Esher Ehieh* (the erroneous "I am who I am" in Exodus III, 13 is partly responsible for the fabrication of a personal deity).

Ahavah and *Ehieh* are two ways of expressing the same fundamental postulate of Qabala and Revelation. The *Sepher Yetsira* states it thus: "Everything with Aleph and Aleph with everything; everything with Bayt and Bayt with everything". Aleph is the timeless energy that no thought can grasp; Bayt is the archetype of all the physical supports. In parallel to this assertion, the timeless Aleph and the archetype Yod of all existences, were revealed to Moses as being both alive.

No human mind can fathom what *Ahavah* and *Ehieh* imply. When Aleph in us and Vayt in us are both alive, we commune with everything that exists, or has existed, or will exist in this our overwhelmingly mysterious space-time continuum. And this communion is the only adequate definition of the word *Ahavah*: love. Likewise, when we understand *Ehieh*, the one, unique Energy appears outside and inside us in its innumerable structures, and duality is no more.

Our meditation can now lead us to compare:

Ahavah: Aleph Hay Vayt Hay
Ehieh: Aleph Hay Yod Hay
YHWH: Yod Hay Waw Hay

(When the two lives Hay and Hay are copulatively related in us the immanent Aleph enters into existence: Yod.)

Our readers can now examine *Ahavah* and *Ehieh* in their

context and see how this beautiful verse, I, 7 (that corresponds so well to its serial number seven) follows logically the preceding one. We will only point out the following words:

Haghidah. Its root is *Ghedi*: "Kid (goat)" or *Gad*: "good fortune" and also "to attack". It is the symbol of a new, young, dynamic life. A *Hagadah* is a legendary or mythical tale, meant to convey the renewal of life. ("The" *Hagadah* is the religious service on Passover night).

Nafshi: "Myself" (Noun Phay Sheen Yod: 50.80.300.10) gives birth to Sheen.

Shalamah: again the word peace.

Tarbeets Betsaharayeem: these two schemata include Tsadde; they deal with the structure of Energy.

I

8 אִם־לֹא תֵדְעִי לָךְ הַיָּפָה בַּנָּשִׁים צְאִי־לָךְ
בְּעִקְבֵי הַצֹּאן וּרְעִי אֶת־גְּדִיֹּתַיִךְ עַל מִשְׁכְּנוֹת הָרֹעִים:

PHONETICALLY: *Im Lo Tedday Lakh Ha'yafah Banasheem Tsei Lakh B'eayqve Hatson We'raay Et Ghediotaykh Aal Meshkenot Haroaym.*
RSV: *If you do not know, O fairest among women, follow in the tracks of the flock and pasture your kids beside the shepherd's tents.*
QABALA: Breath: *If you don't know where I am, most lovely woman, let timelessness come alive for you: bring into duration two lives and two existences in one.*

Im Lo: (Aleph Mem, Lammed Aleph): Aleph diving into Mem, Aleph emerging from Lammed: two flows of energy in inverted directions. This is the answer to the quest of the preceding verse. In many important passages of the Scriptures, the first schema is the equation developed and solved in the verse. If "She" wants to find "Him", she will allow Aleph to penetrate in her (Aleph Mem) then she will give it birth (Lammed Aleph).

(*a*) Her first action will be *Tedday Lakh* (Tav Dallet Ayn Yod: 400.4.70.10, Lammed Khaf: 30.500): in her very essence, as resistance of container of life (400.4) she will be open to all possibilities in action (70.10). *Ha Yafah* (Hay Yod Phay Hay: 5.10.80.5): two lives, Hay and Hay describe her beauty: one acts through Yod upon Phay, the other results from Phay. *Banasheem*: the root of this schema, *Nasha* (Noun Sheen Aleph: 50.300.1), has many opposite meanings, such as life, to bear, sustain, endure, to take away or to receive, to marry or to destroy. We presume that the sequence 50 to 300, and then to 1, is difficult to understand because the Sheen disappearing into Aleph disintegrates every mental picture born of 50 (life in existence). The subtle beauty of *Banasheem* is the insertion of Sheen, between *Ban* and *Eem*, that leads us to the key-words of this action: *Tsei Lakh* (Tsadde Aleph Yod, Lammed Khof), where we see the structurizing Tsadde uniting Aleph and Yod in the organic movement of Lammed. This develops into *B'eayqve* (Bayt Ayn Qof Vayt Yod) with Ayn (70) giving birth to the cosmic Aleph (Qof: 100), and culminates into *Hatson* (Hay Tsadde Aleph Noun) with the triumphant assertion that the life (Hay) of the structurizing process (Tsadde) engenders Aleph and thus completes the cycle of life and existence, with the final Noun (700), the Principle of Principles, the cosmic Indetermination. (In the idiom, *Tson* is only a small flock probably because at that level, this schema conveys a sense of uncertainty.)

(*b*) Her second action is stated by means of the six last schemata, beginning with *We'Raay Et* . . . and ending with *Haroaym*, whose common root is *Raa* (Raysh Ayn: 200.70) meaning to be bad, to break, friend, comrade, vice, wickedness; or (Raysh Ayn Hay: 200.70.5) misfortune, to befriend, to pasture or (Raysh Ayn Yod: 200.70.10) pasture, excrement; or (Raysh Ayn Yod Hay: 200.70.10.5) beloved, wife, friend, pasturing, grazing. When applied to the famous tree of Eden, it is supposed to mean evil, and it is sometimes translated shepherd. In its true sense, the letter Ayn (70) implies a change, a demolishing of structures, an uncertainty open to every possibility. In *Ghediotaykh*, the root *Ghedi* indicates the birth of an organic process: (Tav between two Yod). *Aal* introduces Ayn in Lammed. *Meshkenot* shows Sheen acting on Tav.

I

9   לְסֻסָתִי֙ בְּרִכְבֵ֣י פַרְעֹ֔ה דִּמִּיתִ֖יךְ רַעְיָתִֽי׃

PHONETICALLY: *Lessoossati Berikhvey Pharaoh Dimitikh Raati.*
RSV: *I compare you, my love, to a mare of Pharaoh's chariots.*
QABALA: Breath: *I see you are still under the spell of those with worldly prestige.*

Lessoossati. The root *Sass* (Samekh Samekh: 60.60) means larva. Samekh is the symbol of the female sex.

Berikhvey (Bayt Raysh Khaf Vayt Yod: 2.200.20.2.10) with four times the 2 in every sphere, ending in Yod, expresses a powerfully static container.

Pharaoh (Phay Raysh Ayn Hay: 80.200.70.5) is a combination of two roots: the first *Par* or *Phar*, is a bull; *Perev* means wild, savage, and *Phara* means to be fruitful. The second root Ayn Hay (70 Hay) is not a word but simply 70 alive. It is the "fruit" of Pharaoh's oppression: a revolt, a breaking down, or a departure.

The two last schemata show again Tav between two Yod.

"He" sees "Her" twice female, submissive under the spell of those symbolized by the word *Pharaoh*. Yod and Yod in her ought not to be degraded into Samekh and Samekh. He urges her to wake up.

I

10   נָאווּ לְחָיַיִךְ בַּתֹּרִים צַוָּארֵךְ בַּחֲרוּזִים:

PHONETICALLY: *Naoo Lehhayaykh Batoreem Tsavarekh Bahharoo-zeem.*

RSV: *Your cheeks are comely with ornaments, your neck with strings of jewels.*

QABALA: Breath. *But I shall fertilize your duality: In You will be the whirling of opposites.*

The first two *Autiot, Na* (Noun Aleph: 50.1) are an opening, an offering (idiomatically meaning "please, pray"). He tells her: "please, accept two copulative Waw (*Naoo*: Noun Aleph Waw Waw).

Lehhayaykh: Lammed Hhayt Yod Yod Khaf, for the two lives in you (body and psyche). Or (following his preceding statement): "Instead of degrading your Yod Yod into Samekh Samekh, let me impregnate them with my Waw and Waw".

"She" receives the two Waws and deals with them *Batoreem* (with *Toreem*). The root of *Toreem* (*Tor*) is to tour, to explore to go round and round. The two last schemata contain each a Waw. They operate in two opposite directions. With *Tsavarekh* (Tsadde Waw Aleph Raysh Khaf: 90.6.1.200.500) the structurizing female energy, Tsadde, uses the male power (6) to project Aleph in the universe. The root *Tsavah or Tsovah* of this schema is Tsadde Waw Aleph Hay. In the idiom it means (according to how it is pronounced) command, will, testament, or excrement. Ending with Raysh instead of Hay, it is the neck. In the symbolism of Qabala (see verse VII, 5) the neck is a pipe through which the Fire (that builds the Head) flows and structures the body made of Earth and Water. (In terms of alchemy and Qabala, Water is the formative Element of the belly.)

In the last schema, *Bahharoozeem* (Bayt Hhayt Raysh Waw Zayn Yod Mem) the Waw emerges from the unstructured energy, Hhayt, and acts upon Zayn (7) and Yod. Instead of structurizing Aleph, as in *Tsavarekh*, the Waw, here, destroys with the uncertainty of no. 7 the structures of Yod. Such is their whirl of opposites.

The root *Hharooz*, besides not being the canonical "string of jewels" but a string of beads, is also, idiomatically, verse, rhyme. No. 7 may well be the quality of real poetry.

I

11   תּוֹרֵי זָהָב נַעֲשֶׂה־לָּךְ עִם נְקֻדּוֹת הַכָּסֶף:

PHONETICALLY: *Torey Zahav Naasseh-Lakh Eim Neqoodot Ha'kasseph.*

RSV: *We will make you ornaments of gold, studded with silver.*

QABALA: Breath: *Which will transmute love into gold. But your silver desire will transmute that gold into love.*

There is a subtle difference between *Ba'toreem* of the preceding verse whose root is Tav Raysh, and *Torey*, whose root is Tav Waw Raysh. Both roots have the same idiomatic meaning, (to tour, explore, turn, to seek out). The final Yod in *Torey* is possessive: "My *Tor*" says Breath, is *Zahav* that we make for you (*Naaseh-Lakh*). *Tor* is Waw born of Tav, in copulation with Raysh. To understand it, this schema must be compared with *Awr* (light)

Awr: Aleph Waw Raysh
Tor: Tav   Waw Raysh

Awr is (Gen. i, 3) the first act of Creation: the Copulation of Aleph and of its cosmic "container", Raysh. The Song asserts that Aleph and Tav are two in one. The dialogue is between "Him", Aleph, the one in the two, and "Her", Tav, the two in the one. In the preceding verse, i, 10, "He" offered himself to "Her" under the action of a dual Waw, and "She" saw these two Waw acting in opposite directions. Now "He" says to "Her": "in giving myself to you, I gave you my love: *Ahav* (Aleph Hay Vayt), but through you, love is transmuted into gold, *Zahav*" (Zayn Hay Vayt)

Ahav (Love): Aleph Hay Vayt

Zahav (Gold): Zayn Hay Vayt

This assertion is perfectly correct: in the world of things, the infinitude of love becomes an infinite quantity of things, whose symbolical equivalent is gold.

"But", adds he, "this gold appears with holes punctured (*Naqoodot*) by desires (*Kasseph*)." *Kesseph* or *Kassaph* (Kaf Samekh Phay,) mean idiomatically both silver and desire. This is a reference to her desire for real love and union with the eternal life.

I

12   עַד־שֶׁהַמֶּ֫לֶךְ֙ בִּמְסִבּ֔וֹ נִרְדִּ֖י נָתַ֥ן רֵיחֽוֹ׃

PHONETICALLY: *Aad-Sh'Hamelekh Bi'msiboo Nirdi Natan Rayhho.*

RSV: *While the king was on his couch, my nard gave forth its fragrance.*

QABALA: Psyche: *I am not any more under the seeming eternity of the strong. My sharply awakened senses drive me into the Universal Unknown.*

Aad is a key-word in the Scriptures, and the key-word of this verse. In the idiom, it means Eternity. *Aadah* is one of *Lemekh's* symbolical wives (Gen. IV, 19). When Abimelekh sees Isaac and Rebecca talking in the open (Gen. XVI, 8) he looks at them, *Be-Aaad Ha'hhalawn*, from his temporal eternity. The word eternity is not really conceivable, but it can be stated as the mystery of the existent universe. In the combination *Aad* (Ayn Dallet: 70.4) the symbol Ayn (70) of all possible possibilities, hurls itself against Dallet (4), the archetype of all resistances. The kings in the Scriptures are always agents of the conflict

273

between the concepts of eternity as timeless and eternity as perennial, whether they yield as Abimelekh; resist as Pharaoh and are destroyed; or destroy Jerusalem, as did the king of the Chaldees.

Aad-Sh'Hamelekh Bi'msiboo says that *Aad* thrusts the Breath of Sheen upon the king *Bimsiboo*; (Bayt Mem Samekh Bayt Waw: 2.40.60.2.6). This last schema shows the king firmly established in his protective female shell. In this verse, "She" answers "His" rebuke of verse 1, 9.

The three last schemata *Nirdi Natan Rayhho* mean, idiomatically, "my nard gives its smell". But this is only a weak symbol through which the canonical text leads us to understand that here is a woman explaining to her lover that she is attempting to awaken the king's sensuality while he is on his couch. What she says is exactly the opposite.

Nirdi (Noun Raysh Dallet Yod: 50.200.4.10). The psyche sees itself in its universal totality and realizes that it owes its existence to Dallet (4).

Natan (Noun Tav Noun final: 50.400.700). Through the cosmic resistance (Tav) the duality (Noun and Noun) is transcended in the cosmic Indetermination, 700, of Noun final. *Rayhho* (Raysh Yod Hhayt Waw: 200.10.8.6) as a result of the two preceding schemata, is a projection into Hhayt (8) of the acquired transcendence. This Hhayt is the unstructured energy underlying the inner "nard" or aromatic balsam of the psyche. Symbolically, the ancient nard clearly conveys the meaning of the modern libido.

One of the most interesting themes of the Song is the relation between libido and timeless eternity.

I

13

צְרֹור הַמֹּר ׀ דֹּודִי לִי בֵּין שָׁדַי יָלִין:

PHONETICALLY: *Tsarawr Hamor Dodi Li Bein Shadai Yaleen.*
RSV: *My beloved is to me a bag of myrrh that lies between my breasts.*

QABALA: Psyche: *Because you are in me I am the Holy Apostasy, Breath from the lower depths over against Breath from on high.*

Tsarawr, in the idiom, is something bound in a knot, tied up, preserved. *Hamor* (or *Hamorah*) is a change, an apostasy. *Dodi*: my lover; *Li*: for me; *Bein*: introduce, interpolate; *Shadai*: the Almighty.

Yaleen has no equivalent, and must be interpreted: one Yod with Lammed, one Yod with Noun final (Yod Yod translated God).

All the letters of those schemata, read according to code, justify their meanings: "He" is tied up in her, and given shape; "She" recreates the Breath, thus inserting her action in the Almighty's. This is her apostasy.

Tsarawr must be compared to *Arawr* (curse) and to YHWH

> *Tsarawr:* Tsadde Raysh Waw Raysh
> *Arawr:*   Aleph Raysh Waw Raysh
> *YHWH:* Yod   Hay   Waw Hay

Both *Tsarawr* and *Arawr* oppose Raysh and Raysh to YHWH's Hay and Hay. The Tsadde of *Tsarawr* is the symbolical "female" structural Breath, of the lower depths, as opposed to the mysterious Emanation, Yod, from a "male" Immanence. *Hamor* (Hay Mem Raysh: 5.40.200) postulates a life, Hay, animating the biosphere, and the world in general (as opposed to the Aleph-Hay-Yod-Hay of Moses' Revelation, where Hay, is originated by Aleph).

In *Dodi* (Dallet Waw Dallet Yod) are her two resistances (mentioned by "Him" in verse 1, 2), linked with the copulative Waw. This schema read in Hebrew from left to right is in exact opposition to YHWH.

> *Dodi* reversed Yod Dallet Waw Dallet
> *YHWH*   Yod Hay   Waw Hay

The fact that *Dodi* is a reversed projection of YHWH,

resisting YHWH is in truth a holy apostasy, with tremendous implications. This resistance is a response. So *Dodi* does not mean "my beloved", but, "my response to YHWH". "This, for me," she says, "is (*Bein*) inserted into *Shadai* (Sheen Dallet Yod): the Breath that acts upon Dallet."*

The last schema *Yaleen* (Yod Lammed Yod Noun final: 10.30.10.700) is a condensed repetition and explanation of the theme that is being developed all through the Song. Whereas Yod Yod is, in the Scriptures, an abbreviation for YHWH, *Yaleen* shows one Yod active organically in 30 and one existing in the cosmic Indetermination, 700.

I

14   אֶשְׁכֹּל הַכֹּפֶר | דּוֹדִי לִי בְּכַרְמֵי עֵין גֶּדִי׃

PHONETICALLY: *Eshkol Hakofer Dodi Li Bekharmay Ayn Ghedi.*
RSV: *My beloved is to me a cluster of henna blossoms in the vineyards of En-ged'i.*
QABALA: Psyche: *From contact with my resistances you turn again into yourself in an endless resurrection to new life, which is my knowledge.*

In other words, the Fire born of Aleph is both denied and accepted by her. It resurrects in the fount of ever-new life, which is her knowledge.

Eshkol has two roots: *Esh* (fire) and *Kol* (all, every, or: to comprehend, to measure). In the idiom *Eshkol* is a learned man, because *Esh* (Aleph Sheen) is formative of the head (the intellect) and *Kol* expresses its supremacy.

---

* When the roots are thus studied, they open immense vistas. In *Shadai*, idiomatically God, the Sheen from "above" meeting its resistance Dallet produces Yod. But when on the contrary Dallet gives birth to Sheen, it meets Aleph, and this is *Dasha* (Dallet Sheen Aleph): to sprout vegetation, to grow grass. Here again, in two simple equations, the two Sheen illustrate the one life in its two opposite flows.

276

Hakofer in the idiom is to deny and, contradictorily, to reconcile. The same root pronounced *Kifar* is a village.

We have seen *Dodi* and *Li* in the preceding verses. *Bekharmay Ayn Ghedi* is a reference to the vine she no longer wanted to keep, (see verse 1, 6). Hers is *Ayn* (fount, source, or eye), *Ghedi* (see verse 1, 8).

This verse, 1, 14 (14 = 7 + 7), is known as the verse *Eshkol* (its first schema) or the verse of knowledge. It practically ends Song I, the last three verses being congratulatory. The purpose of QABALA is knowledge, and here we learn in this verse what knowledge is. This is a typical cabalistic writing. No translator has ever been able to read its schemata according to their proper meaning or to link them grammatically in logical sequence, because every one of them is an equation integrated in a whole. With our modern field theory approach, we can well understand the necessity of regarding the problem of knowledge not solely as a succession of units. All the equations introduced by the schema *Eshkol* must be understood simultaneously so as to meet *Ayn Ghedi*, where *Eshkol*, (timeless *Esh* and *Kol* the All), are the eternally fresh and new Sacred Fount.

I

15   הִנָּךְ יָפָה רַעְיָתִי הִנָּךְ יָפָה עֵינַיִךְ יוֹנִים:

PHONETICALLY: *Hinakh Yafah Raayati Hinakh Yafah Ayna'ikh Yoneem.*

RSV: *Behold, you are beautiful, my love; behold, you are beautiful; your eyes are doves.*

QABALA: Breath: *How lovely you are, my friend, how lovely! This rising spring in you speaks for Israel.*

This is a play on the word (or letter) *Ayn* (70): eye and source. Her "eyes" are a reflection of the "source" *Ghedi*, previously mentioned (1, 14). *Yoneem* are doves, but *Yonah*, dove, has always been the symbol of Israel.

The purpose of the plurals *Ayna'ikh* and *Yoneem* is to insert in each the two Yod: the "two in one" that "She" symbolizes.

I

16   הִנְּךָ יָפֶה דוֹדִי אַף־נָעִים אַף־עַרְשֵׂנוּ רַעֲנָנָה׃

PHONETICALLY: *Hinkha Yafah Dodi Aph-Naaym Aph-Aarsenoo Raeinanah.*

RSV: *Behold, you are beautiful, my beloved, truly lovely, our couch is green.*

17   קֹרוֹת בָּתֵּינוּ אֲרָזִים רָחִיטֵנוּ בְּרוֹתִים׃

PHONETICALLY: *Qorawt Batayno Arazeem Rahhiteno Beroteem.*

RSV: *The beams of our house are cedar, our rafters are pine.*

QABALA: Psyche: (16) *What beauty, my loved one! We delight in our newness.* (17) *The place where we rest together cannot be destroyed.*

The last schema of 1, 16, *Raeinanah*, means idiomatically "is our freshness" and not "is green". The two protagonists rest in the indestructible newness of the Source of Life.

In this verse 16 (twice eight), *Raeinanah* has two Nouns, corresponding to the two Dallet of *Dodi*, two *Aph* (Aleph Phay: 1.80) (Aleph penetrating the undifferentiated energy), two Waw; but three Ayn and only one Sheen. The reader can discover and enjoy many other precisions, such as in 1, 17, the first schema *Qorawt* (Qof Raysh Waw Tav: 100.200.6.400), translated "beams". This stupendous equation shows the cosmic Aleph (Qof: 100), through the universal emanation, Raysh (200) in copulation, Waw (6), with its resistant sanctuary Tav (400).

278

Thus ends the first chant. It is mathematically consistent and logical, in every detail, whereas, from beginning to end, the canonical text leaps incongruously from one thing to another: "his name is oil" (1, 3); "She is dark like the curtains of Solomon" (1, 5); she mentions her fragrant nard while the king is on his couch (1, 12); her beloved is a bag of myrrh (1, 13); their couch is green (presumably grass) (1, 15); but why don't they use their house "with cedar beams" (1, 17)?; etc. ... etc. ...

In the Biblical version all the other chants are thus disconnected in erroneous naturalistic descriptions, but we will not comment upon it any further. The essential theme is given. Now the Song will unfold it, to our great delight.

II

1

אֲנִי חֲבַצֶּלֶת הַשָּׁרוֹן שׁוֹשַׁנַּת הָעֲמָקִים:

PHONETICALLY: *Ani Hhebatselat Ha'sharawn Shoshanat Ha'ay-meqeem.*

RSV: *I am a rose of Sharon, a lily of the valleys.*

QABALA: Breath: *I am in your body, depth of the upper Breath, Breath of the depth, double Emanation.*

The schema *Hhebatselet* is a combination of two roots: *Hhab* (Hayt Bayt: 8.2) is the unstructured energy in ourselves and means in the idiom, to be indebted, responsible, guilty; pronounced *Hhob* it is the bosom; with an added Aleph (Hhayt Bayt Aleph) it means to conceal, to hide. The other root is *Tsal* (Tsadde Lammed: 90.30), which means shadow, shade, shelter, but is essentially the structural Tsadde in its organic function.

The root of *Sharawn* is *Sharah* (Sheen Raysh Hay: 300.200.5), idiomatically: to soak, to dwell, to struggle, to persist, persevere.

279

Shoshanat ending with Tav differs from the word rose, spelt *Shoshanah* with Hay. In this schema, "He" explains what he actually is: Sheen Waw Sheen Noun Tav: 300.6.300.50.400 shows the two Sheen so often mentioned, related copulatively one with the other, thus active in "her" factual life (50) and blending in Tav.

Ha'aymeqeem: the depths (plural). The beautiful word *Oomq*, singular, (Ayn Mem Qof: 70.40.100) is "the deep", (so deeply guttural when pronounced correctly). It appears in one of the most exalted passages of *Sepher Yetsira* (1, 5) where the *Sephirot* are described thus: *Ten Sephirot Beli-Mah. Their measure without end. Depth of Beginning. Depth of End. Depth of Good. Depth of Evil. Depth of High. Depth of Low. Depth of Orient. Depth of Occident. Depth of North. Depth of South.*

The depths (plural) mentioned in this verse, II, 1, include all the *Sephirot.* Here they are seen alive in us. We have but to open ourselves to them, to commune with their intense vibrations, where the beginning and the end are One.

II

2   כְּשׁוֹשַׁנָּה֙ בֵּין הַחוֹחִ֔ים כֵּ֥ן רַעְיָתִ֖י בֵּ֥ין הַבָּנֽוֹת׃

PHONETICALLY: *Ke'shoshanah Bein Ha'hhohheem Ken Raayati Bein Ha'banot.*

RSV: *As a lily among brambles, so is my love among maidens.*

QABALA: Lover to woman: *And you are these two Breaths, in existence and life, among unshaped substance.*

In the preceding verse "He" described himself, and now, appearing as her lover, "He" describes her, as he sees her among the other girls. She is *Ke* (Kaf: 20) (objectively) *Shoshanah:* in which the final Hay of Life corresponds to his previously mentioned Tav.

The singular *Hhohh* of *Ha'hhohheem* is, in the idiom, a thorn or a cave. Its spelling Hhayt Waw Hhayt (8.6.8) shows that its best description is, symbolically, a cave where unstructured substances rumble in the dark. It is in striking contrast with "her" Sheen Waw Sheen.

The verse goes on, saying "thus is *Raayati* among *Ha'banot*". *Raayati* means my friend, my companion, not my love. This is an important difference. All through the Scriptures, womanhood is urged to reach the dignity of companion, or "sister" to manhood.

Banot is the plural of *Bat* (Bayt Tav: 2.400) which means daughter, child or girl, and shows the Bayt, the container, the duality, settled and unmoved in a barren Tav.

II

3 כְּתַפּוּחַ֙ בַּעֲצֵ֣י הַיַּ֔עַר כֵּ֥ן דּוֹדִ֖י בֵּ֣ין הַבָּנִ֑ים בְּצִלּוֹ֙
חִמַּ֣דְתִּי וְיָשַׁ֔בְתִּי וּפִרְי֖וֹ מָת֥וֹק לְחִכִּֽי׃

PHONETICALLY: *Ke'tapooahh B'aatsay Ha'yaar Ken Dodi Bein Ha'baneem Be'tsilow Hhimadti We'yashavti Wo'phiriaw Matoq Lehhiki.*

RSV: *As an apple tree among the trees of the wood, so is my beloved among young men. With great delight I sat in his shadow, and his fruit was sweet to my taste.*

QABALA: Woman: *I see you as you appear to me. I was full of joy, inhabiting my body, and there you sprang to life from your tabernacle of glorified dust.*

This verse is a paraphrase of Genesis III, 6-7: *So when the woman saw that the tree was good for food, and that it was a delight to the eyes, and that the tree was to be desired to make one wise, she took of its fruit and ate; and she also gave some to her husband, and he ate. Then the eyes of both were opened, and they knew that they were naked. . . .*

These verses of Genesis, and of the Song, describe a simultaneous awakening of the mind (wisdom or awareness) and of sensuality. The Qabala never separates mind and body: spirit and flesh are one just as Aleph and Tav are one.

This verse, II, 3, shows how the impulse of no. 3 sets "Her" duality into motion. In the next verses "She" will testify to it.

"She" sees "Him" as *Tapooahh* (Tav Pay Waw Hhayt: 400.80.6.8) i.e. as an emanation of Tav, thrust in the unstructured factual energy (80) fertilizing (6) its own archetype (8). This description is the reverse of what the canonical "Breath" is expected to be. She then describes him as *Aatsay* (Ayn Tsadde: 70.90) which means that all his possibilities (70) are being structured (90), as compared to *Yaar* (Yod Ayn Raysh: 10.70.200) meaning both forest and wilderness, where the 70 is simply dissipated in the cosmos.

Be'tsilaw (root: *Tsal*: Tsadde Lammed: structure in organic life) *Hhimadti* (root: *Hhamad*: Hhayt Mem Dallet: to covet, lust, desire: the unstructured Hhayt drives its energy in the biosphere, Mem, so as to feel itself alive). *We'yashavti* (root: *Yashav*: Yod Sheen Waw: to dwell, inhabit: the Yod, archetype of mere existence, calls upon sheen to become fruitful with Waw).

In the context, *Hhimadti* and *Yashavti*, ending with Tav-Yod, indicate the direction and purpose of this intense craving: we must remember that "She" saw him, in the first schema of this verse, as *Tapooahh*: an unstructured but copulative energy emanated from Tav. She craves for Tav, because only in Tav can she meet "Him" unstructured, and structure him, herself, in "*Aatsay*": in her own body, as she is actually.

To find "Him", "She" must dive deeply into herself.

So far, we have three Tav: one from which he emerges and two towards which she is directed. And now comes the fourth, that will reveal the stupendous essence of this lustful love.

The verse concludes thus: *Wo'phiriaw* (Waw Phay Raysh Yod Waw: 6.80.200.10.6): she responds with two Waw to his Waw (see *Tapooahh*). In between her two, is Phay Raysh Yod (in the idiom, pronounced *Pay*: fruit). These *Autiot* show that she opens to "Him" all "Her" own unstructured energy (an important point). And now comes the extraordinary *Matoq* (Mem Tav Waw Qof: 40.400.6.100). The combination Mem Tav, when pronounced *Met* means, in the idiom, death, a corpse, to die, and when pronounced *Mat*, it means a person.

We can meditate on those two meanings. Mem Tav is a magma, a crude mixture of organic matters, a sort of semi-fluid strata under solid earth, lying deep down in the mystery of Tav. In a word: mud. And now in *Matoq*, with simply two signs added, Waw Qof, the miracle explodes as a fantastic hosanna, as a cry of triumph: this mud, transfigured, has given birth to the cosmic Aleph, Qof (100)!

The last schema *Lehhiki*: (Lammed Hhayt Kaf Yod: 30.8.20.10) testifies to the birth in "Her" of this new Life: the organic process of Lammed now animates her, through and through.

II

4

הֱבִיאַנִי אֶל־בֵּית הַיַּיִן וְדִגְלוֹ עָלַי אַהֲבָה:

PHONETICALLY: *Hebi'ani El-Bayt Ha'yin Ve'dag'lo Aalay Ahevah.*

RSV: *He brought me to the banqueting house, and his banner over me was love.*

QABALA: Woman: *You carried me to an intoxication where consciousness must stop or lose itself. But your new life in me is a response to love.*

The schema *Hebi'ani* can be read: *Hebi* (exaggeration, vain talk) *Ani* (me); *El-Bayt* (in the house) *Ha'yin* (of wine). In a symbolical, idiomatic sense, this means that she is intoxicated beyond self-control, exhilarated beyond measure, by the feeling of the new life in her, described in the preceding verse.

Vedaglo (the unconvincing banner) is a humorous play on the key-word of this verse. The schema must be read: *Ve'dag'lo*. It would mean idiomatically "and a fish for him", *Dag* (Dallet Ghimel) meaning fish. But according to Qabala this fish, and the fish that swallowed Jonah, and all the fish and fishing mentioned in the Gospels, have a specific meaning, derived from the confrontation of the *Autiot* Dallet Ghimel (4.3).

In verse I, 8 we met the inverted root 3.4: Ghimel-Dallet (*Ghedi*, meaning kid). It expresses the process of an organic movement, 3, finding its resistance, 4, in a life being born; whereas the sequence 4.3, expresses a resistance inside an active surrounding, 3, symbolizing the firstborn in the sea: the fish.

Both 4.3 and 3.4 are a combination of organic movement and response, without which no organism could build itself and live.

Dallet (4) is the essential point of this verse II, 4; and every one of its *Autiot* contributes to its general meaning: "She" must not allow her consciousness (or psyche) to be swept away in her sensual delight; "He" needs her response as a living Bayt and a living Aleph: from her temporality and from his timelessness, now born in her.

The reader can thus follow all the *Autiot* in their context; appreciate in *Habi'ani* the Aleph between two Yod, and the double life Hay (5) and Noun (50); compare that schema to *Yin*, the wine with its two Yod ending in a cosmic indetermination; then, after *Dag'lo*, consider the Ayn in *Aaley*; etc. . . . etc. . . . and finally meditate again on *Ahavah* (see I, 7).

II

5   סַמְּכוּנִי֙ בָּֽאֲשִׁישׁ֔וֹת רַפְּד֖וּנִי בַּתַּפּוּחִ֑ים כִּי־חוֹלַ֥ת
אַהֲבָ֖ה אָֽנִי׃

PHONETICALLY: *Samkhooni Ba'ashishot Rafdooni Ba'tapoohheem Ki-Hholat Ahevah Ani.*

284

RSV: *Sustain me with raisins, refresh me with apples; for I am sick with love.*

QABALA: Woman: *Oh that I could be strong enough to take your seed into my body! And living Breath in its living support!*

In *Samkhooni,* the Sammekh Mem Khaf, the female (60) biological (40) body in action (20), are none other than the spelling of the letter Sammekh, the female sex. Its idiomatic meaning "support" is therefore correct inasmuch that the female sex is the support, or the physical builder of energy, when the male (Waw: 6) has penetrated it. With the next schema, "She" describes what she wishes that fecundation to be: *Ba'ashishot* (Bayt Aleph Sheen Yod Sheen Waw Tav: 2.1.300.10.300.6.400). This schema is fully explanatory: it contains all the elements that can better express her need: Bayt (the physical support) Aleph (the timeless energy), their two Sheen enclosing the factual Yod, the male energy, Waw, and finally, Tav.

Rafdooni Ba'tapoohheem (see *Tapooahh,* verse II, 3). The *Autiot* Phe Dallet (80.4) in *Rafdooni* introduce in her the resistance that she needs "*Ki'Hholat*". The root of this last schema is *Hhol:* to fall and to writhe, or, rather, to dance. Symbolically, she wants to "dance" Aleph alive and Bayt alive: her love in her living body!

II

6

שְׂמֹאלוֹ תַּחַת לְרֹאשִׁי וִימִינוֹ תְּחַבְּקֵנִי:

PHONETICALLY: *Semolo Tahhat Le' roshi We'imino Tahhabeqni.*
RSV: *O that his left hand were under my head and that his right hand embraced me!*
QABALA: Woman: *His left hand conveys the sacred Name. His right hand is about me and makes me to breathe it.*

The *Sepher Yetsira* describes *Adam-Kadmon*, man perfected facing east, his left arm extended northward, towards the tenth and lowest *Sephirah*, his right southward, towards the ninth *Sephirah*. Left is, idiomatically *Semol* (Seen Mem Aleph Lammed) in which Seen is a weakened Sheen. Sheen Mem: *Shem* is the Name. This left of the lover is shown here *Tahhat* (Tav Hhayt Tav: 400.8.400), leading us to two Tav encircling the undifferentiated Hhayt. The right, *Yemin*, the hand of action, (*Yemin* includes two Yod) leads us to *Tahhabeq* which breathes out the cosmic Aleph: Qof (100).

This verse, under its copulative serial number II, 6, is a deep ontological abstraction of the self-progeny of the One. Its stupendous scale of view, both metaphysical and corporeal, going deeply down into the immeasurable universe and into ourselves, cannot be expressed in words, but must be read in terms of its *Autiot*. In our *Midrash* we have kept midway between its symbolical sphere and the reality of the *Autiot*.

This verse introduces the cabalist in the most secret and sacred depth of the Sanctuary of Life, where time and mind emerge from duration and slumber, where the word is born in a language that no lips can proffer.

II

7 הִשְׁבַּ֨עְתִּי אֶתְכֶ֜ם בְּנ֤וֹת יְרוּשָׁלִַ֙ם֙ בִּצְבָא֔וֹת אֽוֹ בְּאַיְל֖וֹת הַשָּׂדֶ֑ה אִם־תָּעִ֧ירוּ ׀ וְֽאִם־תְּע֥וֹרְר֛וּ אֶת־הָאַהֲבָ֖ה עַ֥ד שֶׁתֶּחְפָּֽץ׃

PHONETICALLY: *Hishbaati Etkhem Benot Yeroshalom Bi'tsebaot Aw Bi'aylot Hassadèh Im-Taayro We'im-Teoreroo Et-Ha'ahevah Aad Shetehhfats.*

RSV: *I adjure you, O daughters of Jerusalem, by the gazelles or the hinds of the field, that you stir not up nor awaken love until it please.*

QABALA: Woman: *Girls of the city! I send you the heavenly company. Do not shut away the universal splendour inside your frozen institutions. Don't dispute it; it IS the Emanation.*

In this seventh verse "She" projects the no. 7 upon the passive girls who had been her companions. *Hishbaati* is this projection of no. 7 *Shibaa* (Sheen Bayt Ayn Hay: 300.2.70.5). This schema is very dynamic: it shows the Sheen breathing the 70 alive into the Bayt (the house).

Bi'tsebaot: "with" *Tsebaot,* the Deity of the Great Fighting Celestial Legions. *Bi'aylot* "with" *Aylot:* strength, power. *Hassadah* is a battle-field. *Im-Taayroo: Ayr* is a city: do not shut away in the city. *Im-Teoreroo:* do not dispute. *Ha'ahevah:* love. *Aad:* eternity.

Shetehhfats (Sheen Tav Hhayt Phay Tsadde: 300.400.8.80.900). This schema shows the Sheen acting upon Tav and extracting 900 from the undifferentiated 8 and 800. The final Tsadde is rarely used. It expresses the Splendour of the Emanation at its highest state of structured Energy.

Briefly, what is meant here, is that the eternal love and the universal splendour cannot be captured in any artificially structured peace.

II

8   קוֹל דּוֹדִי הִנֵּה־זֶה בָּא מְדַלֵּג עַל־הֶהָרִים
מְקַפֵּץ עַל־הַגְּבָעוֹת׃

PHONETICALLY: *Qol Dodi Hineh-Zeh Ba Me'daleg Aal-He'hareem Me'qapets Aal-Ha'gbaot.*

RSV: *The voice of my beloved! Behold, he comes, leaping upon the mountains, bounding over the hills.*

QABALA: Woman: *See, Breath rushes through Space towards me, violently breaks into my strength, rays out inside me.*

The preceding verse elevated the female protagonist to the contemplation of eternal love and beauty, and here comes the response, the *Qol* (Qof Waw Lammed: 100.6.30) from the cosmic Aleph: Qof. It rushes through the immensities of her vision and ejects its Waw so as to put in motion the organic movement of Lammed. *Qol* is not just a voice: it is a voice that penetrates. There are other roots for voicing or uttering, such as *Bitte* (Bayt Tayt Aleph) emanated by the flesh (symbolized, but not named, by Bayt Tayt) towards Aleph. In opposite direction there comes, as a lightning, through all the spheres of Emanation, the cosmic Aleph. "She" feels it *Hineh-Zeh* (Hay Noun Hay Zayn Hay: 5.50.5.-7.5). It is impossible to reach a higher intensity of life in freedom. *Ba* (Bayt Aleph): she receives "Him" in Bayt and emits the Aleph, *Me'daleg* (Mem Dallet Lammed Ghimel: 40.4.30.3), in her actively (functional) resistant bioplasm. *Aal* (70.30) *Ha'hareem* (5.5.200.10.40/600): with 70, "He" can, now, introduce Hay and Hay, the two lives that are mentioned so often. *Me'qapets*: with jumping, leaping. *Qapets* (Qof Pay Tsadde final (100.80.900) is indeed a wonderful jump of "His" Qof through all that is unstructured, meeting "Her" exalted Tsadde.

The root of the last schema, *Gbaot, Gabiya* (Ghimel Bayt Yod Ayn) is the chalice, the consecrated wine cup where the two meet.

II

9 דּוֹמֶה דוֹדִי לִצְבִי אוֹ לְעֹפֶר הָאַיָּלִים הִנֵּה־זֶה עוֹמֵד אַחַר כָּתְלֵנוּ מַשְׁגִּיחַ מִן־הַחַלֹּנוֹת מֵצִיץ מִן־הַחֲרַכִּים:

PHONETICALLY: *Domeh Dodi Li'tsvi Aw Le'oofer Ha'ayaleem Hineh-Zeh Aomed Ahhar Ke'tel'noo Ma'shghiahh Min-Ha'hhalonot Mi'tsits Min Ha'hhrakeem.*

RSV: *My beloved is like a gazelle, or a young stag. Behold, there he stands behind our wall, gazing in at the windows, looking through the lattice.*

QABALA: Woman: *And this radiation is a new birth, original, organic, developing in me.*

The preceding verses have led us into a vast sphere, alive in us, where the cosmic Aleph, Qof, and the universal beauty and love, are united. An infinitesimal new life was born in us, that allowed us to contemplate the holy infinitude of all that is. We are now invited in this verse no. 9 (Tayt) to look at the new cell in "Her", into which "He" has penetrated.

Most of the *Autiot* of this verse have already been explained. So here is only a brief review of the schemata. We will link them together by a loose thread:

Domeh Dodi: the resistance acting upon my organic responses. *Li'tsvi*: is to my thickness. *Aw Le'oofer*: and my dust. *Ha'ayaleem*: a plural of powers. *Hineh-Zeh*: and of lives (Hay Noun Hay Zayn Hay). *Aomed*: this is both an arising and a stop (*Aomed* has both meanings: Breath arises in her and is stopped in her structure). *Ahhar*: a strangeness and a delay (same description through two meanings of a word). *Ke'tel'noo*: as a mound for us (*Tel*: a mound or a hill). *Ma'shghiahh*: of observation and caring (the root *Shagahh*, means to observe, care for, and supervise). *Men-Ha'hhalomet*: from secular openings. *Mi'tsits*: with structure carried to its utmost beauty (*Tsits*: 90.900, means both a bud, i.e. the beginning of a structure, 90, and a crown, i.e. the perfection of 900). *Min-Ha'hhrakeem*: from those that burn (the root *Hharak* means to singe, char, burn): this last schema refers to the great powers that she describes as observation and caring, but *Shghiahh* is fundamentally the action of a burning Sheen.

II

10 עָנָה דוֹדִי וְאָמַר לִי קוּמִי לָךְ רַעְיָתִי יָפָתִי
וּלְכִי־לָךְ׃

PHONETICALLY: *Aana Dodi We'amar Li Qoomi Lakh Raayati Yafati Oo'lkhi-Lakh.*

RSV: *My beloved speaks and says to me: arise, my love, my fair one, and come away.*

289

QABALA: Woman: *Saying "Enter your own organic movement, then go into the world's, towards yourself".*

Note in *Qoomi* the action of Qof on Mem. *Oo'lkhi Lakh* (Waw Lammed Khaf Yod, Lammed Khaf: 6.30.20.10-30.500). See Genesis XII, 1 where YHWH says to Abraham *Lekh Lekha Min Aretskha*, literally: "towards you, into you, (away) from your earth", translated canonically "go from your country".

All those schemata express the action of organic function, Lammed (30) in Khaf (20) or in final Khaf (500): in the person or in the universal life.

II

11   כִּי־הִנֵּה הַסְּתָו עָבָר הַגֶּשֶׁם חָלַף הָלַךְ לוֹ׃

PHONETICALLY: *Ki-Hinah Ha'stav Aabar Ha'gashem Hhalaf Ha'lakh Lo.*

RSV: *for lo, the winter is past, the rain is over and gone.*

QABALA: Woman: *For the sake of shared pleasure, my feminine sex opened the way to Breath. I have gone beyond myself and come to my essence.*

Ki (Kaf Yod: 20.10), idiomatically: since, because, when, sets the action in time and space, in a factual container, 20, in actual existence, 10.

Hinah (Hay Noun Hay: 5.50.5) abundance of life.

Ha'stav. The root *Stav* (Samekh Tav Waw: 60.400.6) shows the female fecundity, Samekh, receding towards its origin, Tav, where it will find a new insemination; Waw. Allegorically, in the idiom, it is autumn, not winter.

Aabar (Ayn Bayt Raysh: 70.20.200) does not mean in the idiom "is past", but to prepare, work out, adapt. The 70 of all new possibilities is introduced in *Bara* (to create).

Ha'gashem; the root *Gheshem* is substance in the idiom. Essentially, it shows Ghimel calling upon Sheen to animate Mem.

Hhalaf (Hhayt Lammed Phay: 8.30.800) inserts the organic drive, 30, between the archetype and the cosmic unstructured stuff, thus piercing the way for a renewal of life. In the idiom, *Hhalaf* means to sprout and to pierce.

Ha'lakh Lo: literally: to you, to him.

This important verse is a general view of the cosmic cycle of the female prolific energy. She loves "Him" in spirit and body, as a young girl identified with the budding spring. Her budding is that of a lover, not that of a virgin bearing a God. The life that is born in her is an awakening of all her faculties. When her time will come for motherhood it will lead her to her autumn. As the fall of leaves fertilize the soil and prepare it for a new semination, "She" will then meet "Him" again, but differently.

II

12

הַנִּצָּנִים נִרְאוּ בָאָרֶץ עֵת הַזָּמִיר הִגִּיעַ וְקוֹל
הַתּוֹר נִשְׁמַע בְּאַרְצֵנוּ׃

PHONETICALLY: *Ha'nitsaneem Nirioo Ba'erets Eyt Ha'zameer Highiaa We'qol Ha'tawr Nishmaa Be'artsenoo.*

RSV: *The flowers appear on the earth, the time of singing has come, and the voice of the turtledove is heard in our land.*

QABALA: Woman: *now I have knowledge of universal impregnation. Constructive energy works in the two lives of nature. Breath is conceived in the flowerbuds and is welcomed by the songs of time.*

This twelfth verse is a development of the preceding one, and completes a circle—as no. 12 does traditionally. The circle began when, in II, 1, "He" declared himself to be two Breaths in her. The "upper Breath" almost intoxicated her, then she understood that she had to go *Lekh Lekha*, towards herself, so as to complete the cycle of womanhood.

Ha'nitsaneem: the buds. The word for bud, is *Nitsan* (Noun Tsadde Noun): the structural Tsadde inside two existential lives, Noun and Noun.

Nirioo and *Ba'erets* are an interesting permutation of Raysh-Aleph in *Nirioo* and Aleph-Raysh in *Erets*. When examined in detail these two schemata reveal a striking condensed picture of the burial of Aleph and its resurrection in Nature. Its Breath is conceived in the flowerbuds.

Eyt (70.400) is the word for time. In Qabala's conception, time is the modification of things. *Eyt* is an adequate description of the flow of possibilities, 70, in the resistant Tabernacle of Emanation, 400.

Ha'zameer: This word for song must be compared to *Sheer*, translated song in the English canonical text. *Zameer* (7.40. Yod Raysh), is an expression of the biosphere, Mem (40) whereas *Sheer* is an expression of Breath, Sheen (300).

The purpose of the combination *Qol-Tawr* (call and turtle-dove) is to illustrate again the relationship between Qof and Tav:

Qol: 100.6.30
Tawr: 400.6.200

II

13   הַתְּאֵנָה חָנְטָה פַגֶּיהָ וְהַגְּפָנִים ׀ סְמָדַר נָתְנוּ רֵיחַ
קוּמִי לָכִי רַעְיָתִי יָפָתִי וּלְכִי־לָךְ:

PHONETICALLY: *Ha'tenah Hhantah Phaghiyah We'hagfaneem Semadar Natnoo Reahh Qoomi Lakhi Raayati Yafati Oolkhi-Lakh.*
RSV: *The fig tree puts forth its figs, and the vines are in blossom; they give forth fragrance. Arise, my love, my fair one, and come away.*

QABALA: Lover: *Everything is made vibrant by Breath, even the fig tree in the dry sands. Get up, beautiful friend, move towards your selfhood.*

The fig tree is a well-known symbol in the Scriptures. Its delicious fruits springing forth from the dry sand where it grows appear as a portent, almost a miracle. The *Autiot* of the name *Tenah* (Tav Aleph Noun Hay:/400.1.50.5) illustrate that fact: the symbol of the fig tree is Tav engendering directly Aleph, in a perpetual life (50.5). Tav Aleph culminate in Noun Hay.

This explains Jesus' mysterious curse upon the unfruitful fig tree (Matt. xxi, 18-22): if it does not give forth the Aleph, it is not a real fig tree, it is an imposture.

In the second schema *Hhantah* (Hhayt Noun Tayt Hay: 8.50.9.5) the flow of life is a response to the first: instead of Tav leading to Noun, here Noun leads to Tayt.

Note in the two following schemata the alternate Phay Ghimel and Ghimel Phay.

II

14 יוֹנָתִי בְּחַגְוֵי הַסֶּלַע בְּסֵתֶר הַמַּדְרֵגָה הַרְאִינִי
אֶת־מַרְאַיִךְ הַשְׁמִיעִנִי אֶת־קוֹלֵךְ כִּי־קוֹלֵךְ עָרֵב
וּמַרְאֵיךְ נָאוֶה׃

PHONETICALLY: *Yonati Be'hhagve Ha'selaa Be'seter Ha'medragah Ha'riyni Et-Ma'raykh Ha'shimiyni Et-Qolekh Ki-Qolekh Aarev Oo'mareykh Naweh.*

RSV: *O my dove, in the clefts of the rock, in the covert of the cliff, let me see your face, let me hear your voice, for your voice is sweet, and your face is comely.*

QABALA: Breath: *I am reborn, Immanence rises from your depths, having passed through a cycle in primordial stuff. Developed forms conceal the living drive within them. Guard against the spell of their rhythm, since you are true perception, mysterious presence of rightness, symbol of Israel. You voice my name.*

This verse has always baffled its interpreters. From the naturalistic point of view, how and why is "She" suddenly hiding in the holes of a rock, and why, in the middle of a conversation, does he say "let me hear your voice"? From the mythical point of view, "He" is the hidden one, to be searched for, not "She".

The verse is divided into three parts. The first explains what her situation is, as it results from the preceding verses. The second expresses the wish that she be seen and heard. The third explains the reason for that wish.

The first part is set in five schemata. The first schema, *Yonati* (my dove) is the name "He" gives "Her". We said (1,15) that the dove is symbol of Israel. To understand it, we must compare *Yonah* and *YHWH*.

> *Yonah:* Yod Waw Noun Hay: 10.6.50.5.
> *YHWH:* Yod Hay Waw Hay: 10.5. 6.5.

Their only difference is the permutation 6.50-5.6, and the fact that 50 is the projection in the concrete, therefore is a symbol of the archetype 5.

Be'hhagve (Bayt Hhayt Ghimel Waw Yod: 2.8.3.6.10), is built on the root *Hhag* (Hhayt Ghimel: 8.3) meaning "to trace a circle". This idiomatic sense is correct: when, in the unstructured energy (8) an organic impulse (3) starts moving and does not find its response, Dallet—as in *Ghedi* or *Dag*, explained earlier—it cannot but whirl round and round.

Ha'selaa (Hay Samekh Lammed Ayn: 5.60.30.70) is a rock. But what kind of a rock? The Sacred Rock of Mount *Hhorev* that gave water when struck by Moses was a *Tsawr*, not a *Selaa*. *Tsawr* as compared to light explains its meaning:

> Light: *Awr:* Aleph Waw Raysh: 1.6.200
> Sacred Rock: *Tsawr:* Tsadde Waw Raysh: 90.6.200

It is the achieved structure of Aleph Raysh. But *Selaa* is only the female sex in an indefinite perpetual movement.

Be'Seter shows again a female Samekh (Samekh Tav Waw: 60.400.6). After having completed its barren circle, as described above, it ends in Tav, where one day a new energy will be born (see II, 11).

Ha'medragah is the final schema of this first part. Its root *Midrag* (Mem Dallet Raysh Ghimel: 40.4.200.3) shows the biosphere giving birth to a new life. In the idiom it is a piercing, and also something gradual, a step, a scale.

In brief, "He" has called her, by her mystical name, to be the spectator of the eternal metabolic circle, whose drive is concealed in the structured forms.

He shows her that complete circle, in which Breath, however present, is still asleep and not apparent. But "She" is different. In her, Breath is awake. Through her, who is symbol of Israel, that symbol must be fully perceived, and the Name clearly heard.

The rest of the verse needs no further comment.

II

15   אֶחֱזוּ־לָ֫נוּ שׁוּעָלִים שֻׁעָלִים קְטַנִּים מְחַבְּלִים
כְּרָמִים וּכְרָמֵינוּ סְמָדַר:

PHONETICALLY: *Ehhezoo Lanoo Shooaleem Shoaleem Qetaneem Mehhableem Keràmeem Oo'kramenoo Smadar.*

RSV: *Catch us the foxes, the little foxes, that spoil the vineyards, for our vineyards are in blossom.*

QABALA: Breath: *Guide the new life that is growing in you. The young foxes ravage the flowering vines. But your vine, ought you to abandon it?*

Ehhezoo is built with the root *Hhazah* (8.7.5). *Hhaz* is a stir (7) in the passive unshaped stuff (8). In the idiom, *Hhazah* is "behold, perceive, foresee". *Ehhezoo* (Aleph Hhayt Zayn Waw: 1.8.7.6) illustrates a strange movement of Aleph, acting upon

Hhayt, and producing the sequence Hayt Zayn Waw in inverted order to Waw Zayn Hhayt of the alphabet. The root *Ahhaz* (1.8.7) means to seize, grasp.

We are facing here one of the deepest and most mysterious operations of the cabalistic thought. This mode of thinking never allows itself to go peacefully along a one-way road from one conclusion to another. Thus, it does not stifle thought in words.

Ehhezoo is the most important action of Aleph, simultaneous to its "going forth", or Emanation: it is its own resistance to it. The resistance of Aleph to itself as Hhayt, is summarized in its number: *Ehhad* (one).

> *Aleph:* Aleph Lammed Phay: 1.30.80
> *Ehhad:* Aleph Hhayt Dallet: 1. 8. 4

Its Dallet (4) is produced by the inverted direction of its flow (expressed by the alphabet in inverted order).

Obviously, if the Universe is the explosion of a concentration of energy, this unique energy is twofold.

With the first schema of this verse, Breath gives a lesson to Psyche. Psyche had discovered in herself that a new life was born: "look at it, perceive it, seize it, grasp it, take care of it", says Breath. In a word: "resist it", so as to be "in the image, after the likeness" of the Creative Powers (Gen. 1, 26). This opening of II, 15 (thrice five) epitomizes the whole verse. It gives, perhaps, the most difficult lesson to learn, the lesson that very few inspired people ever listened to: "do not allow yourselves to be swept away by passion for your revelation: resist it, criticize it, doubt it, and polish with care the shape you give it".

The word *Shoal* for fox (Sheem Ayn Lammed: 300.70.30) must be compared to the barren rock, *Selaa* of the preceding verse.

> *Selaa:* Samekh Lammed Ayn: 60.30.70
> *Shoal:* Sheen Ayn Lammed: 300.70.30

Shoal bristles with uncontrolled life, ready to rouse chaos.

II

16

דּוֹדִי לִי וַאֲנִי לוֹ הָרֹעֶה בַּשּׁוֹשַׁנִּים:

PHONETICALLY: *Dodi Li Ve'ani Lo Ha'raweh Be'shoshaneem.*

RSV: *My beloved is mine and I am his, he pastures his flock among the lilies.*

QABALA: Psyche: *Breath is mine, I am his. Let him stir and guide me. Two Breaths as one.*

"Her" response to "Him" (*Dodi*) is *Li* (Lammed Yod: 30.10) and in her inner being, *Ani*, she is *Lo* (Lammed Waw: 30.6). This is a remarkably condensed assertion, leading us to meditate on the position and significance of Yod and Waw.

We have already seen the schema *Shosshaneem* (lilies for some interpreters, roses for others). It would be better understood if pronounced *Shwa-Shna'im*: Sheen, Waw (or Sheen copulatively active) upon *Shna'im* (meaning two, in masculine absolute): Sheen acting upon Sheen: two Breaths in one.

II

17

עַד שֶׁיָּפוּחַ הַיּוֹם וְנָסוּ הַצְּלָלִים סֹב דְּמֵה־לְךָ
דוֹדִי לִצְבִי אוֹ לְעֹפֶר הָאַיָּלִים עַל־הָרֵי בָתֶר:

PHONETICALLY: *Aad Sheyafooahh Ha'yom Ve'nassoo Ha'tslaleem Sov Damah-Lekh Dodi Li'tsvi Aw Le'ofer Ha'ayaleem Aal-Harey Bater.*

RSV: *Until the day breathes and the shadows flee, turn, my beloved, be like a gazelle, or a young stag upon rugged mountains.*

QABALA: Psyche: *Before the day leads you to an irreversible event, be, my love, the indeterminate freshness of your universal home.*

This is the last verse of the second Chant, the Chant of the Sacred Duality. We have been gradually led to contemplate wider and wider spheres, from the individual to the cosmic, from the temporal to the timeless "Two in One", until we came upon the irreducible Emanation-Resistance, which contains in its Essence every possibility, and appears contradictorily in the one single existence of that which is.

This ascertainment cannot be better condensed than in the first schema *Aad* (70.4) of this last verse. We have tentatively translated it Eternity (see I, 12 and II, 7) although the words eternity, eternal, have no real substance. The juxtaposition of the antithesis 70.4, as "Residue of Residues" of all that is, is dramatic. In this verse, Psyche, wishing for a new, free, fresh life urges both itself and Breath to remain unsoiled: a hopeless battle! Its joys and sorrows, ecstasies and frustrations will be vividly described in the following Chants. We will see how the unpolluted Fount always evades us, even when we battle in it and drink of it.

But now "She" prays to it and invokes it: *Aad Sheyafooahh Ha'yom*: *Aaad* breathes the *Yom* (Yod Waw Mem: 10.6.40). We have seen in "The Cipher of Genesis" that *Yom*, translated "day" is the projection of *Awr* (light), in the emanation Yod, the partner "against" Aleph.

Light: Awr: Aleph Waw Raysh: 1.6.200
Day: Yom: Yod Waw Mem: 10.6.40/600

Ve'nassooo Ha'tslaleem: and escape, depart, disappear, the *Tsaleem*. The singular *Tsalel* (Tsadde Lammed Lammed: 90.30.30) must be understood as the structure (Tsadde) of two Lammed, or of *Lailah*, night, whose *Autiot* are all in *Ha'tsaleem*. In the idiom, Tsalel has different contradictory meanings, as often happens when the root expresses an ontological fact: to sink and to settle, to grow dark, and to tingle, to prickle. Those meanings describe adequately the new life that sinks and settles in the dark recesses of her mind and her sensations. We extensively commented upon the two Lammed, two lives operating in *Leilah*, when that word appeared in Genesis. Night has always been considered in the ancient tradition as the regeneration of both the physical and the psychological lives.

With those schemata, Psyche described the contradictions and conflicts that, during the day, dispel, the unifying pureness of the night.*

We must now keep in mind that "She" is not addressing a mystical Breath located in an imaginary heaven, but Breath, as it is "conceived" (in both senses of the word) in her. "She" is not pregnant with child: the incarnation described in the Song will not give birth to any pagan child-God. It will stir womanhood in body and mind, and culminate in "conceptive" intelligence.

Here are the explanatory schemata: *Sov* (Samekh Bayt: 60.2): she addresses her own sex in her body. *Damah-Lekh*: think yourself. *Li'tsvi*: the idiom, unknowingly, gives one of the keys to the root *Tsvi*, when we put together its apparently unrelated meanings: "gazelle, glory, beautiful colour". *Tsviah* means simply female. The key that relates this word to the essential meaning of this verse and to the general meaning of the Song, is its structural Tsadde (Tsvi: Tsadde Bayt Yod). *Aw Le'ofer Ha'ayaleem*: or else, perhaps, the dust's powers, *Aal Harey Bater*: acting upon the characteristic, individual aspect, will dissect it, cut it in two.

---

* In this respect, we are prompted to quote the famous "vanity of vanities" of Ecclesiastes (a cabalistic author), and his "a time for every matter under heaven"... (... a time to do this, and a time to do something else etc.). The Word he uses for "vanity" is none other than *Hevel*, Cain's mythical brother, known in English as Abel. When read with the code, what Eccleciastes says is: the breath of Sheen in the living world has in it every possibility, but, as time flows, it only actualizes one thing after another, eliminating all the other would-be possibilities. This, by the way, explains Abel's disappearance, and this is what "She" has just been saying in cabalistic language.

In résumé, Psyche warns itself against disintegration in everyday existence.

III

1

עַל־מִשְׁכָּבִי בַּלֵּילוֹת בִּקַּשְׁתִּי אֵת שֶׁאָהֲבָה
נַפְשִׁי בִּקַּשְׁתִּיו וְלֹא מְצָאתִיו:

PHONETICALLY: *Aal Mishkabi Ba'leilot Bi'qashti Et Sh'ahavah Nafshi Be'qashtiv We-lo Mitsativ.*

RSV: *Upon my bed by night I sought him whom my soul loves; I sought him but found him not; I called him but he gave no answer.*

QABALA: Person: *I heard him, he came into me, but I am still looking for him. His breath and my body are united, yet I do not know where this union took place. His presence in me was radiance; so bright—how could I catch hold of it?*

The *Autiot* of the first equation read one by one, explain the events following Psyche's invocation, as stated in the preceding verse: *Aal* (Ayn Lammed) idiomatically: upon, height, toward, beside, near, etc. . . . projects upon 30 all that it is capable of (70). *Mishkabi* (Mem Sheen Kaf Bayt Yod) idiomatically "my couch", expresses "Her" biological response, Mem, projecting Sheen in her body. *Ba'leilot* idiomatically "by nights" (Bayt Lammed Yod Lammed Waw Tav: 2.30.10.30.6.400) shows how the body, Bayt, having received the impact of Sheen, engenders two Lammed that fertilize their origin Tav. (For explanations of the schema *Leilah* (night) see verse II, 17 and "The Cipher of Genesis".) *Bi'qashti* (Bayt Qof Sheen Tav Yod: 2.100.300.400.10) shows the effect of the fertilization: it inserts Sheen between Qof (the cosmic Aleph), and its tabernacle of cosmic resistance, Tav.

Sh'ahavah: Sheen upon Aleph alive and Vayt alive! This schema is the conclusion of the process just described. (We remember that *Ahavah*, in the idiom, is Love.)

COMMENTARIES

In spite of this fulfilment, "He" evades "Her": *Nafshi
Be'qashtiv*: "with my whole person, my soul, my breath (Sheen),
I have obtained a cosmic communion of Qof and Tav".

We-lo Mitsativ "and yet, the organic Aleph, I have not been
able to structure".

In the last schema *Mitsativ*, the structuring Tsadde, acting
upon Aleph, is of no avail: Aleph-Tav remained linked together
as a total unfolded mystery.

III

אָק֫וּמָה נָּא וַאֲסוֹבְבָה בָעִיר בַּשְּׁוָקִים֙ וּבָרְחֹב֔וֹת 2
אֲבַקְשָׁ֕ה אֵת שֶׁאָהֲבָ֖ה נַפְשִׁ֑י בִּקַּשְׁתִּ֖יו וְלֹ֥א מְצָאתִֽיו׃

PHONETICALLY: *Aqoomah Na Wa'assov'vah Ba'ayir Ba'shvaqeem
Oo'va'rhhobot Avaqshah Et Sh'ahavah Nafshi Bi'qashtiv We-lo
Mitsativ.*

RSV: *I will rise now and go about the city, in the streets and in the
squares; I will seek him whom my soul loves. I sought him, but found
him not.*

QABALA: Person: *I set out to look for him among the items of my
work, contradictory they turned me round and round upon
myself and I did not find him.*

Aqoomah: (Aleph Qof Waw Mem Hay) the root Qom (Qof
Waw Mem) is a rising by the action of Cosmic Aleph (Qof)
upon Mem; here, "She" is doubly prompted to arise, by Aleph
and Qof. They activate her so as to bring forth the following
schema, *Na*, in which Aleph springs forth, through her.

Wa'assov'vah: Aleph, thus freed, acts upon her sex (Samekh),
and fertilizes two Vayt alive, two containers, mind and body.
No schema could better express a self-generating process. It
can be interpreted as "walking around oneself".

Ba'ayer: *Ayer* (70.10.200) is, in Genesis, Cain's first action.
To "build a city" is to give existence and shape to a container

of the possibilities offered by Ayn (see II, 17). In spite of the potential energies being present during the night, in *Leilot*—nights—"She" did not capture "Him"; now she must face her own structures.

This second verse illustrates the inescapable conflict of duality in which one is caught when trying to clutch at the Unseizable. In the "city" of her structures "She" goes round and round, from *Shvaqeem* to *Rhhobot*. These two schemata are better seen in numbers: 300.6.100.10.600. and 200.8.2.6.400. The first shows a stream of life from Sheen, and for the idiom, *Shoq* is something active, as a market; the second is passive; its root *Rehhav* is a space, a width.

The end of the verse is identical to that of the preceding one.

III

3   מְצָא֙וּנִי֙ הַשֹּׁמְרִ֔ים הַסֹּבְבִ֖ים בָּעִ֑יר אֵ֣ת שֶׁאָהֲבָ֔ה
נַפְשִׁ֖י רְאִיתֶֽם׃

PHONETICALLY: *Metsa'ooni Ha'shomareem Ha'soveveem Ba'ayir Et Sh'ahavah Nafshi Reytem.*

RSV: *The watchmen found me, as they went about in the city. "Have you seen him whom my soul loves?"*

QABALA: Person: *Their energies swirled about in self-protection, closing in, pressing upon me as I went on asking: where is my love?*

Met'sa'ooni is a very strong word. Its root, *Mitsah* or *Matsah* means to drain, to squeeze, to wring out, to exhaust; it is also the unleavened bread, deprived of watery substance. The *Shomareem* are the "guardians". As so often happens, the root *Shamar* or *Shemer*, gives us, through its apparently unrelated meanings, a key to what is really meant, psychologically, by "guardian": *Shemer* is the word for yeast, *Shemareem* are dregs, sediment. Yeast introduced in dough, produces a fermentation, i.e. an effervescence, a heat, an inflation. The dregs are the last remnants of fermentation in wine. The schema *Shemer* (Sheen Mem Raysh: 300.40.200) shows the movement of Sheen introduced in a biological substance, and disappearing in Raysh: a simple fermentation.

The verse could be condensed thus: The energies that ferment in the structures built by men rejected me in order to protect themselves, as I went on asking: where are my Aleph alive and my Vayt alive?

III

4
אֶת שֶׁמָּצָאתִי עַד מֵהֶם שֶׁעָבַרְתִּי כִּמְעַט
שֶׁהֲבֵיאתִיו עַד אַרְפֶּנּוּ וְלֹא אֲחַזְתִּיו נַפְשִׁי שֶׁאָהֲבָה
הוֹרָתִי: חֶדֶר וְאֶל אִמִּי בֵּית אֶל

PHONETICALLY: *Kimaat Sh'aavarti Mehem Aad Sh'matsati Et Sh'ahavah Nafshi Ahhaztiv We'Lo Arfenoo Aad-Sh'hevetiv El-Bayt Imi We'el Hheder Horati.*

RSV: *Scarcely had I passed them, when I found him whom my soul loves. I held him and would not let him go until I had brought him into my mother's house, and into the chamber of her that had conceived me.*

QABALA: Psyche: *They emptied me out. Then I found him who was being born, found him in the cell that was engendering me: a union of two who were because they were not yet.*

Psyche has now learned that all that had given her substance, volume and weight was simply a fermentation, that had assailed her, but had not been able to penetrate in her. She resisted it and found herself completely empty. An empty psyche is as if it were not born. Yet, because it knows itself to be empty, it is ready to commune with Breath.

Kimaat, is idiomatically: "as soon as". But the *Autiot* (Kaf Mem Ayn Tayt: 20.40.70.9) say that her physical body animates her sex with 70.

Sh'aavarti: the root *Aavar* or *Eever* or *Ayber* or *Aabarah* or *Iyvri*, etc. . . . has such varied meanings that it meets the requirements of many different interpretations. We will limit our reading to its *Autiot*: Ayn Vayt Raysh: 70.2.200. The complete schema, ending in *Ti* (Tav Yod: 400.10) brings the action back to her, grammatically, and "into" her, ontologically.

Mehem: Two Mem including life (Hay). *Aad*: "towards" the eternal equation 70.4. *Sh'matsati*, a remarkable schema: "Her" Sheen acts upon *Matsati* ("my" flatness, or "my lack of substance"). The *Autiot* Mem Tsadde Aleph Tav Yod show the structural Tsadde emerging from Mem and uniting Aleph and Tav in manifestation (Yod).

Et: Aleph Tav (the beginning and the end) in one.

In the remaining schemata, the interplay between Aleph and Tav is apparent. All the *Autiot* bring their contribution to our understanding the necessity of emptying ourselves of our psychological structures.

III

5 הִשְׁבַּ֨עְתִּי אֶתְכֶ֜ם בְּנ֤וֹת יְרוּשָׁלִַ֙ם֙ בִּצְבָא֔וֹת א֖וֹ בְּאַיְל֣וֹת הַשָּׂדֶ֑ה אִם־תָּעִ֧ירוּ ׀ וְֽאִם־תְּעֽוֹרְר֛וּ אֶת־ הָאַהֲבָ֖ה עַ֥ד שֶׁתֶּחְפָּֽץ׃

PHONETICALLY: *Hishbaati Etkhem Benot Yeroshalom Bi'tsebaot Aw Bi'aylot Hassadeh Im-Taayroo We'im-Teoreroo Et-Ha'ahevah Aad Shetehhfats.*

RSV: *I adjure you, O daughters of Jerusalem, by the gazelles or the hinds of the field, that you stir not up or awaken love until it please.*

QABALA: Woman: *Daughters of the false styles of peace! I send the Heavenly Hosts against you. Love which is not a source is only unsatisfied desire.*

This verse is the exact repetition of II, 7 and as such has been commented upon many times, in many ways, with no positive result as to making sense out of it. It is not in the rules of Qabala to repeat anything without purpose. If we go back to II, 7 and read it in its context, we see that it deals with abstract generalities. If we read again this III, 5, keeping in mind the verses that precede it, we find ourselves in the actual source of life, where the two flows of Aleph and Tav are operating and awake. The verse, II, 7 is a vision of reality; III, 5, if we have lived psyche's inner call, is its blossoming.

In brief, love, *Ahavah*, Aleph alive and Vayt alive, is the double process of the One in us. In the psyche, Aleph alive destroys in succession all the structures of the mind, so as to keep it constantly free and agile. In the body, Vayt alive rebuilds in succession, the structures of the body so as to keep it whole and in good health.

When the two inverted directions of Energy are free to operate in us, their process is *Ahavah*, love, because we commune with Aleph and with Bayt in everything that is.

III

6-11

מִי זֹאת עֹלָה מִן־הַמִּדְבָּר כְּתִימֲרוֹת עָשֵׁן מְקֻטֶּרֶת מֹר וּלְבוֹנָה מִכֹּל אַבְקַת רוֹכֵל׃ הִנֵּה מִטָּתוֹ שֶׁלִּשְׁלֹמֹה שִׁשִּׁים גִּבֹּרִים סָבִיב לָהּ מִגִּבֹּרֵי יִשְׂרָאֵל׃ כֻּלָּם אֲחֻזֵי חֶרֶב מְלֻמְּדֵי מִלְחָמָה אִישׁ חַרְבּוֹ עַל־יְרֵכוֹ מִפַּחַד בַּלֵּילוֹת׃ אַפִּרְיוֹן עָשָׂה לוֹ הַמֶּלֶךְ שְׁלֹמֹה מֵעֲצֵי הַלְּבָנוֹן׃ עַמּוּדָיו עָשָׂה כֶסֶף רְפִידָתוֹ זָהָב מֶרְכָּבוֹ אַרְגָּמָן תּוֹכוֹ רָצוּף אַהֲבָה מִבְּנוֹת יְרוּשָׁלָ͏ִם׃ צְאֶינָה וּרְאֶינָה בְּנוֹת צִיּוֹן בַּמֶּלֶךְ שְׁלֹמֹה בָּעֲטָרָה שֶׁעִטְּרָה־ לּוֹ אִמּוֹ בְּיוֹם חֲתֻנָּתוֹ וּבְיוֹם שִׂמְחַת לִבּוֹ׃

PHONETICALLY: *Mi Zot Oola Min-Ha'midbar Ke'timarot Aashan Meqooteret Mor Oo'lvonah Mi'kol Avaqit Rokhel.*

Hini Mitato Sheli'shlomoh Shisheem Ghiboreem Saviv Laha Mi'gborey Israel.

Koolam Ahhouzev Hherey Meloomdi Mi' lhhamah Iysh Hharbo Aal-Yerekho Mi'pahhad Ba'leylot.

Apiryon Aassah Lo Ha'melekh Shlomoh Me'atstey Ha'lvanon.

Aamodov Aassa Kessef Refidato Zahav Merkavo Argheman Tokho Ratsmof Ahevah Mi'benot Yeroshalom.

Tseynah O'reynah Benot Tsion Ba'melekh Shlomoh B'atarah Sh'itrah Lo Imo Be'yom Hhatonato Oo'be'yom Shimhhat Libo.

RSV: *What is that coming up from the wilderness, like a column of smoke, perfumed with myrrh and frankincense, with all the fragrant powders of the merchant?*

Behold, it is the litter of Solomon! About it are sixty mighty men of Israel.

All girt with swords and expert in war, each with his sword at his thigh, against the alarms by night.

King Solomon made himself a palanquin from the wood of Lebanon. He made its posts of silver, its back of gold, its seat of purple; it was lovingly wrought within by the daughters of Jerusalem.

Go forth, O daughters of Zion, and behold King Solomon, with the crown with which his mother crowned him on the day of his wedding, on the day of the gladness of his heart.

QABALA: Poet: *At a certain distance from the false styles of peace I see another false peace: of passiveness. What smoke rises from that desert? King Solomon, whose name is pretended Peace, for whom the quintessence is what perfumers make, burns day and night those scented extracts, a pretended residue. He puts himself, as it were, in a box, a pretended stately conveyance. War-men to the number of 60 (the number of the female sex), the bravest of Israel, watch over his night fears, for he does not resist life with suppleness and rigidly he resists death. His passiveness holds Emanation in check. When Breath enters into him, he will burst. The shell concealing him depends on the stuff of female submission. They are busy about his inertia. Pretended royalty is on his head. Crowned by his mother on his wedding day, this Solomon, this pseudo-king is the female Queen!*

This personage is ludicrous. He is described with a dismal, cruel sense of humour. The accumulation of details is deliberately incongruous: what is he doing, in his palanquin, in a desert, burning all the products of perfumers, lying crowned with an absurd crown given by his mother, the day he married? And why is he terrified? The text does not say that the warriors surround him "against the alarms by night" but *Mi'pahhad Ba'leylot*: because of the nocturnal terrors (*Pahhad* is fear, awe, dread, to be frightened).

The word crown, as it is often met in *Sepher Yetsira* is *Keter* (20.400.200). But Solomon's maternal crown is *Aatarah* (70.9.200.5) including *Tayt* (9) the female sex. In Exodus, the two columns of light and smoke guiding the people are *Aamoodeem* but Solomon's scented columns of smoke are *Timarot* (beginning and ending with Tav). *Hhatonato* again from Tav to Tav. *Mitato* blends Tayt and Tav. *Apiryon*, of hellenistic sound, thrusts Aleph into Pay, deprived of its organic element Lammed, without which it cannot live. Its action upon Pay, however, culminates in the final Noun of *Apiryon*: the cosmic indetermination. In the process, Solomon will be destroyed. Many details are meant to corroborate the general picture, namely the assiduous attention of the girls upon that enormous palanquin, so similar to the licking of the queen bee's belly.

IV

1   הִנָּךְ יָפָה רַעְיָתִי הִנָּךְ יָפָה עֵינַיִךְ יוֹנִים מִבַּעַד
לְצַמָּתֵךְ שַׂעְרֵךְ כְּעֵדֶר הָעִזִּים שֶׁגָּלְשׁוּ מֵהַר גִּלְעָד:

PHONETICALLY: *Hinakh Yafeh Raayati Hinakh Yafeh Aynaikh Yonim Mi'baad Le'tsomatekh Shaarikh Ke'ayder Ha'azeem Shegleshoo Ma'har Ghilaad.*

RSV: *Behold, you are beautiful my love, behold you are beautiful! Your eyes are doves behind your veil. Your hair is like a flock of goats, moving down the slopes of Gilead.*

307

QABALA: Lover: *How beautiful you are, my friend, how beautiful! Through the veil of appearance your eyes are the fountain of Israel. You are the vision where time and timelessness meet, to be prized as a multitude that springs from eternity.*

The fourth Chant, except for the last verse said by the Person, is entirely "His" description of "Her", whether we name him Lover, Poet or Breath. The fact that she is materialized is in accordance with the serial number of this Chant. No. 4 (Dallet) is the symbol of the resistance of all the Bayt to timeless Aleph. Qabala has always considered the apparent physical supports to be a reversed projection of timeless, infinite Energy. In this fourth Chant, "He" declares her to be different: Breath is seen to be present in her, through the veil of her physical appearance.

From now on, the play on words (on appearance) will be uninterrupted. The readers will have to choose the idiomatic roots that are nearest to the meaning of the *Autiot*.

The beginning of the verse is a repetition of 1, 15: he sees once more, but this time, *Mi'baad Le'tsomatekh*: "through, or on behalf of your thirst" (the root *Tsama*: Tsadde Mem Aleph means thirst). This is a direct reference to her ardent desire to structure him through Tsadde.

Shaarikh: your price, value, or measure, *Ke'ayder Ha'azeem*: as a mighty flock of goats, *Sheglashoo* (Sheen Ghimel Lammed Sheen Waw: 300.3.300.6) boiling over. This is the key to the whole verse, with its two Sheen, one acting upon the archetype of organic movement, the other emitted by factual organic life. This dual process culminates in Waw.

Ma'har: from a mountain top. *Ghilaad* is a combination of the above mentioned Ghimel, Lammed, and *Aad*: eternity.

This symbolic description is a repetition of the leitmotiv we now know so well: "She", born in the lower depths, is also multitude emerging from the higher depths "boiling over" from animality into eternal life.

IV

2

שִׁנַּיִךְ כְּעֵדֶר הַקְּצוּבוֹת שֶׁעָלוּ מִן־הָרַחְצָה
שֶׁכֻּלָּם מַתְאִימוֹת וְשַׁכֻּלָה אֵין בָּהֶם׃

PHONETICALLY: *Shneykh Ka'ayder Ha'qtsovot Shealoo Min-Ha'rahhtsah Shekoolam Mat'i'mot We'shakoolah Ain Ba'hem.*

RSV: *Your teeth are like a flock of shorn ewes that come up from the washing, all of which bear twins, and not one among them is bereaved.*

QABALA: Poet: *Such is the dominance of your femininity. The second female aspect of your energy I have seen represented by a pompous and nervous actor wearing a crown, who lay on a scented cloud. His hands are full of wealth but he carefully washes them. Compare him to a flock of sheep, dead though not dead, without understanding.*

Shneykh: "your 2", in the masculine construct, is a reference to the male personage described earlier, whose character is female. "He" sees through "Her" the dual femininity as a whole: colloquially, the higher and the lower, the spirit and the flesh. Spirit is traditionally thought to be holy and male, flesh vile and female. In many religions, women have only recently been granted a soul and are not considered fit for sacerdocy. "She" of the Song has conquered spirit through her sex, and in striking contrast a hideous, frightened, lazy, greedy female is hidden under the appearance of a mighty king, whose hands are full of wealth but carefully washed.

This *Shneykh* is *Ka'ayder*: as a flock of sheep, *Ha'qtsovot*. The root *Qatsav* (Qof Tsadde Vayt: 100.90.2) shows the cosmic Aleph captured, limited, conditioned, by Tsadde into a container, Bayt. Those ewes are "shorn" indeed: deprived of their fleece. *She'aloo*: idiomatically, *Shoaal* (Sheen Ayn Lammed: 300.70.30) is a handful. *Min-Ha'rahhtsah*: coming from a washroom; *Shekoolam*: and all of them, *Mat'i'mot* are dead-but-not-dead, *We-Shakoolah* (*Shakal*: to be wise) and wisdom, or proper understanding, *Ain Ba'hem*: is not with them.

IV

3

כְּחוּט הַשָּׁנִי שִׂפְתוֹתַיִךְ וּמִדְבָּרֵיךְ נָאוֶה כְּפֶלַח
הָרִמּוֹן רַקָּתֵךְ מִבַּעַד לְצַמָּתֵךְ:

PHONETICALLY: *Ke'hhoot Ha'shney Sh'ptaotaykh We'midbarekh Naweh Ka'pelahh Ha'rimon Raqatekh Mi'baad Le'tsometekh.*

RSV: *Your lips are like a scarlet thread, and your mouth is lovely, your cheeks are like halves of a pomegranate behind your veil.*

QABALA: Poet: *This second aspect of your femininity is dullness, like a sin, separating you from yourself, a flaw behind the smooth exterior.*

Ke'hhoot: as a sin. The root *Hhot* (Hayt Tayt: 8.9) made of a vague element Hhayt, and an unstructured element Tayt, with no organic energy, shows that the real sense of the words sin, transgression or violation, is that lack of response to life.

Ha'shney: the 2 (above mentioned). *Sh'ptaotaykh*: which is your dullness (the root *Pteot* (Pay Tav Yod Waw Tav: 80.400.10.6.400) shows a shapeless stuff, Pay, going from Tav to Tav as in a deep slumber. Hence the idiomatic "foolishness".

We'midbarekh: (whilst) your utterances, *Nawah*: are beautiful. *Ka'pelahh*: (this dullness) is as a cleavage, *Ha'rimon* in a pomegranate, *Raqatekh* (and is) your exception (or flaw) *Mi'boad Le'tsomatekh* behind the veil of your appearance (or structure).

In this verse, the intelligent woman is described as being other than the primitive she-female.

IV

4

כְּמִגְדַּל דָּוִיד צַוָּארֵךְ בָּנוּי לְתַלְפִּיּוֹת אֶלֶף הַמָּגֵן
תָּלוּי עָלָיו כֹּל שִׁלְטֵי הַגִּבּוֹרִים:

PHONETICALLY: *Kemigdal David Tsawarekh Bano Le'talpiot Aleph Ha'maghen Taloo Aalav Kol Shiltav Ha'gaborim.*

RSV: *Your neck is like the tower of David, built for an arsenal, whereon hang a thousand bucklers, all of them shields of warriors.*

QABALA: Poet: *You are different from that, supple and strong, for your two resistances fructify one, another. They build a stronghold for Aleph, the defender of those that rest in Him, the All powerful.*

This verse comments on the preceding one, by laying stress upon the two resistances in "Her": Dallet, Dallet (4.4). "Two resistances call to me from you" (1, 2) were "His" very first words to "Her". Now, in the serial number IV, 4, a developed symbol is cleverly introduced by the play on the name *David* (Dallet Waw Yod Dallet: 4.6.10.4). It is not for the purpose of comparing a pretty neck to an enormous tower full of warrior's shields, but rather to explain why the name of the ambivalent king *David* contains two Dallet. They are in perfect contrast to the static resistance of king Solomon, recoiled in his absurd shell.

The only difference—slight but. significant—between the word *Dodi*, that we have met several times, and *David*, is a permutation of Yod and Dallet:

> Dodi: Dallet.Waw.Dallet.Yod
> David: Dallet.Waw.Yod. Dallet

The key-word to the whole verse is *Tsawarekh*: your neck. We will see in verse VII, 5 the neck is instrumental in conveying the exalted Fire, "formative of the head",* to the body. Through it is the operation that structures Fire into earthly heat. Reciprocally, through it, the bodily heat nourishes Fire: *Esh* (Aleph Sheen). Another name for Fire, is Light: *Awr* (Aleph Waw Raysh). Let us now compare *Tsawar* (Tsadde Waw Aleph Raysh and *Awr*:

> Neck: Tsadde Waw Aleph Raysh
> Light: Aleph Waw Raysh

---

* This symbolical terminology is common to Qabala and Alchemy.

In the cabalistic manner of thinking, the neck is factually the structural element, Tsadde, that operates a permutation in Light: Aleph becomes Waw and Waw becomes Aleph. This opens a remarkable field of relations between Light, Breath and Fire.

In praise of "Her", the poet says that she structures Light so as to build, *Bano Le'talpiot Aleph*, a stronghold for Aleph. From now on, the reader will easily follow both the *Autiot* and the idiomatic corresponding roots: from this stronghold, Aleph is the defender of those that depend on it; it has the power of the Mighty Ones.

IV

5

שְׁנֵי שָׁדַיִךְ כִּשְׁנֵי עֳפָרִים תְּאוֹמֵי צְבִיָּה הָרוֹעִים
בַּשּׁוֹשַׁנִּים׃

PHONETICALLY: *Shney Shadaykh Ki'shnev Aaphareem Teomey Tsebiah Ha'roieem Ba'shoshaneem.*

RSV: *Your two breasts are like two fawns, twins of a gazelle, that feed among the lilies.*

QABALA: Poet: *In and through your two resistances the Breath of Life and the Breath of Existence are at the same time taken in and given out.*

In this fifth verse, we note five Sheen, meaning that Sheen, so often mentioned, is actively alive. The first *Shney* (two in the masculine construct) is related to *Shadaykh*, translated your breast. Its real meaning is your Almighty. "This two, your Almighty" cannot surprise us more than the plural *Elohim*, naming the same deity. Considering that "She" is the duality, this "two", her *Shadai*, is justified.

Among the many idiomatic connotations of the root Sheen Dallet (such as breast or robbery) the most remarkable are *Shed* (Sheen Dallet): the devil, *Shadai* (Sheen Dallet Yod): the Almighty, and *Shadad* (Sheen Dallet Dallet): to plunder,

despoil. Qabala explains them: Sheen and Dallet are two contrasting forms of Energy. Sheen is the "breath" of a cosmic
organic motion, Dallet is a resistance. When Dallet obtains a
deadlock, it is the "devil"; when Dallet prevails, the contest
ends in a "plunder"; when Sheen prevails, the Yod of existence
comes into being.

The second *Shney* of this verse is applied to *Aaphareem*. We
have seen the schema *Aaphar*, pronounced *Oofer*, in II, 9 in one
of its idiomatic meanings: dust. It also means fawn. The association dust and fawn is due to the fact that Phay is the raw
material into which Aleph (Aleph Lammed Phay) introduces
the organic motion of Lammed. The fawn is a very young life,
mobile as dust.

Thus, the first *Shney* of the verse IV, 5 is applied to "Her"
Shadai, her highest state of Energy, and the second to her
lowest energy, not yet structured. Over and over again, tire-
lessly, the Song sings the blending of the End and the Beginning.

IV

6 עַד שֶׁיָּפֹוּחַ הַיֹּום וְנָסוּ הַצְּלָלֵים אֵלֵךְ לִי אֶל־הַר
הַמֹּור וְאֶל־גִּבְעַת הַלְּבֹונָה׃

PHONETICALLY: *Aad Sheiaphooahh Ha'yom Ve'nassoo Ha'tsalaleem
Elekh Li El-Har Ha'mor We'el-Ghibaat Ha'lvoonah.*

RSV: *Until the day breathes and the shadows flee, I will hie me to the
mountain of myrrh and the hill of frankincense.*

QABALA: Breath: *Before the dull day takes me from what is possible
and makes it irreversible, I give life to your two aspects. One
is your holy uncertainty, the other will go back to unshaped
substance.*

The first five schemata of this verse are a repetition of the
first five of II, 17. But now, until IV, 15, "He" is the one who

speaks. In their colloquial sense, the meanings of the following words are disconnected:

Elekh: towards you. *Li*: to me. *El-Har*: towards the mountain. *Ha'mor*: the exchange, or change of religion. *We'el*: and the Almighty. *Ghibaat*: puts in a cast. *Ha'lvoonah*: the whitening (or the grinding).

Ghibaat idiomatically is also a hill, and *Lvoonah* frankincense, but Mor, spelt Mem Waw Raysh, is not myrrh (spelt Mem Raysh). This key-word must be compared to *Awr* light:

Awr: Aleph.Waw.Raysh

Mor: Mem. Waw.Raysh

It expresses a state of Energy belonging to the biosphere: a materialized projection of Aleph Waw Raysh.

We can now connect to this projection the beginning of the verse: *Aad Sheiaphooahh Ha'yom Ve'nassoo*. *Yom* (Yod Waw Mem) is also a materialization of Aleph Waw Raysh. The sequence *Yom-Mor* is: Yod Waw Mem—Mem Waw Raysh. Thus *Mor* starts from Mem and reverses the direction of the Energy *Yom*.

We have seen, in commenting II, 17, that the action of *Yom* is the disappearance (*Nasso*) of *Tsalaleem*: whereas those symbolical shadows structure, by Tsadde, two Lammed in Mem, *Nasso* (Noun Samekh) thrusts back that energy in a womb, Samekh. This, says Breath in IV, 6, must not happen. Lammed is Aleph's active agent. Its action must not be destroyed. So the verse proceeds: *Elekh*: *Al* upon final Khaf (500: cosmic life); *Li* (Lammed upon Yod, the existence) *El-Har*: *Al* and Hay Raysh, life of the emanation. The Sacred Language is all-inclusive. The most exalted abstract meaning is conveyed in its physical support. "She" receives the impact of *Al*'s energy, and indeed reverses the flow called *Yom*. Then *Al* appears again, and, metaphorically, puts her in a cast, moulds her purity. (In *Ghibaat*, the uncertainty of Ayn is projected in Tav.)

This is perhaps the most mystical of all the verses of the Song. It relates what is known as the Gnostic Nuptials.

IV

7

כֻּלָּךְ יָפָה רַעְיָתִי וּמוּם אֵין בָּךְ:

PHONETICALLY: *Koolakh Yaphah Raayati Oomoom Ain Bakh.*
RSV: *You are all fair, my love; there is no flaw in you.*
QABALA: Breath: *You, my dear one, are the beautiful transfigured
sanctuary of my indetermination.*

The serial no. 7 of this verse is the number of indeterminate
possibilities, now open to "Her" by her conversion described
in the preceding verse.

The first schema *Koolakh* (Kaf Lammed Khaf: 20.30.20-500)
illustrates an alternative: when Khaf is only its number (20),
the energy acts upon itself; when that Khaf assumes its final
value (500) in the name Koolakh, the action is cosmically alive.

The key-word of the verse is *Oomoom* (Waw Mem Waw Mem:
6.40.6.600) in which the male energy is seen as being doubled
by two Waw, so as to meet the duality. One Waw is received
by the biosphere Mem (6.40) and the other is projected cosmically, still retaining its male quality (6.600). This happens when,
mystically speaking "the flesh gives birth to, or becomes spirit".

IV

8

אִתִּי מִלְּבָנוֹן כַּלָּה אִתִּי מִלְּבָנוֹן תָּבוֹאִי תָּשׁוּרִי |
מֵרֹאשׁ אֲמָנָה מֵרֹאשׁ שְׂנִיר וְחֶרְמוֹן מִמְּעֹנוֹת אֲרָיוֹת
מֵהַרְרֵי נְמֵרִים:

PHONETICALLY: *Iti Mi'lvanon Kalah Iti Mi'lvanon Taboi Tashoori
Me'rosh Amanah Me'rosh Shneer We'hhermon Mi'mo'onot Arayot
Me'harerey Nemireem.*

RSV: *Come with me from Lebanon, my bride; come with me from
Lebanon. Depart from the peak of Ama'na, from the peak of Senir and
Hermon, from the dens of lions, from the mountains of leopards.*

QABALA: Breath: *Come with me, come and contemplate our common origin. Your person is double and so is your lunar symbol. I bury myself in you and I come out from you: one act in two opposite directions.*

The play on words such as mountain peaks, dens of lions and leopards has a dreamlike quality, well befitting a verse dealing with the hidden layers of consciousness, Hhayt (8), its serial number.

Iti (Aleph Tav Yod: 1.400.10), translated not erroneously "come with me", is the wished-for meeting of "Him" (Aleph) and "Her" (Tav) in factual existence (Yod).

Mi'lvanon is one of the fundamental words used in the Song to convey different meanings, and to mislead the non-cabalist readers. It has no connection with Lebanon. The root *Lavan* (Lammed Vayt Noun) means white. Its components: Lammed, the organic motion, Vayt, the container, and Noun with its double meaning as 50 (life in existence) or 700 (cosmic indetermination) constitute an abstract unsolved equation of a double process. *Lvanah* is also the moon, or a stone slab, generally used as a tombstone.

We are led here in the deepest layers of our consciousness in connection with the Zodiac. Hhayt (8), serial number of this verse, "forms", in the Zodiac, Cancer named *Sartan* (Samekh Raysh Tayt Noun: 60.200.9.700). It is the dwelling place, or habitat of the Moon. The Moon, formed by Tav (400), has two opposite qualities that cohabit in the same constellation. According to the Sepher Yetsira their names are *Aabadot*, textually the slaves, in which the dynamic (male) Energy deeply sinks, and *Memshelah*, sometimes seen as Messianic, from which that same Energy springs forth.

The first three schemata *Iti Mi'lvanon Kalah* describe "their" meetings in which "He" sinks; and the three following, *Iti Mi'lvanon Taboi* (Tav culminating in Aleph Yod) describe their "Meeting" in which "He" arises. Such is "their" common origin, where "He" disappears and reappears in contrary directions.

In our *Midrash* we did not enter into all the elaborate details of this verse. We are dealing here with a double exploration of the origin of Life, in the ovule and in the Zodiac, by means of a complex semantic code, and an analogical way of thinking through which the *Autiot* can find their way into us. When this happens, those powerful centres of Energy release the Revelation that is said to be Abraham's.

Those elucidations must be clearly understood before we attempt to follow "Her" where she is led to "look" and to "see". Here are a few notes that will be as signs on the way:

Tashoori. The root—verb or noun—*Shor* (Sheen Waw Raysh: 300.6.200) has idiomatically many different meanings, such as ox, wall, acrobat, enemy, to see, behold, observe, to turn aside, to depart, to tumble, to wrestle. Its real sense is mysterious, because, as in *Sheer Ha-Sheereem* (Song of Songs) the Sheen in *Shor* precedes Raysh, whereas in the alphabet, the Raysh precedes Sheen. Moreover, *Tashouri* (Tav Sheen Waw Raysh Yod: 400.300.6.200.10) clearly shows a Breath (Sheen), as the active agent of Tav, giving birth to the Emanation (200.10). This schema is in absolute opposition to the notion of a Breath emitted by a deity. It is the point where "She" has been led—by the first six schemata—to "see, behold, observe" the One double origin of Life, in her and in the Universe. It is a power (ox), a wall, an enemy (a resistance), and, indeed, a state where we, as structured entities, must tumble and wrestle and turn aside, and depart acrobatically. Thus all the idiomatic connotations are true, unconsciously: our idioms and creeds appear, from this point of view, as solid dreams.

This panoramic view is *Me'rosh Amanah, Me'rosh Shneer. Rosh* (Raysh Aleph Sheen) has always been translated head, principle, or beginning. In *Me'rosh* (Mem Raysh Aleph Sheen) we see Aleph being born of Mem. In *Amanah* (Aleph Mem Noun Hay) we witness the reverse: Mem being born of Aleph. In *Me'rosh Shneer* we have a complete whirl of temporal and timeless energies giving birth to each other: a really "acrobatic" exercise for the mind!

In *Mi'mo'onot*, we note two Mem projecting Ayn (70) into Tav.

In *Arayot*, Aleph projects itself through Raysh, into Yod so as to fertilize Tav.

Me'harerey is the result of this penetration: two Raysh: two worlds, temporal and timeless, existing and alive!

Finally, *Nemireem*, with its two Mem, pictures the biological process of growth.

IV

9
לְבַבְתִּנִי אֲחֹתִי כַלָּה לְבַבְתִּנִי בְּאַחַד מֵעֵינַיִךְ
בְּאַחַד עֲנָק מִצַּוְּרֹנָיִךְ׃

PHONETICALLY: *Lebavtini Ahhoti Kalah Lebavtini Be'ehhad Me'aynaykh Be'ehhad Aanaq Mi'tsavronaykh.*

RSV: *You have ravished my heart, my sister, my bride, you have ravished my heart with a glance of your eyes, with one jewel of your necklace.*

QABALA: Breath: *Sister of Breath, your organic life redoubles my unity. You are able to build me and still be one with me.*

Lebavtini is a variant of *Milvanon* (IV, 8), of *Halvonah* (IV, 6) of *Lvanah* (the moon) and of *Levav* (the heart). All those schemata are references to the organic process Lammed, in its physical support Bayt. In this ninth verse (nine is the archetype of the living cell), Breath asserts that "His" wish to incarnate in "Her" is fulfilled because in "Her" the dual process of the one Energy is alive.

All the schemata of this verse are mathematically accurate, and easily read when the general theme of the Song is kept in mind. *Lebavtini* (30.2.2.400.50.10: the organic motion of double two in Tav factually alive) is written twice. The first time it is followed by a word qualifying "Her": *Ahhoti* (Aleph Hhayt Tav; *Ehhat* means two in the feminine). The second time, it is followed by a word qualifying "Him": *Be'ehhad* (Aleph Hhayt Dallet; *Ehhad*, means One in the masculine) *Me'aynaykh* (Mem Ayn Yod Noun Yod Khaf: 40.70.10.50.10.500) shows her biological life as it projects the 70 in two existences (10.10) alive factually (50) and cosmically (500). As a counterpart, *Be'ehhad* repeated, projects, with the schema *Aanaq* (Ayn Noun Qof: 70.50.100) the cosmic Aleph, Qof, by means of 70 and 50.

Mi'tsavronaykh (see also, in IV, 4, the word *Tsawar*), its root *Tsor* or *Tsar*, or the verb *Yotser*, and their idiomatic derivations, are all connected to the notion of structures.

IV

10

מַה־יָּפוּ דֹרַיִךְ אֲחֹתִי כַלָּה מַה־טֹּבוּ דֹרַיִךְ מִיַּיִן
וְרֵיחַ שְׁמָנַיִךְ מִכָּל־בְּשָׂמִים:

PHONETICALLY: *Mah Yafoo Dodaykh Ahhoti Kalah Mah Tovoo Dodaykh Mi'yayeen Wereyehh Shemanaykh Mi'kol Be'shamaim.*

RSV: *How sweet is your love, my sister, my bride! How much better is your love than wine, and the fragrance of your oils than any spice!*

QABALA: Breath: *Companion of Breath, my Fire in the Earth is only wine but you breathe me out and this breathing surpasses the whole content of the skies.*

All the schemata of this verse—except the last—have been met with and explained. The reader will therefore have no difficulty in following the *Autiot* one by one. In the canonical Hebrew, the letter-vowels have distorted the last word, *Shamaim*, into *Samim*, translated spices or aromas.

In our *Midrash*, we have given it its symbolical sense: the skies, although fundamentally *Shamaim* is the action of Sheen upon *Maim* (Mem Yod Mem), symbolically, the Waters.

IV

11

נֹפֶת תִּטֹּפְנָה שִׂפְתוֹתַיִךְ כַּלָּה דְּבַשׁ וְחָלָב
תַּחַת לְשׁוֹנֵךְ וְרֵיחַ שַׂלְמֹתַיִךְ כְּרֵיחַ לְבָנוֹן׃

PHONETICALLY: *Nofet Titofnah Siftotaikh Kalah Debash We'hhalav Tahhat Leshonekh We'reihha Shalmotaikh Ke'rihha Lvanon.*

RSV: *Your lips distil nectar, my bride; honey and milk are under your tongue; the scent of your garments is like the scent of Lebanon.*

QABALA: Breath: *Companion of Breath, blessedness of the perceived Incarnation, you sustain organic movement and are that organic movement itself. You are, from depth of your origin to depth of your presence now, an endless movement of contraries. You are the peace of that movement.*

The union of Aleph and Tav is now complete; the inner light of Breath radiates through the body described as "Hers"; her body is seen, so to speak, "beyond" itself. (Going "beyond" is symbolized, in Qabala, by no. 11, the serial number of the verse.) If we have looked into the hidden layers of our consciousness, as "She" has been directed to do (IV, 8), we have seen that the "lover" and the "loved" are both in us; their dialogue calls for the echo of our inner voice. The honey and milk under the tongue are a degraded symbol of that voice; her scented garments a play on the word Peace. (The word *Shalmotaikh* translated garments must be read *Shalom-taikh*: your peace; we have explained earlier the name *Lebanon*.)

The first three schemata are developments concerning the letter Phay (80), the unstructured (unconscious) hidden energies underlying the mind and body. In *Nefet* Phay dives into its origin Tav; in *Titofnah* Tav engenders Tayt and Phay; in *Siftotaikh*, the lower Breath (Sheen, pronounced Seen) acting upon Phay, redoubles Tav.

The focus of this endless—and complex—vibration between the origin and the person "now", is the schema *Kalah* (20.30.5), translated bride, and whose meaning is as wide apart as annihilation and completeness. The juxtaposition of 20 and 30 is an unsolved equation. It cannot be "thought", but it can be put in motion.

IV

12

גַּן ׀ נָעוּל אֲחֹתִי כַלָּה גַּל נָעוּל מַעְיָן חָתוּם:

PHONETICALLY: *Gan Naool Ahhoti Kalah Gal Naool Ma'ayan Hhatoum.*

RSV: *A garden locked is my sister, my bride, a garden locked, a fountain sealed.*

QABALA: Breath: *To look at what exists is to look at absolute mystery. To look at you is to open oneself to the mysterious metabolism of Emanation, for your presence creates it.*

The preceding verse invited us to put in motion an equation, in which the co-existence of Kaf (20: the physical supports) Lammed (30: the organic motions) and Hay (5: life) was stated as a fact that can be lived but not explained. It is a fantastic vibration between the "Source" and the appearance of the "now". It animates the two mysterious metabolisms of the living cell (its life in and out). Its mere being is the absolute Mystery of the existence of whatever is. Life and shape are one single phenomenon, self-engendered. "She" of the Song, being the radiation of form and the form of radiation, is both Creation and Emanation: a perceptible but sealed Mystery in the universe and in the person.

> *Gan* (Ghimel Noun: 3.700) and
> *Gal* (Ghimel Lammed: 3.30)

The archetype of metabolism, Ghimel (3) is active in the cosmic indetermination (700) and factually in its very self (30).

321

The two last schemata: *Ma'ayan Hhatoum* are revealing. They begin and end with Mem, thus closing the cycle of the biosphere. *Ayn*, the eye, or source, is projected into Hhayt and rests in the final Tav, from which the cycle starts again; in a "sealed" circuit.

IV

13　שְׁלָחַיִךְ פַּרְדֵּס רִמּוֹנִים עִם פְּרִי מְגָדִים כְּפָרִים עִם־נְרָדִים:

PHONETICALLY: *Shelahhaikh Pardes Rimoneem Aym Peri Magadeem Kefareem Aam-Neradeem.*

RSV: *Your shoots are an orchard of pomegranates with all choicest fruits, henna and nard.*

QABALA: Breath: *You are the apple of the tree and the sensuous taste of it. You are fragrance of fruit and of stimulating drugs.*

Shelahhaikh is Sheen Lammed acting upon Hhayt Yod Khaf (300.30-8.10.500): Breath activating "Her" unstructured energies. The root *Shelahh* means to extend, to send away, to send forth, to set free.

Pardes, idiomatically an orchard spelt Phay Raysh Dallet Samekh (80.200.4.60) expresses an unconscious energy (80) related through 200.4, to the female fecundity (60). The next schemata, *Rimoneem*, is pomegranates, and the following ones compare "Her" to all the choicest fruits. This calls our attention to Genesis II, 9 (note no. 9: Tayt, the ovule) where *grow every tree that is pleasant to the sight and good for food* and Genesis II, 6 (not no. 6: Waw the male sex) *when the woman saw that the tree was good for food, and that it was a delight to the eyes, and that the tree was to be desired to make one wise, she took of the fruit and ate . . .*

Nardeem, plural of *Nard*, is a symbol of stimulating drugs, as is shown by the last letter Dallet, a resistance, meaning a response.

IV

14

נֵרְדְּ ׀ וְכַרְכֹּם קָנֶה וְקִנָּמוֹן עִם כָּל־עֲצֵי לְבוֹנָה
מֹר וַאֲהָלוֹת עִם כָּל־רָאשֵׁי בְשָׂמִים׃

PHONETICALLY: *Nerde We'kharkom Qaneh We'Qinamon Aym Kol-Eytse Levonah Mir We'ahalot Aym Kol-Roshi Be'shamaim.*

RSV: *Nard and saffron, salamus and cinnamon, with all trees of frankincense, myrrh and aloes, with all chief spices.*

QABALA: Breath: *In you are the fruits of the Earth that go back into the elements. In you are the Principles of the waters animated by Breath: in you also is the intelligence which conceives those Principles.*

This verse is divided in two parts. The first part states two double equations:

> *Nerde We'kharkom* (50.200.4 and 20.200.20.40)
> *Qaneh We'Qinamon* (100.50.5 and 100.50.40.6.700)

In the double equation beginning with 50 all the following numbers are containers and their biological resistances; it expresses the absorption of life in fruitfulness. The other double equation begins with 100 (cosmic Aleph) and shows an intense life (50.5.50) achieving its process (40.6) in the cosmic indetermination (700): it is the end of fruitfulness, when the elements are scattered throughout the Universe.

This first part of the verse ends with *Aym Kol-Eytse*. *Eytse* (Ayn Tsadde Yod) meaning idiomatically tree, but expressing in a general way any existential structure.

The second part of the verse deals with Principles. We have seen several times the schema *Levonah, Lvanah, Lvanon* or *Mi'lvanon*, the lunar principle in which Aleph is buried and resurrected. *Mir* is the root of *Mareh* (sight, view, appearance, vision); *Ahalot* is ungrammatically, the feminine plural of *Ohel* (tabernacle) whose plural is *Oheleem*: a permutation of *Elohim*. Likewise, *Ahalot* is a permutation of *Elohot*, a feminine "deity".

323

For the believers in a male deity, it is a sacrilege, an unthinkable apostasy. However, when the equations are seriously examined, it appears as a logical formula: *Ahalot* (Aleph Hay Lammed Waw Tav: 1.5.30.6.400) is none other than the process through which Aleph meets Tav.

The last schemata, *Aym Kol-Roshi Be'shamaim* can be roughly translated: "all the Principles animated by the universal Breath". The word *Maim* (the waters) calls for the development of the following verse.

IV

15   מַעְיַן גַּנִּים בְּאֵר מַיִם חַיִּים וְנֹזְלִים מִן־לְבָנוֹן:

PHONETICALLY: *Meayn Ganeem Bir Maim Hhaim We'nozleem Min-Lvanon.*

RSV: *A garden fountain, a well of living water, a flowing stream from Lebanon.*

QABALA: Breath: *The double movement of the waters rises in the wells and comes down from the hills.*

The Sheen upon waters (*Shamaim* of the preceding verse) is stated here as being double: one Sheen is an impulse from "below" (Tav) springing upwards; the other is a rush from "above" (Aleph), symbolically from the hills of "Lebanon", but essentially from *Lvanon*, her Principle, or Essence (see the preceding verse).

IV

16   עוּרִי צָפוֹן וּבוֹאִי תֵימָן הָפִיחִי גַנִּי יִזְּלוּ בְשָׂמָיו
    יָבֹא דוֹדִי לְגַנּוֹ וְיֹאכַל פְּרִי מְגָדָיו:

PHONETICALLY: *Oori Tsefon We'boi Timan Hefihhi Gani Izloo Be'semav Yavo Dodi Le'gano We'iokhal Peri Be'gadav.*

324

RSV: *Awake, O north wind, and come, O south wind! Blow upon my garden, let its fragrance be wafted abroad. Let my beloved come to his garden, and eat its choicest fruits.*

QABALA: Person: *May the depth of depths free the depths of Indetermination! May my twofold organic resistance enter the organic life of Breath! And Breath live its own life!*

This verse 16 (2 × 8: twice Hhayt) concludes Chant IV (Dallet), the Chant of her response—or resistance—to Breath, through the awakening of her Hhayt, or Phay. It conveys an important, and perhaps a disappointing conclusion. "She" has tried to capture "Him" in her structure, and has failed. She now realizes that she is that structure itself: she is Tsadde, not Tav. Aleph and Tav are One, irreducibly so. She cannot identify herself to Tav and seek for Aleph; she must yield, allow both Breaths to "blow upon her garden": to blow her up, so to speak.

The following Chants will describe the human drama of achievements that are failures, of failures that are unfoldments, of errors that are truths, of discoveries that are mistakes: no Revelation can ever be captured!

The verse reads thus: "Awake me *Tsefon*! Enter into me, *Timan*! Breath me, *Gani*! He disregards *Yavo* by his Name; *Dodi* is in *Gani*; Yod-Aleph are all my fruitfulness."

Tsefon and *Timan* are the North wind and the South wind, meaning the Breaths that blow from the depth of North and from the depth of South. Those depths are, according to the *Sepher Yetsira*, respectively, the ninth and the tenth *Sephira*.

The ninth *Sephira* is the fulcrum of the female energy whose archetype, no. 9, is Tayt, and whose development is Tsadde (90). North wind, *Tsefon* (Tsadde Phay Waw Noun: 90.80.6.700) shows the depth of Tsadde liberating the cosmic Indetermination, 700.

The tenth *Sephira* is the welding of the projected Aleph (Yod) and Tav. The south wind, *Timan* (Tav Yod Mem Noun: 400.10.40.700) shows the depth of Tav-Yod also liberating the cosmic Indetermination, 700.

In our *Midrash* we have not mentioned the complex details of the subsequent schemata. *Hefihhi* (Hay Phay Yod Hhayt Yod: 5.80.10.8.10) is "breathe me" only metaphorically. It shows the breath of life (Hay) acting upon Phay, and revealing Hhayt set between two Yod. *Gani* has been explained several times. *Be'semav* is a modification of *Be'shemo*: by "His" Name. *Yavo*, (Yod Vayt Aleph: 10.2.1), idiomatically to come, to enter, is the reverse of *Avi* (Aleph Vayt Yod: 1.2.10): my father. The appearance of this schema illustrates her conversion, or change of direction.

V

1 בָּאתִי לְגַנִּי אֲחֹתִי כַלָּה אָרִיתִי מוֹרִי עִם־
בְּשָׂמִי אָכַלְתִּי יַעְרִי עִם־דִּבְשִׁי שָׁתִיתִי יֵינִי עִם־חֲלָבִי
אִכְלוּ רֵעִים שְׁתוּ וְשִׁכְרוּ דּוֹדִים:

PHONETICALLY: *Baoti Le'gani Ahhoti Kalah Ariti Mori Aym Be'shemi Ikelti Yaari Aym Dileshi Shetiti Yini Aym Hhalavi Ikhloo Reaim Sheto We'shikroo Dodim.*

RSV: *I come to my garden, my sister, my bride. I gather my myrrh with my spice. I eat my honeycomb with my honey. I drink my wine with my milk. Eat, O friends and drink: drink deeply, O lovers.*

QABALA: Breath: *I have gone into my bodily support. In response to your call I have gathered in you what is mine. I have gathered my exchange money—30 pieces—which you kept inside my name. I have used what wildness still remained in you. I have founded the unity of my work. The beginning and the end are one. You who hear me, be happy!*

This verse deals with the penetration of Aleph in the biosphere and with its reappearance. It calls the attention of the reader by its rhythm, by the repetition of *Aym*, by the words in which appear both Aleph and Tav, by such words as *Shetiti* (Sheen upon Tav-Yod-Tav-Yod) and *Sheto* (Sheen upon Tav-Waw; etc. . . .).

Baoti (Bayt Aleph Tav Yod) is Aleph penetrating through Bayt, and meeting Tav in existence (Yod). *Le'gani*: Lammed being the biologically active agent of Aleph (Aleph Lammed Phay). *Baoti Le'gani* means that Breath has entered actively in its (or in "His") bodily support, now that "He" is free to do so (see preceding verse).

Ahhoti Kalah (Aleph Hhayt Tav Yod—Kaf Lammed Hay: 1.8.400.10-20.30.5). Here *Ahhat* is "One" feminine, rather than "sister" (the word for sister, *Ahhowt*, is spelt with a Waw), and *Kalah*, means whole. These schemata testify to her response to his penetration: "She" is entirely "His One".

Ariti Mori Aym Be'shemi. In *Ariti* (Aleph Raysh Yod Tav Yod: 1.200.10.400.10) Aleph meets Tav for the third time in this verse. The root *Arah* means to pluck, to gather fruit. The schema *Ariti* states a fruitful relationship between Aleph-Raysh (a unitary emanation), and Yod-Tav-Yod (the duality that contains it and that responds to it); in brief, "He" gathers what is his.

Mori (Mem Waw Raysh Yod: 40.6.200.10) is not myrrh (Mem Raysh). its root is *Morah* or *Moreh*, both with Waw. Its many connotations are all related to an idea of exchange, or of a miraculous event, or of a teacher, or of fear and terror. In fact, the Aleph who, under the symbol of Breath, or otherwise, is supposed to be talking here, is describing the mysterious event of its incarnation.

In Genesis, the first Emanation was "light": *Awr* (Aleph Waw Raysh). We are now contemplating *Mor* (Mem Waw Raysh). Aleph is "exchanged" for Mem, the biosphere; and this has happened through its own action (30). The L, kept inside "His" name, *Al* (idiomatically the deity), is the "price" (30) paid by Mem for receiving "Him". It means that inertia pays the price, 30, for being set in motion.

Ikelti Yaari Aym Dibshi. The root *Ikel*, idiomatically, is not simply to eat, but also to consume, to burn. *Ikelti* (Aleph Kaf Lammed Tav Yod: 1.20.30.400.10), fourth meeting of Aleph and Tav, expresses the strongest possible action of Lammed, consuming all its obstacles. *Yaari* (Yod Ayn Raysh Yod:

10.70.200.10), means idiomatically my forest, or my wilderness. *Dibshi* (Dallet Bayt Sheen) as a verb, suggests a ferment that has been spoiling him.

Shetiti (Sheen Tav Yod Tav Yod: 300.400.10.400.10) is the unity of Breath living in its dual Foundation. *Iyni*: hence, three Yod in factual life; and *Hhalavi*: the Hhayt gives birth to Lammed! (The end is in the beginning.)

V

2

אֲנִי יְשֵׁנָה וְלִבִּי עֵר קוֹל | דּוֹדִי דוֹפֵק
פִּתְחִי־לִי אֲחֹתִי רַעְיָתִי יוֹנָתִי תַמָּתִי שֶׁרֹאשִׁי
נִמְלָא־טָל קְוֻצּוֹתַי רְסִיסֵי לָיְלָה:

PHONETICALLY: *Ani Yishena We'libi Ayr Qol Dodi Dofeq Pit'hhi-Li Ahhoti Raaiati Yonati Tamati She'roshi Nimla-Tal Qevootsotai Risseissi Lailah.*

RSV: *I slept, but my heart was awake. Hark! my beloved is knocking. "Open to me, my sister, my love, my dove, my perfect one; for my head is wet with dew, my locks with the drops of the night."*

QABALA: Person: *Though I am asleep in Duration I perceive my heart-beats and the world's heart-beats in identical discontinuity: that of living and dying Breath. He lives and dies: lives dying, dies living. He says: "Open yourself for me, from you I am being born".*

The root of *Yishena* is *Yashen*, to sleep; Yod Sheen Noun. It is a permutation of the letter Sheen spelt in full (Sheen Yod Noun). Another permutation is *Shnei* (Sheen Noun Yod), meaning two in the masculine. *Shanah* (Sheen Noun Hay) is a year (a lapse of time) and also means opposedly, to repeat and to change. Qabala includes all those connotations into one single concept: when time sleeps in duration, time is not; when it awakes, it is only a continual modification of appearances.

328

We cannot refrain from quoting here the beautiful opening of *The Stanzas of Dzyan*, as given by Madame Blavatsky in her *Secret Doctrine:*

1. *The Eternal Parent, wrapped in her Ever-Invisible Robes, had slumbered once again for Seven Eternities.*
2. *Time was not, for it lay asleep in the Infinite Bosom of Duration.*
3. *Universal Mind was not, for there were no Ah-Hi to contain it.*

Before the existence of the Universe, there was no "Ah-Hi": no Aleph Hay-Hay Yod: no Aleph alive in living Yod.

The two "partners for and against each other", Aleph and Yod must be both alive, or else nothing is,* except the "deep slumber of Seven Eternities". This, in other words, is the cabalistic *Ain-Soph* (Aleph Yod in cosmic indetermination—final Noun, 700—and Samekh Waw: female and male energies in unstructured state: Phay, 80). When *Ahyeh Esher Ahyeh* revealed itself to Moses, the "Universal Mind" entered into him through the direct perception of all that is and all that is not: *Ahyeh* (Aleph Hay Yod Hay) means Aleph alive, Yod alive.

We must comment still further upon this verse, v, 2 (life of duality); it being the very centre, the heart of the Song of Songs.

From the scientific point of view, the Universe is an explosion that may have begun some four or five billions of years ago, due to a fantastic accumulation of Energy. How could such a concentration of Energy happen, if not by an equally fantastic pressure upon it?

Let us not try to understand how it is that Energy exists at all: this is the Ultimate Mystery of Mysteries, present in every speck of dust. Let us not name it, but let us understand its living process, and "be it", as did "our father Abraham"†

Let us, to that effect, contemplate, both outside and inside us, the two Powers (Breaths or Sheen), of Compression and Explosion (of Tav and of Aleph). They are not contradictory. They are every appearance, and the Residue of Residues of all

---

* *The Cipher of Genesis.*   † *The Sepher Yetsira.*

appearances. They are the containers and the contained of all that has been, of all that is, of all that will be. They are the One Life, the One Mystery: not the life of the mystery, nor the mystery of life, but a single self-generating Immanence, permanently pervading Itself.

The self-relationship of the One within Itself is the co-existence of its two living aspects: Yod as a continuity of changes, where things that do not last appear to last, and Aleph as a discontinuity of life and of death in the pulsation life-death, life-death, of a heart-beat.

Happy are those who, in their everyday existence, are aware that their heart-beats are at one with the heart-beats of the Universe!

The schemata of this verse contain a double Dallet, three double Yod, a double Tav, a double Sheen, a double Waw, a double Samekh and a double Lammed. The key-word, translated "knocking", is *Dofeq* (Dallet Waw Phay Qof: 4.6.80.100): pulse.

The head (fire), the locks (structures growing from it), the being wet (water), the drops (or rather fragments in double female sex: Samekh) the night; all those symbols are easy to read.

V

3 פָּשַׁטְתִּי אֶת־כֻּתָּנְתִּי אֵיכָכָה אֶלְבָּשֶׁנָּה רָחַצְתִּי
אֶת־רַגְלַי אֵיכָכָה אֲטַנְּפֵם׃

PHONETICALLY: *Pashateyti Et-Kootanti Ey'Khak'ha El'ba'sheni Rahhatsti Et-Raglai Ey'khakha Atanfem.*

RSV: *I had put off my garment, how could I put it on? I had bathed my feet, how could I soil them?*

QABALA: Person: *He says: "I am stripped of the symbols that disguised me. I have no appearance, for any form would exclude others. But your form is purified by the emptiness which begat me. Therefore you can evolve in duration and yet be clean.*

We have read over and over again that Aleph cannot be structured. All structures are of Yod, and inside them Aleph is more or less asleep, more or less alive. "She" had heard "His" heart-beat in her own heart-beat, whilst sleeping the sleep of Time in Duration. Now her innermost voice tells her that she was not mistaken, that Breath is indeed alive in her, alive but not structured, alive in the primitive condition of an original living element.

Pashateyti Et-Kootanti, can be translated colloquially: "I have discarded that which was disguising me". The root *Peshet* (Pay Sheen Tayt: 80.300.9) is the extreme simplification of unstructured energy (80), through Breath (300), in a single element (9). The two Tav acting upon each other in *Kootanti* are, so to speak, the Resistance of Resistances, or the Duality of Duality. Energy cannot possibly go further in the act of opposing itself. The *Autiot* Kaf Tav Noun Tav Yod: 20.400.50.400.10 are an amazing combination, well apt to evoke the "Ever-Invisible Robes of the Eternal Parent" (*The Secret Doctrine*). They are permanently discarded by virtue of single, infinitesimal living particles, in which Breath is hidden.

Ey'Khak'ha: this Aleph and Yod, in two living containers, are alive. *El'ba'sheni*: and *Al* is alive in the Sleep of Duration and also in the process of Time, that co-exist in Emanation.

The rest of the verse must not be read according to its grammatical idiomatic construction: "I" had bathed "my" feet etc. . . . but must be deciphered with the code, and understood according to the ontological meaning of the roots. The attention of the cabalist is first called upon by the two Raysh of *Rahhatsti* and *Reglai*.

The bathing of the feet is an important semitic symbol. Jesus washed the feet of his disciples. In the Moslem religion, this washing is compulsory before prayer. And we must not forget (*Sepher Yetsira* VI, 4) the Covenant between *Adon Hakol* and Abraham, "fitted in his ten toes, and it is the Covenant of Circumcision".

An exhaustive exegesis on that matter would be beyond our

present scope. The feet (foot: *Regl*: Raysh Ghimel Lammed: 200.3.30) are symbolic of humanity's march in and through time. Humanity is born of Raysh, and develops its organic functions (Ghimel) as far as Lammed, Aleph's active agent. Men walk on the Earth, *Eretz* (Aleph Raysh Tsadde), where Aleph is buried in a peaceful cohabitation with Raysh, the result being the natural and unconscious proliferation of proto-types, *yielding seed according to their own kinds* (Gen. 1, 12).

The binomial Raysh Tsadde is a state of Energy far below the human level. So is mud, *Bots* (Bayt Tsadde). The bathing, *Rahhats* (Raysh Hhayt Tsadde) introduces the missing link: the unstructed Hhayt, the unconscious element that the humans can and must structurize. It is worth noting that in the idiom, the toes are "the fingers of the feet". In the word finger, *Etsbaa* (Aleph Tsadde Bayt Ayn) Aleph is so dynamic that it reverses the sequence Bayt Tsadde of *Bots*, (mud) and opens the way for Ayn (70).

V

4   דּוֹדִי שָׁלַח יָדוֹ מִן־הַחֹר וּמֵעַי הָמוּ עָלָיו:

PHONETICALLY: *Dodi Shelahh Yado Min-Ha'hhor We'meyi Hamo Aalav.*

RSV: *My beloved put his hand to the latch, and my heart was thrilled within me.*

QABALA: Woman: *My love makes him resilient. As soon as he appears in the richness of my body, he disappears in the empty places of my mind. A contradictory movement! He goes inversely to his coming, yet the cave of my being is quickened by his vibration.*

Our *Midrash*, here, is somewhat more explanatory than it generally is, the Hebrew text being idiomatically obscure. An authorized Jewish version in French gives it as "My beloved withdraws his hand from the garret-window, and my entrails are moved in his favour".* The King James' version sees it as: "My beloved put in his hand by the hole of the door and my bowels were moved for him".

A hand put in, a hand withdrawn; a heart that is thrilled; bowels that are moved; a latch, a garret-window, a hole in the door; and none make sense. Let us clarify the context. In the last verse of the preceding Chant (IV, 16), "She" had expressed a wish: *May my twofold organic resistance enter the organic life of Breath!*

Breath answered (V, 1) that such a wish could not be fulfilled because Aleph has no organic life of its own. Alive as Aleph may be, at times, in a human body, whatever is felt, understood, said, taught, written, made or built, is not IT, but its "exchange money": symbols, myths, creeds, theologies, or any other equivalent of Aleph in terms of human minds. Breath had added that IT had consumed what wilderness still remained in "Her". The result of that consummation was that no thought remained in her mind, so "She" knew herself to be "asleep in Duration" (V, 2), yet perceiving Breath (or Aleph, or Timeless Energy) as the continuous discontinuity of a Cosmic Pulse, reflecting itself in her own heart-beat: a tremendous Revelation, the deepest that the deepest layers of unconscious consciousness can be aware of! And the innermost inner voice acknowledged the fact (V, 3): "Yes, all images gone, this is the throb of Life, born unborn".

We now come upon V, 4, with a chance to understand it.

In *Dodi*, the two Dallet are, by this time, so united by Waw, and so real in Yod, that the scheme includes both "Him" and "Her", or rather, their Essence, in which both "He" and "She" are, so to speak, dissolved. As all schemata, *Dodi* has evolved with the evolution of its components. The *Autiot* are living focalized energies; each single combination has as many meanings as are offered by the interplay of forces.

---

* "Mon bien-aimé retire sa main de la lucarne et mes entrailles s'émeuvent en sa faveur." From the Zadoc Kahn version of the Bible published by the French Rabbinate (Paris 1899-1906).

Such is the key-word *Shelahh* (Sheen Lammed Hhayt:
300.30.8). When Breath (300), active through organic functions
(30), permeates the unstructured, unconscious energy (8) in us,
it either comes through, or withdraws, depending on Hhayt's
receptivity. In fact, it appears and disappears as a heart-beat.
This contradictory movement is illustrated by the schemata
Dodi and *Yado*, with their *Autiot* in reverse order: Dallet Waw
Dallet Yod-Yod Dallet Waw. In going backwards, one Dallet
falls into *Ha'hhor*, idiomatically a cávern. Her "entrails", *Mei*
(40.70) transform 4 into Mem (40), her biological response.
Hamo (5.40.6) is the assertion of that life in her, and *Aalav*
(70.30.10.6) projects all the possibilities of 70 into the retrieved
Lammed.

This v, 4 (4 is Dallet) is a mathematically accurate investigation in one of the most mysterious aspects of Life: its resistance
to itself.

V

5

קַמְתִּי אֲנִי לִפְתֹּחַ לְדוֹדִי וְיָדַי נָטְפוּ-מֹור
וְאֶצְבְּעֹתַי מֹור עֹבֵר עַל כַּפּוֹת הַמַּנְעוּל:

PHONETICALLY: *Qamiti Ani Le'pitoahh Le'dodi We'yadai Nat-foo-
Mor We'etsbeotai Mor Eebar Aal Kapot Ha'mano'ol.*
RSV: *I arose to open to my beloved, and my hands dripped with myrrh, my
fingers with liquid myrrh, upon the handles of the bolt.*
QABALA: Woman: *I was set going by his Breath, so that I should give
birth to something without blemish. But his seed is impaired
by his being fixated on me: everything I touch is of the past.*

We are now midway through the Chants, at a turning point
where the essential theme will express more and more realistic-
ally the dramatic human search for an ever-elusive Absolute.
As we know most of the words "She" uses in the beginning of
this verse, we will simply paraphrase them: "I was set going

334

(*Qamiti Ani*) by Qof, the cosmic Aleph: *Le'pitoahh*: to develop, to loose that which was unstructured in me, so as to bestow *Le'Dodi*: an organic life to my two resistances; my action (or my hand: *Yadai*) revealed my fundamental Dallet between two Yod; here starts my life, in *Natfoo-Mor* (Noun Tayt Phay Waw-Mem Waw Raysh); it is the biological development of Tayt: my "exchange money".

The schema *Mor* is the one "He" had used in v, 1, meaning his exchange money. Here, she realizes that her quest for Aleph, the Timeless, the Unpolluted, will always fail, will always remain in her biological sphere.

The rest of the verse conveys the same idea, with words carefully chosen for their multi-symbolical meanings.

We'etsbeotai: the word *Etsbe'a* (Aleph Tsadde Bayt Ayn) finger, is a remarkable combination of Aleph and *Tsebe'a* (Tsadde Bayt Ayn), colour, paint. The meanings of those *Autiot* offer us a vast field of meditation: Aleph is hidden in the action of our fingers, just as it is hidden in Adam's blood. The question is whether we can "paint it" alive.

There is no verb between *Etsbotai* and *Mor*: "My fingers actually are *Mor*".

The following schema *Eebar* (Ayn Bayt Raysh) has so many connotations, that we can either select the one that is most agreeable to us, or include them all in a synthetic view given by the *Autiot* 70.2.200. *Aavrah* is a sin; *Ever* a side; *Avar* means to pass, or to pass away; *Aiber*, to make pregnant; *Avar* is the past, and the past tense; *Aavrah* is a ford or a transition; *Eevrah*: anger, rage; *Aivri* a Hebrew, a Jew . . . etc. . . . We can observe that in that root, Ayn-Vayt is in reverse order to Bayt-Ayn in *Tsebe'a* (finger).

Aal (70.30) is a compulsion upon Lammed, introducing in it an element of doubt and insecurity.

The root of *Kapot*, is simply the letter *Kaf*, which, as a word, means hollow, a cave, or *Kafah*, an open hollow such as a door-way. *Ha'mano'ol* designates something that locks, such as a bolt. That which is "locked in her cave" is the seed of Aleph and it already belongs to the past (Avar) because of her pregnancy (*Aiber*): the structured seed is "Her", not "Him", in spite of "He" being in it.

V

6 פָּתַ֨חְתִּֽי אֲנִי֙ לְדוֹדִ֔י וְדוֹדִ֖י עָבַ֣ר חָמָ֑ק נַפְשִׁי֙
יָֽצְאָ֣ה בְדַבְּר֔וֹ ·בִּקַּשְׁתִּ֙יהוּ֙ וְלֹ֣א מְצָאתִ֔יהוּ קְרָאתִ֖יו
וְלֹ֥א עָנָֽנִי׃

PHONETICALLY: *Patahhti Ani Le'dodi Hhamaq Aavar Nafshi Yotsah Be'dabro Be'qashtihoo We'lo Mitsaotihoo Qeratio We'lo Aanani.*

RSV: *I opened to my beloved, but my beloved had turned and gone. My soul failed me when he spoke, I sought him and found him not: I called him but he gave no answer.*

QABALA: Woman: *I am open to my love, Breath has gone back to its origin, has disappeared. Through hearing his Word I found that origin. There, among the creative Forces, I invoked our Union, and two lives spoke to me.*

The verse v, 5 was the turning point where "She" began to experience directly the impossibility of communing with Aleph. V, 6 corroborates it, but only as prelude to a hopeless, frenzied search, a dreamlike mental derangement, in which "He" will appear to her as an idol.

Patahhti Ani: 80.400.8.400.10-1.50.10: "I opened myself to Him by reverting my unstructured 80 and 8 to their origin, 400 and 400, thus allowing Aleph to live in me".

We'dodi Hhamaq: "From my two resistances, Dallet Dallet, my Hhayt, through Mem, bounces back and reaches Qof, the cosmic Aleph".

Aafar Nafshi Yotsah: "I returned to the past where my structure had began to take shape; *Be'dabro*: through the action of his speach, and in virtue of our Covenant: *Be'qashtihoo*". The root *Qeshet* (Qof Sheen Tav: 100.300.400) is the rainbow,

336

symbol of a covenant in the Bible, a stupendous union of Qof and Tav, operated by Sheen.

The verse ends with two declarations: *Lo Mitsaotihoo* and *Lo Aanani*, considered idiomatically as negations, but not so by the Qabala. *Lo* (Lammed Aleph), in the idiom means no, not, but is in essence a flow of Energy springing from Lammed and giving birth to Aleph. It is *Al* flowing in its opposite direction, returning unto itself: an important factor in the discovery of the double Breath, that leitmotiv of the Song. According to the idiom, we are invited to understand that "He" is not found and that "He" does not answer. In fact, that which is found and that which answers is the double life of Duality, animated by what we have referred to as the "Lower Breath".

Mitsaotihoo is a combination of two contrasting Energies: a structuring Mem Tsadde (40.90) and an absolute Aleph Tav (1.400) resulting in a plenitude of factual life (Yod Hay Waw: 10.5.6).

Aanani (Ayn Noun Noun Yod: 70.50.50.10) introduces the archetype of indetermination in her double life.

V

7   מְצָאֻנִי הַשֹּׁמְרִים הַסֹּבְבִים בָּעִיר הִכּוּנִי
פְצָעוּנִי נָשְׂאוּ אֶת־רְדִידִי מֵעָלַי שֹׁמְרֵי הַחֹמוֹת׃

PHONETICALLY: *Metsaooni Ha'shomreem Ha'soveveem Be'yir Hikooni Phetsaooni Nassoo Et-Redidi Mealai Shomrei Ha'hhamot.*

RSV: *The watchmen found me, as they went about in the city; they beat me, they wounded me, they took away my mantle, those watchmen of the walls.*

QABALA: Woman: *The Powers-that-be who in burying Breath build their cities send their agents against me: strip me of my latest form. See me now naked and free. The veil of my appearance is lifted showing the visible One to be twofold.*

In her sleep, "She" had called for the One. She had felt that the pulsation of the cosmic life was attuned to her own pulse; but two lives had answered her. Now she is awake and the two lives appear in the reality of their contrasting actions. Her perception of the One is so vivid as not to allow her to seek an escape. She wants to find "Him" where she knows him to be battling against the structures of a symbolic city. Here the text is too logical to say that the guardians of structures attack her in order to despoil her of her structures. On the contrary, she describes the meeting as "*Metsaooni*" (Mem Tsadde Aleph Noun Yod), they attack her with the intent of structuring (by Tsadde) the Aleph, and of thrusting it into its "partner against", Yod. The root *Matsa* (Mem Tsadde Aleph), among other connotations, means to find; *Hemtsa* to be supplied with; *Tsah* (Tsadde Aleph Hay) is filth, to soil, which means that to apply a structure to Aleph is to soil it. That is what the guardians, *Shomreem*, (Sheen Mem Raysh Yod Mem), who are turning around *Soveveem* (Samekh Vayt Vayt Yod Mem) are trying to do: they insert Sammekh, the female sex, in two Vayt, two containers. This strong pressure upon her, squeezes, so to speak, her structured life out of her: "My veil" (*Redidi*: Raysh Dallet Yod Dallet Yod) "From upon me" (*Mealai*) "that protected me" (*Shomrei*) from *Ha'hhamot*. The root of this last schema is *Hham*; idiomatically heat.

The veil of appearances is here identified with the degradation of pure Light into Heat (see the first *Sephira*).

V

8   הִשְׁבַּעְתִּי אֶתְכֶם בְּנוֹת יְרוּשָׁלַͅם אִם־תִּמְצְאוּ
אֶת־דּוֹדִי מַה־תַּגִּידוּ לוֹ שֶׁחוֹלַת אַהֲבָה אָנִי:

PHONETICALLY: *Hishbaati Etkhem Benot Yaro'shalom Im-Timtseoo Et-Dodi Mah-Taghidoo Lo Shehholat Ahavah Ani.*

RSV: *I adjure you, O daughters of Jerusalem, if you find my beloved, that you tell him I am sick with love.*

QABALA: Woman: *Girls of the misleading peace of cities, if you meet him I love, tell him that what I built in myself has disappeared. My love for him is no more than the rhythm of a holy dance.*

As far as "the girls of the cities" are concerned, see verses I, 5, II, 7 and III, 5. The key-word here is *Shehholat* (Sheen Hhayt Waw Lammed Tav: 300.8.6.30.400). Its root *Hhol* (Hhayt Waw Lammed) does not mean "being sick", but to fall, to dance and to writhe.

When the unstructured energy Hhayt (8) becomes copulatively active (Waw) in relation to the organic movement of Lammed, the result is an uncontrolled agitation, a falling, a dancing, a writhing. But in "Her" statement: *Shehholat*, she is "Sheened" all through, stirred by Breath as far as Breath can go, hurling itself against Tav.

This verse V, 8 (Hay Hhayt) is the culmination of all the preceding verses that dealt with the awakening of the unconscious mind. "She" has become creative, as the Holy Rhythm of the Cosmic Life is creative. Her whole body is attuned to it as was her heart to the Heart of the World. She will dance it.

V

9   מַה־דּוֹדֵךְ מִדּוֹד הַיָּפָה בַּנָּשִׁים מַה־דּוֹדֵךְ
מִדּוֹד שֶׁכָּכָה הִשְׁבַּעְתָּנוּ׃

PHONETICALLY: *Mah-Dodekh Mi-dod Ha'yafah Be'nasheem Mah-Dodekh Mi-dod Shekakhah Hishbaatanoo.*

RSV: *What is your beloved more than another beloved, O fairest among women? What is your beloved more than another beloved, that you thus adjure us?*

QABALA: Girls of the cities (singing):

> *Mah-Dodekh Mi-dod:* rhythm 3.2.
> *Ha'yafah Be'nasheem:* rhythm 3.3.
> *Mah-Dodekh Mi-dod:* rhythm 3.2.
> *Shakakhah Hishbaatanoo:* rhythm 3.5.
> *To this incantation she dances the rhythms. (She dances the interrogation of the girls as follows)* "Who is your lover among lovers, most beautiful among us? Who is your lover among lovers, that you so cry out to us?"

3.2 Translated in letters: Ghimel Vayt, suggests that the movement of Ghimel is projected in a container, Vayt; 3.3 (Ghimel Ghimel) suggests the elevation of a double movement; 3.5 (Ghimel Hay) is Ghimel alive.

V

10

דוֹדִי צַח וְאָדוֹם דָּגוּל מֵרְבָבָה׃

PHONETICALLY: *Dodi Tsahh We'edom Dagol Marvavah.*

RSV: *My beloved is all radiant and ruddy, distinguished among ten thousand.*

QABALA: Feminine sex: *From the pinnacle of my depths, I see my Love. Edom, son of Earth, of royal birth, He is the cell united with mine, to elaborate earthly strength. He and I are two bodies in one.*

This verse and her further descriptions are ample proofs that her vision of "Him" is purely subjective. Her statement *Dodi Tsahh* (Tsadde Hhayt) describes that which has happened in her: her Hhayt has found itself to be structured (Tsadde). After so many changes in direction this response is still another reversal. How could "She" have avoided it, after having danced her love, giving it rhythm and bodily motion? She has been so true to "Him", she has so adhered to "Him", she has been so united to "Him"! Can she be expected to remember her earlier revelations? Can she still feel that whatever she does and touches is nothing but herself, never "Him"?

She says "*Dodi* is also *Edom*": *We'edom*. We know that *Edom* is *Esau* (see Gen. XXXVI, 1). Edom-Esau, as opposed to Jacob. Adam is son of the primordial earthly powers, whereas Jacob is son of YHWH. Among the descendants of Esau is King Herod, among those of Jacob is Jesus, whom Herod wanted to murder.

The text goes on saying that Edom is *Dagol* (Dallet Ghimel Waw Lammed). This schema is an inverted *Gadol* (great). Its root, *Dag*, is a fish. *Dagol* is a proliferation (by Lammed) of primitive flesh. That multiplication is corroborated by the last schema, *Marvavah* (40.200.2.2.5), where the biosphere Mem generates two Vayt, none of them fertilized. Two Vayt, are two bodies, intimately linked. This is well apt to deceive her.

V

11 רֹאשׁוֹ כֶּתֶם פָּז קְוֻצּוֹתָיו תַּלְתַּלִּים שְׁחֹרוֹת כָּעוֹרֵב:

PHONETICALLY: *Rosho Ke'tam Paz Qevootsotav Taltaleem Shehhorot Ka'orev.*

RSV: *His head is the finest gold; his locks are wavy, black as a raven.*

QABALA: Phylum: *The Principle of Breath, Fire in Matter, is Adam, of perfect red and pure gold. But as soon as he penetrates the formative structure he is Edom. Woman, his emanation, shoots spirally in the shadows of the womb.*

"She" has dreamt "Him" as an idol, and in her description, many symbols appear, that she does not understand. Our *Midrash* introduces their explanation as seen by the Qabala, uttered by the Phylum, and subsequently by the Poet. Her dream will last until the end of Chant V and during all Chant VI, when she will finally awake and confess (VI, 12) that in her slumber she had "not known".

The translation of her vision is easy enough: his head is gold, his locks are wavy, his body is ivory, etc. . . . . The fact that his legs are set "upon bases of gold" (V, 15) amply proves that in her dream, "He" has become an image used as an object of worship.

The sentence *Rosho Ke'tam Paz,* understood concretely, means: his head is as pure gold. Essentially, the schema *Rosh* (Raysh Aleph Sheen), is a combination of Raysh, meaning the whole of the existent Universe, and Aleph Sheen meaning Fire.

Ke'tam means "as" *Tam. Tam* (Tav Mem) is a mysterious schema. It is the reverse of *Met* (Mem Tav) Death. It qualifies Jacob in Genesis xxv, 27, *We'yaaqov Eesh Tam,* where it is translated by the Revised version: Jacob was a "quiet" man. The King James' says: Jacob was a "plain" man. According to a Catholic French version, Jacob was "harmless'. According to a Jewish French canonical text, he was "peaceful", whereas the same version translates this verse: His head is as "pure" gold. As for the code, *Tam* is the biosphere, Mem, generated by Tav. It illustrates the materialization of Breath in a man, and "She" attributes it to her idol in her dream.

Qevootsotav (Qof Waw Tsadde Waw Tav Yod Waw), idiomatically "his curls", are (symbolically) structured spirals winding out of the "fiery" head. The schema is a complete equation, showing "Her" perennial wish to structurize the cosmic Aleph (Qof) and to carry its fruitfulness into Tav.

In her dream those spirals (*Taltaleem*) are locks, black (*Shehhorot*) as a raven (*Orev*), which is paradoxical, they being curls of a "golden head". The Phylum recognizes them in the act of winding their way into the darkness (*Erev*) of her womb. In short, she unknowingly describes an erotic dream with her partner, Edom.

342

V

12

עֵינָיו כְּיוֹנִים עַל־אֲפִיקֵי מָיִם רֹחֲצוֹת בֶּחָלָב
יֹשְׁבוֹת עַל־מִלֵּאת:

PHONETICALLY: *Aynav Ke'iyweneem Aal-Afiqei Maim Rahhatsot
Be'hhalav Ishbot Aal-Milet.*

RSV: *His eyes are like doves beside springs of water, bathed in milk,
fitly set.*

QABALA: Poet: *The brilliance of his eyes is as wet mud bathed in milk
so as to appear purified. He makes his home among the
shapeless human mass.*

"She" proceeds with her description of Edom, mistaken for
Adam, in words humorously chosen so as to confuse the would-
be translators. This is what the poet is actually saying: *Aynav:*
his eyes; *Ke'iyweneem:* as mire (liquid mud); *Aal-Afiqei Maim:*
on the border of waters, *Rahhatsot:* washed; *Be'hhalav:* with
milk; *Ishbot* they swell, *Aal-Milet* in the multitude.

V

13

לְחָיָו כַּעֲרוּגַת הַבֹּשֶׂם מִגְדְּלוֹת מֶרְקָחִים
שִׂפְתוֹתָיו שׁוֹשַׁנִּים נֹטְפוֹת מוֹר עֹבֵר:

PHONETICALLY: *Lehhayav Ka'aroogat Ha'boossem Migdelot Mer-
gahheem Siftotav Shoshanaim Notfot Mor Oover.*

RSV: *His cheeks are like beds of spices, yielding fragrance. His lips are
lilies, distilling liquid myrrh.*

QABALA: Poet: *He revives his life with ointment and drugs, as one
might give new scent to the petals of withering flowers which
are losing their smell.*

The ironical description continues by means of a play on
words. The verse can be read, colloquially, thus: "As far as his

vigour is concerned, he is as a flower-bed where the scent of
spices is amplified by perfumers, he is as remains of roses from
which drip aromatic juice".

V

14   יָדָיו֙ גְּלִילֵ֣י זָהָ֔ב מְמֻלָּאִ֖ים בַּתַּרְשִׁ֑ישׁ מֵעָיו֙ עֶ֣שֶׁת
שֵׁ֔ן מְעֻלֶּ֖פֶת סַפִּירִֽים׃

PHONETICALLY: *Yadav Ghelilei Zahav Memoolaim Be'tarsheesh
Maav Ayshet Shen Mailefet Sapireem.*

RSV: *His arms are rounded gold, set with jewels. His body is ivory work,
encrusted with sapphires.*

QABALA: Woman: *With turn of his hand he changes love to gold and
the Sepher to Sapphires, for in him are two Breaths. What
would become of the upper Breath if the Tabernacle of Edom
had not the lower Breath to resist it?*

Yadav: his hands. The hand, *Yad* (Yod Dallet) expresses the
Existence, Yod (Yod Dallet) and its quality of Resistance,
Dallet. It is by the action of the hand that mankind resists life
and dominates nature. But while dreaming her idol, the woman
sees his hands *Ghelilei* (3.30.10.30.10) in a circuit. This movement results in gold: *Zahav* (see I, 11 concerning love, *Ahav*
transmuted into *Zahav*). *Memooleim* (Mem Mem Lammed Aleph
Yod Mem) is an intense biological medium through which the
life supposed (by "Her") to be Breath's is conveyed to the
senses.

An important key-word is *Tarsheesh* (Tav Raysh Sheen Yod
Sheen), idiomatically a precious stone. It shows Tav, through
Raysh, emitting the two Breaths: two Sheen. *Maav* (Mem Ayn
Yod Waw): his belly, *Ayshet* means strong, idiomatically; it
expresses here a projection of the possibilities of Sheen into Tav.
Whether *Shen* (Sheen Noun: 300.700) means ivory or tooth is
irrelevant: it shows Sheen culminating in the final cosmic

Indetermination. *Mailefet* is a complete equation. The sequence Mem Ayn Lammed Phay Tav: 40.70.30.80.400, expresses the entire biological process in its relation to Tav. It is mysterious and has been said to be "frightening". Its root *Ayleph*, Ayn Lammed Phay, is a permutation of Aleph:

$$\text{Aleph:} \quad 1.30.800$$
$$\text{Ayleph:} \quad 70.30.800$$

its idiomatic meaning is to cover, to wrap, to be frightened, weak, faint. Some rabbis thought it to be the very expression of sacrilege. What better corroboration of that meaning than the last schema, *Sapireem*, the *Sepher* changed to Sapphires? (In Exodus, XXIV, 9-10, Moses and others "see" the God of Israel with a pavement of sapphire under his feet.)

V

15

שׁוֹקָיוֹ עַמּוּדֵי שֵׁשׁ מְיֻסָּדִים עַל־אַדְנֵי־פָז
מַרְאֵהוּ כַּלְּבָנוֹן בָּחוּר כָּאֲרָזִים׃

PHONETICALLY: *Shoqav Aamodei Shesh Meyossadeem Aal-Adoni-Paz Marahoo Ka'lvanon Be'hhoor Ka'erezeem.*

RSV: *His legs are alabaster columns, set upon bases of gold, His appearance is like Lebanon, choice as the cedars.*

QABALA: Woman: *I see him, a marble idol on a golden plinth.*

Poet: *In truth, his legs go in opposite directions, one from back to front, the other from front to back, he pivots continually on himself.*

The important assertion in this verse is that his legs are columns of *Shesh* (Sheen Sheen) meaning idiomatically marble, but we have learnt that one Sheen goes from Aleph to Tav, the other from Tav to Aleph. All the other schemata of this verse have been commented upon, or are easy to decipher.

345

V

16

חִכּוֹ מַמְתַקִּים וְכֻלּוֹ מַחֲמַדִּים זֶה דוֹדִי וְזֶה
רֵעִי בְּנוֹת יְרוּשָׁלִָם:

PHONETICALLY: *Hhiko Mamtaqeem We'kkoulo Mahhamadeem Zeh Dodi We'zeh Reayi Benot Yero'shalom.*

RSV: *His speech is most sweet, and he is altogether desirable. This is my beloved and this is my friend, O daughters of Jerusalem.*

QABALA: Woman: *If I did not see him as an idol I would not see him: if he did not modify Breath I would not hear him. But he speaks and arouses my desire. Such is my love, such is my Shepherd, daughters of the cities.*

Idiomatically *Hhiko* (Hhayt Kaf Waw) means his palate, *Memtaqeem*: (is) sweetmeats. Why have the canonical interpreters refrained from this translation, after having written in I, 2, "O that you would kiss me with the kisses of your mouth"?

VI

1

אָנָה הָלַךְ דוֹדֵךְ הַיָּפָה בַּנָּשִׁים אָנָה פָּנָה
דוֹדֵךְ וּנְבַקְשֶׁנּוּ עִמָּךְ:

PHONETICALLY: *Onah Halakh Dodekh Ha'yafah Be'nasheem Onah Panah Dodekh Oo'nbiqshenoo Aaymakh.*

RSV: *Whither has your beloved gone, O fairest among women? Whither has your beloved turned, that we may seek him with you?*

QABALA: Poet: *Where has he gone, beautiful woman? You called him, visited him, and you have seen only an idol that turned love to gold. Answer my cry! What has become of Breath?*

Onah (Aleph Noun Hay) means idiomatically to lament; to mourn, to wrong, to befall, rather than the simple interrogation "where?" It shows Aleph being thrust into the existential life of Noun Hay, buried so to speak, therefore mourned and sought. This opening schema epitomizes the whole verse.

Onah appears twice: first in association to *Halakh* (5.30.500), idiomatically a flowing or a road (from 5 to 500); then with *Panah* (80.50.5), idiomatically an emptiness or a corner, or as a verb, to turn from, to remove.

VI

2

דּוֹדִי יָרַד לְגַנּוֹ לַעֲרֻגוֹת הַבֹּשֶׂם לִרְעוֹת בַּגַּנִּים
וְלִלְקֹט שׁוֹשַׁנִּים:

PHONETICALLY: *Dodi Yarad Le'gano Li'aaroogot Ha'be'shem Li'reavot Ba'ganeem We'lilqot Shoshaneem.*

RSV: *My beloved has gone down to his garden, to the beds of spices, to pasture his flocks in the gardens, and gather lilies.*

QABALA: Psyche: *He has gone down into himself in the organic sphere: There he nourishes the human herd with pure sap and takes hold of two Breaths that exist and live together. True, I dreamed an idol, but beyond that idol I recognized him.*

Yarad (Yod Raysh Dallet) to go down, to descend. "He", the Aleph, has become Yod, and answers the unruffled Psyche. Compared to *Onah*, *Yarad* shows three permutations:

$$\frac{1 \quad 50 \quad 5}{10 \quad 200 \quad 4}$$

Aleph-Yod, Noun-Raysh and Hay-Dallet.

Le'gano: we have often seen that the root *Gan* (Ghimel Noun), garden, is a "container" in the biosphere.

Li-aaroogot and *Li'reavot* are respectively: 30.70.200.3.6.400 and 30.200.70.6.400. Both schemata project 30 in 400, but with 70 occupying two different positions in relation to 30. 70, thus expressing two different directions of Energy.

347

In *Lilqot* (Lammed Lammed Qof Tayt) these directions are wide apart: Lammed Qof (30.100) meets the cosmic Aleph, Qof, and Lammed Tayt (30.9) the elemental cell.

Thus, once again we come, with the last schema, upon *Shoshaneem*, two Sheens: the double flow of the One Energy, so often repeated.

VI

3   אֲנִי לְדוֹדִי וְדוֹדִי לִי הָרוֹעֶה בַּשּׁוֹשַׁנִּים:

PHONETICALLY: *Ani Le'dodi We'dodi Li Ha'roaah Be'shoschaneem.*
RSV: *I am my beloved's and my beloved is mine; he pastures his flock among lilies.*
QABALA: Woman: *I have found unity again: the intemporal and the temporal are two Breaths in one.*

Unity is rediscovered. The temporal Psyche blends two lives in one life. The two Sheen of *Shoshaneem* appear again, emerging from the two opposite directions, Aleph and Tav. But though Aleph is Tav, and Tav Aleph, Aleph has a quality as a signal, as an exalted shout, leading towards the freedom of all possibilities. *Rooaa* (Raysh Waw Ayn: 200.6.70), idiomatically, is such a shout, and is a shepherd only in a lower, symbolical sphere.

VI

4   יָפָה אַתְּ רַעְיָתִי כְּתִרְצָה נָאוָה כִּירוּשָׁלָ͏ִם אֲיֻמָּה
            כַּנִּדְגָּלוֹת:

PHONETICALLY: *Yafah At Raayati Ke'tertsah Navah Ki'yaro'shalom Ayaomah Ka'nidgalot.*
RSV: *You are beautiful as Tirzah, my love, comely as Jerusalem, terrible as an army with banners.*

QABALA: Lover: *My dear one, you are as beautiful as the solution of a difficulty. Your life as lived creates Breath, like peace descending; and Breath creates you, an intense proliferation.*

The root of *Tertsah* (Tav Raysh Tsadde Hay), *Terets*, means, idiomatically, to answer, to solve a difficulty. The difficulty here was to know what happened to Aleph when it disappeared in the biosphere; and "She" had answered it in the preceding verses. When compared to *Erets* (the *Earth* as symbol of the biosphere) the root *Terets* shows that Aleph has simply become Tav:

The Earth, *Erets:*   Aleph Raysh Tsadde
the Solution, *Terets:* Tav   Raysh Tsadde

The two Schemata *Navah* and *Ayomah*, translated "comely" and "terrible" (but why should she be terrible?) express two inverted flows of Energy. In *Navah* (Noun Aleph Waw Hay), the existential life, Noun, gives birth to timeless Aleph, and in *Ayomah* (Aleph Yod Mem Hay) Aleph is projected in the time-process of Yod.

We have met and explained *Diglo*, the root of *Nidgalot*, in verse II, 4.

VI

5

הָסֵבִּי עֵינַיִךְ מִנֶּגְדִּי שֶׁהֵם הִרְהִיבֻנִי שַׂעְרֵךְ
כְּעֵדֶר הָעִזִּים שֶׁגָּלְשׁוּ מִן־הַגִּלְעָד:

PHONETICALLY: *Hessevi Aynayekh Me'neghedi She'hem Hirhiboni Shaarekh Ke-eder Ha'ayzeem Shegalshoo Min Ha'ghilaad.*

RSV: *Turn away your eyes from me, for they disturb me—Your hair is like a flock of goats, moving down the slopes of Gilead.*

QABALA: Lover: *Let me sink in your stream of energy. You offer all that's possible, all the possibilities opened by your two*

349

*resistances to life: your biological existence and your Breath
breathing with mine.*

Hessev is the life (Hay: 5) of the female sex (Sammekh: 60) in
its body (Vayt: 2). In the idiom, *Hessev* is a banquet. As a verb
it means to transfer, not to turn away. *Aynayekh* means "Your
two eyes", but also "your two sources". *Me'neghedi*: colloquially
"from my presence" (not from "me"). *Neghedi* (Noun Ghimel
Dallet Yod: 50.3.4.10) is his objective existence as an organic
process (Ghimel Dallet: 3.4). It is "Him" as flesh.

In other words, the lover tells "Her" that she has transferred
her sexual appeal, from his physical body to something that
the verse, read sign by sign, will now describe (and thus
explicate its serial number, VI, 5—Waw Hay—as archetypes).

She'hem: Sheen (Breath) Hay (Life) Mem (Biosphere). This
schema expresses the living action of "Her" Sheen (through the
referred duality of her Sources) upon the biosphere.

Hirhiboni (5.200.5.10.2.50.10) is a complete equation. It
shows one life (Hay) in the cosmos (Raysh), one life (Hay), in
factual existence (Yod), a body (Bayt) fully alive (Noun), in its
existence (Yod). The two Hay and two Yod active in the body,
illustrate the union of "His" and "Her" lives.

Shaarekh: idiomatically "your hair". We have translated this
word "your price, value, or measure" (see I, 4). All the connotations of its root (Sheen Ayn Raysh: 300.70.200) emphasize
either the powerful movement of Sheen, as in *Shaar*: to storm,
to sweep away, to shudder, a tempest; or the uncertainty of
Ayn as in *Shaar* or *Shier*: price, value, to calculate, measure,
reckon, suppose, imagine; or, symbolically, *Shear*, hair: an
overflowing of Sheen from the head, supposedly a "breathing-
out of power" from the fire, *Esh* (Aleph Sheen), "builder" of
the Head, Principle of all things.

Ke-Eder Ha'ayzeem and the last schema *Ha'ghilaad* offer three
more Ayn: three further possibilities; and *Shegalshoo* two Sheen:
two Breaths.

This verse is "His" answer to "Her" statement (VI, 3): *Ani*

COMMENTARIES

Le'dodi We'dodi Li: *Ani*: Aleph in my existence; *Le'dodi*: the organic process Lammed applied to my two Resistances; *We'dodi*: copulatively my two Resistances; *Li*: in organic process. In answer to this, VI, 5 reveals five Ayn (70) and four (twice two) Sheen.

VI

6

שִׁנַּ֙יִךְ֙ כְּעֵ֣דֶר הָֽרְחֵלִ֔ים שֶׁעָל֖וּ מִן־הָרַחְצָ֑ה
שֶׁכֻּלָּם֙ מַתְאִימ֔וֹת וְשַׁכֻּלָ֖ה אֵ֥ין בָּהֶֽם׃

PHONETICALLY: *Shnaikh Ke'eder Ha'rhheleem She'aloo Min'ha'rahhtsah Sheklam Mat-yi-mot We'shekoolah Ayn Behem.*
RSV: *Your teeth are like a flock of ewes, that have come from the washing, all of them bear twins, not one among them is bereaved.*
QABALA: Breath: *The female that underlies your femininity is like a flock of sheep, a biological magma, unfertilized by me. Among the sheep, some will go back into primal substance, others into the evolutionary flow, being innocent and pure.*

The beginning of this verse is almost a repetition of IV, 2 with the exception of the third schema *Ha'rhheleem* instead of *Ha'qtosovot*. At that earlier stage *Shnaikh* ("your two" in the construct masculine) was a reference to King Solomon, who because of his corruption, and in spite of his carefully washed hands, appeared as *a flock of sheep, dead though not dead, having no proper understanding.*

"She" is now shown, on a deeper level, what the primal substance is: that pure energy, still unfertilized, is sexless. The female that underlies her femininity is a simple biological magma that cannot be referred to in the feminine. Some of it will go back into primal substance, and some of it, in perfect innocence, will become female in the evolutionary process.

The roots of *Ke'eder Ha'rhheleem She'aloo Min'ha'rahhttsah* are idiomatically:

351

Eder (Ayn Dallet Raysh: 70.4.200) flock, herd
Rehhel (Raysh Hhayt Lammed: 200.8.30) ewe
Sho'al (Sheen Ayn Lammed: 300.70.30) handful
Rahhats (Raysh Hhayt Tsadde: 200.8.90) to wash, bathe

We see in them all the unconscious biological process at work, building its structures in a state of uncertainty.

VI

7

כְּפֶלַח הָרִמּוֹן רַקָּתֵךְ מִבַּעַד לְצַמָּתֵךְ׃

PHONETICALLY: *Ka'phelahh Ha'rimon Raqatekh Mi'baad Le'tsometekh.*

RSV: *Your cheeks are like halves of a pomegranate behind your veil.*

QABALA: Breath: *But you, pure like them, fertilized by me, safeguard universal indeterminancy, strong because you are the residue of successive forms.*

Ka-phelahh: as an organic substance not yet structured, *Ha'rimon* (but), copulatively linked with the cosmic indetermination; *Raqatekh*: the union in you of Qof-Tav; *Mi'baad*: opens through your appearance every possibility; *Le'tsometekh*: by the evolution of your structural energy tending towards its fulfilment.

VI

8 & 9

שִׁשִּׁים הֵמָּה מְלָכוֹת וּשְׁמֹנִים פִּילַגְשִׁים
וַעֲלָמוֹת אֵין מִסְפָּר׃ אַחַת הִיא יוֹנָתִי תַמָּתִי אַחַת הִיא
לְאִמָּהּ בָּרָה הִיא לְיוֹלַדְתָּהּ רָאוּהָ בָנוֹת וַיְאַשְּׁרוּהָ
מְלָכוֹת וּפִילַגְשִׁים וַיְהַלְלוּהָ׃

PHONETICALLY: *Shesheem Hemah Melakhot Oo'shmoneem Pilagsheem We'aalamot Ein Mi'sfar.*

*Ahhat Hi Yonati Tamati Ahhat Hi Leimah Barah Hi Le'ioladtah
Raooha Benot We'ashrooha Melakhot We'filagsheem Wa'yehalelooha.*
RSV: *There are sixty queens and eighty concubines, and maidens without
number.*

*My dove, my perfect one, is only one, the darling of her mother, flawless
to her that bore her. The maidens saw her and called her happy; the
queens and concubines also, and they praised her.*

QABALA: Lover: *There are 60 queens: the female sex figure; there are
80 concubines: the figure of undeveloped substance. But you
are unique, in you is the ever virginal beginning. To me you
are the ideal of a pure woman.*

Sixty, *Sammekh*, fifteenth letter of the Hebrew alphabet, is,
idiomatically a support. According to Qabala, it is the female
sex; indeed, the "support" of all flesh.

Shesheem, by two Sheen, expresses the double energy that
activates the elaboration of forms. Eighty (Phay) is the number
of unstructured substance.

The symbol of the Mother has been mentioned in III, 4 and
III, 11. Here we have translated the canonical *darling of her
mother: in you is the ever virginal beginning.* The reading of the
Autiot deepens the general meaning of the verse, without
altering it.

VI

10

מִי־זֹאת הַנִּשְׁקָפָה כְּמוֹ־שָׁחַר יָפָה כַלְּבָנָה
בָּרָה כַּחַמָּה אֲיֻמָּה כַּנִּדְגָּלוֹת׃

PHONETICALLY: *Mi-Zot Ha'nishqafah Kemo-Shahhar Yafah Khal-
vanah Barah Ka'hhamah Ayomah K'nidgalot.*
RSV: *"Who is this that looks forth like the dawn, fair as the moon,
bright as the sun, terrible as an army with banners?"*

QABALA: Poet: *What is this dark unearthly light? It is energy going down into the female and rising in the male. Between them is uncertainty.*

It is illogical to associate the dawn and the moon. The interpreters should have known that this verse deals with astrology, because the sun is referred to by its astrological name, *Hhamah,* whereas colloquially, as in I, 6, it is *Shamesh.*

Hhamah (Hhayt Mem Hay: 8.40.5) shows two aspects of life; Hhayt is the passive energy that is set in motion by Hay, and Hay is the active energy that finds in Hhayt the substance upon which it can act. Thus can Hhayt enter the biosphere Mem, and thus can Mem come alive with Hay. But this creative quality, *Barah,* of the Sun has its opposite: the Sun also dries up, burns, destroys all life. It is *Ayomah* (Aleph Yod Mem Hay). This root means, in the idiom, to frighten, to threaten; it is something horrible, terrible. The name *Hhamah* (Hhayt Mem Hay) thus explains the two Sheen of *Shamesh:* one is the Breath that disintegrates structures in the undifferentiated Hhayt, the other blows in the direction of Hay, the archetype of Life.

We have noted earlier that the astrological Moon has also two aspects: the dynamic Energy is both submerged and leaping forth. It dies in it and it resurrects from it.

In this verse, "She" appears to the Poet as *Shahhar* (Sheen Hhayt Raysh: 300.8.200), idiomatically both dark and light, similar to the creative aspect of the Moon and to the destructive aspect of the Sun. The word is well chosen: it is a most ambiguous unsolved equation. We do not know which of the two Sheen is acting upon Hhayt, nor do we know how Hhayt responds to it. The idiom, unknowingly, reflects that uncertainty: *Shahhar* (or *Shahhor*) as a verb means to seek, to search for, to rise at dawn or to become black. In I, 5-6, we noted Psyche saying to Breath: *you take me from the daylight . . . Blackness of the sun puts conflict into me . . .* and to the girls of the cities: *uncertainty is my peace.*

354

VI

11

אֶל־גִּנַּת אֱגוֹז יָרַדְתִּי לִרְאוֹת בְּאִבֵּי הַנָּחַל
לִרְאוֹת הֲפָרְחָה הַגֶּפֶן הֵנֵצוּ הָרִמֹּנִים׃

PHONETICALLY: *El-Ghenat Egoz Yaradti Li'reot Be'avi Ha'nahhal Li'reot Ha'ferhhah Ha'ghefan Ha'netsoo Ha'rimoneem.*

RSV: *I went down to the next orchard, to look at the blossoms of the valley, to see whether the vines had budded, whether the pomegranates were in bloom.*

QABALA: Psyche: *I am this uncertainty. Who am I in whom the two poles of life meet? I have sunk into my biological sphere to see if the Principle which bore me has endowed me with its rising sap. In the Father's vineyard I have seen Breath put under the ground, there meeting with its universal Tabernacle, its bounding through the whole Creation, its reburial, its setting-out again, and I knew that that very pulsation was the life of all nature.*

El-Ghenat Egoz Yaradti must be read as the ancient scriptures were read, without interruption, all the *Autiot*, one by one in their full significance, without any grammatical construction:

1.30.3.50.400.1.3.6.7.10.200.4.400.10.

We see, in this succession of numbers, two trajectories from Aleph to Tav. At first, Aleph sinks in the biological sphere where the ever receptive nature gives birth to its prototypes, each according to its seed, and that Energy is resisted by Tav (400). Then, from Tav, Aleph springs forth into the unpredictable no. 7 and meets an existence (No. 10) through which the universal emanation (200) resists its own Energy (4) and rebounds from Tav (400).

The subsequent schemata describe the perpetual cycle of Energy buried and resurrected: the Psyche sinks into the biological sphere to discover "Her" Father's heritage. (*Hahhal* means to inherit.)

355

The word for vine, here, is *Ghefan* (Ghimel Phay Noun: 3.80.700). It is the "Father's Vine", a well-known symbol, leading to the cosmic Principle of indetermination, 700. In 1, 6 the vine she *didn't want anymore* was *Karm* (20.200.40), a static possession in the realm of the sons of Mother Earth.

VI

12   לֹא יָדַעְתִּי נַפְשִׁי שָׂמַתְנִי מַרְכְּבוֹת עַמִּי נָדִיב:׃

PHONETICALLY: *Lo Yadaati Nafshi Samatni Markevot Aami Nadiv.*
RSV: *Before I was aware, my fancy set me in a chariot beside my prince.*
QABALA: Psyche: *In my dream I did not know it. I was still under the spell of those with worldly prestige.*

This conclusion of Chant VI is a clear reference to "Her" dream where she had idolized *Edom*. In a deep sense, *Lo Yadaati* means that she had neglected to project Ayn (70) in Tav.

VII

1   שׁוּבִי שׁוּבִי הַשּׁוּלַמִּית שׁוּבִי שׁוּבִי וְנֶחֱזֶה־בָּךְ
מַה־תֶּחֱזוּ בַּשּׁוּלַמִּית כִּמְחֹלַת הַמַּחֲנָיִם:

PHONETICALLY: *Shoovi Shoovi Ha-sholamit Shoovi Shoovi We'nehhezeh-Bakh Mah Tehhezoo Ba'sholamit Ki'mehholat Ha'mahhenaeem.*
RSV*: *Return, return, O Shu'lammite, return, return, that we may look upon you. Why should you look upon the Shu'lammite, as upon a dance before two armies?*
QABALA: Poet: *Return, return, but to lived reality, you whose name chimes with Peace. Return, return . . . I have made you*

* In the Revised Standard Bible, this verse is numbered VI, 13. We have observed the Hebrew Scripture's numeration, and will therefore be one number ahead for every verse of Chant VII.

*speak and your voice came now from one sphere, now another.
It is time you came to earth, so that we could see you, and
that Breath restored me to my exact self. Why did I see you
like a hesitation between two Breaths? I want to sing my love.*

From the first Chant to the sixth, "She" appeared sometimes
as a young woman, either talking or being described; sometimes as the universal symbol of femininity, or of Psyche, or of
Structures; sometimes wandering in the prototype of Cities;
sometimes asleep, yet aware of her heart and of the Heart of the
World; then disappearing in the Zodiac, in a state of uncertainty; and finally descending in an orchard where only
Qabala could see her meeting the "Father's Holy Vine".

The magic of that fluidity so carefully erased her image
before it could crystallize in the mind of the reader, that the
simple act of following it was in truth the double contrasting
movement of Sheen and Sheen: of *Sheer Ha-Sheereem* (Song of
Songs).

Now the poet wants to see her as a real woman. He wants to
live his love in the exquisite reality of a dream come true.
Shoovi, Shoovi, Shoovi, Shoovi: this repetition is an invocation, an
exhortation. The name he gives her, *Scholamit* is none other than
Shalom, Peace, in Tav. The end of the verse is a reference to
her state of uncertainty between the two Breaths, described
throughout, particularly in vi, 10.

VII

2

מַה־יָּפוּ פְעָמַיִךְ בַּנְּעָלִים בַּת־נָדִיב חַמּוּקֵי
יְרֵכַיִךְ כְּמוֹ חֲלָאִים מַעֲשֵׂה יְדֵי אָמָן׃

PHONETICALLY: *Mah-Yafoo Beamaikh Ba'naaleem Bat-Nadeev
Hhamooki Yerekhaikh Kemo Hhalaeem Maasseh Yedei Aman.*
RSV: *How graceful are your feet in sandals, O queenly maiden! Your
rounded thighs are like jewels, the work of a master hand.*

357

QABALA: Poet: *Noble girl: how beautiful has been your evolution, as your looks show! The curves of your hips seem to torment themselves as if they wished to be independent even of what made them.*

The feet are a symbol of humanity's evolution through time. The *Sepher Yetsira* states that Abraham's Covenant with the Cosmic Energy, the circumcision at eight days, is "in his ten toes". The ancient Rabbis never gave in their written texts the keys to the assertions that were not meant to be taken literally. Their teaching was based on an oral tradition that offered to the students an analogical way of thinking.

The roots of *Peamaikh Ba'naaleem* are *Paam* (Pay Ayn Mem: 80.70.40) idiomatically to impel, a beat, time, step, foot; its *Autiot* show the undifferentiated Energy, 80, evolving by means of all its possibilities (70), in the biosphere (40). And *Naal* (Noun Ayn Lammed: 50.70.30), a shoe, is also, as a verb, to bar, bolt, lock; its *Autiot* show an existential life (50), evolving, by means of all its possibilities (70), organically (30).

The word *Yerekh* means hip as well as thigh. The root of *Hhalaeem* is *Hhal* (Hhayt Lammed): to fall, to dance, to tremble, or *Hhala* (Hhayt Lammed Aleph): to be ill, diseased. (The word for jewelry, *Hhalayot*, is different.)

Aman means to rear, to nurse.

VII

3

שָׁרְרֵךְ֙ אַגַּ֣ן הַסַּ֔הַר אַל־יֶחְסַ֖ר הַמָּ֑זֶג בִּטְנֵךְ֙
עֲרֵמַ֣ת חִטִּ֔ים סוּגָ֖ה בַּשּׁוֹשַׁנִּֽים׃

PHONETICALLY: *Srarakh Aghen Ha'sahar Al-Yehhsar Ha'Mazag Betnikh Aaromat Hhiteem Soogah Be'shooshaneem.*
RSV: *Your navel is a rounded bowl that never lacks mixed wine, your belly is a heap of wheat encircled with lilies.*

COMMENTARIES

Q̲ABALA: Poet: *You rule over the borderline of the lunar crescent in its shrinking phase, you rule over the lunar energy which fills the bellies of women: you control births according to your wisdom: your anger is that of Sarah face to face with the woman-slave Agar.*

We beg our readers to visualize a navel as a rounded bowl full of wine on a belly like a heap of wheat surrounded with lilies, and to meditate on that solemn interpretation of a sacred text.

In the preceding verse, we have done away with the voluptuous rotundities of the oriental women. The young woman described here is fully mature and reigns upon the "Waters", formative of the bellies (see the *Sepher Yetsira*). The Waters, in astrology and in alchemy are associated with the Moon.

Srarakh: you reign, rule, prevail, have control over. (The root *Sarar*: Seen Raysh Raysh: 300.200.200 shows an action upon two worlds.)

Aghen (or *Oghen*): Aleph Ghimel Noun: 1.3.700. is a navel only symbolically. Its Aleph in the biological primitive Garden: *Gan* (Ghimel Noun) is a central point of anything projected in the cosmic indetermination, 700. The combination 3.700 is not an evolutionary process: the organic movement, 3, disappears in 700. Thus was *Gan Eden*, the famous garden that never was: an unstructured immovable state, on the borderline of evolution. *Aghen* in the idiom is a brim, a border, an edge, or analogically, a navel, the remains of a border point of two lives that were linked through the umbilical cord.

Sahar (Sammekh Nay Raysh: 60.5.200) in the idiom is the crescent moon. *Yehhsar* (Yod Hhayt Sammekh Raysh) means to decrease. The root *Hhassar*, in all its connotations is a lack, a want, a poverty, to decrease, to be defective, lessened, short of.

Ha-Mazag: idiomatically, to pour water. *Betnikh*, your belly, can be read *Be'tnikh*: in your bowl. *Tanan* is to become moist. We see here the above mentioned symbolic relation between water and belly.

359

Aaromat Hhiteem. These two words can mean a heap of wheat, or the nakedness of a restrained anger, or of a purifying of a guilt or sin, according to which root (*Hhita* or *Hhata* or *Hhatam*) we care to choose. The Qabala asserts that this veiled passage is a reference to *Sarah* (compare her name to the root *Sarar*) in restrained anger, facing the pregnant slave woman *Agar*: the morally and intellectually elevated women control the Moon in its shrinking phase, control the "Waters", control their bellies. In a word, they control the births according to their judgement.

Soogah (Sammekh Waw Ghimel Hay) is yet another reference (with *Sahar* and *Yehhsar*) to the female sex.

Lastly, *Shooshaneem* brings us back to the action of two Sheen that we have often seen.

VII

4   שְׁנֵי שָׁדַיִךְ כִּשְׁנֵי עֳפָרִים תְּאֳמֵי צְבִיָּה׃

PHONETICALLY: *Schnei Shadaikh Kishnei Aaphareem Taamei Tsbe'yah.*

RSV: *Your two breasts are like two fawns, twins of a gazelle.*

QABALA: Poet: *Your divinity is in you. It forms two free Emanations, from four Elements.*

The first four schemata and the sixth are the same as in IV, 5. The fifth, *Taamei* differs in spelling: it has no Waw between Aleph and Noun. The two last schemata of IV, 5 are omitted. This has led us to a different, more abstract *Midrash*, and to mention the four Elements. (We remind the reader that a *Midrash* is a commentary, not a translation.)

In Chant IV, we were following an evolutionary process. The context, here, is different: the poet is describing his ideal woman, or, rather, he is creating her, analogically, with the knowledge of the cosmic significance of the different parts of the human body.

The *Sepher Yetsira* gives several charts of the structured states of Energy as they co-exist in the Zodiac, in the human body and in the calendar. That very ancient science is forgotten today. We compare, for instance, a head to other heads, but we do not classify the heads as particular cases of a universal structure.

In the ancient times, the four Elements were used as a convenient elementary classification. Having linked, in the preceding verse, the belly, the Waters and the Moon, we will follow the text on that basis.

VII

5 צַוָּארֵךְ כְּמִגְדַּל הַשֵּׁן עֵינַיִךְ בְּרֵכוֹת בְּחֶשְׁבּוֹן עַל־שַׁעַר בַּת־רַבִּים אַפֵּךְ כְּמִגְדַּל הַלְּבָנוֹן צוֹפֶה פְּנֵי דַמָּשֶׂק:

PHONETICALLY: *Tsav'orekh Ke'migdal Ha'shen Aynakh Brakhot Be'hhissavon Aal-Shaar Bat-Rabeem Afekh Ke'migdal Ha'lavnon Tsofeh Pnei Dam'sheq.*

RSV: *Your neck is like an ivory tower, Your eyes are pools in Heshbon, by the gate of Bathrab'bim. Your nose is like a tower of Lebanon, overlooking Damascus.*

QABALA: Poet: *Your head is Fire. The Air, through your neck, nourishes the temporal part in your body made of Earth and Water. The length of your neck is a measure of Time. Your eyes flash with the essence of intemporal Fire. They give benediction. Your bright thought waits for the iron bars to open behind which are the rabbis. Your anger is as a great whiteness facing the spilt blood.*

The neck, *Tsavor* (Tsadde Waw Aleph Raysh) has always been considered by Qabala as a structurizing element. It is a passage through which the exalted Fire, or Light, belonging to the head is reduced to bodily heat. The three letters, Waw Aleph Raysh, that follow Tsadde, are a permutation of Aleph Waw Raysh (*Awr*: light).

361

Ke'migdal: as a great. *Ha'shen*: duration (we have seen the root Shen, Shnei, Shana, etc. . . .). It also means tooth; the canonical translation, "ivory" is an equivalent for "big tooth"; the teeth, in many idioms, are associated with ideas of struggle, memory, effort, reproach, mostly linked to time and duration.

Aynakh: your eyes, or founts; *Brakhot*: are blessings; *Be'hhissavon*: with, or due to, thought; *Al-Shaar*: by the gate; *Bat-Rabeem* of the suburb of the Rabbis; *Afekh*: your anger (*Af* in the idiom is both nose and anger); *Ke'migdal*: as a great; *Ha'lavnon*: whiteness; *Tsofah*: flooding; *Pnei*: at the face of; *Dam-sheq*: blood flowing.

VII

6

רֹאשֵׁךְ עָלַיִךְ כַּכַּרְמֶל וְדַלַּת רֹאשֵׁךְ כָּאַרְגָּמָן
מֶלֶךְ אָסוּר בָּרְהָטִים׃

PHONETICALLY: *Roshekh Aalaykh Ka'Karmel We'dallet Roshekh Ka'argamon Melekh Assoor Be'rhateem.*

RSV: *Your head crowns you like Carmel and your flowing locks are like purple; a king is held captive in the tresses.*

QABALA: Poet: *Earthly fire is active in your fertile body. The fire of your thought transmutes the blood in a way unknown to kings.*

Roshekh: your head or summit. The spelling of *Rosh*: (Raysh Aleph Sheen, when Raysh is read in full (Raysh Yod Sheen) not only reveals two Sheen, but shows Aleph born of Raysh (timeless Energy engendered by the existent Universe). The opening of Genesis, *Bereshiyt*, can be understood that way, among others.

Karmel is a fertile soil; *Dallet-Roshekh* is none other than the letter Dallet, as a word, meaning here the resistance of her "head", as centre of fiery intelligence.

Argamon (Aleph Raysh Ghimel Mem Noun: 1.200.3.40.700), translated purple, is a marvellous equation in which is pictured

362

the descending of Aleph in its cosmic container Raysh; its putting in motion the archetype of organic movement, Ghimel; its penetrating the biosphere, Mem; and resurrecting in the cosmic indetermination, Noun final: 700. The purple as colour is symbolic of that transfiguration. It is as blood purified and exalted. Adam means red and Edom is red. The historical conflict around the colour red or purple, between kings and the human masses, will only cease when the blessing of Woman's intelligence will be active, as "Hers" is in the Song.

VII

7

מַה־יָּפִית וּמַה־נָּעַמְתְּ אַהֲבָה בַּתַּעֲנוּגִים׃

PHONETICALLY: *Mah Yafeet Wo'mah-Naamet Ahavah Bat'aanogheem.*
RSV: *How fair and pleasant you are, O loved one, delectable maiden!*
QABALA: Poet: *The blend of Breath and its vessel, how actively organic it is: blending in you, girl of delight.*

The spelling *Yafeet* (Yod Phay Yod Tav: the undifferentiated Phay between two Yod meeting Tav) is deliberately different from the *Yafeh* we already know. Likewise, the spelling of *Naamet* ending in Tav, is not the expected feminine *Naamah*; *Ahavah* is love, not "the loved one"; *Bat'aanogheem* is girl of delight. *Bat* introduces a third Tav (a trinity of Tav) and *Aanog* a second Ayn (a double range of indefinite possibilities).

This concise verse (no. VII, 7) shows Tav set in a trinitary motion by the blending of "His" and "Her" delights.

VII

8

זֹאת קוֹמָתֵךְ דָּמְתָה לְתָמָר וְשָׁדַיִךְ לְאַשְׁכֹּלוֹת׃

PHONETICALLY: *Zot Qomatekh Damtah Le'tamar We'shadaikh Le'esh-Kolot.*

RSV: *You are stately as a palm tree, and your breasts are like clusters.*

QABALA: Poet: *You grow straight upwards as if your blood were transfigured, omnipotent as if the Fire of knowledge burned in you.*

Zot (Zayn Aleph Tav: 7.1.400) is a concentrated equation of the general theme of the Song: the indetermination (7) presiding over the blending of Aleph and Tav.

Qomatekh: your springing up; *Damtah*: in the image of, or, in a deeper sense: *Dam* (blood) *Tah* (Tav alive); *Le'tamar*: as a palm-tree. The same root *Timer* is a smoke rising straight up. Its *Autiot* reveal the essence of these connotations: *Tamar* (Tav Mem Raysh: 400.40.200) is a power of cosmic resistance active in Emanation.

The schemata *Zot Qomatekh Damtah Le'tamar* can be translated (said by the Poet to his ideal woman): "this uncertain blending of you and me springs forth from the resistance of life to itself as a palm-tree from the soil or as a column of smoke from burning substance."

The verse ends with *Shadaikh*: your dual divinity; *Le'eshkolot*: is as a bunch of grapes, or, fundamentally, as *Eshkol*, a learned person; *Ot* (Waw Tav): fertilizing Tav. (Symbolically a bunch of grapes, as the wine, or the vine, reveals the hidden knowledge of the Exalted Fire buried in the Earth.)

VII

9   אָמַ֙רְתִּי֙ אֶעֱלֶ֣ה בְתָמָ֔ר אֹֽחֲזָ֖ה בְּסַנְסִנָּ֑יו וְיִֽהְיוּ־
נָ֤א שָׁדַ֙יִךְ֙ כְּאֶשְׁכְּל֣וֹת הַגֶּ֔פֶן וְרֵ֥יחַ אַפֵּ֖ךְ כַּתַּפּוּחִֽים׃

PHONETICALLY: *Amarti Eaaleh Be'tamar Oohhazah Be'sansinav We'ihoo-Na Shadaikh Ke'eshkelot Ha'ghefen We'reiahh Afekh Ka'tafoohhhim.*

RSV: *I say I will climb the palm tree and lay hold of its branches, Oh, may your breasts be like clusters of the vine, and the scent of your breath like apples.*

QABALA: Poet: *I said to myself: "Rise to this high condition, take this twofold fullness, that it may become Omnipotence for you, where all branches of knowledge meet. Let the one of the beginning be as the many of the end."*

"I said to myself: climb on that palm-tree; take hold of its palms." The palm, *Sansin* (Sammekh Noun Sammekh Noun: 60.50.60.50) is a double female existence, abundantly alive.

The next schemata are untranslatable: in *We'ihoo Na Shedaikh. We'ihoo* (Waw Yod Hay Yod Waw) is the sacred Yod Hay Yod, or Yod Hay Waw; and we need not ponder again on *Shadai.*

Eshkelot Ha'ghefen: symbolically, the wisdom of the "Vine". Idiomatically, *Reiahh Afekh* means the smell of your nose, in its most degraded connotation. We have, earlier, translated *Af* anger. This schema: Aleph Phay is compared here with *Tafoohhim*, plural of Tav Phay Hhayt (apple). We must extract the essentials of both schemata: Aleph Phay for *Af* and Tav Phay for *Tafoohhim*. (In the canonical Hebrew, the Phay is dotted and pronounced Pay; this simply hardens it without altering its cabalistic meaning.) The archetype Hhayt (8) in *Tafoohh* or [*Tapoohh*] and the plural *Im* justify our *Midrash*: let the one of the beginning (Aleph Phay) be as the many of the End [Tav Phay Hhayt Im plural].

VII

10

וְחִכֵּךְ כְּיֵין הַטּוֹב הוֹלֵךְ לְדוֹדִי לְמֵישָׁרִים
דּוֹבֵב שִׂפְתֵי יְשֵׁנִים:

PHONETICALLY: *We'hhikakh Ke'yin Ha'tov Holekh Le'dodi Le'mishareem Dovev Siftei Yesheneem.*

RSV: *and your kisses like the best wine that goes down smoothly, gliding over lips and teeth.*

365

QABALA: Poet: *My love, your desire is wine to me . . .*
Woman: *. . . wine that goes towards the one I love. Its utter rightness makes words come from our sleeping lips.*

Idiomatically, a kiss is *Neshikah*, to kiss is *Nashak*; it is not the word used in this verse.

The root *Hhekh* is the palate, *Hhikah* is to hope, to wish. "Her" desire for "Him" is expressed both by her words and her lips.

Le'mishareem: the root *Yashar* (Yod Sheen Raysh) means straightness, rightness, equity. We find it in *Isra-El. Dovev* (Dallet Waw Vayt Vayt: 4.6.2.2) with its resistant Dallet acting upon the two and two, meaning to cause to awake, to speak up, to assert.

Siftei: the lips; *Yesheneem* who sleep in duration.

VII

11

אֲנִי לְדוֹדִי וְעָלַי תְּשׁוּקָתוֹ׃

PHONETICALLY: *Ani Le'dodi We'alai Teshooqatoo.*
RSV: *I am my beloved's and his desire is for me.*
QABALA: Woman: *I am his. But his desire weighs upon me.*

The schema *Teshooqatoo* (Tav Sheen Waw Qof Tav Waw: 400.300.6.100.400.6) shows Tav emitting Sheen, acting upon Qof, and projected back upon itself. It is a complete circuit from Tav to Tav, that cannot be deeply understood in its idiomatic meaning. Its root *Shooq* is the oriental market. On an everyday level, the ideal woman answers the poet that she gives herself to the man she loves, but that he treats her as an object to be bought and sold.

The falling back of Tav upon Tav is, for her, a tragedy.

VII

12

לְכָה דוֹדִי נֵצֵא הַשָּׂדֶה נָלִינָה בַּכְּפָרִים׃

PHONETICALLY: *Lekhah Dodi Netse Ha'sadeh Nalinah Be'kafareem.*
RSV: *Come, my beloved, let us go forth into the fields, and lodge in the villages.*
QABALA: Woman: *It depends on you, my love, whether our union can reconcile the contraries.*

We are nearing the end of the seventh Chant. Through the preceding ones, the Poet had lived a stupendous experience; his mind had explored all the realms of Emanation in terms of symbols, abstractions, projections; he had understood the Sacred Dialogue between the two extreme Poles of Creative Energy. Whether we call that adventure knowledge, mysticism or revelation is irrelevant. However total it seems to be, it is still unsatisfactory for the Poet. He no longer identifies himself with the beloved; the male protagonist has disappeared. The Poet in flesh describes his ideal woman and longs to meet his Shalomite "in lived reality". With an exceptional awareness, he does not imagine her according to the ancient oriental proto-type. She is tall and thin as a palm-tree, almost aerial as a column of smoke, her intelligence awakes "the sleeping lips", but she is also most desirable sensually.

The blending of Gnostic Nuptials and physical love is an essential theme of the Song, and perhaps one of the most diffi-cult to live. In Genesis, beginning with the allegorical apple of the Garden of Eden, the understanding and evolution of sen-suality linked to intelligence is of the woman. She sees that the fruit is both a delight and "makes one wise".

The Poet knows the necessity of that evolution, and that, historically, the women have been and are subdued, given an inferior status, exploited and considered mostly in their capacity of awakening and satisfying the lust of men. Following his description of the ideal woman, he moves her to answer with the desperate cry: "his desire weighs upon me" (VII, 11).

The schema *Netse* (Noun Tsadde Aleph) means to fly away, to escape. The root of *Ha'sadeh* is *Shad* (Sheen Dallet): to ravage, despoil, violence, ruin. *Nalinah* means let us sleep overnight; *Be'Kafareen*, in the villages. The apparent meaning of this invitation is (in relation to the preceding verse): "I love you but you only desire me; let us run away from that violence; let us sleep together overnight, so that you may love me."

But this is only an interpretation on a very low level of the constant theme of the Song. In *Netse*, the Noun (50) expresses a life in existence, and the following Tsadde Aleph state again her wish to give structure to the Timeless Energy; *Shad* is Breath thrust upon a resistance; *Nalinah* with its two Noun and Lammed Yod Hay means two lives living together; as to *Kafareem*, its root is *Kifer*: to atone, to expiate, to forgive.

VII

13 נַשְׁכִּ֫ימָה לַכְּרָמִ֗ים נִרְאֶ֤ה אִם־פָּֽרְחָ֣ה הַגֶּ֔פֶן פִּתַּ֣ח הַסְּמָדַ֗ר הֵנֵ֙צוּ֙ הָרִמּוֹנִ֔ים שָׁ֛ם אֶתֵּ֥ן אֶת־דֹּדַ֖י לָֽךְ:

PHONETICALLY: *Naskimah Le' krameem Nereh Im-Parhhah Ha'ghefen Pitahh Ha'smadar Henetsoo Ha'remoneem Shem Eten Et-Dodai Lakh.*
RSV: *Let us go out early to the vineyards, and see whether the vines have budded, whether the grape blossoms have opened and the pomegranates are in bloom. There I will give you my love.*
QABALA: Woman: *Come with me, let us go and see if the spring is yet here. I shall reveal the names of things as they are renewed, and you will learn who you are.*

This verse is a reference to the sinking in the biological sphere described in VI, 11.

Shem Eten means: the name of Aleph Tav united in the completion of Noun final (700), the cosmic Principle of Indetermination.

VII

14

הַדּוּדָאִים נָתְנוּ־רֵיחַ וְעַל־פְּתָחֵינוּ כָּל־
מְגָדִים חֲדָשִׁים גַּם־יְשָׁנִים דּוֹדִי צָפַנְתִּי לָךְ׃

PHONETICALLY: *Ha'doodaim Natnoo-Reahh We'aal Petahhenoo Kal-Megadeem Hhadasheem Gam-Yeshaneem Dodi Tsafanti Lakh.*

RSV: *The mandrakes give forth fragrance, and over our doors are all choice fruits, new as well as old, which I have laid up for you, O my beloved.*

QABALA: Woman: *The flowers of earthly love give off their scent. Everything exquisite is at our doors. But my love for you is not in these aspects of Duration.*

The mandrakes are the flowers of earthly love, symbols of exquisite fruits "new and old", that is, belonging to Time. Her love for him is beyond all transient feelings, beyond all appearances.

VIII

1

מִי יִתֶּנְךָ כְּאָח לִי יוֹנֵק שְׁדֵי אִמִּי אֶמְצָאֲךָ
בַחוּץ אֶשָּׁקְךָ גַּם לֹא־יָבוּזוּ לִי׃

PHONETICALLY: *Mi Itenkha Ka'ahh Li Yoneq Shadai Imi Emtsakha Be'hoots Eshaqkha Gam Lo-Yavoozoo Li.*

RSV: *O that you were like a brother to me, that nursed at my mother's breast! If I met you outside, I would kiss you, and none would despise me.*

QABALA: Woman: *Who will teach you to be for me like a newborn brother not yet depraved by time? I would quench your thirst in the realms of space and, moreover, do so as a free woman.*

This verse develops "Her" impressive reproach of VII, 11: "his desire weighs upon me". We have seen in Genesis* that the woman must evolve so as to acquire the status of "sister". If her historical development is inadequate, is it not the fault of the males, who do not know how to be, in the image of Breath, perpetually young, fresh, not yet depraved by their own structures?

"Who will teach you to be for me" *Yonek* (a bud) *Shadai Imi* (of the All-mighty maternal Power)?

Emtsakha: I would encourage you; *Be'hoots*: in the open spaces—or beyond yourself; *Eshaqkha*: I would give you to drink (from the root *Shaqah*); *Gam Lo-Yavoozoo Li*: and moreover I would not be contemptible (as a woman slave).

VIII

2

אֶנְהָגְךָ אֲבִיאֲךָ אֶל־בֵּית אִמִּי תְּלַמְּדֵנִי
אַשְׁקְךָ מִיַּיִן הָרֶקַח מֵעֲסִיס רִמֹּנִי:

PHONETICALLY: *Enhagkha Abiakha El-Bayt Imi Talamdini Ashqekha Mi'yin Ha'reqahh Mi'ayessiss Rimoni.*

RSV: *I would lead you and bring you into the House of my mother and into the chamber of her that conceived me. I would give you spiced wine to drink, the juice of my pomegranates.*

QABALA: Woman: *I would unite your incessant beginnings beyond time with my perennial inheritance through the generations. Living together we would mingle these two streams ...*

Symbolically: "I would talk to you, I would live with you in the house where my mother taught me; I would give you wine mixed with fruit-juice".

The six Aleph (the copulative number) and the eight Yod (the number of unstructured energy) in this verse illustrate her intense wish to blend the timeless and the temporal primordial

* *The Cipher of Genesis.*

370

Energies. The wine mixed with fruit-juice is a good image for that union. The wine, as we know, is a symbol of male Energy. In Hebrew, *Yin* (Yod Yod Noun: 10.10.700) is a strange schema, Yod Yod meaning, colloquially God. The fruit-juice, *Yessiss*, contains two Sammekh, the female sexuality (Ayn Sammekh Yod Sammekh).

The last schema, *Rimoni*, is not spelt as *Rimoon*, the pomegranate, which contains an extra Waw, and moreover, it is not a plural. It is a play on two contrasting roots: *Rim* (Raysh Mem: to rise, to be high, exalted) and *Ni* (Noun Yod: to lament).

VIII

3   שְׂמֹאלוֹ תַּחַת רֹאשִׁי וִימִינוֹ תְּחַבְּקֵנִי:

PHONETICALLY: *Semolo Tahhat Roshi We'imino Tehhabeqeni.*
RSV: *O that his left hand were under my head, and that his right hand embraced me!*
QABALA: Woman: *But his left hand brings me the Sacred Name while his right hand embraces me: one hand does not know what the other hand is doing.*

This verse is a repetition of II, 6, with the only difference of *Roshi* instead of *Le'roshi*. By suppressing the organic Lammed, the woman in flesh rejects the ambiguous action and desire of her male partner.

VIII

4   הִשְׁבַּעְתִּי אֶתְכֶם בְּנוֹת יְרוּשָׁלַם מַה־
תָּעִירוּ | וּמַה־תְּעֹרְרוּ אֶת־הָאַהֲבָה עַד שֶׁתֶּחְפָּץ:

PHONETICALLY: *Hishbaati Etkhem Benot Yero'shalom Mah-Taavroo We'mah-Teareroo Et-Ha'ahevah Aad Shetehhfats.*

RSV: *I adjure you, O daughters of Jerusalem, that you stir not up nor awaken love until it please.*

QABALA: Woman: *By the living Seven, girls of false peace, why in your cities, in your fortified cities, do you wall up love in a non-stop state of desire?*

This verse partly repeats II, 7, with a difference: *Mah* interrogative, instead of *Im*: do not. The last schema, *Shetehhfats* must be read here in the context of her dramatic revolt: why are the girls dependent on the desires of men? Why is love walled, so to speak, and desecrated in the cities of lust?

VIII

5

מִי זֹאת עֹלָה מִן־הַמִּדְבָּר מִתְרַפֶּקֶת עַל־
דּוֹדָהּ תַּחַת הַתַּפּוּחַ עוֹרַרְתִּיךָ שָׁמָּה חִבְּלַתְךָ אִמֶּךָ
שָׁמָּה חִבְּלָה יְלָדַתְךָ:

PHONETICALLY: *Mi Zot Oolah Min' Ha'midbar Mitrapeqet Aal-Dodah Tahhat Ha'tapooahh Oorartikha Shamah Hhiblatkha Imekha Shamah Hhiblah Yeladotkha.*

RSV: *Who is that coming up from the wilderness, leaning upon her beloved? Under the apple tree I awakened you, there your mother was in travail with you, there she who bore you was in travail.*

QABALA: Voice: *Who is this woman who stands up in a place where there are no cities, in a desert quite different from the desert where Solomon lies in his palanquin? She is by herself, sustained by her only love.*

Woman: *Breath, through my love I woke you under the tree where pure juice rises, where your mother Earth kept you in holy sleep till I came.*

The woman who is coming up from a desert is not leaning upon her beloved: she is alone, leaning upon *Dodah* (Dallet Waw Dallet Hay: 4.6.4.5), her two resistances in living fruition. She is *Tahhat Ha'tapooahh* (Tav Hhayt Tav-Hay Tav Phay Waw

Hhayt: 400.8.400-5.400.80.6.8). This means that she is letting herself go in a state of total abandon (unstructured 8 between two Tav), in communion with the pure sap of a living tree, where Tav rests in a happy vegetal slumber. After all her struggles and searches the fact of being in a state of awareness is her only possibility of awakening the Aleph asleep in the Earth (Eretz: Aleph Raysh Tsadde).

VIII

6

שִׂימֵנִי כַחוֹתָם עַל־לִבֶּךָ כַּחוֹתָם עַל־
זְרוֹעֶךָ כִּי־עַזָּה כַמָּוֶת אַהֲבָה קָשָׁה כִשְׁאוֹל קִנְאָה
רְשָׁפֶיהָ רִשְׁפֵּי אֵשׁ שַׁלְהֶבֶתְיָה׃

PHONETICALLY: *Shimeni Ka'hhootam Aal-Lebekha Ka'hhootam Aal-Zeroekha Ki-Aazah Kamavet Ahavah Qasha Ki'sheol Qinah Reshafeiha Rishfei Esh Shalhevetiah.*

RSV: *Set me as a seal upon your heart, as a seal upon your arm; for love is strong as death, jealousy is cruel as the grave. Its flashes are flashes of fire, a most vehement flame.*

QABALA: Breath: *Let me be as a seal in the centre of your being, a seal on the arm of your doing. Love is powerful as death, absolute as the grave, excluding what is unreal. Its heat is that of the Fire, the Fire of the daughter of Yah.*

Liv (Lammed Vayt: 30.2), the heart, is the organic motor (30) of the body (2). The arm *Zaroc* (Zain Raysh Waw Ayn: 3.200.8.70) is the same word as sowing, seed. It synthesizes all productive action.

The translation: cruel (or absolute) as "the grave", for *Sheol*, is acceptable, although in the idiom *Sheol* generally means "hell". If, in this verse, love is compared to *Sheol* and to *Esh* (fire) it is because those two schemata are respectively spelt Sheen Aleph (followed by Waw Lammed) and Aleph Sheen, thus showing two opposite directions of the same Energy; meaning that Love is a Totality.

VIII

7

מַיִם רַבִּים לֹא יוּכְלוּ לְכַבּוֹת אֶת־הָאַהֲבָה
וּנְהָרוֹת לֹא יִשְׁטְפוּהָ אִם־יִתֵּן אִישׁ אֶת־כָּל־הוֹן
בֵּיתוֹ בָּאַהֲבָה בּוֹז יָבוּזוּ לוֹ׃

PHONETICALLY: *Maim Rabeem Lo Yookloo Le'Khabot Et-Ha'ahavah Oo'neharot Lo Ishtefooha Im-Iten Yish Et-Kol-Hon Bayto Ba'ahavah Boz Yavoozoo Lo.*

RSV: *Many waters cannot quench love, neither can floods drown it. If a man offered for love all the wealth of his house, it would be utterly scorned.*

QABALA: Lover: *This love cannot be extinguished by water, even rivers of water could not put it out. A man who tried to get it with heaps of money would be met with contempt.*

The Fire that cannot be extinguished by water is a fire that does not reduce its energy to heat. (See Ex. III, 2, the bush that *was burning, yet it was not consumed.*) There is a direct link between *Ahavah* (love) and YHWH, as can be seen in the permutations of the two schemata:

YHWH: Yod   Hay Waw Hay
Ahavah: Aleph Hay Bayt Hay

VIII

8

אָחוֹת לָנוּ קְטַנָּה וְשָׁדַיִם אֵין לָהּ מַה־נַּעֲשֶׂה
לַאֲחֹתֵנוּ בַּיּוֹם שֶׁיְּדֻבַּר־בָּהּ׃

PHONETICALLY: *Ahhot Lanoo Qetana We'shadaim Ayn Lah Mah-Naasseh La'ahhotenoo Ba'yom Sheidobar-Bah.*

RSV: *We have a little sister, and she has no breasts. What shall we do for our sister, on the day when she is spoken for?*

QABALA: Woman: *Our sister, a woman-child not yet awakened by Breath, what will we do about her when she receives Breath?*

374

The word *Ahhot* (Aleph Hhayt Waw Tav: 1.8.6.400) meaning
sister, is the symbol of accomplished womanhood. It qualifies
the exalted *Rebekah* (Gen. xxiv, 59-60). As a schema, it is most
expressive: it shows a complete circuit, structured and fruitful,
between Aleph and Tav.

When womanhood is not yet mature, the historical woman
is *Qetana*: small. This schema (Qof Tayt Noun Hay: 100.9.50.5)
shows the cosmic Aleph animating a simple cell. The canonical
little sister that has no breasts is only a particular case of a general
field. The play on words such as *Shadaim*: two breasts or a dual
divinity (*Shadai*, as we have already seen, is idiomatically *God*)
is an example of the cabalistic way of thinking based on the
ancient field theory.

VIII

9

אִם־חוֹמָה הִיא נִבְנֶה עָלֶיהָ טִירַת כָּסֶף
וְאִם־דֶּלֶת הִיא נָצוּר עָלֶיהָ לוּחַ אָרֶז:

PHONETICALLY: *Im-Hhomah Hi Nevneh Aaleiha Tirat Kesseph
We'im-Dallet Hi Natsoor Aaleiha Loahh Arez.*

RSV: *If she is a wall, we will build upon her a battlement of silver; but
if she is a door, we will enclose her with boards of cedar.*

QABALA: Breath: *If she is only organic matter, she will be shut away
in her desires. If she is responsive, circumstances will help me
to shape her.*

Hhomah (Hhayt Waw Mem Hay: 8.6.40.5) is, idiomatically,
a wall. The *Autiot* of its root *Hham* (8.40), meaning heat, are a
picture of unstructured energy, 8, in the biosphere. The
idiomatic *Hhomerah* means matter. Breath saying of an immature
womanhood "if she is a wall" can only mean: "if she is only
unconscious matter: an obstacle to me".

Tirat (Tayt Yod Raysh Tav) is a tent, an enclosure. *Kesseph*
means to desire, to long for. *Dallet* is simply the letter Dallet:

resistance. *Natsoor*, from the root *Yotser*, is structure, meaning I would structure.

Aaleiha: with her, or upon her. *Loahh*: in this context is a calendar. *Arez* (1.200.7) meaning, idiomatically, to pack, to put things together hopefully opens, with Zayn (7) every possibility.

VIII

10   אֲנִי חוֹמָה וְשָׁדַי כַּמִּגְדָּלוֹת אָז הָיִיתִי
בְעֵינָיו כְּמוֹצְאֵת שָׁלוֹם:

PHONETICALLY: *Ani Hhomah We'shadai Ka'migdalot Az Ha'iyti Be'aynav Ke'motzet Shalom.*

RSV: *I was a wall, and my breasts were like towers; then I was in his eyes as one who brings peace.*

QABALA: Woman: *I am organic matter, but I am all powerful and give answer to Breath. In this twofold existence, as far as concerns Breath, lies the origin of his Peace.*

Her gallant assertion: I am that *Hhomah* (not I was) is a powerful epitome of the entire Song of Songs. "She" *is* matter, she *is* a resistance to "Him". The inspired Poet lends those words to a woman in flesh, identified with that matter, with that resistance, that awareness, that recognition. "She" and "He" are the two poles of the One Single Holy Energy, and with this Revelation, undoubtedly lived by him, the unknown Author bestows on us an understanding and a stupendously active Peace.

VIII

11   כֶּרֶם הָיָה לִשְׁלֹמֹה בְּבַעַל הָמוֹן נָתַן אֶת־
הַכֶּרֶם לַנֹּטְרִים אִישׁ יָבִא בְּפִרְיוֹ אֶלֶף כָּסֶף:

PHONETICALLY: *Kerem Haiah Le'shlomoh Be'baal Hamon Natan Et-Ha'Kerem Le'notreem Eesh Yavi Be'firio Eleph Kesseph.*

RSV: *Solomon had a vineyard at Ba'al-Ha'mon; he let out the vineyard to keepers; each one was to bring for its fruit a thousand pieces of silver.*

COMMENTARIES

QABALA: Woman: *Among his other riches Solomon had a vine. He had its fruit pressed by country workers. Each gave a thousand coins for his share of the grapes.*

This verse and the following are as an addendum, a final "cadenza" at the close of a symphony.

King Solomon's vine is under the protectorship of the pagan God of Plenty, *Ba'al-Hamon.*

The thousand coins, are *Eleph Kesseph. Eleph* (one thousand) is none other than *Aleph. Kesseph* (see VIII, 9) is a longing, a desire. Thus is Aleph bartered by King Solomon.

VIII

12

כַּרְמִי שֶׁלִּי לְפָנָי הָאֶלֶף לְךָ שְׁלֹמֹה
וּמָאתַיִם לְנֹטְרִים אֶת־פִּרְיוֹ׃

PHONETICALLY: *Karmi Sheli Le'fanay Ha'eleph Lekha Shlomoh Oo'mataeem Le'notreem Et-Pirioo.*

RSV: *My vineyard, my very own, is for myself; you, O Solomon, may have the thousand, and the keepers of the fruit two hundred.*

QABALA: Woman: *My vine is organic Breath and my organic life. Yours, Solomon, the thousand coins, and two hundred coins for those who keep the fruit.*

"My vine": *Sheli* (Sheen Lammed Yod: 300.30.10) is her organic Breath (300) and her organic life (30) in factual existence (10): in brief, her whole living body.

VIII

13

הַיוֹשֶׁבֶת בַּגַּנִּים חֲבֵרִים מַקְשִׁיבִים לְקוֹלֵךְ
הַשְׁמִיעִנִי׃

PHONETICALLY: *Ha'ioshevet Ba'ganeem Hhavereem Maqshiveem La'qolekh Ha'shimyini.*

377

RSV: *O You who dwell in the gardens, my companions are listening for your voice let me hear it.*

QABALA: Breath: *Woman symbol of all life and you who listened to my call, hear me . . .*

This is Breath's desperate cry, when Aleph, the Timeless, the ever-Uncaptured, is already gone. Have we even heard its Voice, or was only its echo apprehended and moulded for our benefit into the signs of the Sacred Language?

VIII

14

בְּרַח ׀ דּוֹדִי וּדְמֵה־לְךָ לִצְבִי אוֹ לְעֹפֶר
הָאַיָּלִים עַל הָרֵי בְשָׂמִים׃

PHONETICALLY: *Berahh Dodi Oo'dimeh-Lekha Litsvi Oo. Le'Oofer Ha'eialeem Aal Harey Be'shamaim.*

RSV: *Make haste, my beloved, and be like a gazelle or a young stag upon the mountain of spices.*

QABALA: Person: *He is gone! . . . Go out, my love! Be like the Armies of Breath who transcend the Heavenly Hosts.*

The schema *Tsvi* translated gazelle is, idiomatically, also a glory. *Oofer Ha'eialeem* is the dust, or scattered elements, of the Mighty Ones. The last schema *Shamaim* means the Heavens, and not "mountain of spices". The root *Oofer* (70.80.200), translated "fawn" or "young stag" in canonical versions, means dust. In Genesis, whereas all living creatures on earth are made out of earth, Adam is made of *Oofer*, which means that every possibility of development (70) is granted to what in him is unstructured (80) and allows him to attain the cosmic 200.

In this last verse, the *Oofer* of *Shamaim*, qualified glorious (root *Tsvi*) and mighty (root *Eial*) in its appearance (root *Harey*) justifies our *Midrash* "Heavenly Hosts". The action *Berahh* of Breath is to flee, to go beyond.

378

We have only given a first reading of this most beautiful text, as an introduction to the Sacred Language of the *Autiot*. No idiom, no explanations, no one-way thought, (tributary to time and space) can fathom the *Residue of Residues*. Yet a passage can be opened through those delightful poems which have enchanted so many generations: a passage to the Holy of Holies, their rightful place.

BOOK III
The Sepher Yetsira
INCLUDING THE
ORIGINAL ASTROLOGY
ACCORDING TO THE QABALA
AND ITS ZODIAC

Introduction

ALTHOUGH *The Sepher Yetsira* is the fundamental text book
of the Qabala, most, if not all, of the cabalists are baffled by
this work, finding it mysterious, occult and well-nigh incomprehensible. One would expect that a text book giving a clear
and simple résumé of the subject should be intelligible to
"specialists," but the majority has no idea of what the Qabala
is about. In this they are not very different from the general
public who has vaguely heard about the Qabala. For the more
it is discussed, the more it becomes entangled with the extraordinary complications of mediaeval, Jewish theology whose
obsolescence is respected or despised, according to prejudice.

In actual fact, the Qabala is essentially Hebraic, although
no one, not even the Jews, can say exactly what its mystery is.

Despite all the assertions of living and past cabalists I do
not agree with the saying that "The Qabala is the Zohar." I
consider that the three great cabalistic works are *Genesis, The
Song of Songs* and *The Sepher Yetsira*.

These three works have had very different fates. *Genesis* has
been translated into twelve hundred languages and even today is selling in millions of copies annually. About a third of
humanity is hypnotised by its stories masquerading as history
and by its characters who have never existed: Adam, Eve,
Cain, Abel, Noah, and so on. Some of them, such as Abraham,
Isaac or Jacob may, perhaps, have an historic basis, but they
are much more the heroes of an epoch than real persons. *The
Song of Songs* is firmly and absurdly attributed to Solomon,
and nobody knows, or wishes to know, why this love story is
included in the "Holy Bible." I have done my best to present

the true nature of these writings to the public.[1] Here, therefore, is the third volume in this series, which should complete a first elementary study of the Qabala, according to my interpretation.

★

I begin our study by saying that the Qabala is a science and that *The Sepher Yetsira* is a precise and accurate treatise on the structure of cosmic energy, written in a hidden code. This should not be a surprise; all the physical sciences are, nowadays, written in cipher codes. If the code referring to the letters E, M, C was unknown, Einstein's equation, $E = MC^2$, could not be understood. The mystery of the Qabala is simply due to the fact that the cabalists are not aware of what its language is, and to their ignorance both of the analogical mode of thought characterising this language, and of the necessity of connecting this text with modern scientific research, instead of with the archaic stages of a science. In this they are like people who call themselves great physicians because they spend their time studying Archimedes, or mathematicians because they know Euclid by heart. This kind of scholarship is no more than an intellectual diversion, contributing nothing to our strife-riven world, or to our present consciousness which has lost its past mythological illusions and is in the process of bridging religion and science.

It is this very bridge that is being offered to those who wish to study the Qabala seriously. *The Sepher Yetsira,* with the two other Cabalistic texts mentioned above—*Genesis* and *The Song of Songs* (even if archaic in form and surpassed in the observation of phenomena by modern science) —belong to a cycle when knowledge of the cosmic forces playing upon human consciousness was directly and intuitively perceived. Historical evolution has developed the brain's so-called "objec-

[1] *The Cipher of Genesis* (Shambhala, Berkeley, and Stuart & Watkins, London 1970) *The Song of Songs* (Shambhala, Berkeley and London 1972).

tive" powers of thought. It is high time that these powers
break through some of the barriers they have erected to prevent cosmic energy from penetrating the psyche.

Our faculty of scientific observation, by means of finely perfected instruments, penetrates the galaxies, the atoms and the
infinitesimal genetic elements, and is contending with the
mystery of mysteries, the phenomenon of consciousness, about
which it admits it understands nothing. Psychology, enclosed
in its own analytical world, with a vocabulary of its own, is
incapable of freeing itself from its own verbiage.

In studying the Qabala, and *The Sepher Yetsira* in particular, one must be prepared to think in a new way, entirely
different from one's usual, habitual manner, because its language is analogical and inclusive: each letter must be understood within a field surrounding a particular aspect of energy
at all its cosmic and human levels, as well as symbolically. For
example, one reads that the letter *Bayt* "forms" day One,
Shabatai, Saturn in the Zodiac, and the right eye. Such assertions and many others have been and still are ridiculed by the
representatives of "enlightened Judaism," partisans of "rational theology." These are the people who rank as authorities.
They classified the *Yetsira* as mysticism, and when they happen to quote a passage they quote it askance.

It is true that the anonymous authors of this curious writing did nothing to help the reader understand it. As a matter
of fact, they wrote it to refresh the memory of those who know,
and to mislead those who do not. Those who know, in the full
sense of the word, can "read" not only the letters of the code
in cipher, not only the ontological significance of the numbers,
but also the permutations which the anonymous authors
"played," so to say, in order to baffle those who were not
capable of formulating them in their real meaning. (Readers
will see an example of these permutations in our commentary
on verse I,12.)

It is also true that we are not, even yet, able to verify if one
part of the body corresponds to such and such a planet, or if

some Sephira corresponds to some direction in Space (due to science's present abysmal ignorance of man's place in the universe). However, one cannot prevent oneself from feeling a shiver, almost of horror, on reading that the letter Tayt forms the hebrew month Av. Tayt is number 9. It is the symbol of a cell, and Av is the birth of a new cycle following the destruction of the old. And it is a fact that all the great disasters of the Jews, including the final destruction of the Temple, happened so persistently on the 9th of the month of Av, that that date has become a day of mourning in the State of Israel. The Jews bewail the destructions and, naturally, do not hail the recurring new births of which they only know the repeated, excruciating pain. The Tayt, formation of Av, as asserted by *The Sepher Yetsira,* is enough to ask ourselves, in a kind of a daze, if the whole story of the Jews is a projection of the Qabala on the world scene, as understood by anonymous initiates!

To gain this knowledge for ourselves, we must, let us repeat, learn to read, know, what each letter and number means. We must, at least, know how to decipher certain combinations which, in the three writings with which we are concerned, have become, traditionally and idiomatically, totally different from their real meaning.

It is not surprising, one realises, that the authors of these texts have hidden themselves behind their anonymity and have hidden what they had to say in a play on words containing their secret key. Their knowledge contrasted strongly with traditional religion, which, even in these days, is only the mythological projection engendered by the impact of truths that have been misunderstood, and not by the expression of these truths themselves.

It is therefore no longer surprising that *The Sepher Yetsira* has given rise to most fantastic interpretations, from which we must completely free ourselves if we wish to understand this text directly. To start on this way of thinking, its postulates must be understood, its mode of reflection and expression be penetrated and its constituent elements known. To bring this about, it is necessary to purge the Qabala of all the proliferations of the cabalists seeking, over the ages, to express their own conditioning centered on their religious myths.

In particular, the majority of cabalists are Jews enslaved to the Torah, and they have always asserted that one cannot know how to be a cabalist without practising the Mosaic law. In this way Mosaism both annexed and rejected the Qabala and made it unrecognisable.

But the Qabala is not a derivative from, or a superstructure of, or a Heresy of Mosaism. The contrary is true: Moses was directed to give out this very ancient knowledge antedating Judaism in an historical sequence (and it is undeniable that the people who received it became its protective shell).

The Sepher Yetsira leaves no doubt as to its anteriority and its cabalistic method: it never refers to Moses, or to his laws or to the historical Jewish people. It is outside the flow of time. Its only contact with history—in language that has nothing anecdotal about it—is the legendary Abraham.

It speaks to those who know its code in the following words that conclude the book (VI,4): Schetsefa Abraham, our father, may he rest in peace (when he was set on emitting a flux, on participating in the vital flow) he looked, he saw, he explored, he articulated, he mapped out, he heaved, he combined, he structured, he raised his hand and Adon Hakol, blessed be his name, filled him to overflowing, revealed himself to him, received him in his bosom, kissed him on the head, called him my friend and made a covenant with him and his descendants, which he authenticated with Hay (Abram becoming Abraham) and meeted out justice to him (gave him an exact measure). And concluded with him a covenant between the ten toes of the feet, and it is the covenant of circumcision, and between the ten fingers of the hand, and it is the covenant of the Tongue, and attached to his tongue twenty-two Autiot and revealed Yassoden (their foundation) and soaked them in water, singed them by fire, shook them by blowing, consumed them by the seven and guided them by twelve constellations.

PART ONE

THE PRIMARY ELEMENTS

1

The Framework of the Book

THE SEPHER YETSIRA is composed of about 250 lines divided into six chapters. The first has 14 verses; the second, 6; the third, 8; the fourth, 12; the fifth, 4; and the sixth, 4.

The first 8 verses of the first chapter deal with the Sephirot (transformers of energy) in general. The following verses, to the end of the chapter, deal individually with the concept of "transformers" of infinite energy on all planes of existence.

The second chapter, in its six verses, describes the function of the twenty-two letters, known as the *Autiot*. The fifth verse, in particular, says that the states of living energy designated by Aleph and Bayt are contained in and contain everything that exists.

The third chapter establishes the basis of the letters (or Autiot). It describes the nature of three of them, Aleph-Mem-Sheen, called "Mothers."

The fourth chapter concerns the seven double letters. These are: *Bayt-Vayt, Ghimel-Gimel, Dallet-Thalet, Kaf-Khaf, Pay-Phay, Raysh-Raysh* and *Tav-Thav.* (The doubles differ from one another according to whether they have a dot or not, and generally are pronounced differently.) These 7 doubles "trace" 7 extremities, 7 "days" of the year, 7 planets, as well as the 7 orifices of the face.

The fifth chapter deals with the 12 simples which complete the alphabet. They connect with the different functions of the human body as well as with the 12 ridges of the space-cube which "open and go towards eternity and are the world's arms," and with the 12 signs of the Zodiac.

Finally, the sixth chapter is about the "Three Fathers" and

associates them with fire, air and water. It refers back to the
7 doubles and the 12 simples, and finishes with the verse concerning Abraham, which has been cited above.

It is useful and interesting to note what different authors
have said about The Sepher Yetsira.

According to Mr. Enel (Trilogie de la Rota ou Roue
céleste, Editions Paul Derain, 1960), The Sepher Yetsira is
"A superhuman work" (p. 121), because "in its allegories,
numbers and correspondences it contains all the cosmological
sciences and their reflection in man, the prototype of the universe."

In writing (p. 59) that The Sepher Yetsira is about "the
creation of the world," Mr. Enel commits a grave error in his
premises: this work deals with the "formation," or structuration, of energy and does not mention the creation of the world.

Besides, it is difficult to see how Mr. Enel can assert that
"The Cabbala is a philosophical system upon which all the
sciences are based, and whose laws it formulates" (op. cit.,
p. 60). It seems more exact to say that the Qabala could (and
no doubt should) be the base of the unifying epistemology
that is missing from our physical sciences and from our
attempts at an ontology. The concept of unity, which was the
original source of primitive knowledge, got lost during the
beneficial process of evolution. It is true that we could, by
detaching ourselves from certain archaic mental habits, re-
discover this unity in the Qabala, in Genesis and in The
Sepher Yetsira. But Mr. Enel, who comes so close to the correct perception of the ciphered code, drowns us again in a
dubious theology, from the fact that instead of deciphering, by
means of the code, the equation Elohim, he translates it God,
"thinking" it God, and remains in the myth of "a divine individual spirit incarnated in matter."

According to Mr. Henri Serouya (La Kabbale, Grasset,
1947): "The language of The Sepher Yetsira is very obscure.

Its propositions are aphoristic" (p. 41). However, he does recognise its importance: "This fundamental work has given rise to numerous commentaries, some of which are most penetrating, on Judaic literature . . . ideas coming from this doctrine have much relevance to metaphysics . . . its expressions tend to be too abstract, even too detailed, in deliberately and radically brushing Anthropomorphism aside. It appears to have no resemblance to Pythagoras' ideas . . . Its inspiration seems to come directly from the Bible (especially from *Genesis* and *Job*) and not from Greek philosophy" (p. 129). "*The Sepher Yetsira* is not . . . the simple symbolism of ten numbers and twenty-two letters of the alphabet . . . Neither is it a simple homily: it is a philosophical system. However analogous its cosmogony is with Clement's and the Gnostics' its gnosticism is no more harmful than theirs, because it does not propound any religious or philosophical dogma, and it protects itself from all the extravagances of the Gnostics" (p. 137).

The "innocent" character of this gnosis, its radical and deliberate rejection of all anthropomorphism, its distinctness from religious doctrine are well brought out by Mr. Serouya.

In his excellent little book, *Rabbi Simeon Bar Yochaï et la Cabbale* (Editions du Seuil, 1961), Mr. Guy Casaril gives a succinct and accurate exposition of the Qabala, enlightening the reader on its aim if not on its knowledge: "Through the intermediary of *The Sepher Yetsira* (Book of Formation) the cabbala studies by letters the ancient doctrine of the genesis of the world, as well as the concept of the hierarchy of the Sephirot" (p. 39). From pages 43-49 Mr. Casaril gives a partial translation of *The Sepher Yetsira*, differing from the one upon which we are relying. Thus, he translates the verse we have cited, *Adon Hakol*, as "Master of All." (In the present degraded condition of our language he is not to be reproached for this.) His version ends thus: "and he said of him: 'Before even having formed you in the womb I knew you' " (Jeremiah I,5). This interpolation is not in the least astonishing. Never

having been a canonical work *The Sepher Yetsira* has undergone so many versions that not one of them can claim to be
the original. Let us acknowledge that Mr. Casaril gives Yetsira
its real meaning: Formation.

The different versions of *The Sepher Yetsira* are not really
a hindrance. Mr. S. Karpe explains this in his *Etudes sur les
origines et la nature du Zohar* (Alcan, Paris 1901): "There
have always been very divergent texts of *The Sepher Yetsira*.
The one translated and commented on by Saadyah is far from
being identical with Sabbataï Donolo's, which, in turn, is
widely different from Jehudah bar Barzilai's. Given these
divergencies we adopt the prevailing version in the Jewish
tradition, although it is probably not the original version. For
us it is more a philosophical than a philological study; in this
connection the version we have adopted is of very great interest. To confront all the variations would require a volume
to itself. That is not our aim . . ." (p. 138). Nor is it ours. We
have glanced at two or three versions and chosen the one that
seems to be best known; its imprint is: *Copyright by Lewin-
Epstein Ltd., Printed and Published in Israël, Jerusalem
P O B 1020.* But the choice is of little importance. Does not
the text invite the cabalist "to understand, to meditate, to
examine, to experiment, to speak to the Creator" and "to
restore the moulder of forms to his rightful place"? (I,4).

The cabalist is someone who, without preconceived ideas,
freely "plays the game" of Aleph-Bayt without an intermediary:
"He speaks to the creator of the Sephirot." In other words,
he joins in the unique creative movement. But we must understand that contact is where our "name" is, in "the rightful
place" of our structure. It is up to the cabalist to discover his
"name," to know his "sphere." He is a psychologist, or an
artist, or philosopher, or interested in social questions. In
short, the entrance to "the game" begins when the cabalist becomes aware of his own individuality. At the same time he
must stop reiterating religious or other teachings. The "game"
will reveal itself to him from the way he treats its elements: it

is a movement, a vibration of the different living forms which "come and go" (*Sepher Yetsira* I,8), and the cabalist can become the receiver and transmitter of this cosmic movement. Then the Qabala, in all its complexity, becomes comprehensible.

One sees why the Qabala came to be synonymous with obscurity. Its source has been polluted by everything foreign to it—Mosaism, Christianism or scholasticism. Probably unprejudiced people did not wish, or were unable, to reveal it.

The elements of the "game," we now know, are letters and numbers. Concerning this S. Karppe states (op. cit. p. 161): "There are no clear traces of Pythagorism in *The Sepher Yetsira*. Pythagorism makes number itself the material and form of the world. But in *The Sepher Yetsira* number in itself is nothing; it is neither the material nor the form of number; it does not determine the quality of number; it determines only the Sephirot and the letters, and it is the Sephirot and the letters which are the essence of things."

This seems to be a correct but incomplete explanation. It is true that numbers define the meaning of the letters and the Sephirot, but each number has a name and these names have their meanings. Karppe's analysis ends on a confused note: "*The Sepher Yetsira* contains no trace of pantheism; The Sephirot are 'bound to one another,' but in their entirety are cut off from God" (p. 162).

The last assertion contradicts the very basis of the Qabala which considers that the universe and its life are a single endogenous phenomenon. Introducing monotheism, in default of finding pantheism in it, is equivalent to separating life from living beings. Not much is known of this "God" mentioned here, "entirely cut off" from the Sephirot, which are states of life.

In his work *Le Miroir de la magie* (Editions Fasquelle), Kurt Seligman, quoting from Judas Halévi on *The Sepher Yetsira*, writes: "This book teaches us that only one God exists, by showing that amidst variety and multiplicity there are a harmony and a sequence which derive from a single co-ordinator. *The Sepher Yetsira* reveals the formation of the Universe created and maintained by the One, and of everything emanating from him" (p. 270).

That is true, provided that the word *God*, which "mythifies" the Name without explaining it, is suppressed, for it inevitably transforms it into a person. As for the Qabala, one can write down the equations *Ayn-Sof, Yah, YHWH,* and many other complex ones, without giving them a thought, just as in mathematics one automatically writes the sign ∞ of infinity.

The works of Professor G. G. Scholem must now be mentioned: *Les Grands Courants de la mystique juive* (Payot, Paris, 1950), and *La Kabbale et sa symbolique* (Payot, Paris, 1960). Representing "enlightened Judaism of the nineteenth and twentieth centuries," and siding with "rational theology," Mr. Scholem provoked the exaggerations to which this way of thinking gave rise, classifying everything under the false category of "mysticism."

Mr. Francis Warrain, in the preface to *La Théodicée de la Kabbale* (Vega, 1949) begins by examining this mode of expression and thought as objectively as possible: "The ancients expressed themselves in concrete terms; their knowledge was more intuitive than ours and automatically they had a tendency towards synthesis, the natural end of thought . . . therefore it is necessary to discover an equivalent abstract conception in concrete terms, and in images conforming to those in the ancient doctrines. Attempting to find a parallel does not imply that the ancients wished to disguise an abstract conception under a concrete symbol. It does not claim to make us discover how the ancients thought about the metaphysics which they were describing; *it seeks for an abstract idea, conforming to our mental attitudes, which correspond with the things they have indicated.*"

Cabalists and alchemists often disguised their thoughts from fear of being arrested and condemned as heretics, but that does not affect the elements of the problem. Whether one is a cabalist, student, or historian, it is clearly necessary to understand which truth it is that our utterly different way of thinking has to be connected to.

Undoubtedly, one of the worst excrescences to have caused the loss of *The Sepher Yetsira's* meaning is the legend of the *Golem,* the living robot in Judeo-Polish and Hungarian folklore, who the records say was created by more or less heretical rabbis, with the help of a secret key contained in that Sepher. Mr. Scholem makes much of it: "The creation of Golem," he writes (op. cit., pp. 113-114), "was, so to say, a particularly sublime experience felt by the mystic once he was absorbed in the mystery of the alphabetical combinations described in 'The Book of Creation' (sic)." No doubt he means "The Book of Formation."

In *Le Nombre d'or* (Gallimard, 13th edition, 1959), Matila C. Ghyka writes: "Dating from the Xth century one can find the legend of the creation by 'geometrical greatness' of an homunculus with the help of the Sepher Ietzirah, expressed in letters taken from the 'Schem Hamephoras' (divine names in the sephirotic triangle)" (note on page 155 T:1.) and (ditto, pp. 153-154). "The technique of creating the 'homunculus' by the inbreathing of 'pneuma' and by the insertion of a magic written word into the clay doll has gone without alteration into the hebraic Kabbalah through the Sepher Ietzirah, or Book of Creation (sic), and has been the source of the legends of the creation of an homunculus in the Middle Ages, especially of the whole 'Golem' cycle in Prague."

These anecdotes have no connection with our subject. What is important is to become aware of a very ancient knowledge and see to what extent it has qualities of perception which we lack. Thus, Mr. Francis Warrain writes: "Ancient knowledge and modern knowledge are somewhat as opposite as are geometrical drawings and mathematical analysis. What the one expresses with lines the other defines abstractly . . . only by reading the texts and, above all, by meditating on them could we enter into communion with the idea in the ancient doctrine. It is by re-thinking the text, and not by following the literal meaning that this assimilation will come about . . . conceptions having more or less the same narrow parentage as the Sephirot are to be found throughout all the esoteric doctrines of antiquity . . . If this parentage has an identical source, the fact that this doctrine has been universally accepted shows that it offers the most satisfactory solution to the problem of the Absolute" (p. 70). This reasoning is not satisfying. But even this "solution" (a perplexing word) should be understandable and intelligent.

2

The Language

The Autiot

BEFORE READING *The Sepher Yetsira* it is best to consider the primary elements constituting the text: the Autiot (plural).

This name in Hebrew (singular, Aut), denotes not only a "letter" (of the alphabet), but also a sign, a proof, a symbol and even a miracle revealing its forgotten ontological origin. (Likewise, so many words of this language are profane.)

Contrary to our letters which are simple elements (A, B, C, etc.), the Autiot are names that must be spelt. The official teaching of Hebrew has its own spelling, but cabalists have adopted several others which are not concordant. Those we have worked out seem to correspond well with the twenty-two structures of energy signified by the twenty-two signs.

The Autiot

Name	Number
Aleph	1
Bayt Vayt	2
Ghimel	3
Dallet	4
Hay	5
Vav or Waw	6
Zayn	7
Hhayt	8
Tayt	9
Yod	10
Kaf Khaf	20
Lammed	30
Mem	40
Noun	50
Sammekh	60
Ayn	70
Pay Phay	80
Tsadde	90
Qof	100
Raysh	200
Scen Sheen	300
Tav	400
final Khaf	500
final Mem	600
final Noun	700
final Phay	800
final Tsadde	900

3

An Explanation

THE PRESENT writer, being obliged to use our language in order to make himself understood, cannot offer the reader the truth of the One Cosmic Energy, but only images of that truth. Our language has a sensuous origin. Through it we can understand only by means of imagery. But we shall do our best not to wander off into illusory beliefs and dreams of the supernatural.

Let us now concern ourselves with the individual Hebrew letter numbers according to the code (see chart p. 24).

The first nine letters are the archetypes of numbers from 1-9.

Aleph, number 1, is the unthinkable life-death, abstract principle of all that is and all that is not. It lives and is timeless, yet all time is in it. It is beyond measure, beyond understanding, yet all measures and all understanding have their roots in it.

Bayt[1] (or Vayt), number 2, is the archetype of all "dwellings," of all containers: the physical support without which nothing is.

Ghimel, number 3, is the organic movement of every Bayt animated by Aleph.

Dallet, number 4, is the physical existence, as response to life, of all that, in nature, is organically active with Ghimel. Where the structure is inorganic, Dallet is its own resistance to destruction. It acts as a door that can be open or shut.

Hay, number 5, is the archetype of universal life. When it

[1] We consider this spelling more correct phonetically than the usually adopted Beth.

is conferred upon Dallet, it allows it to play the game of existence, in partnership with the intermittent life-death process.

Vav (or Waw), number 6, expresses the fertilising agent, that which impregnates. It is the direct result of Hay upon Dallet.

Zayn, number 7, is the conclusion of every vital impregnation: this number opens the field of every possible possibility.

Hhayt, number 8, is the sphere of storage of all undifferentiated energy, or unstructured substance. It expresses the least evolved state of energy, as opposed to its freedom completed in Zayn.

Tayt, number 9, as symbol of the primeval, female energy, draws its life from Hhayt and builds it gradually into structures. It is the archetype of the cell.

The nine following letters, from Yod, number 10, to Tsadde, number 90, describe the process of the nine archetypes in their factual, conditioned existence: their manifested projections are always multiples of 10.

The nine multiples of 100 express the exalted archetypes in their cosmic states.

The number 1000 is written with an enlarged Aleph (Aleph in Hebrew actually means a thousand), but is seldom used. It expresses a supreme power, a tremendous cosmic energy, all-pervading, timeless, unthinkable. Such, very briefly outlined, are the elements of the "covenant of the tongue."

The study of these nine and their multiples by 10 and by 100 is therefore the study of the very archetypes in their various spheres of emanation. The student will find it useful to examine them, so to say, vertically: 1.10.100—2.20.200, and so on.

The choice of Kaf (20) for 500, of Mem (40) for 600, and of Noun (50) for 700 in finals of schemata means that those numbers acquire corresponding cosmic values when they unfold in human beings. Thus, Adam is 1.4.40 when immature, and achieves 1.4.600 when attaining his full maturity.

AN EXPLANATION

Here is a brief general view of the relationship between the archetypes and their multiples:

Aleph-Yod-Qof (1.10.100). Whereas Aleph (1) is the beat or pulsation, life-death-life-death, Yod (10) is its projection into temporal continuity. So Yod (in Hebrew, the hand) is the opposite of Aleph, its partner playing against it the game without which nothing would be. In brief, one can say that Aleph lives and does not exist, whereas Yod exists and only lives in Aleph. The Qof (100) is the most difficult symbol to understand. It includes Aleph exalted in its principle, yet acting, though its projection, against itself, and thereby being cosmically deathless. It is best seen in Qaheen (Cain), that mythical destroyer of illusions.

Bayt-Kaf-Raysh (2.20.200). Whereas Bayt (2), the archetype of all containers, has its roots in the cosmic resistance to life, Kaf (20) — in Hebrew the hollow of the hand — is ready to receive all that comes, and Raysh (200) the cosmic container of all existence, has its roots in the intense organic movement of the universe.

Ghimel-Lammed-Sheen (3.30.300). These three letter-numbers express a movement in progressive enlargement, from the uncontrolled functional action of Ghimel (3), through the controlled connecting agent Lammed (30), going as far as the universal Sheen (300), mythically considered to be the "spirit" or "breath" of God; in fact, the organic process of the cosmic life.

Dallet-Mem-Tav (4.40.400). The physical resistance of structures, Dallet (4), finds its purveyor in the maternal waters, Mem (40), where all life originates. Tav (400) is the exaltation of the entire cosmic existence in its utmost capacity to resist life-death. The root Dallet-Mem (Dam) is "blood" in Hebrew, and the root Mem-Tav (Met) is "death." Thus the two together express the complete cycle of existence.

Hay-Noun-Kaf in finals (5.50.500). The universal life, Hay (5), is condensed in individual existences as Noun (50), and is exalted cosmically as Kaf (500) in terminals.

Waw-Sammekh-Mem in finals (6.60.600). Waw (6) is the male agent of fertility, Sammekh (60) the female. Mem when in terminals (600) is the cosmic achievement of fruitfulness, both in the intelligent or immaterial part of man and in the flesh. In Hebrew Waw maintains its character grammatically as copulative or connecting agent.

Zayn-Ayn-Noun in finals (7.70.700). Zayn (7) as an opening towards all possible possibilities has its source and its vision in Ayn (70), which is the word for "eye" in Hebrew. It is exalted in Noun (700): this number expresses the very principle contended for in the interplay of energies throughout the universe: the Principle of Indetermination in which life itself is at stake. Here we find Cain again.

Hhayt-Pay-Phay in finals (8.80.800). In every sphere of emanation, from the densest to the most rarefied essence, these numbers stand for the primordial substance, the unfathomed reserve of undifferentiated, unstructured energy.

Tayt-Tsadde-Tsadde in finals (9.90.900). These ideograms express a progression ascending from the simplest and most primitive cell (or female structural energy) up to the transfigured symbols of womanhood, social and mythical.

A Spelling of the Autiot

1	Aleph	Aleph-Lammed-Phay (1.30.80)
2	Bayt (Vayt)	Bayt-Yod-Tav (2.10.400)
3	Ghimel	Ghimel-Mem-Lammed (3.40.30)
4	Dallet	Dallet-Lammed-Tav (4.30.400)
5	Hay	Hay (5)
6	Waw (Vav)	Waw-Waw (6.6)
7	Zayn	Zayn-Yod-Noun (7.10.50)
8	Hhayt	Hhayt-Yod-Tav (8.10.400)
9	Tayt	Tayt-Yod-Tav (9.10.400)
10	Yod	Yod-Waw-Dallet (10.6.4)
20	Kaf (Khaf)	Kaf-Phay (20.80)
30	Lammed	Lammed-Mem-Dallet (30.40.4)
40	Mem	Mem-Mem (40.40)

50	Noun	Noun-Waw-Noun (50.6.50)
60	Sammekh	Sammekh-Mem-Khaf (60.40.20)
70	Ayn	Ayn-Yod-Noun (70.10.50)
80	Phay (Pay)	Phay-Hay (80.5)
90	Tsadde	Tsadde-Dallet-Yod (90.4.10)
100	Qof	Qof-Waw-Phay (100.6.80)
200	Raysh	Raysh-Yod-Sheen (200.10.300)
300	Sheen	Sheen-Yod-Noun (300.10.50)
400	Tav	Tav-Waw (400.6)

Some authors write Hay, Hay-Aleph; others Hay-Yod. I think that life (Hay) must not in any way be limited. Moses' revelation, Ehiayh-Asher-Ehiayh (Aleph-Hay, Yod, Hay), means "Aleph living, Yod living." These equations contain all the Revelations.

In studying the Autiot one must learn how to open them completely so as to have pictures of their anatomy.

Here are the pictures of Aleph and Bayt:

Aleph (1)

Bayt (2)

ב-י-ת-ו-ו-ו

ו-ו-ו

ד-ל-ת-ו-ו-ו

מ-מ-מ

ד-ל-ת-ו

מ-מ-מ

ד-ל-ת

It is very instructive to make a comparative study of the processes indicated by the anatomic pictures of the whole Autiot. It is also useful to see which Aut enters another Aut, and which does not, and how many times each intervenes in the whole twenty-two, and why. What does it mean that Bayt, Dallet, Hhayt, Tayt end at Tav? Is there a special connection between them? Why does Phay go only with Hay? Why (and this is important) is Sheen (the mythic Breath of Elohim) introduced by Raysh? There are many other questions whose answers show the depth of cabalistic thought with remarkable clearness, such as the difference between Seen and Sheen. They are the same number yet their functions are not the same.

The further the Autiot are studied the more it is realised that they are the complete Qabala, and that it is not advisable to lose oneself by reading two or three thousand ancient texts in search of knowledge which is distorted by conceptions unconnected with the cipher-code of the Autiot.

One also realises that cabalistic thought is monolithic and that the expression closest to its source is *The Sepher Yetsira*.

This is why the book remains mysterious for people who

call themselves cabalists but who lack the basis of the Autiot.

It is a complex study, consisting of a scripture, symbols and a language relating to the science of the structure of Energy, *but never separate from the fundamental postulate of Unity.*

The Meaning of the Words

The greatest difficulty for a student of the cabalistic revival stems from not thinking of enough questions to ask. We are so accustomed to take for granted that table means table and chair means chair that we have forgotten that the words are not the object. The word *house* has no real connection with a house, nor, in French, with the word *maison,* nor, in Italian, with the word *casa.*

But if Aleph is Aleph, and not Aret or Anek, or any other combination, it is because Lammed and Phay, added to the first unpronounceable symbol, have a tremendous meaning that these Autiot, Lammed and Phay, alone possess.

In this monolithic thought the meaning of each Aut in any equation is important, as each fragment contains the whole. We are familiar with holograms — photographic plates taken by a laser. When the plate is broken up each fragment contains an image of the whole. More familiarly, we know that if a child resembles some trifling details of his father's looks it is because everything that makes up a person is contained in one genetic cell.

It is the same with the Autiot — the sacred language of the cycle of civilisation — because their essential equations given in the three great cabalistic texts that I have named are thought projections of cosmic energy, and not just words formed by idiomatic usage. As, primarily and above all, *The Sepher Yetsira* is about the Autiot, let us begin reading this book by learning to read this word.

In the singular Aut is written Aleph-Waw-Tav, an equation formed similarly to light, Aur: Aleph-Waw-Raysh. We have seen that Aur is a projection of Aleph, the infinite, in Raysh, its container (in which Aleph becomes unconscious of its life), and that Aleph and Raysh are connected by the copulative sign Waw. Aleph fertilises Raysh.

The word Aut says the same thing, with all the difference that there is between Raysh and Tav. For Raysh (200) is the name of the cosmic "house," but Tav (400) is the resistance to the container of Aleph: a resistance necessary to contain this energy, but which, what is more, engenders an energy of an equal but contrary character.

Here we are touching on one of the essential ideas of the Qabala: the living energy of Aleph is not just absorbed in the projection of the Universe; it is reflected and returned to Aleph in such a way that universal life is a dual flow of energy, the One being twofold in its emanation. In short, Tav is, simultaneously, resistance to Aleph, its tabernacle, and eventually Aleph in disguise.

When YHWH wishes to confer immortality on Cain (Quayn: Qof-Yod-Noun) he names him with an Aut (*Genesis* Book One). If one is satisfied by reading that he put a "sign" on him, one fails to know what it means. Such is this unfortunate way of reading the Bible, for, in fact, he confers Aleph-Waw-Tav on him; hence the double-flowing energy of life. In other words he defined Cain as mankind's creative genius, always triumphant whenever attempts to extinguish it are made.

In the roots of Hebraic idioms it is not surprising to discover an unconscious memory and an unconscious knowledge of the real meaning of the biblical text, since Aut is sign, proof, symbol and even miracle in one.

When, idiomatically, Aut designates a letter of the alphabet its plural, strangely, is Yod-Waw-Tav, instead of being Waw-Tav, like all the other feminine plurals.

The introduction of this Yod is extremely important, although it has never been understood. However, if it is understood it means that one is really aware of the heart of *The Sepher Yetsira*.

Likewise, as I have said above, the Revelation of Moses,

Aleph-Hay-Yod-Hay, indicates that Aleph and Yod are alive. In short, the Autiot express the following equation:

$$\frac{\text{Aleph} - \text{Waw} - \text{Tav}}{\text{Yod} \quad - \text{Waw} - \text{Tav}}$$

That is to say, the Autiot are the active agents fertilising Tav by Aleph and by Yod.

We are now at the origin of the Sacred Language, having glanced at the second chapter of *The Sepher Yetsira*, particularly at II,5, where it is stated that all that is formed and uttered proceeds from the Name One. Here again is the idea of the Word as creator of all structures.

The Sepher Yetsira, or "book," or "sphere" of Formation, confines itself to the study of structures. It is implied that this limitation is imposed by our understanding, that we are immersed in an impenetrable mystery and that we are this mystery. But it is averred that the twenty-two "letters" are, nevertheless, intended to make us enter into this vital movement that braces all structures, including ours. (For the moment we will not tackle the ten Sephirot which are "transformers," of the energy of Aleph in Yod.) The twenty-two Autiot are the "workmen" who make them function. By virtue of this their general meaning is included in Aleph-Waw-Tav-Yod-Waw-Tav, because, simultaneously, they all share in the action of Aleph and Yod; that is to say, in the non-structured, intemporal life-death, and in existant life. These two lives act *in coniunctio oppositorum* upon Tav, the cosmic force of resistance. Thus the joint participation of the Autiot in the Aleph and Yod, energising the metaphysics of the Qabala, plays the role attributed in some theologies, to angels, intermediaries between "God" and men.

From the second verse *The Sepher Yetsira* mentions the 22 Autiot. "Yassod" (Yod-Sammekh-Waw-Dallet: 10.60.6.4) and *Yassod* almost always returns coupled with the Autiot. Usually it is translated as "fundament," which explains nothing and introduces a proposition that is not in the text. Rather, the two equations should be read as they are, without an intermediary agent: one as feminine plural; the other as masculine singular. This is not the only instance: is not Elohim a plural taken as a singular? The correct procedure is to treat the Autiot similarly, because they form a whole, all of whose elements are components closely bound together.

Yassod, (Yod-Sammekh-Waw-Dallet) qualifies the Autiot and makes their ambivalent character clear. Here Yod, the existence, manifests Sammekh (60), feminine generative force, and Waw (6), male generative force, and their resistance (or foundation, or substructure), Dallet (4). Here again is a feature common to the Autiot and to angelic cohorts. *Yassod* expresses something solid, a massing of elements which constitute a whole. This multiple and single intermediary messenger, *Autiot Yassod,* entering the world of Aleph and Yod, seems much more like Jacob's ladder than the angels who are supposed to go up and down it: the coming and going movement is the making of the ladder's substance. It is an internal process.

This interior movement is the base (or fundament) of the cabalistic tongue and distinguishes it from all the profane languages. Its internal process is a continual requestioning, a continual regrouping of fixed elements, a moving weft by means of which the cabalist is free to understand, in his own way, not only concepts, symbols, signs and names, not only to interpret their combinations according to his own judgment, but to abandon himself to the play of forces vital to new combinations, and, in his contemplations, making use of them to discover in himself and in the cosmic play of life, death and existence, depths hitherto unsuspected. In short, the cabalist is a creator.

Autiot and Sephirot

The Sepher Yetsira is a summary of knowledge taken for

granted by cabalists. The enigmas which it poses are directed at the experienced cabalist as a school book sets problems to the student who knows his subject and is supposed to be able to understand them. But as my intention is to present a wider public with an introduction to this work, certain basic ideas, which are not mentioned in it, but on which it relies, must be expounded.

Above all, the *Autiot Yassod* must be understood thoroughly in order to recognise their character, their profound constitution, so that their origin and their connection with Elohim are revealed, enabling us to integrate them with our own consciousness.

The text reminds us that they are engendered by the second Sephira. Let us say provisionally that the first Sephira is the turn-table operating the first transmutation (or graduation) of infinitely energising life into an energy that is projected into structures; and that the second Sephira is the return shock, the feed-back, the response of structured energy. In symbolic language it is "the breath of breath." Translated into Hebrew its name, *Hhokmah*, means consciousness, knowledge, intelligence, wisdom. Read according to the code (Hhayt-Kaf-Mem-Hay: 8.20.40.5), it expresses life emanating from what can be called nondifferentiated energy, powerfully prominent in its individual, corporeal existence. The word that best describes the second Sephira is "consciousness." One realises that consciousness is taken to be a structured energy formed by the energising life in physical form. And this consciousness begets the *Autiot Yassod* whose function is "to go against the stream," so to say, towards unity, in one dynamic movement. Indeed, during the course of our reading we shall see some of the Autiot "going against" lower Sephirot, up to the first Sephira, *Keter,* which "crowns" all degrees of construction.

In the Autiot the essential movement of this unifying idea characterising the Qabala is already there. Furthermore, this movement of infinity to number and from number to infinity is discernible in each component of the written text, which-

411

ever passage is being studied: each part, each component of the sacred language is this very movement and, consequently, reveals the whole. All things considered, this scripture always repeats this movement (which is life) on different scales.

As the Autiot are feminine plural, their substance has a female character. In Hebrew the masculine plural *Im* (Yod-Mem) and the feminine *Aut* (Waw-Tav) sometimes have transpositions that are apparently disconcerting. Actually, these endings express two different states of the construction of energy. Yod-Mem, that is, 10.40, has a solid existence, while Waw-Tav, feminine, is made of masculine centrifugal Waw (6) joined to cosmic Tav (400). Between Waw and Tav there is no communication. Tav is the end which contains the beginning. Like Aleph, it is an absolute. Now the symbol of the feminine is the development in continuity. The structured "masculine" must fertilise the "feminine" forcefully, and the feminine becomes structured and structural energy simultaneously.

The Autiot — feminine plural — constitutes a masculine singular unity, Yassod. It is an endogenic, self-fertilising organism. Its intense to-and-fro movement through the ten Sephirot binds them to one another, and thus puts them in motion, in such a way that *their end is without end . . . they flow and come, rush headlong like a tempest and bow down before the throne of Elohim . . . Their end is made fast to their beginning and their beginning is made fast to their end . . .* These translations of verses I,6-7, can give the reader an overall view of the theme elaborated by *The Sepher Yetsira.* For is it not necessary to behold a building in its entirety, to understand its function, to have an idea of the materials of which it is made, before examining it in detail?

For the moment we are discussing only the Sephirot as formed by the Autiot. *The Sepher Yetsira* investigates them one by one, hierarchically, in the numerical order of 1 to 10, but that does not mean that they have been created one after another, in the sense of entering matter in depth: they are co-eternal in Elohim, and we know that Elohim is the method by which One, the Unique, the "Al" in its Aleph function, becomes Yod (10) by projection. In Elohim, the Sephirot are therefore an ever-changing method of construction, a method analysed by *The Sepher Yetsira*.

The graphic signs which specify the Autiot, these initials of the names constituting the Hebraic alphabet, have, as phoneme, characters distinct enough for us to see if they should be pronounced on the lips, in the throat, or with the breath, etc. This somatic aspect of the letters is hardly dealt with in *The Sepher Yetsira* which also, in other respects, fails to explain their graphology (said to be designed by Ezra). In the course of ages this has undergone transformation. The current graphology is not uninteresting. All the signs have Yod at the beginning, as a clue, since the Autiot always refer to the constructed states of life-in-existence, never to speculations about the unreal. These states do not only cast themselves in mental representations: they show themselves in signs which reflect them in the world of appearances. The study of these signs is therefore allied to physiognomy.

We will give one characteristic example; the graphic sign for Aleph. Does not its design, with a diagonal line symbolising the mysterious origin of life, express the element which, according to biologists, breaks the symmetry of crystallisations and thus instigates a life-engendering movement? Is not the hammer-like stroke surmounting the diagonal the presence of the world within it, and is not the stroke below, to the left, like a leg, the symbol of the future coming into existence? Is not the whole sign a curiously alive, moving cross, simultaneously separating and reuniting two worlds that are really one? Such a symbolical whole is not fortuitous. It sums up the meaning of the Autiot. Cabalists have always said that Aleph contains them all.

Let us add that this sign, contrary to the opinion of some people who translate it as A, is not pronounced. The accompanying vowel signs in postmassoretic scriptures fix its pronunciation as A, E, I, or U, according to the usual conventions of language, but which the cabalist is not obliged to obey. Often Aleph is not pronounced at all.

Another subject for study is the connection between the names of the Autiot and their numbers, and the names of the numbers. For example, Aleph is 1, but is called *Ehhad* (Aleph-Hhayt-Dallet: 1.8.4). As is seen from the meaning of the numbers according to the code, *Ehhad* sets a fixed equation. 1 is face to face with the archetypal, undifferentiated 8, and with the archetypal, extant force of resistance 4. On the other hand, the word Aleph (1.30.8) introduces the organic movement of 30 into 8. In short, *Ehhad* (the name of number 1) is an anatomical survey, and Aleph (the sign of number 1) is a biological survey of the said 1.

The relations between the anatomy and the biology of numbers is sometimes inverted. For example, the sign of number 2, Bayt, shows itself in the guise of a static, anatomical image (2.10.400). Nevertheless, the names of this number (*Schnei, Schtei, Schnaim* or *Schtaïm,* according to whether they are in the masculine, or feminine or not in the "absolute") reveal by their Sheen (300) the cosmic movement animating them.

Résumé and Conclusion

Once again let us state that it is impossible to speak of the unknown in our common tongue (including Hebrew), without changing it arbitrarily into recognisable images. This artificial device is at the bottom of all "proofs of the existence of God." It is inevitable that our tongues desecrate all that they discuss, because they have their being only in the measurable, in images, appraisements, comparisons. If they were not like this (by virtue of their nature) they would be useless for our *modus vivendi,* which cannot operate without having an accurate language at its disposal. We know that the decay of these instruments brings social disorders in its train. It is less easy to understand that these disorders also originate from the introduction of profane language into religious matters. (Hebrew, which uses only the initials of the Autiot as an alphabet — B for Bayt, etc. — is as profane as other tongues.)

In assembling clearly defined words, in surrounding, explicitly stating and isolating the subject under discussion, our languages proceed by methodical exclusion: a subject is defined and clearly indicated by the elimination of everything extraneous to it. This is evident from the fact that thinking dependent on these languages always acts by comparisons.

The language of *The Sepher Yetsira* is anything but this. It treats objects — water, fire, human bodies, planets, the zodiac — only in terms of their situation and of their rôle within an infinitely multiple, hierarchical, systemisation of the one energising life force. The equations indicating these objects consequently designate, on all planes, all the structures which exist, or could exist, in the innumerable, known or unknown, conjugations of this hierarchical system, from the most material to the most rarefied, from the least to the highest state of consciousness. It is an all-inclusive language which has no equivalent in ours. It propounds a deeply religious mode of thought, in as much as it offers the cabalist the opportunity to find, on all existent levels, the secret bond which ties everything ontologically to the mysterious equation of the Unfathomable.

As everything that this language speaks about is a state of energy, and as energy is movement, nothing is a "thing" offering itself to spirit. On the contrary, spirit must pursue it through the metamorphoses of its groupings. But what happens to this language when its elements are themselves representative of differently structured conditions of this movement?

Instead of consisting of letters having no significance of their own (as are the letters of our alphabets) the language of the Qabala fully expresses itself in the whole Autiot, for the Autiot are projections of the vital movement that is both within and without Man who is the subject of *Genesis* and of *The Sepher Yetsira*.

Therefore, this sacred language is not an ordinary instrument capable of pointing something out, but incapable of conveying its meaning. (The words "music" and "colour" and, *a fortiori*, "God" and "Eternity" do not make music heard, colours visible, etc.) This language is a moving projection of what it is dealing with. It can be compared to a perfect documentary film which shows us an unknown world "as if we were there," but there is more to it than that: we *are* there. It is not "as if." We are in this projection, we are this projection; this documentary is our own situation, our own rôle, what we are and what we could be in the hierarchy of structures. But there is one further step in the adventure offered to us by this language, the possibility of effecting, producing new combinations with the Autiot. The cabalist who is steeped in contemplation of the Autiot and who becomes, in projecting their movement into himself, both this movement and the creator of new spheres, inevitably loses his sang-froid if his spirit is not completely free of religious myths (for then he feels he is a prophet), or of all will for power (for then he imagines he is a magician). If one is interested in these questions it is important to "play the game," without giving up one's critical faculties, because after all (or in spite of all), the Qabala is a matter of common sense.

4

The Equations

*Equations which do and Equations which do not
point out their Solution*

A GREAT mistake is to think that *The Sepher Yetsira* is a book
that can be understood after reading it once. Those most
qualified — not to read but to study it — are physicists engaged
in advanced scientific research. By showing that the energising
properties of the Autiot have a dual cosmic flow, the way to
an essential stage of modern physics is cleared: the study of
consciousness, in its material manifestations, as energy.

Lately I have had the opportunity to explain to physicists,
such as Fred Wolfe[1] and Jack Sarfatti,[2] that it is possible to
work this out with the "3 Mothers," Aleph, Mem, Sheen (and
Seen) *S Y III, 1-8*, and I think it will not be long before the
Autiot will replace the letters used arbitrarily in physics today.

The Autiot therefore arrange themselves in equations, not
words, which, by virtue of their complexity, can be studied in
several ways, according to the greater or lesser involvement of
the Autiot in them.

Without fear of self-deception, we can think of the anonymous authors of *The Sepher Yetsira* as knowing the numbered
code. In their minds the whole work is a commentary, in the

---

[1] *Dr. Fred Alan Wolfe*, Ph.D. in theoretical physics from the University of
California at Los Angeles, holds a joint appointment at Birkbeck College,
University of London, and at the Ionic Collisions Laboratory at the University
of Paris-Orsay.

[2] *Dr. Jack Sarfatti*, Ph.D., University of California. Formerly on faculty of
Physics Department of San Diego University and Honorary Research Fellow
at Birkbeck College, Department of Physics, University of London, and of the
Institute for Theoretical Physics, Trieste.

light of certain fundamental postulates of the Qabala, on the first verses of *Genesis*.

Too many people have read this scripture without realising that it is only an aide-memoire for those who have already undergone the necessary stages of preparation. Some of the quotations given earlier in this essay show the lamentable confusion which is prevailing.

Following the method pointed out above, I think that with adequate preparation the serious student in the course of his reading can make headway, without too great a need of commentary on the text.

Above all one must avoid starting out in a false direction from the first line of *Genesis*. Whereas it is always read *Bereshyt Bara Elohim* . . . etc., there is no reason why it should not read: *Bara-Shyt-Bara-Elohim,* as the three first Autiot are repeated. It is then realised that this equation, *Bara* (Bayt-Raysh-Aleph), which is banished after its first appearance, has a meaning which can be discovered by expanding its 3 Autiot.

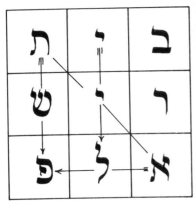

A first development of Bayt, Raysh, Aleph, the three Autiot by which the Bible begins.

Yod-Yod, often written as the name of a deity, appears here as: 1) the existence of any container (Bayt) and as: 2) the existence of the cosmic container (Raysh). This second Yod is the centre of a diagonal Tav-Aleph (everything that is, says the Qabala, is between Aleph and Tav). A flow of energy from Yod-Yod gives motion to Lammed, the organic drive. Phay, the unstructured energy, is activated by Aleph's Lammed and by Tav through Sheen (which is engendered by Raysh). Tav acts upon Sheen as a compression aimed at Phay.

Thus it is seen that the equation *Shyt* (Sheen-Yod-Tav) is one of the very important ones laying out the data of the problems, without revealing how to solve them. In fact the repetition of *Bara,* leading to *Elohim,* harks back to the question, which, in the equation *Elohim,* contains its own solution and solves *Shyt.* The two equations can be described as referring to a process of Energy in a space-time continuum.

One equation which is very important because it pertains to the fundamental data of the Qabala invested in *Genesis* and *The Sepher Yetsira,* is *ET* (Aleph-Tav), but when translators meet it in the very first line of Genesis (*ET Ha-Shamaïm We-ET Ha-Eretz*) they say it means nothing and pass it by in silence, though when Hhevah begets Cain and says *Qanyty Iysch ET YHWH,* it does not prevent them from writing: *I have gotten a man from the Lord,*[1] because they cannot understand that, from Aleph to Tav, Cain is YHWH.

If Adam is the name given to Man, by what curious transformation does this schema become a "pottage," in words attributed to Esau when he tells Jacob before his tent that he feels he is dying if he does not have *Ha-Adam, Ha-Adam Hazeh,* translated: *Feed me, I pray thee with that same red pottage?*[2] Is Adam Man or pottage?

When, in Ecclesiastes, we read *Hevel Heveleem* why does "poor Abel (whose name is Hevel), killed by his wicked brother," suddenly become Vanity?

Sepher and Yetsira

Before grappling with the text let us say something about the title.

In Hebrew the word *"Sepher"* indicates the article — book, leaves, scroll — on which a scripture is written and, in a wider sense, the text itself, as when we say, for example, "The Book of Job."

The three letters, Sammekh, Phay, Raysh, forming *Sepher* have a meaning which throws light on its origin. Sammekh (in full, Sammekh-Mem-Khaf) is a "support." Phay (or Pay), among other things, means "mouth." Raysh (Raysh-Yod-Sheen) is "poverty." Writing can be thought of as a support

---

[1] *Genesis,* IV,1 (King James' Version)
[2] *Genesis,* XXV,30

in former times to the oral tradition, to vouch for it, to prevent its decadence.

Pronounced according to the different vowel-points, the same word, *Sepher* or *Saphar*, means code. It is the root of the word *chiffre* in French. This tallies with the fact that this scripture is written in code: that is to say, that the letters serve not only as codes, but that the codes have as much meaning as the language.

In a still larger meaning *"Sepher"* makes "an orb," and, in the figurative sense, embraces a wide range of knowledge, as well as a field of action or influence (sphere). Here, it is the field of Yetsira, translated as "formation," to which "structuration" can be added without further explanation. As *The Sepher Yetsira* is a commentary on *Genesis* it is necessary to read *Genesis* carefully from the beginning in order to understand the root of the word *Yetser,* seeing it in a particular context.

We are making it clear that in chapter one of *Genesis* the verbs which play an important part during the 6 "days" — crowned by the 7th — are *Bara* (Bayt-Raysh-Aleph: 2.200.1) and *Aassah* (Ayn-Seen[1]-Hay: 70.300.5), which are translated as "to create" and "to do."

Not until chapter two, after the appearance of *Ad* engendered by *Eretz,* does YHWH-Elohim *Yitser* "form" *Adam-Aafar-Men-Ha'Adamah.*[2] This verb returns in the following verse (II,8), where it is said that YHWH-Elohim places in Eden the Name *(Schem)* of Adam whom he has formed *(Yatsar),* and to verse II,19 where it is said that "all the animals of the field" are formed *(Yitser)* from *Adamah.*

The three verbs, *Bara* (to create), *Yaass* (to do) and *Tsar* (to structure), must be compared.

Tsar has so great a content and value that it is only after a profound study of *Genesis* and *The Sepher Yetsira* that its meaning becomes consistent. Let us concentrate on the fact

---

[1] Seen or Sheen: the number is the same, but, as said above, their function and pronunciation are different.

[2] In the vulgate: dust of the earth.

that this Sepher is about the structuration of man and his environment, and proceed to see how Adam is envisaged in the Bible.

The idea of "making Adam" appears in *Genesis* I,26. The number 26 is the total of Yod, Hay, Waw, Hay. Although YHWH appears only in *Genesis* II, the "idea" of that equation appears simultaneously with the "idea" of the equation Adam. Verse I,26 is translated: ". . . and God said: let us make man in our image." The actual words are *Elohim Yomer*. The verb *Yomer*, translated "said" (Yod-Aleph-Mem-Raysh), is a projection or emanation, of Yod and Aleph upon substance, Mem. This emanation "projects" — in the true sense of the word — a potential act of "making" (*Naasseh*) *Adam Betsalmenou-Kidmothnou.*[1]

But in the following verse, *Elohim* "*Ivra*" (created) *Adam Betsalmeno* only. *Kidmothnou* and *Aassa* are missing. The verb *Bara* is conjugated three times and *Iselem* twice: "And *Elohim* created *Eth-Ha-Adam-Betsalmo: Betselem Elohim Bara Oto* (with *Tselem Elohim* created him) *Zakar Ve-Nekiva* (male and female) *Bara Otam* (created them).

Next (I,28) he *Yevarekh* (blesses) them. The verb *Barekh*, to bless, (Bayt-Raysh-Khaf) differs from *Bara*, to create, only by the substitution of the Aleph final for a Khaf (20 or 500).

At *Yom*, 7 completes everything that *Elohim* has Aassa (made). Day 7 is blessed and sanctified.

The strange verse of *Genesis* II,4 announces: *These are the generations of Schamaïm and of Eretz when they were "created" in the day that Yod-Yod-Elohim made Eretz and Schamaïm.*

Finally we come to the verse mentioned before (II,7: note the 7), where Adam is "formed."

The prophet Isaiah distinguishes the three verbs in question (XLII.1): *Thus now speaks YHWH who has "created"*

---

[1] In common language: according to our image and our likeness.

you, O Jacob, and he who has "formed" you, O Israel. In the same chapter, verse 7: . . . *all those who witness to my Name, all those I have "created" for my glory, I have "formed" and also (Ef) (with greater reason) have I made.* Further on we shall see how these 3 verbs correspond to 3 spheres of the Tree of Life.

Karppe (op cit., p. 252) notes that Ibn Gabirol has emphasised this verse of Isaiah and that Ibn Ezra, quoting Ibn Gabirol, has said on the subject of the three verbs: *Therein lies the mystery of the universe.*

We think that the mystery of the universe is impenetrable by the human spirit, but we are in it, we are it, and we have the capacity to study its structure outside and inside ourselves, and therefore to partake of its flow of life, as it is said that Abraham did.

The mystery therefore does not lie in Isaiah. Neither *Genesis* nor *The Sepher Yetsira* are so absurd as to pretend to "explain" it, but a careful study of the Autiot, the verbs and the names in the text allow us "to see, to consider, to go into it deeply, to understand" the interplay of the different aspects of integral life and ourselves to engage in this game.

Our contemporary scientific research is already tending to think of the Revived Qabala in the terms in which I am introducing it, free of its religious myths and laws. So far only a few scientists are aware of it, but I have reason to believe that in a not too distant future the Autiot will be used as symbols in different disciplines, such as physics, biology, and others, instead of our conventional, lifeless, letters.

A new sphere of thought is being opened up, and it is left to us to make our own discoveries. The joy of discovery is part of the game, and there is an infinite number of profound combinations to be thought out. The verbs *Bara, Aassa,* and *Tsar* open up unlimited perceptions.

Here are some free commentaries on the 3 fundamental verbs and on a few important words necessary for the understanding of *The Sepher Yetsira.*

Bara. Let us recall the field of thought which, straightaway, from the first Autiot of *Genesis* (Bara: Bayt-Raysh-Aleph), projects us into the mystery of Aleph. This mystery is the first two Autiot of Aleph: Aleph-Lammed and AL have become a divinity in the Mosaic tradition. In fact, they are the equation of the broken balance (I,30) which distinguishes an organism from an aggregate, 30 being an organic movement born in Phay (80), undifferentiated matter, completing the schema Aleph.

The Sepher Yetsira asserts (II,6) that Aleph and Bayt combine with everything and that everything combines with them. In other words, infinite life is everywhere and everything is in Bayt, a "container" in the very largest meaning of the word: form, vibration, undulation, a physical prop.

Aleph cannot be seen, it cannot be directly proved, but its action can be seen and verified. This is shown in the alphabet by the letter Sheen (300). Sheen is one of the principle themes of *The Sepher Yetsira*. It often appears either directly or in the schemas *Rouahh Elohim* (the breath), whose letters make a total of 300.

This "breath" is traditionally attributed to Elohim. Since Elohim is being constantly deified, commentators tend to forget that Sheen is introduced into the alphabet by Raysh (200), the twentieth letter of the alphabet, whose meaning is 2×100: the cosmic "house" or container of Aleph. Sheen comes only as the twenty-first letter. In other words, "the breath" is begotten of the universe itself as a "container" (200).

A first development of *Bara* shows nine Autiot: Bayt 2.10.400 — Raysh: 200.10.300 — Aleph: 1.30.80. It is a series of equations that reveal, when properly combined, many complexities, such as a joint action of two Yods in an organic process, a flow of life from Tav through Sheen meeting in Phay Aleph's action through Lammed, etc. A second development shows a combination of nineteen elements. The developments have no end. We then see how meaningless is the vernacular "to create."

Tsar, Yetsira. Note at once the preponderating role of the letter Tsadde (90) in everything concerning the structuration (Yetsira) of energy. This letter whose number is 90 (9 × 10) expresses the fertilised feminine who has evolved from the primordial stage (9) of the cell to a "formative-form" in actual process of growth.

The rôle of the development of the feminine is one of the principle elements in the whole of Hebraic-Christian mythology (see "The Cosmic Marriage" of *Aïn-Sof*, numerous gnostic writings, etc.). We have seen it represented by Ischah in Eden, by Mary of Magdala,[1] and we find it again in other myths, for example, under the name of Psyche.

Tsadde is in *Yotser* (to structure), in *Tselem* (making Adam according to our *Tselem* "says" Elohim), in *Tselaa* (the mythical extraction from "the side" of Adam), in *Ets* (the tree whose fruit plays such an important part), in *Erets,* etc. Now we will go back to verse I,26, where Elohim "purposes" to "make" an Adam according to *Tselem* and *Kidmot.*

Tselem, as root (Tsadde-Lammed-Mem) expresses the fact that the structured and structurating feminine (90) engender an organic movement (Lammed, 30) in "the primordial waters" of Mem.

But this action is not sufficient for "making" an Adam. Again, the greatest possible resistance to life must be met. And this is just what the root Dallet-Mem-Tav (4.40.400) of *Kidmothnou* expresses. (Khaf is a prefix and Waw and Noun have a grammatical character.)

Beyond the fact that it expresses, with Dallet-Mem, Dam (blood) and with Mem-Tav (death) the whole process of animal existence, this equation is a violent assertion of 4 on all levels. We saw it transfixed by the cosmic Aleph of Cain when Cain withdrew *Qidmath Eden* (translated "to the east of Eden"). We know that this powerful mobilisation of 4 is the indispensable counterpart to the highest kind of life that this planet can produce, corresponding to Cain, the incarna-

---

[1] See *The Cipher of Genesis*

tion of YHWH, perfected man, possessed of an unconditioned conscience.

In verse I,26, "making" man, etc., must not be seen as a conscious or unconscious completion. All completion has to take place in a period of time. In spite of the evolution that this "intention to make" seems to indicate when wrongly read, we must grasp what *The Sepher Yetsira* says about the Sephirot (I,7): their end is in the beginning and *their beginning is in their end.*

This "end" is laid down in verse I,26 of *Genesis,* by the number 26, which makes us aware that the completion of YHWH is present from the beginning of human evolution, although it was not apparent at the beginning, nor is it even now, alas, in the present condition of humanity.

Aassa, Genesis II,3, must be clarified. It says that Elohim *Ebarekh* (blesses) the seventh day *Ve-Yeqadesch* (hallowed it) because he *Schavath* (Sheen-Vayt-Tav: untranslatable: this verb has been replaced by the misleading "reposed") from all *Melaktou* (his work) that Elohim *Bara* (created) *Leaasoth* (in order to "make").

The question is: to make what? Exactly, for *Aass* (Ayn-Seen, is 70.300, in its lowest root), that is to say, to confer on Seen the 70 of all the possible possibilities. And *Aassa* (Ayn-Seen-Hay) adds the Hay (5) of life to *Aass.*

Remember the meaning of *Bara*: the presence, face to face of Bayt and Raysh. That is, in full power, Bayt-Yod-Tav and Raysh-Yod-Sheen, where the Tav (400) and the Sheen (300) confront each other as an opposition to be resolved. This opposition, this clash between the static universal Tav and the dynamic universal Sheen causes Aleph to rise, in the form of an equation that needs to be understood.

We have seen that Sheen is engendered, not by a divinity acting upon its world, but by "the house," the container, the 200 which expresses energy at a dead end.

The equation is resolved when the Elohim process results in 70, which opens all possibilities to Raysh. At this moment "creation" is absolutely self-governing because it is animated by the movement of 70, which is full release. In *Schavath,* Sheen and Vayt live in symbiosis from the fact that Bayt (house) is between Sheen and Tav, the co-existing, reconciled opposites.

In other words — and the story that the Autiot, the Sephirot, the Yom, the equations, the ciphers, the numbers tell is always the same — the Elohim process by which Aleph manifests itself, operates from the interior of the extant universe: Raysh.

This is how it works: from Raysh (200), "cosmic house," rises a vital movement, which is the return shock of the movement fertilising everything that is static. This "breath of breath" seen in the second Sephira surges back to its source through the medium of consciousness.

This fertilisation consists of the following postulate: the universe in general and human consciousness in particular possess the *Baraka* of the seventh number. It confers self-government upon them. The source is within. The source of unity is within us, and we have the power to evoke it. This is *Aassa,* "the making."

Aassa re-unites making, creating and structuring into a single cluster. The three are one.

In the next chapter we will grapple with the text of *The Sepher Yetsira,* in Hebrew and English, while reminding readers that Hebrew is a degenerate form of the Autiot language. We have said enough about the powerlessness of our languages to penetrate linguistics. Therefore we have little choice: we will transcribe in English the equations necessary for the general understanding of the verses, and into Hebrew the words that their traditional English homologues only misrepresent. Afterwards we will re-read the significant equations in terms of the Autiot, or of the figures which constitute them.

Our intention is to sift from this text the things which directly concern people whose minds are uncluttered by mythology, and who are interested in the essential question that conscience asks regarding the universe and itself.

It is certainly true that the best informed cabalists have all, without exception, borne witness to different branches of belief in a personal god, in one form or another. But is this divinity mentioned by *The Sepher Yetsira* anything else than an often transparent veil? The vital movement that the Autiot cast into the mind has an image-less intensity, and man is invited to work out his own revelation for himself, so that, objectively, the notion of "God," so indispensable to translators, is fundamentally wrong.

The cabalist can slip through the mesh. He can annihilate the person of "God," but for the translator of profane language this is impossible. If, to forbid the pronunciation of YHWH the tradition transforms it into Lord, *The Sepher Yetsira,* far from compelling us to do so, tells us to put "the formator" (the *Yotser*) in place of it (I,4) after cogitating on it intelligently, scrutinising it and going into it deeply.

It is worth stating again that this book, which for so many centuries has been taken to be obscure and unfathomable, is plain to any reader with an open mind.

Recapitulation

Bara and *Aassa* appear with Elohim in the first chapter of *Genesis.*

Bara, Bayt-Raysh-Aleph, are the very first three letters of the first verse of *Genesis* (Bereschyit). They cause Aleph to rise from Bayt and Raysh.

In the first verse Bara is joined to *Schamaïm* and *Erets,* while upon its first appearance (in verse 7) *Aassa* is associated with *Raqia,* which is between "the waters above" and "the waters below."

Aassa (Ayn-Seen-Hay: 70.300.5) comprises all the possible possibilities with the 70, and with 300 the movement of every existing thing, in order to produce 5, life, conferred on everything extant.

Bara and *Aassa* operate successively and sometimes jointly to produce or to maintain the kind of life that *Genesis* calls

Nefesch Hhaya or *Hhayath ha-Erets* (the breath of the living or the life of the earth).

Yetser appears with YHWH-Elohim in the second chapter, after the completion of the seven "days." By its presence YHWH joins its action to Elohim's. Its immanence compels recognition and is translated in the Yod (10) of *Yetser* (10.90.200). By the intervention of Tsadde (90) — the fertilised and therefore supporting feminine — this Yod causes 200 to rise anew, to receive a new breath, called *Nischmath Hhavim.*

Nischmath (Noun-Sheen-Mem-Tav) shows Sheen-Mem (Schem) between Noun (50), individual life; and Tav (400), cosmic resistance which allows life to manifest in lavish variety.

Note *Yetser* well: $10+90+200=300=$ Sheen-Rouahh-Elohim. It can be said that YHWH-Elohim operates with Rouahh-Elohim through *Yetser.*

Again, note well that the word *Yod* or *Yad,* the hand, euphemism for the phallus, often goes with *Aassa,* which leads one to think that *Aassa* connects either with what is handled or with what is engendered.

The three verbs *Bara, Aassa* and *Tsar* have given rise to the idea of an earlier "emanation" that would cause the three methods of functioning just mentioned. The first emanation is indicated by the word *Atsiloth,* meaning literally, "nobility, aristocracy." These four hierarchical differentiations of the same evolutionary process have been called the four worlds of the Qabala.

Consequently a sephirotic, geometrical tree can be made of the four worlds. The design will be given in chapter 6.

Before meeting the text we must throw some light on *Ayn-Sof (Aleph-Yod-Noun-Sammekh-Waw-Phay)* and *Aur Aëlion.*

Addressing itself to cabalists, *The Sepher Yetsira* leaves out the equations of pre-structured energy known to them, but which do not enter the sphere of *Yotser,* or formation. As it is our intention to explain the cabalistic mentality to the general public, the equations must be examined before going on to a translation that would otherwise be lacking in its essential basis.

The ten *Sephirot* are transformers of energy, breaking it down until it becomes completely materialised.

As a preliminary to this structuring of energy, the Qabala recognises two double equations of infinite energy: *Ayn-Sof* and *Aur-Aëlion*. In Hebrew *Ayn-Sof* means "without end," or "infinite," and *Aur-Aëlion* means "light," the highest or uplifted state of mind.

Read according to the code, the two double equations disclose the fundamental postulates of the Qabala, and contain an epitome of the whole.

Ayn-Sof. Ayn: Aleph-Yod-Noun (1.10.700) is a negation in Hebrew: "There is not." Strangely, this equation, on the contrary, expresses the whole, because it consists of Aleph and Yod, which are intemporal energy and its temporal projection: that is to say, the two partners in this interplay of cosmic life, death and existence. However, it is understandable why, due to the sense-based origin of the vulgate, *Ayn* is a negation. Noun final (700) which defines the stake of the cosmic part as being the Principle of Indetermination is an irresoluteness, an openness to all possibilities, to all that can come about unforeseen, beyond thought, from the not yet created: that is to say, to all that is still non-existent. This extraordinary abundance of freedom is a whirlpool of nothingness for the psyche (which feels in its element only through the familiar or the past). *Ayn* originates the metaphysical: "God created the world *ex nihilo*."

Read in full, Aleph (Aleph-Lammed-Phay: 1.30.80), Yod (Yod-Waw-Dallet: 10.6.4) and Noun (Noun-Noun: 50.700) show that the action of Aleph is to confer an organic movement (30) upon undifferentiated energy (80); that existence expressed by Yod is a fertilising (6) of opposing life (4); and that the life-in-existence of Noun (50) results in the freedom of the indeterminate (700).

Sof (Sammekh-Waw-Phay: 60.6.80) repeats and completes *Ayn* by the introduction of Sammekh (60) which, according to the code, is centripetal, fertilising energy. *Sof* is a double energy: centripetal by Sammekh and centrifugal by Waw (which evolve into female and male). These two contrary energies highlight the Phay (80) which was discovered in *Ayn* only when opening out Aleph (Aleph-Lammed-Phay). In short, *Ayn* is an anatomical equation which lays down the three elements of prime importance in this mode of think-ing — Aleph-Yod-Noun final. *Sof* is a biological equation ex-pressing the setting in motion of differentiated energy, Phay (80), by two thrusts. One of them, Sammekh, picks up energy in the cellular centre, and the other, Waw, emanates from the centre and projects itself to the outside.

Aur-Aëlion. Even though *Ayn-Sof* is the most abstract double equation in the Qabala, *Aur-Aëlion* is a turn-table in the universe, between the finite abstract and infinity. Never-theless it should be noted that, according to the Qabala, in-finity is not represented at all. The explanations of these two double equations are, therefore, only analogous ideas, and the images arising from them are only symbols. This preciseness is necessary because with *Aur,* translated as light, we are com-ing near to the biblical legend about its creation.

Aur (Aleph-Waw-Raysh: 1.6.200) expresses the clash be-tween Aleph, the infinite in motion, and Raysh (200) which physically supports all that exists. The support has mass, strength, "number": the physical equation of the universe gives rise, according to the Qabala, to the greatest speed of which existence is capable. The function of the universe's mass is speed, which is determined by its resistance to the in-finite in movement emanating from itself. Wrongly or rightly, this is taken to be the speed of light. But in *Aur-Aëlion* it is magnified.

Aëlion, as a matter of fact, shows how the infinite comes from number. Its Autiot (Ayn-Lammed-Yod-Waw-Noun final: 70.30.10.6.700), express the fact that all the possibilities in being (70) endow existence (10) with organic life (30), and thus fecundate all cosmic possibilities (700). Here we see how the cosmic 700 is begotten of the existential 70: it is indeed a "magnification" of *Aur* and a demonstration of what was implicit but secret in *Ayn-Sof*. However, it is advisable to go back to *Ayn*, which, pronounced as written, does not reveal the Lammed and the Phay contained in Aleph. Only when conducted by Ayn (70) into *Aëlion* do Phay and the action of Lammed become visible.

Such are the first ideas which emerge from *Ayn-Sof* and *Aur-Aëlion*. These equations lead the way to levels of knowledge for each person to discover, because one can meditate on them endlessly, and they lay down the primary notion of the Unity of being and substance of the universe.

PART TWO

THE TEXT

5

The First Two Verses

משנה א בשלשים ושתים נתיבות פליאות
חכמה חקק יה יהוה צבאות
אלהי ישראל אלהים חיים ומלך עולם אל שדי
רחום וחנון רם ונשא שוכן עד מרום וקדוש
שמו וברא את עולמו בשלשה ספרים בספר
וספר וספור

By thirty-two Nativot-Phayliot Hhokmah carved (established or limited) Yah YHWH Tsebaot Elohi Israël Elohim Hhaïm Wemelekh Oulam El Schaddaï merciful clement magnified raised up (or respected) (who) lives (in) eternity (of) elevation (and) Holy (is) his name (which has) created his universe with (or by) three Sepharim (:) with Sepher Sepher and Sipour.

In beginning the *Yetsira* with Bayt, the first sign in Genesis, its authors show their firm intention to start with Bara, which propounds a scientific study of the relations between Aleph, Intemporal Consciousness, and Bayt, their physical framework. If the *Yetsira* is a commentary on *Genesis* it adds to the subject of Beresheet by treating it from the inside; that is to say, by beginning with the meaning of the Autiot. But as the cipher of the code got lost, *Genesis* became a canonised mythology whose only relation to the original meaning is to be its opposite, whilst the *Yetsira* has been left out of the rabbinical tradition. And as it is not canonical there are various, differing versions of it. Perhaps there is no harm in that, for (see I,4) it invites us to reflect on it personally, rather than find in these pages a documentation which it would suffice to consult. Are not all religions and all the sciences quests — and more or less mistaken assertions — for the relationship between the Universe and ourselves?

In putting Aleph in a pre-eminent position, the Qabala develops a rational and logical thought. Aleph, Consciousness both in intemporal and Universal life, is everywhere and in everything but acts in our space-time continuum only through two agents, Sheen and Seen (300). We have defined the Autiot often enough not to have to stop at every turn (as we had to do in *The Cipher of Genesis*). However, let us establish the fundamental role of Sheen, from the beginning, and note that the sign is written twice in the first line of Beresheet, three times in the first line of the *Yetsira* and four times in the first line of *The Song of Songs*: these are three ways of approaching the same subject, which it is up to the reader to understand.

Let us begin by reading the first verse: Beschlaschîm Weschaïm: times 32 . . . but take care: Shtaïm is the feminine absolute of No. 2 (the masculine being Shnaïm). As to the Schlaschïm we realise that it means 30 only in reading it, because, thanks to the code, the attribute of this language is that the meaning of words is given only by the hand-writing. Note that the first Sheen (agent of Aleph, and therefore of Cosmic origin) acts through Lammed as agent of Aleph, and that a second Sheen, put in motion by Lammed, acts on the extant Yod. The third Sheen is introduced into Shtaïm by the fertilisation of Mem by Waw: it acts on Tav and completes the circuit. These indications are sufficient to define the intellectual significance of the Qabala. It takes into consideration all energy and consciousness, which is energy, as returning to itself in a process of self-induction, and not at all a single emanation originating from demiurgic creation, as the monotheistic tradition has it. Now let us re-read the first words of the first verse: *By thirty-two Nativot-Phayliot.*

In order to understand these two words let us eliminate their feminine plural endings. *Nativ*: Noun-Tav-Yod-Vayt (50.400.10.2) is clearly a Bayt (Bayt-Yod-Tav) spelt in reverse and preceded by a Noun. *Phaylia*: Phay-Lammed-Yod-Aleph

(80.30.10.1) is no less clearly an Aleph (Aleph-Lammed-Phay) also spelt backwards, into which a Yod, preceding the Aleph, is inserted.

Recalling verse II,5, where it is said: *Aleph with all, and all with Aleph, Bayt with all and all with Bayt,* what does it mean here?

Let us suppose that we are facing through a pane of glass a tremendous flow of living energy, coming from the highest level, which is composed of the inconceivable, intemporal Aleph, and of Bayt including all physical frameworks.

Therefore, supposing we "see" that vital energy coming towards us, and writing its two names, Aleph and Bayt, on the pane: On the right side is written Aleph-Lammed-Phay, and on the left, Bayt-Yod-Tav, in letters of light (written from right to left, following Hebrew script).

We obviously see these Autiot in reverse. But, furthermore, Tav-Yod-Vayt must have a living existence in order to pass through these transformers. For this purpose it is preceded here by a Noun (50) expressing this life. And there must also be the Yod (10) of existence, in which Phay-Lammed-Aleph "lowers itself." It is in its exact place there, between Lammed and Aleph.

Nativot-Phayliot are feminine plural, just like the Sephirot and Autiot (we have explained the Waw-Tav above). They constitute the category in which the twenty-two and the ten can be added together. This category is the level where things appear in reverse, in harmony with the vital energy. Our consciousness (Hhokmah) [1] belongs to this level. Things which have a most solid appearance (stones, metals) are the deepest "sleep" of Aleph. Aleph fully "awake" is beyond our perception. In brief, the living infinite Energy has its manifestation reversed: an important postulate to start with.

Thus Aleph and *Phayliot,* Bayt and *Nativot* have opposite meanings.

[1] *Hhokmah* is the name of the 2nd Sephira which, according to the Qabala, begot the Autiot.

437

Going on with our mental picture we have now to study *Phayliot* and *Nativot* acting as a vital current flowing in the opposite direction to that which we have shown. This two-fold current of life corresponds to Jacob's ladder, to the action of the Autiot as has been defined above, as well as to the essential narratives in the myth, such as Jonah's dive to "the roots of the mountain," Jesus's descent into the ground for three days, etc.

If Aleph-Lammed-Phay show that the essential function of Aleph is to instigate an organic movement in the undifferentiated energy of Phay, *Phayliot* (Phay-Lammed-Yod-Aleph-Waw-Tav) shows that the motion of the evolutionary framework engendered by Phay acts on the existential Yod, thanks to which the buried Aleph comes back to life. The feminine plural suffix frees abstract thought from its purely conceptual scope and brings it into concrete manifestation.

Bayt-Yod-Tav shows that Bayt, "the containing," is, by the very fact of its existence, a single element of Tav (400): that is to say, of all cosmic resistance to life, without which there would be no life. *Nativot* (Noun-Tav-Yod-Vayt-Waw-Tav) shows that life is realised (Noun=50) fully in the universe, and that this existence (Yod) is conferred on the perpetually changing body of the universe.

In short, the first four words of the first verse, *Beschlaschim Weschtïm Nativot Phayliot* invite us to study thirty-two elements binding the energy of intemporal life to the visible universe, as conceived and thought in human knowledge: that is to say, they are turned into the contrary of the real value of their energy and life.

We see how misleading, superficial and indeed senseless are the generally accepted translations of Nativot (paths, pathways, roads) and Phayliot (wonderful, mysterious, incomprehensible). The obviousness of 32 being the sum of 22 Autiot and 10 Sephirot appears as a screen or a snare to bewilder the amateur cabalists. Not only is the summing-up of Sephirot and Autiot, as roads, inadequate, but adding them together is rather like adding a number of electric transformers to the voltage which lights them. In number 32 there is a secret key which it was very important not to hand over to the non-initiated, because it opens the door to a conception of the first 4 Sephirot, respecting creative energy, that is hardly canonical. We will examine it in discussing Verses I,3 to I,8.

We come to the fifth word of our verse, and it is logical that it is *Hhokmah* (Hhayt-Kaf-Mem-Hay: 8.20.40.5), which defines intelligence as, at one and the same time, a feminine symbol, knowledge and wisdom; in short, as awoken consciousness. The Autiot forming the equation *Hhokmah* express the reservoir of undifferentiated, primordial energy asserting its active existence from which the developing flow surges in search of the lost unity.

Such is the role of consciousness, as it is of the 2nd Sephira which, as we have said, begets the Autiot; *Hhokmah* shows reality upside down. To show it thus is to present it in the way that an imprint is the hollow of a plenum, or the plenum of a hollow, left by a shape given to a body. If the surface is supple, living and active it reflects the energy which has punched it out. This return shock is the language of the Autiot uttered by thought which receives and drives along the game of life, death and existence.

The same flow, stream and intensity of life strikes consciousness and is reprojected by it, overtaken in its closest secret by the maturation which overthrows its bulwarks. It can no longer deny that the interplay of the Autiot is different from their intimations. The identity of meaning and its significant number, as 2nd Sephira, which we emphasise, is a mysterious passage across "a psychic high frequency," a continuous perception due to an ultra rapid and constant vibration: life-death-life-death of conscious being.

The shock of life to awoken consciousness-non-conscious being, and the return shock, are the two fulgurations of *Hhaqaq* (Hhayt-Qof-Qof: 8.100.100), the equation following *Hhokmah*. It is translated, very badly, as "limited" or "pitted."

Hhaqaq is a verb. In Hebrew the word expressing action precedes the name of the active agent. We will now examine this name. But let us recall what has been read up to here: *Beschlaschim Weschtaïm Nativot-Phayliot Hhokmah Hhaqaq....*

Though having by no means completely solved these equations, we think we have clarified them enough to allow students to study them further. Next come the names of the active agent (in the myth, "God"). They are given in nineteen equations, eleven of which are, strictly speaking, "The Name," and eight of which are attributes.

In the first eleven "names" fifteen Autiot are composed so as to become, with certain repetitions, forty-two signs.

In the eight which follow, eleven Autiot become thirty signs.

The forty-two signs of "Names" are the forty-two often mentioned by the cabalists. According to the Zohar all forms in the world come from the forty-two letters crowning the sacred Name. The world has been moulded by the letters of the sacred Name; therefore their role in the Name is the reverse of what they are in the world. (We have already made this reverse rôle clear.)

These forty-two, to which thirty are added, compose "The Name of seventy-two letters" which has given rise to numerous speculations about angels. This is not surprising as we have seen that the Autiot, mediating between intemporal and temporal, serve the function attributed to angels in deistic mythology. As to the assertion that the Autiot — according to the Zohar — have "a role the reverse of what they are in the world" (sic) we have just seen that when the symbolism is reduced to its essentials, it refers to the reality of *Hhokmah,* reflected consciousness.

The names transcribed into forty-two Autiot are: *YAH, YHWH, TSEBAOT, ELOHI, ISRAEL, ELOHIM, HHAIM, WAMELEKH, OULAM EL,* and *SCHADDAI.* When decoded they show as from within, the diminution of Energy operated by the ten Sephirot.

YAH: Yod-Hay expresses life alive.

YHWH. We know this equation.[1] Briefly, it expresses Life fulfilled, perfected by the mutual fertilisation of its two lives, Hay and Hay (container and contents, etc.) In the world of becoming *YHWH* is immanent in potentiality of being.

TSEBAOT, too often translated "Lord of Hosts." This equation is, by the entry of Tsadde (90), the logical continuation of the preceeding one, *YHWH*, one of whose two Hay, of necessity refers to the "feminine," vital flow, in the widest meaning. *Tsebaot*: Tsadde-Bayt-Aleph, with the feminine plural suffix Waw-Tav, expresses the constructive action of Tsadde (90) in causing Aleph to emerge from Bayt. Remember that Aleph is buried in *Erets* (Aleph-Raysh-Tsadde). *Tseba* is inverted. Its Hebrew meaning of "gathering," or "reunion" is quite close to "construction."

ELOHI ISRAEL. These two words do not need a lengthy explanation. *Elohi* (Aleph-Lammed-Hay-Yod) expresses the fact that Aleph confers an organic movement (Lammed) on life (Hay) and the living (Yod). As for *Israel* (Yod-Seen-Raysh-Aleph-Lammed) it expresses the answer of the living (Yod) to Aleph-Lammed, through Seen and Raysh.

ELOHIM HHAIM. Eloh spreads by means of the masculine plural suffix. *Elohim* is energy living in the constructive process. The final Mem indicates that the process has completed its course, so to say, in getting in touch with the origin of all operative organic life. *Hhaïm* (Hhayt-Yod-Yod-Mem) which accompanies it is strange. *Hhai* (Hhayt-Yod) means "living," in Hebrew. Here, as in *Elohim,* it is a plural called singular. It is the presence of the two Yod in it that matters. The binomial *Elohim-Hhaïm* (which we shall meet again in the 1st Sephira) indicates the double direction, "the going and coming," of the flow of cosmic life. Having reached Mem, the vital current sets out again from Hhayt (8), from undifferentiated life, having acquired two Yod (two structures),

---

[1] See *The Cipher of Genesis.*

and rejoins *Elohim* in the fertilised Mem. (We have seen that the suffix *Im* indicates a structuring energy.)

WAMELEKH OULAM means "and king of all" in Hebrew. Actually *Melekh* (Mem-Lammed-Khaf, that is, 40.30. 20/500) results from the previous equation. It shows that the Lammed of organic life is conferred on Mem, the former passing from 20 to the final 500 of cosmic life. And *Oulam* (Ayn-Lammed-Mem: 70.30.40/600) in fact expresses "the whole," but by elucidating what this "whole" is: the 70 of all realised possible possibilities, the 30 of all organic life and the final Mem affirm it. (Note that the root of the schema, *Melekh,* is the tenth and last Sephira, *Malkout.*)

EL SCHADDAI, Aleph-Lammed-Sheen-Dallet-Yod. This is the last equation of this enumeration. It is easily decoded as it says what the Qabala never ceases repeating in a thousand different ways from different points of view. Here we see the action of *Al* (Aleph) exerting itself on Dallet and Yod through Sheen.

It is not necessary to overload an account of the eight following words with an analysis (as has just been done for the "Name" in forty-two Autiot). These "attributes" — *Rahhoum Wehhanoun, Ram Wenascha Schokan Aad Maroum Wegadosch* — can be deciphered by the usual code. Their thirty signs add nothing significant to the forty-two preceding them. Moreover, the Qabala considers that the "Name" is more important in forty-two Autiot than in seventy-two.

Now we come to *Schemou,* translated as "His Name." But in order not to lose the thread of the first phrase of *The Sepher Yetsira,* let us summarise it by substituting the meaning (so to speak, the infinite meaning of these equations) for the words that serve our purpose: *By thirty-two intermediaries YHWH projects Schem.*

Schemou (Sheen-Mem-Waw: 300.40.6) is such a shrewd digest that it has given rise to the notion that every individual is a personification of the name he bears, a notion whose origin can be seen in the ontological meaning of the Autiot. Sheen expresses the action of the universal, organic movement. Mem is the material of the subject. Waw is the fertilisation of this substance by Sheen. This direct bond between a subject and living cosmic energy is, as we have seen in this linguistics, its method of description: the subject is defined according to the function of the position it occupies in the hierarchy of structures. The ensembles being countless, when a name is pronounced, it has analogous repercussions at the same level of structuration throughout the possible entities. If the Qabala is not interpreted with this way of thinking it is a dead letter and the Bible discloses nothing.

Now the *Schem* of *YHWH-Elohim* is at a level of perpetual, intemporal creation, always new, flowing in space and time, whose nature eludes human awareness. It is, in fact, illustrated by *Bara* (Bayt-Raysh-Aleph) which follows *Schemou: We Bara Eth Oulamou* ("created he all"). These words are familiar to us.

The last assertion that ends the 1st verse is: "Created he all with three Sepharim: *Sepher,* and *Sephour* and *Sipour*" (*Sephour:* that which is counted; *Sipour,* that which is related).[1]

The reader has in front of him the gamut of interpretations of the signs of the world gathered together into their whole. Does not one speak of "The Book of Nature"? Does not one speak of "Interpreting the Universe"? Is not the celestial "sphere," putting the observer in the middle of his own space, a current expression?

We recognise the three Sepharim of the world in perpetual creation: they are the sphere of numbers where everything is in mathematical equations; the physico-chemical sphere of formulae for the constitution of bodies and their transformations, and, finally, the Sipour where the events of life, death and existence are inscribed.

Thus ends the first verse.

---

[1] As the text has no vowels (points) one can introduce those considered to be the most adequate.

I,2 מ״ב עשר ספירות בלי מה ועשרים ושתים
אותיות יסוד שלש אמות ושבע כפולות
ושתים עשרה פשוטות:

The second verse is strictly limited to these words: *Ten
Sephirot Beli-Mah* and *twenty-two Autiot-Yassod; three
Mothers, seven doubles and twelve simples.* All the following
verses, to the end of the first chapter, deal with the Sephirot
exclusively, the Autiot intervening only as agents. The direct
study of the classification of the Autiot (3, 7 and 12) only begins in the second chapter.

Therefore let us examine the meaning of *Sephirot-Belimah.*
We see that the root of the Sephirot is the same as Sepherim's.
Yet there is one Yod more: Sammekh-Phay-Yod-Raysh, instead of Sammekh-Phay-Raysh, and the suffix is feminine
plural, instead of masculine plural, to express their character:
they reduce the potential energy and shepherd it into differentiations relative to existence as actually experienced.

In the text of *The Sepher Yetsira, Belimah* is sometimes
written in one word, sometimes in two: *Beli-Mah.* In one
word, in Hebrew, it signifies a restraint, a fetter, an obstacle.
In two words: *Beli* "without," *Mah,* "what?" This proposition
is most enigmatic but also perhaps the most suggestive.

The key of *Belimah,* however, is not in the Hebrew tongue
whose ontological origin is forgotten. We have said that the
Sephirot are derived from the energy of Elohim. Let us present the schemas *Elohim* and *Belimah* together:

Elohim: Aleph-Lammed — Hay-Yod-Mem
Belimah: Bayt-Lammed — Yod-Mem-Hay

This relation illustrates the double organic movement of
life in a state of being. In fact, reading these two series of
Autiot by the code it is seen that *Belimah* is the response of
Bayt, the archetype of all physical support, to the Elohim
process. The Aleph-Lammed-Hay-Yod-Mem (1.30.5.10.40) of

444

Elohim indicates that Aleph (1), in exerting its biological action, Lammed (30), on life, Hay (5), enters into existence, Yod (10), in the midst of Mem, (40), where the whole of organic life is born. The Bayt-Lammed-Yod-Mem-Hay of *Belimah* shows how, in return, the organic movement Lammed (30) is engendered by Bayt (2). In these sequences the inversion of their three finals is most remarkable: Hay-Yod-Mem for *Elohim* and Yod-Mem-Hay for *Belimah*. In one, life confers existence on Mem; in the other, the existence of Mem engenders life.

Often the Ancients secretly put their knowledge of the One in the minutest detail.

Verses 3 to 12

VERSES I,3 to I,8 treat of the ten Sephirot in general, sometimes called *Beli-Mah*, sometimes *Belimah*. We will give the
Hebrew version of them here, and attempt to interpret them,
while reminding readers that *The Sepher Yetsira* has frequently been distorted, and thus none of these versions is
entirely trustworthy. Moreover, in terms of the code, we will
study only the most important equations which principally
appear from verse I,9 onwards where the Sephirot are treated
in detail, one by one.

I,3   עשר ספירות בלימה מספר עשר **מ"ג**
אצבעות חמש כנגד חמש וברית יחיד
מכוונת באמצע כמלת הלשון וכמילת מעור:

*Ten Sephirot Belimah according to the number of ten fingers.
Five opposite (or: as in the presence of) five. And (the) covenant (of) the One, adapted (or, directed) in the midst of (or,
by means of) (the) word (of) the tongue and as (the) circumcision witnesses.*

I,4   עשר ספירות בלימה עשר ולא תשע, **מ"ד**
עשר ולא אחת עשרה , הבן בחכמה
וחכם בבינה, כחון בהם וחקור מהם והעמד
דבר על בוריו והשב יוצר על מכונו:

*Ten Sephirot Belimah. Ten and not nine. Ten and not eleven.
Understand with Hhokmah. Meditate with Binah.[1] Examine*

---

[1] *Hhokmah* (translated Wisdom) *Binah* (translated Intelligence) are the
2nd and 3rd Sephirot.

*them. Delve into them and experiment with them. And the
one who is there (standing) speaks to his creator and puts the
maker of form in his rightful place (or, his foundation).*

I,5

מ״ה עשר ספירות בלי מה מדתן עשר שאין
להם סוף עומק ראשית ועומק אחרית
עומק טוב ועומק רע עומק רום ועומק תחת
עומק מזרח ועומק מערב עומק צפון ועומק
דרום אדון יחיד אל מלך נאמן מושל בכולם
ממעון קדשו ועד עדי עד :

*Ten Sephirot Beli-Mah. Their measure without end. Depth
of beginning. Depth of end. Depth of Tov. Depth of Raa.
Depth of above. Depth of below. Depth of East. Depth of
West. Depth of North. Depth of South. Adon Yahhid true
King (or eternal) has dominion over the Universe of (the)
Holy Abode. Eternity of eternity immemorial.*

The equation translated "depth," Ayn-Waw-Mem-Qof
(70.6.40.100), is important as it shows that by 70, that is, the
activation of all possibilities, Mem causes the cosmic Aleph
(Qof:100) to arise. That means to say that the "depth" of
cosmic energy has its source in the element of indetermination
acting within the biological sphere.

I,6

מ׳ן עשר ספירות בלי מה צפייתן כמראה
הבזק ותכליתן אין להן קץ ודברו בהן
ברצוא ושוב ולמאמרו כסופה ירדופו ולפני
כסאו הם משתחוים:

*Ten Sephirot Beli-Mah their apparition (or, aspect) as light-
ning (or the vision of lightning) their aim has no end. Its
utterance with (or, in) them with its course and return and
when its word (is) like the tempest they descend (go underneath) in front of the throne and "they" carouse.*

The usual translations of this verse do not take into account the masculine (Im), "they," with which it ends. Perhaps it does not exist in other Hebraic versions. Up to now we have not found the translation of "to carouse" for *Mischthhavim* anywhere else, although *Mischteh* in Hebrew signifies banquet or feast. The words "they carouse" seem to have no meaning in this context.

However, we are aware that, further on, *The Sepher Yetsira* comments at great length on three "Mothers" and ends (Ch. VI.1) abruptly at "Three Fathers." Here we have a description of a cause and of a "return" of Sephirot glorified as lightning, which then "descends." As always, it is a question of the double energising movement coming simultaneously from "above" and "below": it concerns an endogenous energy that is both "female and male." Here, there does not seem to be a "fall" into calamity, but a "descent," a change of pole, and rejoicings.

I,7

מֶ"ן עשר ספירות בלי מה נעוץ סופן בתחלתן
ותחלתן בסופן כשלהבת קשורה בנחלת
שאדון יחיד ואין לו שני ולפני אחד מה
אתה סופר :

Ten Sephirot Beli-Mah. Their end is fixed (or, inserted) at the beginning, their beginning at their end, as the flames from glowing embers She-Adon Yahhid (unique) (which has) no second and in front (or, to) its face One, who are you? (or, what do you know?) (or, of what account are you?)

I,8

כֶּ"ח עשר ספירות בלימה בלום פיך מלדבר
ולבך מלהרהר ואם רץ לבך שוב
למקום שלכך נאמר והחיות רצוא ושוב.
ועל דבר זה נכרת ברית :

Ten Sephirot Belimah. Shut (or, restrain) your mouth and do not speak (or, enclose the word) and your heart and do not think (or, let your heart enclose its thought) and if your heart

*begins to run, return to the place where it is said: lives run
and come back, and on this word (the) covenant is made.*

This verse which concludes the general survey of the Sephirot, is explicit on its thought processes: "If your thought
runs in one direction," it says, "return in the opposite direction, for what is alive has two opposite dimensions: it is on
this that the covenant is based."

The Sephirot 1, 2, 3, 4

I,9   מ״ט עשר ספירות בלימה, אחת רוח אלהים
חיים ברוך ומבורך שמו של חי
העולמים קול ורוח ודבור וזהו רוח הקדש:

*Ten Sephirot Belimah. One: Rouahh Elohim Hhaim, blessed
and glorified his Name belonging to the life of worlds (space-
time). Qol (voice) Ve-Rouahh (breath) Ve-Dabor (word) and
it is Rouahh Haqadosch (the saint).*

I,10   מ״י שתים רוח מרוח חקק וחצב בה ישרים
ושתים אותיות יסוד שלש אמות ושבע כפולות
ושתים עשרה פשוטות ורוח אחת מהן:

*Two: Rouahh Merouahh, Hhaqaq Vehhatsav (legislates or
organises and chisels or cuts with). Twenty-two Autiot Yassod,
three fundamentals and seven doubles and twelve simples and
Rouahh One with (in) them.*

I,11   מי״א שלש מים מרוח הקק וחצב בהן תהו
ובהו רפש וטיט חקקן כמין ערונה
הציבן כמין חומה סככם כמין מעזיבה:

*Three: Maim Merouahh Hhaqaq Vehhatsav (legislates or
organises and chisels or cuts) with (in) them Tohou and Bohou*

(Genesis: I,ii: Erets was Tohou and Bohou. It is seen that The Sepher Yetsira radically contradicts the generally accepted translation, "formless and empty." In Refesch (mud) and Tith (clay), organised as a kind of flower-bed (garden), hewn as a kind of wall, covered as a kind of roof.

I,12

מי"ב ארבע אש מטים חקק וחצב בה כסא
הכבוד שרפים ואופנים וחיות הקודש
מלאכי השרת ומשלשתן יסד מעונו שנאמר
עושה מלאכיו רוחות משרתיו אש לוהט :

Four: Esch Memaim. Hhaqaq Vehhatsav (legislates, organises and chisels or cuts) the glorious throne (with) (the) Seraphim and (the) wheels and the Hhaivoth (holy lives) auxiliary messengers (angels), and with these three founded his dwelling as it is said: he made of his messengers the breaths (winds) and (the) blazing fire of his servants.

Here follow complete specifications of the first four Sephirot, including their names, which *The Sepher Yetsira* does not give, but which are derived from other sources, and their qualitative descriptions as stated in verse I,5.

The 1st Sephira
   Number: *Ehhath* (Aleph-Hhayt-Tav).
   Name: *Keter* (Khaf-Tav-Raysh).
   Quality: *Oomq Reschiyth.*
   Energy: *Rouahh Elohim Hhaim* (Breath of Elohim alive).
The 2nd Sephira
   Number: *Schtaim* (Sheen-Tav-Yod-Mem).
   Name: *Hhokmah* (Hhayt-Kaf-Mem-Hay).
   Quality: *Oomq Ahhriyth.*
   Energy: *Rouahh Merouahh* (Breath of Breath).
The 3rd Sephira
   Number: *Schelesch* (Sheen-Lammed-Sheen).
   Name: *Binah* (Bayt-Yod-Noun-Hay).

Quality: *Oomq Tov.*
Energy: *Maim Merouahh* (Waters of Breath).
The 4th Sephira
Number: *Arbaa* (Aleph-Raysh-Bayt-Ayn).
Name: *G'dolah* (Ghimel-Dallet-Waw-Lammed-Hay).
Quality: *Oomq Raa.*
Energy: *Esch Memaim* (Fire of Waters).

The First Four Sephirot (their complete specifications)

One	Its Number	אחת
	Its Name	כתר
	Its Quality	עומק ראשית
	Its Potential Function	רוחאלהיסחייס
Two	Its Number	שתים
	Its Name	חכמה
	Its Quality	עומק אחרית
	Its Potential Function	רוח מרוח
Three	Its Number	שלש
	Its Name	בינה
	Its Quality	עומק טוב
	Its Potential Function	מ'ס מרוח
Four	Its Number	ארבע
	Its Name	גדולה
	Its Quality	עומק רע
	Its Potential Function	אש ממיס

The energising process which passes through the Sephirot,
at one and the same time, determines and is determined by
them, as is expressed by: *Rouahh-Elohim-Hhaim, Rouahh-
Merouahh, Maim-Merouahh* and *Esch-Memaim.* This formative phenomenon being the subject of *The Sepher Yetsira,*
these equations must, before taking anything else into consideration, be decoded.

Rouahh Elohim Hhaim: (Raysh-Waw-Hhayt. Aleph-Lammed-Hay-Yod-Mem. Hhayt-Yod-Yod-Mem).

Rouahh Merouahh: (Raysh-Waw-Hhayt. Mem. Raysh-Waw-Hhayt).

Maim Merouahh: (Mem-Yod-Mem. Mem-Raysh-Waw-Hhayt).

Esch Memaim: (Aleph-Sheen. Mem-Mem-Yod-Mem).

These are their original signs:

The 1st Sephira has 12 signs   רוח אלהים חיים

The 2nd Sephira has 7 signs   רוח מרוח

The 3rd Sephira has 7 signs   מים מרוח

The 4th Sephira has 6 signs   אש ממים

Total: 32 signs

The number 32 for the structuration of energy, seen previously as 10 + 22, ten Sephirot added to twenty-two Autiot, is again met, in its entirety, in the first four Sephirot. These "form" the perfected man, *Adam Qadmon*, into whom the whole evolutionary process entered. Therefore the thirty-two signs in the first four Sephirot are the projection of the thirty-two within the combined ten.

Reading the words: Breath of Elohim, Breath of breath, Waters of breath, and Fire of Waters, it is difficult to see them as a description of the structuration of energy emanating from *Ayn Sof* and *Aur-Aelion*.

Without excluding other arguments and other possible combinations, let us ask ourselves if it is not rational to start

452

from *Aur-Aelion,* the source, infinite light, and to see how *Rouahh-Elohim-Hhaim* can constitute the first stage, the first device, by which light is rendered measurable and perceptible.

By a permutation of the letters of Rouahh-Elohim-Hhaim let us look at *Aur,* light, and see if a combination signifying a reduction of energy can be found. We discover that *Aur* and *Hhalah* (Hhayt-Lammed-Hay) are expressing it. Hebrew provides proof, as Hhalah means both a weakening and "sabbatical bread."

What a confirmation of the fact that the infinite, the intemporal, become "sacred food" in confining and diminishing themselves! Here again is one example, amid so many others, of discoveries which could construct semantics focussed on the main points.

Let us follow the combinations and see if a diagram can give us a result:

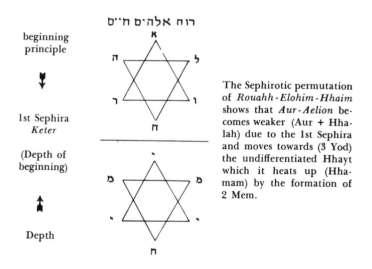

רוח אלהים חיים

beginning principle

1st Sephira
Keter

(Depth of beginning)

Depth

The Sephirotic permutation of *Rouahh - Elohim - Hhaim* shows that *Aur - Aelion* becomes weaker (Aur + Hhalah) due to the 1st Sephira and moves towards (3 Yod) the undifferentiated Hhayt which it heats up (Hhamam) by the formation of 2 Mem.

This diagram which has never, to my knowledge, been made public, does not give merely one result, but a great number of converging combinations. Vertically, Aleph and Hhayt are

moving in Yod and Hhayt. It can also be read: *Al We Hharah*
(*Al* and a blight), or *Aloahh,* an infection, etc. The lower tri-
angles contain *Hhai,* living, and *Maim,* the waters, but we
leave our readers the pleasure of studying and enlarging, on
all planes of existence, the countless effects from the confrontation of Aleph with Hhayt in Tav, cosmic resistance (its
number is *Ehhath* in this Sephira). Its name, *Keter* (20.400.
200), translated "crowns," in fact, summarises the capture of
the universe by one-and-indivisible-life.

As for *Oomq-Raschiyt,* which is the qualitative description
of this Sephira, we think it pointless to analyse the equation
Raschiyt, as it has been investigated in *Genesis.*[1] It is translated as "beginning," although Raysh-Aleph-Sheen-Yod-Tav
are anything but a word, and as untranslatable as all the other
equations. *Oomq* (Ayn-Waw-Mem-Qof: 70.6.40.100) is common to the ten Sephirot (see verse I,5). It shows that the 100,
or cosmic Aleph, rises from Mem (40) when the latter is fertilised by the 70 of all the possibilities which have been
affected.

The diagram which produces the 2nd Sephira is simple and
comes directly from the process released by the 1st. This is
how *Rouahh Merouahh* is actually arranged:

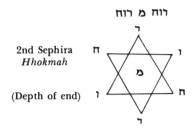

רוח מ רוח

2nd Sephira
Hhokmah

(Depth of end)

The Sephirotic permutation
of Rouahh Merouahh shows
that the 'descent' of Aur
came to its end, through the
coagulation of Mem. The
energy assumes two aspects:
the nucleus and the eddy
surrounding it.

Here we are seeing the consequences, on all levels of existence, of the shock which simultaneously joins and separates
the static and dynamic poles of energy. In the atom it forms

[1] *The Cipher of Genesis.*

454

the nucleus (illustrated here by Mem) and the eddy of the electrons which surround it: Rouahh-Rouahh. . . .

The congealing of the central nucleus is the formation of a centre of consciousness on the psychic plane. The name *Hhokmah* (8.20.40.5) is indicative of this. Consciousness, whose origin is lost in the background of undifferentiated substance, accumulates and leads to an affirmation of existence: that is to say, to a resistance aware of itself, coping with life.

The name *Hhokmah* indicates that this Sephira relates to mankind. There is no consciousness in the nucleus of the atom, even though the energising process is analogous to the formation of a conscious centre. The analogous thought which includes these two formations enables the rôle and the nature of the human psyche to be discerned. The qualitative description, *Oomq Ahhriyt,* translated as "depth of the end," ought not to refer to an end, in the true sense of this word. *Ahhriyt* can be a future, as well, or even a resting place.

Referring to what has already been said about the Autiot, they are generated by *Hhokmah,* as rays reflected by the centre, Mem returning to the source.

The 3rd Sephira shows how this phenomenon is produced. Its name is *Binah (Know with Hhokmah and apply the knowledge with Binah,* says the text of verse I,4).

מים מ רוח

3rd Sephira
Binah

(Depth of *Tov*)

The Sephirotic permutation of *Maim-Merouahh* shows that the substance of Mem is tripled and partially centrifugal: 2 Mem brought by Rouahh become Maim, yet only one nucleus re-forms.

This Sephira is the third: *Schlesch* (Sheen-Lammed-Sheen). The numbers of those Autiot, 300.30.300, express motion within a double cosmic movement, 300. The name of this

Sephira, *Binah,* intelligence, (Bayt-Yod-Noun-Hay: 2.10.50.5)
is a twofold life — a life in a state of existence (50) and an
archetypal life (5) — conferred on the being of Bayt. But the
qualitative description of this Sephira, *Oomq Tov* (depth of
Tov) shows that Adam Qadmon is not yet completed, for we
know that Tov (400.6.2) is a congealed structuration recurring
ad infinitum. This word is always translated "good," because
the psyche which is caught in its own structure considers that
its own "good" consists in settling down for ever.

The 4th Sephira is *Esch Memaim,* translated by such phrases
as "fire originating from water." Let us examine it:

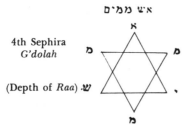

אׁש ממׁים

4th Sephira
G'dolah

(Depth of *Raa*)

The Sephirotic permutation of *Esch
Memaim* shows that Iysch, the archetype of the perfected human, is born
here. In fact, with the "Depth of *Raa*"
he becomes one of us (*Genesis* III,22),
says YHWH-Elohim: *Ki Ahhad Mim-
enou* through the consciousness of *Tov*
and *Raa.* Mem, its substance, is trinitarian, and the central nucleus has gone.
Cosmic unity is rediscovered.

It may be asked why the second name of this Sephira,
Hhessed (Mercy) is often preferred to *G'dolah* (Splendour),
which is a better term for the birth of *Adam Qadmon.*
(*Hhessed*: Hhayt-Sammekh-Dallet: 8.60.4 expresses a very
primitive life.)

As to the qualitative description of this Sephira, depth of
Raa (Raysh-Ayn 200.70), we know that from the time of the
famous tree in the Garden of Eden the schema 200.70, considered as evil, is the guardian of the spontaneous creation of
life, because it expresses the destruction of badly constructed,
or lapsed, or exhausted, organisations: the "dead" aspects of
"life."

The symbolic meaning of verses I,9; I,10; I,11; I,12 can now
be read.

VERSES 3 TO 12

Alternative Permutations for the first 4 Sephirot

First Sephira

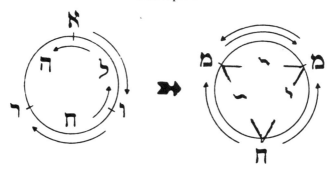

Second Sephira

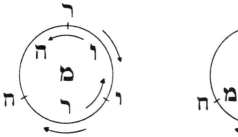

Third Sephira

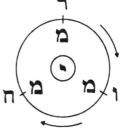

Fourth Sephira

Verse I,9 describes the projection of what, for lack of words, can be called infinity in number. In addition to the equations which we know, we meet *Qol* (Qof-Waw-Lammed: 100.6.30), translated as appeal, or voice, but which expresses the prolific scintillation of Cosmic Aleph, and *Dabor* (Dallet-Vayt-Waw-Raysh: 4.2.6.200) expressing the echo or the voice which reverberates from the solid substance struck by *Qol.*

Verse I,10 says that the 2nd Sephira beget the Autiot, as response (*Rouahh Merouahh*) to "breath."

Verse I,11 mentions Maim for the first time: Water as the "Prime Element" (in the alchemical sense) of formation. *Maim Merouahh* is a condensation of living energy. Next, referring to *Genesis,* the text takes *Tohou* and *Bohou* into account as substance without form. The element "water" cannot, in fact, take any form of its own. Consequently, in order to have a primary formation, mud (or ooze) arises. The equations used by the verse are *Refesh* (Raysh-Phay-Sheen: 200.80. 300), which is remarkable, 80 being the undifferentiated substance of life; and *Tit* (Tayt-Yod-Tayt), that is, 9.10.9, a twofold female energy in life. (*Tit* is always clay in alchemical symbolism.)

Thus, symbolic or inner space is formed. It is shown by three symbols: a "flower-bed" (or a lawn), symbol of the horizontal, a "wall," symbol of the vertical, and a "kind of roofing," a diagonal marking the third dimension of space.

Verse I,12 is the symbol of "Fire" in its two rôles: it hardens and stabilises the clay, and this completes the "formation" of an object, but it is also the blazing force, the "formative" element of *Kisse* (Kaf-Sammekh-Aleph) or celestial "throne" which "serves" the hierarchy of *Seraphims, Auphanims, Hhaivot Haqadosch* and assistant angels. The names of all these messengers and servants who are continually traversing the universe as blasts of wind and fire, are easy to decode and to "de-mythologize."

We are now at the end of the description of the first 4 Sephirot, which readers can study at leisure. It is advisable to note, in particular, that the first formation of three dimensional space occurs in the 3rd Sephira (Oomq Tov), from the rising of *Tohou We-Bohou.*

The 4th Sephira transposes and magnifies the notion of space into "the sacred dwelling of the Ineffable." Hence the intervention of legions of angels (Seraphims who burn, Aufanims who whirl around) and "holy lives." Their *Rohho* (spirit) is messenger and *Esch* (fire) is servant of *Rouahh-Elohim-Hhaim,* the first Sephira, of which the 4th (the whole man) is the projection.

The angels have a shadowy rôle in *Genesis.* When Jacob returns to the country of his birth after a life of hard labour in exile he is "accosted" or "attacked" by angels (*Genesis* XXXII,2). The verb used here, *Pagaa* (80.3.70) has two meanings: to meet, to attack. In fact, it refers to an inner experience on the deepest level of the unconscious (80) and gives it an organic life (3) leading towards its fulfillment, 70. The magnified space of the 4th Sephira is still within, and "the angels" are its craftsmen. In short, the first four Sephirot give birth to Interior Space in Human Consciousness.

7

The Sephirot 5-10

מי"ג חמש שלש אותיות מן הפשוטות חתם
רום ברר שלש וקבען בשמו הגדול
יה"ו . וחתם בהם שש קצוות ופנה למעלת
וחתמו ביה"ו . שש חתם תחת ופנה למטה
וחתמו ביו"ה . שבע חתם מזרח ופנה לפניו
וחתמו בהי"ו . שמנה חתם מערב ופנה לאחריו
וחתמו בהו"י . תשע חתם דרום ופנה לימינו
וחתמו בוי"ה . עשר חתם צפון ופנה לשמאלו
וחתמו בוה"י :

*Five: three Autiot among the simples. Sealed (the) height (or
apex). Three chosen. Solidified them with his great Name:
Yod-Hay-Waw. And sealed with six extremities. Turned
towards the upper, sealed it with Yod-Hay-Waw. Six: sealed
the lower, turned towards the underneath and sealed it with
Yod-Waw-Hay. Seven: sealed the East, turned towards his
(own) face and sealed it with Hay-Yod-Waw. Eight: sealed the
West, turned behind it and sealed it with Hay-Waw-Yod.
Nine: sealed the South and turned to his right and sealed it
with Waw-Yod-Hay. Ten: sealed the North, turned to his left
and sealed it with Waw-Hay-Yod.*

מי"ד אלו עשר כפירות בלימה אחת רוח
אלהים חיים ורוח מרוח ומים מרוח
ואש ממים ורום מעלה ותחת מזרח ומערב
וצפון ודרום :

סליק פרקא

These are the ten Sephirot Belimah (that are) *One: Rouahh Elohim Hhaim and Rouahh Merouahh and Maim Merouahh and Esch Memaim and Height glorified and low, East, West, North, South.*

(End of Chapter I)

Commentaries

In the preceeding chapter we have seen the first Sephira transforming light into graduated heat; the second begetting a central nucleus around which "the breath" whirls; the third splitting the nucleus into two parts, one of which, being centrifugal, combines with the whirlwind of *Rouahh*; the fourth projecting the Fire into the Waters and, by that operation eliminating the nucleus.

The last symbol finishes the "descending" cycle of living energy and its immersion in its opposite, "The Waters" which were but itself. The essential theme of the Qabala is again met here. We have seen that by a sephirotic permutation this "fire," *Esch* (entering Maim) produces *Iysch,* the archetype of the perfected human being.

The name of perfected *Adam* is *Adam Qadmon.* The root of the second word, *Qadam* (Qof-Dallet-Mem) is none other than *Adam* in which Aleph is replaced by Qof (100), the cosmic Aleph. In Hebrew this refers to what is anticipated, to what is coming, and also to the East (the direction of the rising sun). Seven is the number designating the uncertainties of life. Therefore in the 7th Sephira we see cosmic man looking towards the East, facing his own image as he projects it in the future.

When this psychological East is understood, we can follow the cabalistic "Spatial Cube"[1] introducing the human being in an inner space constituted by the first four Sephirot and in the outer space made of the six other Sephirot, every one of them pointing to one of the six directions of that space.

[1] See chart.

In short, the first four Sephirot give form to *Adam Qadmon* and his inner space. The other six form his outer space. He looks to the East, he is upright, his head touches the 5th Sephira, his feet are on the 6th, his gaze on the 7th, his back towards the 8th, the arms extended right and left, the right pointing towards the 9th (the South), the left towards the 10th (the North).

The six directions of space are "sealed." They are the six surfaces of a cube, as shown in the diagram.

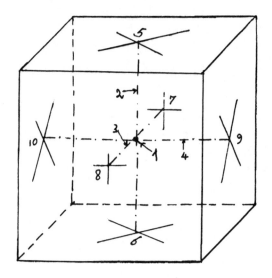

The text does not give the layout of the first four Sephirot. We place them thuswise: the first at the centre-point, the second on the vertical, the third on the West-East horizontal, the fourth on the South-North horizontal. Further on we shall see the twelve angles of intersection "grow, move apart and become the arms of the world," by the intervention of the twelve Autiot simples.

As a symbol this space cube corresponds to a psychological fact: we have our "noble" values, our gods are "on high in heaven": by contrast we have our "basic" values, sometimes grossly materialistic, sometimes diving underground into "hell." Most people anticipate their future by simply projecting their past (we will comment on that later on). Politically they are of the "right" or "left," and for two thousand years *Adam Qadmon,* the half human, half-divine symbol waits for permission to re-appear.

Thus everybody lives inside an enclosed and bounded cube locking inner space in a package.

But let us return to the Sephirot.

The 5th Sephira (on the top surface of the cube)
  Quality: *Oomq* (depth) *Rom* (Romah: height)
The 6th Sephira (on the ground surface)
  Quality: *Omq* (depth) *Tahhat* (below)
The 7th Sephira
  Quality: *Omq* (depth) *Mizrahh* (East)
The 8th Sephira
  Quality: *Omq* (depth) *Maarav* (West)
The 9th Sephira
  Quality: *Omq* (depth) *Tsafon* (North)
The 10th Sephira
  Quality: *Omq* (depth) *Darom* (South)

The last four Sephirot must be examined with regard to the position of Adam Qadmon face to face with himself, as well as this "himself" who is the observer.

Remember that in verse I,5 the last two Sephirot are named in this order: Depth of the North and Depth of the South. This means that the 9th is in the North and the 10th is in the South. At verse I,13, the 9th is in the South and the 10th in the North. In the summary in the following verse (I,14 which ends the chapter) the North is again mentioned before the South. It has been alleged that this is a scribe's mistake. We do not think that it is. We think that for Adam Qadmon the 9th is indeed the South and 10th the North, and that the transposition of verses I,5 and I,14 relate to the way in which the image of Adam Qadmon is supposed to see them when face to face with himself. The student, who is not yet a complete man (although made in his image), turns his back to the East and looks to the West, towards the past, projecting on it what he imagines to be his future. Indeed, everyone who is not yet Adam Qadmon has his compass the wrong way round. It is him of which verse I,5 is a study, and whose lesson is recapitulated in verse I,14, but in verse I,13 Adam Qadmon is alive.

Looking towards the West the unperfected man, in his imagination, sees Adam Qadmon, across the distance separating him from his maturity, lit by the reflection of the sun, which he faces. For his part, Adam Qadmon sees the future in the East, actually lit by the sun, and the past, Westwards, behind his back.

Give your attention to the connection between the following:

Mizrah	40.7.200.8	East	(7th Sephira)
Maarav	40.70.200.2	West	(8th Sephira)

In the East (the future) 7 is an archetype, in the West (the past) 70 is a reality. The East acts on 8, the undifferentiated, the West on 2, the house.

Yamin (the right): Yod-Mem-Yod-Noun, with its two existential Yod, is the side where action takes place in the physical world. It receives the 9th Sephira, *Yassod*, signifying, as we have seen, the foundations which support the Autiot.

Schmol (the left), Sheen-Mem-Aleph-Lammed, is none other than *Schem-El*, the name of Elohim. It is directed towards the last Sephira which is numbered Yod, existence, and is called *Melkot*, the realm of infinite power infinitely magnified, endowed with the name of the first Sephira, *Keter*, crown.

Thus, by *Schem-El*, integrated man loops the circumference of the Sephirot, uniting the end to the beginning and the beginning to the end. (In this language *Schem-El* becomes Semol, left, by a substitution of Sheen in Seen.)

Verse I,13 describes the "sealing" of the Cube in a most precise, subtle and illuminating way, with three "chosen" Autiot: Yod, Hay, Waw. They are, of course, the three that, with Hay repeated, compose YHWH. We must consider here that Yod stands for "existence," Hay for "life" and Waw for any connecting agent that we can think of. Therefore, those three Autiot summarize the fundamental problem of existence alive, or life in existence, or of an active agent engendering both life and existence. The extraordinary "sealing" of the Cube is meant to illustrate the fact that all three coexist simultaneously without any order of precedence, but that we can "think" them in different orders according to different points of view.

The first seal covers generally the 6 "extremities" with Yod,Hay,Waw, and rests again on the 5th Sephira, which, thus, is sealed twice with the same seal. This is important, because that 5th acts as a hinge, or joint, between the four inner Sephirot, inside the cube, and the six outer. We can meditate indefinitely on the significance of those two seals by Yod,Hay, Waw.

The student will now follow attentively the change of relative positions of the three chosen letters, as they "seal" the five remaining Sephirot according to their locations on the faces of the Cube, and to their different meanings, as I have outlined them.

They are sealed thus:

                    the 6th with Yod.Waw.Hay
                    the 7th with Hay.Yod.Waw
                    the 8th with Hay.Waw.Yod
                    the 9th with Waw.Yod.Hay
                    the 10th with Waw.Hay.Yod

It is up to the student to go deeply into this shuffling until it becomes obvious.

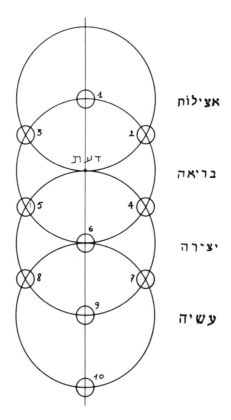

The Tree of Life

The Sepher Yetsira does not give the traditional names of
the *Sephirot,* nor does it mention The Tree of Life (or Sephirotic Tree). That Tree has been the subject of much speculation and given rise to a vast literature, generally theological,
which, compared with *The Sepher Yetsira's* views, is most unsatisfactory.

However, it could be suggested that the decoding of The
Tree reveals certain perspectives. It illustrates a scale of Energy derived from Ayn-Sof, an equation which I have, to a
certain extent, explained, and its reading can begin there. It
is clear that the four Sephirot which are located vertically on

466

a line that can be considered as the trunk (or the spine) of The Tree are none other than the opening of the equation *YHWH*: Keter (1), Tipheret (6), Yesod (9) and Malkout (10) are $1+6+9+10=26$, Yahweh's number. They show how number 1, Aleph, connects or fertilises through number 6, Waw, the cell, Tayt (9) and gives it existence 10, Yod.

The vertical line drawn by the traditional location of the four Sephirot crosses all spheres of the Tree: Keter (1) on top is the world of *Atsilot* (Emanation); Tipheret (6) is in the next world, just below *Bria* (Creation); Yesod (9) in the next, the *Yetsira* (Formation); and lastly Malkout (10) is in the world of *Aassa* (Action).

I would advise the student to be very cautious when giving a meaning to the ten Sephirot described as being: (1) a crown, (2) wisdom, (3) intelligence, (4) clemency, (5) rigour, (6) beauty, (7) triumph, (8) glory, (9) foundation, (10) sovereignty.

Note on Genesis II,7 and II,19

Adam is *Itser* (formed) of Aafar (70.80.200) "dust" of *Adamah*, though the *animals are formed from Adamah*.

The word "dust" evokes something quite different from its meaning here. The 70 of all possible possibilities, allied to the 80 of undifferentiated substance able to be worked, opens to Adam infinite possibilities unavailable to the animals. "You are only dust" is a complete mistranslation. The *Nischmet-Hhaim* which receives Adam—who becomes *Nefesch Hhaya*—proves this overwhelmingly.

Note on Menora (light)

There is no difficulty in connecting the cube of space, as we have drawn it showing the constituent parts of the Sephirot, with the schematic tree of life. But one cannot help thinking that the two representations are like the well-known symbol of the candlestick with seven branches, as described in the Bible.

(Keeping in mind the description of the lines of the cube, "They expand, they diverge throughout Eternity and are the world's arms" (S.Y.V.I.), and associating the candle's light with it, we propose to call the cube *Ayn Soph Aur*.)

As it is said in Exodus XI, 24.5, the light was put in the meeting tent: *He put the light in the meeting tent, opposite the table, on the southern side of the tabernacle, and lit the lamps in front of YHWH, as he had been ordered.*

This lamp (see Exodus XXV, 31-40 and XXXVII, 17-24) was *of pure gold and made in one piece* (on the subject of the Sephirot see *Sepher Yetsira* I,7: *their end is in their beginning and their beginning in their end*). It had six branches, three on one side and three on the other, like the six faces of the cube, High-Low, East-West, North-South, in opposite pairs. On each branch were three chalices, corresponding to the different positions of the three letters Yod-Hay-Waw (Sepher Yetsira I,13). The stem, or support, corresponding to the three interior axes of the cube, *with its four chalices, its buds and flowers conveyed knowledge*: there was a bud at the beginning of each pair of branches. It is repeated that *it was fashioned in one single piece of gold*.

It is advisable to note that there was no chalice on the stem of the light. It corresponds to the point designating the centre of the cube, and therefore cannot be drawn, being in the position of the 1st Sephira, *Rouahh Elohim Hhaim.*

There were seven lamps: six corresponding to the six faces of the cube and the 7th corresponding to the 4th Sephira, *Esch Memaim,* or, as the inner light, to the 1st.

The light, or *Menora,* has been carried out by Betsalel, son of Auri (my light), son of Hhaur.

For all these reasons the cube can be called "The Cube of *Ayn Soph Aur,*" or "The Luminous Cube," or "The Cube which illuminates."

8

The Three Mothers

CHAPTERS II and III of *The Sepher Yetsira* are about the twenty-two Autiot and especially about Aleph-Mem-Sheen, called "The Three Mothers." They investigate the different aspects which co-ordinate and complete the whole, in the 6+8 verses forming these chapters.

II,1

פ"ב מ"א עשרים ושתים אותיות יסוד
שלש אמות שבע כפולות
ושתים עשרה פשוטות . שלש אמות אמ"ש
יסודן כף זכות וכף חובה ולשון חק מכריע
בינתים :

Twenty-two Autiot Yassod. Three Amot (Mothers) seven doubles and twelve simples. Three Mothers: Aleph-Mem-Sheen. Yassodan (based on) Kaf Zakot-We-Kaf Hhovah. And Lischon, the tongue Hhaq Mekaryi between the two.

Literally, these three Mothers are founded on a rock (cave or vault), hollow of acquittal (of merit, privilege or credit), *Kaf Zakot,* and on another duty (guilt or sale) *Kaf Hhovah,* and the tongue *Lischon* limits them "kneeling" between the two, *Hhaq Mekayi. (Karyi:* 20.200.10.70: an existence between the definite and the indefinite.)

In simple language (for we shall see these letters again later on) the Three Mothers represent: 1. Aleph, the greatest energy; 2. Mem (Water), minimum energy; 3. Sheen, the action of Aleph on Mem. The seven doubles are pointed or nonpointed, such as Bayt and Vayt. They represent elements which, according to circumstances, reflect Energy, or let it go by. We shall see them forming the 7 planets and the twelve simples forming the twelve signs of the Zodiac.

The foundation of the Three Mothers on "a hollow rock" symbolises all physical support. In fact, we know that the most solid body, seen atomically, is apparently empty.

These "solids" which contain only "hollows" express two united and contradictory states of energy: symbolically, credit (full), debit (empty); or worth (full) and guilt (empty). (This is applicable, in general, to mankind who appears so positive yet is so empty inside.)

This is expressed by *Zakot* and *Hhovah*:

Zakot	(full)	Zayn-Kaf-Waw-Tav:	7.20.6.400
Hhovah	(empty)	Hhayt-Waw-Bayt-Hay	8. 6.2. 5

One is part of the undetermined 7, and the other is part of the undifferentiated 8.

The tongue fixes their limits (or rules) between the two extremes. The word for tongue, *Lischon*, (30.300.6.700) is remarkable for its movement, fertility and intelligence.

The word *Hhaq* (Hhayt-Qof: 8.100) expressing this fixing is repeated in the subsequent verses, where it will be analysed.

II,2   מ"ב עשרים ושתים אותיות חקקן הצבן
שקלן והמירן צרפן וצר בהם נפש כל
כל היצור ונפש כל העתיד לצור:

Twenty-two Autiot Hhaqaqan (graven) *Hhatsavan* (carved) *Schaqalan* (weighed) *and Hamiran* (inverted) *Tsarafan* (amalgamated) *and formed with Nefesch* (character, personality) *of all* (that is) *formed, and Nefesch of all* (that is) *to be formed in the future.*

There is nothing there that we do not know already, but there is some advantage in numbering the equations which define the transformations of the Autiot, and in observing that they all end in 700, cosmic indetermination.

THE THREE MOTHERS

1) Hhaqaqan   8.100.100.700
2) Hhatsavan   8. 90. 2.700
3) Schaqalan   300.100. 30.700
4) Hamiran   5. 40. 10.200.700
5) Tsarafan   90.200. 80.700

This sequence expresses one single structural process:

1: double intervention of the cosmic Aleph (100) in the un-differentiated 8
2: advent of the structurising Tsadde (90)
3: advent by the 30 of organic motion in all spheres
4: manifestation by 5 of life in the biosphere
5: the structurising energy of Tsadde (90) taking charge of the process

II,3   מ"ג עשרים ושתים אותיות יסוד חקוקות
בקול חצובות ברוח קבועות בפה
בחמשה מקומות אחה"ע בומ"ף ניכ"ק
דטלנ"ת זסשר"ץ :

This verse classifies the Autiot phonetically.

4 gutturals	Aleph, Hhayt, Hay, Ayn
4 labials	Bayt, Waw, Mem, Phay
4 palatals	Ghimel, Yod, Kaf, Qof
5 linguals	Dallet, Tayt, Lammed, Noun, Tav
5 dentals	Zayn, Sammekh, Sheen, Raysh, Tsadde

22

II,4   מ"ד עשרים ושתים אותיות יסוד קבועות
בגלגל ברל"א שערים וחוזר הגלגל פנים
ואחור וזהו סימן לדבר אין בטובה למעלה
מענג ואין ברעה למטה מנגע :

471

Twenty-two Autiot Yassod fastened Belgalgal (to a turning wheel) *by two hundred and thirty-one Schaarim* (portals, values or measures) *and the wheel turns forwards and backwards. It is a token of the language. Nothing in Tov is superior to Aanag* (pleasure or coitus) *and nothing in Raa is inferior to Nagaa* (plague or leprosy).

A wheel which causes the Autiot to revolve two hundred and thirty-one times in two directions turns it $2 \times 231 = 462$ times. This is the number derived from combining each of the 22 with the 21 others. The text adds that the key to this language is "The front and the back." For example, the combination Aleph-Bayt leads towards structuration; the combination Bayt-Aleph goes in the opposite direction. This key must always be used when interpreting the words as equations.

The to-ing and fro-ing of the Autiot passes from one pole of energy to the other, keeping the balance. One of the poles is Aanaq: 70.50.3. It is the trajectory from the indeterminate that is going to animate the archetype of organic movement. The other is *Nagaa*: it leaves the existence of organisms in order to reach indetermination: 50.3.70.

Here they are facing one another:

Aanag: 70.50. 3
Nagaa: 30. 3.70

This dual current is constructive and no "Tov" (good) is superior to it: it is destructive and no "Raa" (evil) is inferior to it. What is interpreted as Good and Evil are two sides of the one vital energy in motion, and that motion is apparent in the language of the Autiot.

II,5   מ"ה כיצד שקלן והמירן אל"ף עם כלם וכלם
עם אל"ף , בי"ת עם כלם וכלם עם בי"ת
וחוזרת חלילה נמצא כל היצור וכל הדבור
יוצא בשם אחד :

472

(This is) *how Aleph* (is) *weighed, combined with everything and everything with Aleph. Bayt with everything and everything with Bayt. They return in a circular movement* (turn by turn) *to where all that is formed and uttered is found coming out of the One Name.*

Intemporal life and physical support in everything existing and in everything coming into being, including the word. Whirlwinds of energy born of One.

II,6

מ"ן יצר מתהו ממש ועשה אינו ישנו וחצב
עמודים גדולים מאויר שאינו נתפש וזה
סימן צופה וממיר עושה כל היצור ואת כל
הדברים שם אחד וסימן לדבר עשרים ושתים
(מניינים) [חפצים] בגוף אחד :
סליק פרקא

Yatsar (formed) *with Tohou Mamasch* (material reality) *and Aassa* (made from) *its Ayn* (Aleph-Yod-Noun, general equation of the universe) *Yaschnou* (its slumber) *and hewed* (or chiselled) *great pillars* (or pages of a book) *with the air* (or atmosphere) *for its Ayn to seize* (plural) *and that is the proof* (or sign) *of the watcher (Tsofah). With what is being projected is made everything that is formed* (just as) *the words* (everything is) *One Name and the proof of the saying: twenty-two elements in a single body.*

This last verse of the second chapter concerns emanation, one of the principle themes of the Qabala and of the Hebraic tradition in general, in virtue of which monotheism, although it is a deviation, never fell into pantheism.

The key words in this verse are, in the first place, *Ayn*, the whole, officially translated as nothingness (just as we have seen above), and *Yaschnou* (from *Yoschan*: old age, antiquity, or, rather, from *Yaschen*, to sleep, more suitable to this context, we think). We are thus a long way from the recognised translations, according to which "he" made "nothing from something." The text does not require personal first names, and for grammatical reasons we have avoided introducing them. This sleep is not Brahma's mythical sleep. It is the stasis state of energy living in inorganic matter.

(End of Chapter II)

III,1   פ"ג מ"א שלש אמות אמ"ש יסודן כף
חובה וכף זכות ולשון חק
מכריע בינתים :

Three Mothers: Aleph Mem Sheen. Yassodan, Kaf Hhovah and Kaf Zakot and the tongue kneeling between the two.
Repetition of verse II,1, except that Hhovah and Zakot are named in reverse order.

III,2   מ"ב שלש אמות אמש סוד גדול מופלא
וטכוסה והתום בשש טבעות וממנו
יוצאים אש ומים מתחלקים זכר ונקבה
שלש אמות אמ"ש יסודן ומהן נולדו אבות
שמהם נברא הכל :

Three Mothers: Aleph Mem Sheen Sod Gadol, Mev Phaylay Vemakossa sealed by six seals (or hall marks) and from them are derived Fire, Waters divided (into) male and female. Three Mothers: Aleph Mem Sheen. Yassodan and from them the Fathers, the creators of everything, are born.

The words Sod Gadol derived from *Yassod* (base or foundation), less the Yod indicating existence, here mean "great secret." The following *Mev* (with, but, however), rests on this "great secret" in introducing *Phaylay*, "marvel." This equation is none other than the complete Aleph, written backwards, a characteristic of a subtle language which becomes clear only within. If, like all the other Autiot, the preceding verse qualified Aleph-Mem-Sheen by Yassodan, it transposed *Hhovah* and *Zakot*, the hollow and the solid, in order to place the "Three Mothers" inside the manifestations they engender. Here they are secret, pre-existing *Sod*. And the "marvel" is Phay-

474

Lammed-Aleph (80.30.1), by which the reverse Aleph, emanated by undifferentiated Phay, accomplishes its own birth.

The meaning of the following text is uncertain. *Vemakossa* can mean "is covered." Numbered 6.40.20.6.60.5 it shows centrifugal energy (6) going deeply into 40 and 20 and emerging twice as strong: 6 and 60 and 5 alive. In the continuation of the verse this energy becomes, in fact, male and female: *are sealed* by (the) six spaces of the six Sephirot, (sealed as has been seen) *and from these seals* (or stamps) *comes forth Esch* (fire) and *Maim* (waters) *divided into male and female.*

The verse ends with the Three Mothers, *Yassodan* (here we are back into the sphere of appearances) *engendering the Fathers from whom everything is created* (or, their names from which everything is created).

III,3   מ"ג שלש אמות אמ"ש בעולם אויר מים אש
שמים נבראו תחלה מאש וארץ נבראת
מטים והאויר מכריע בין האש ובין המים:

Three Mothers, Aleph, Mem, Sheen. In the universe: Avir Maim Esch (air, water, fire). *Schamaim are created first by Esch* (fire) *and Eretz* (earth) *created Memaim* (by the waters) *and Ha-Avir* (air) *kneeled down* (sloped) *between Ha-Esch* (fire) *and Ha-Maim* (waters).

Avir	Aleph-Waw-Yod-Raysh: 1.6.10.200
Maim	Mem-Yod-Mem: 40.10.40
Esch	Aleph-Sheen: 1.300
Schamaim	Mem-Yod-Mem: 300.40.10.40
Eretz	Aleph-Raysh-Tsadde: 1.200.90

Schamaim traditionally translated as *Heaven*, is the action of Sheen on *Maim*. *Esch* (fire) is the action of Aleph-Sheen. Aleph buries itself in *Eretz*. *Maim* has Yod between two Mem. *Avir*, having Aleph and Yod, is "inclined" towards both *Esch* and *Maim*.

475

It is interesting to notice that the Three Mothers form, symbolically, three Elements. The Earth is not taken to be an Element.

III,4

מ"ד שלש אמות אמ"ש בשנה אש ומים
ורוח חום נברא מאש קור ממים
ורויה מרוח מכריע בינתים . שלש אמות
אמ"ש בנפש אש ומים ורוח ראש נברא מאש
ובטן נברא ממים וגויה נברא מרוח מכריע
בינתים :

Three Mothers: Aleph Mem Sheen. Be-Schinah (in trans-formation): Esch and Maim and Rouahh. The word *Schinah* or *Schanah* (Sheen-Noun-Hay) signifies transformation or change. In current language it means "year," doubtless as a measure of duration, since time is measured by change. Next we read *Hhom* (Hhayt-Waw-Mem, translated as "heat," al-though heat is *Hham:* Hhayt-Mem without Waw) *is created by Esch; Qor:* Qof-Waw-Raysh (translated "cold") *by Maim and Rvaia* (Raysh-Waw-Yod-Hay), translated "surfeit," *by Rouahh "knelt down" between the two. Three Mothers: Aleph-Mem-Sheen. In Nefesch* (Noun-Phay-Sheen in Hebrew is breath, spirit or the individual: here it is understood by the last meaning). *Esch and Maim and Rouahh. Rosch* Raysh-Aleph-Sheen: the head created by Esch, and *Batn* (Bayt, Tayt, Noun) the abdomen *by Maim and Gvyia* (Ghimel-Waw-Yod-Hay, torso) *by Rouahh "kneeled down" between the two.*

Read in everyday Hebrew, and all the more so in transla-tion, this verse is superficial. But the cabalist's attention is drawn to the Waw of *Hhom,* which should not be there if it only concerns *Hham,* heat. Is it not a question of the trans-formation of the Autiot? And must the sky and the earth be explored in order to state that fire engenders heat? (In verse VI.1 we shall comment on the concrete reality of fire-heat, water-cold and the air.)

The Three Mothers, Aleph, Mem, Sheen summarise the

whole process of energy. They beget themselves mutually, project themselves into existence and, first and foremost, into the human individual. This is the central concern of *The Sepher Yetsira,* which considers man as the focal point of all cosmic energies. Aleph, Mem, Sheen express simultaneously the essence, appearance and movement of everything. It is important to see these at work in the totality of everything that it is possible to mean. For the authors of *The Sepher Yetsira* the most important thing is to show how the two poles of energy (essence-appearance, spirit-matter, etc., etc.) are One. As follows:

Fire, *Esch,* 1.300, transforms itself into *Hhom,* 8.6.40; water. *Maim,* 40.10.40, transforms itself into *Qor,* 100.6.200.

Esch, beyond our conception, becomes substance 8, undifferentiated, fertilising (6) the Mem (40), and *Maim* becomes cosmic Aleph, 100, fertilising (6) the cosmic 200 (Raysh, as we have seen, engenders Sheen). In short, Aleph becomes Mem and two Mem become cosmic Aleph. We are here in the whirling round of the Autiot which we come to feel in our minds and even in our bodies. By Raysh-Aleph-Sheen, Aleph-Sheen enters the head (*Rosch*), *Maim* enters "the dwelling house," Bayt-Tayt-Noun (2.9.50), of the abdomen, and *Rouahh,* the breath, unites the two through *Gvyia* the torso, whose components are an eye-opener: Ghimel and Waw-Yod-Hay, the three Autiot of *YHWH* brought by Ghimel, 3, archetype of organic motion (in the order in which they seal the 9th Sephira). This verse opens up endless opportunities for contemplation.

III,5   מ"ה שלש אמות אמ"ש חקקן וחצבן וצרפן
וחתם בהן שלש אמות בעולם ושלש
אמות בשנה ושלש אמות בנפש זכר ונקבה:

Three Mothers. Aleph Mem Sheen; Hhaqaqan Ve-Hhatsavan-Ve-Tsarafan (graven, chiselled, cast; see II,2) and sealed with: Three Mothers Be-Oolam (in the universe) and

Three Mothers Be-Schana (in time or change) *and Three Mothers Be-Nefesch* (the individual) *male and female.*

III,6

מ"ז המליך אות אל"ף ברוח וקשר לו כתר
וצרפן זה עם זה וחתם בהן אויר
בעולם ורויה בשנה וגויה בנפש זכר באמ"ש
ונקבה באש"ם :

Hamalikh (conferred kingship) *on* (the) *Aut Aleph by Rouahh and fastened a crown to it and Tsarafan* (combined) *Zeh Maa Zeh* (this with that), *and sealed with it: Avir in the universe and Rvaia in Schana and Gvyia in Nefesch* masculine with *Aleph Mem Sheen* and feminine with *Aleph Sheen Mem.*

All these words have already been read and explained. Gvyia which synthesises the existence and life of humanity on all levels, is formed of an energy which begins from Aleph, passes through Mem and ends at Sheen in man; begins with Aleph passes through Sheen and ends at Mem in woman.

III,7

מ"ז המליך אות מ"ם בטים וקשר לו כתר
וצרפן זה עם זה וחתם בהן ארץ בעולם
וקור בשנה ובטן בנפש זכר ונקבה במא"ש
ונקבה במש"א :

Hamalikh (conferred kingship) *on* (the) *Aut Mem by Maim and fastened a crown and Tsarafan* (combined) *Zeh Maa Zeh* (this with that) *and sealed with it: Eretz in the universe and Qor in Schana and the abdomen in Nefesch* masculine and feminine, with *Mem Sheen Aleph.*

The words Qor in *Schana* are always translated "the cold of the year," which is hardly satisfactory. *Qor*: Qof-Waw-Raysh must be related to Aur: Aleph-Waw-Raysh. It becomes visible as a light magnified by the Qof (100) which is instead of the Aleph of *Aur* (light). We have said that *Schinah,* or Schanah, indicating the transformation of things, defines passing time.

Cosmic light, *Qor,* is here jointly sealed with Maim, altering appearances.

III,8   מ״ח המליך אות שי״ן באש וקשר לו כתר
וצרפן זה עם זה וחתם בהן שמים בעולם
וחום בשנה וראש בנפש זכר ונקבה :
סליק פרקא

Hamalikh (conferred kingship) on (the) Aut Sheen by Esch and fastened a crown to it and Tsarafan (combined) Zeh Maa Zeh (this with that) and sealed with it: Schamaim in the universe and Hhom in Schinah and Rosch (the head) in Nefesch masculine and feminine.

Commentators have seen the summer in Hhom and the year in Schinah. We are referring to the comment on verse III.4: Hhom is the transformation of *Esch,* just as *Qor* is of *Maim.*

(End of Chapter III)

479

9

Seven Doubles and Twelve Simples

The Seven Doubles

IV,1

פ״ד מ״א שבע כפולות בג״ד כפר״ת
(מתנהגות בשתי לשונות), יסודן
חיים ושלום וחכמה ועושר חן וזרע וממשלה,
ומתנהגות בשתי לשונות ב״ב נ״ג ד״ד כ״ב
פ״פ ר״ד ת״ת תבנית רך וקשה תבנית גבור
וחלש כפולות שהן תמורות . תמורת חיים
מות תמורת שלום רע תמורת חכמה אולת
תמורת עושר עוני תמורת חן כיעור תמורת
זרע שממה תמורת ממשלה עבדות :

SEVEN DOUBLES: Vayt, Djimel and Thalet,[1] Khaf, Phay, Raysh
and Tav[2] (offer two pronunciations) *founded on: Hhaim and
Schalom, Hhokmah and Oosser, Hhan and Zare and Mem-
schelah and offering two pronunciations: Vayt-Bayt, Djimel-
Ghimel, Thalet-Dallet, Khaf-Kaf, Phay-Pay, Raysh-Rhaysh,
Thav-Tav and are constructed in Raa and Qascha* (softened
and hardened) *constructed in powerfulness or weakness. They
exchange their dwellings by substitution. Contrary: Hhaim-
Mot, contrary Schalom-Raa, contrary Hhokmah-Olet, contrary
O'sser-O'ni, contrary Hhan-Kior, contrary Zar'-Schemama,
contrary Memschela- Aabadot.*

We will examine these contraries concerning the dwelling
places in twelve Zodiacal signs of the seven Planets, where the

---

1 Pronounced as the soft English Th: *the; thus,* etc.
2 Pronounced as the hard English Th: *thunder, thought,* etc.

Seven Doubles appear either barren, or hardened (taking the place of nocturnal and diurnal aspects in traditional astrology). We will give their names, their opposite qualities and their houses in the Zodiac, in Hebrew signs, so as to understand their meaning. In this present chapter we will not translate the words transcribed from the Hebrew. To bring out their meaning, would require involved comments which would obscure the text rather than clarify it. Nevertheless, we consider that reading these words, as given here, will help readers to become aware of them and recognise them when they appear in the Zodiac.

IV,2

מ״ב שבע כפולות בנ״ד כפר״ת שבע ולא
שש שבע ולא שמונה בחון בהן וחקור
מהן (וצור וחשוב) והעמד דבר על בוריו
והשב יוצר על מכונו:

Seven Doubles: Vayt-Djimel-Thalet (and) *Khaf, Phay, Raysh, Thav. Seven and not six. Seven and not eight. Behhon Behen We Hhagor Mehen: (a tower or strong structure with them and an investigation (important) into that structure, and arise the word reverse* (or close to) *its creator, and restore* (the) *form-maker to its place* (or in its function).

To go thoroughly into the essential being through the strength of appearances. To maintain the integrity of the word. To perceive the method of formations (or structurations). But above all to understand the meaning of number 7 and why the seven are doubles.

IV,3

מ״ג שבע כפולות בנ״ד כפר״ת כנגד ז'
קצוות מהם ו' קצוות מעלה ומטה מזרח
ומערב צפון ודרום והיכל הקדש מכון באמצע
והוא נושא את כולן.

Seven Doubles: Vayt, Djimel, Thalet (and) *Khaf, Phay, Raysh, Thav as in the presence of Seven extremities, six of*

*which — height, depth, East, West, North and South — and the
holy sanctuary* (which) *directs them from the middle* (or kernel) *and it is the Aleph-Tav theme of everything.*

Aleph-Tav, union of the beginning and the end: central
theme, as seventh invisible direction of the intemporal, holy,
sanctuary.

IV,4

מ״ד שבע כפולות בנ״ד כפר״ת חקקן חצבן
צרפן וצר בהם כוכבים בעולם וימים
בשנה ושערים בנפש ומהן חקק שבעה
רקיעים ושבע אדמות ושבע שבתות לפיכך
חבב שביעי תחת כל השמים :

Seven Doubles: Vayt, Djimel, Thalet (and) *Khaf, Phay,
Raysh, Thav, Hhaqaqan Hhatsavah Tsarafan* (see these words
in II,2) *Vetsar* (formed) *with Kawkabim* (plural of Kawkab:
Kaf-Waw-Kaf-Bayt, which will be seen, further on, is the name
of Mercury, "messenger of the gods," here indicates, in plural,
the seven astrological planets combined, in their capacity of
inverted emanations of the YHWH principle). Resuming:
Kawabim Be-Olam (in the universe) *Ve Yamon Beschinah:*
the seven aspects of transformation which gave rise to the
myth of the seven days of creation. *Yamom* is the plural of
Yom, and Yom is the transformation of *Aur* (light)[1] in the
sphere of appearances:

Yod-Waw-Mem: "day"
Aleph-Waw-Raysh: "light"

Veschierim Benefesch (the tempests in the breath, or, by
analogy, the individual's speculations and imagination) *and
from them carved* (or enacted) *seven spaces and seven Adamot*
(this word plural of Adamah, expresses the hiding of Aleph in
the resistance Dallet-Mem-Tav) *and seven Schabatot* (this

1 *The Cipher of Genesis.*

plural of Schabath — the Sabbath — expresses the organic action of Sheen on the physical formations Bayt, Tav) *and consequently loved Schabyi under all the Schamaim.*

Schabyi (seventh) is what Elohim sanctifies and blesses in *Genesis* II,2 and 3. *Schamaim,* traditionally "heaven," is the action of Sheen on *Maim,* the waters.

In the seven following verses of this IVth chapter each of the Doubles acquires "kingship" and forms one of the seven astrological planets, one of the seven "days" of *Schinah* and one of the orifices of the face (two eyes, two ears, two nostrils and the mouth).

In the next chapter we will see the Twelve Simples acquiring their "kingship" over the twelve signs of the Zodiac, the twelve months of the Hebraic year and different parts of the human body. Each of the signs of the Zodiac will appear at the extremity of the trajectory of one of the ridges of the cube of space when, upon the rupture of the cube, its ridges extend so far as to become "the arms of the world." The Vth chapter of *The Sepher Yetsira* is given to this nomenclature. The VIth and last chapter is a brief general recapitulation of the whole of the text.

By means of analogical equations the last chapters sum up the unifying formation of space, time, and the human body. To obtain an idea of it, all the equations must be solved, and the literal meaning given to them in Hebrew must be abandoned. For example, it is useless to know that *Ein Yamin* means "right eye," but it does matter that we understand the combined 70.10.700.10.40.10.700 that these two united equations constitute. They can then be put in the presence of the letter Bayt (2.10.400) which, according to the text, "forms" the right eye, and also *Shabatai* (Saturn). Careful study of the meaning given by the Qabala to the Hebrew characters will help readers to solve the import of the analogical connections put forward by this text, until such time as scientific research

discovers by experiment the relations between such and such
Planets and parts of the human body, etc.

IV,5 מ"ה כיצד המליך אות ב' בחיים וקשר לו
כתר וצר בו שבתי בעולם ויום ראשון
בשנה ועין ימין בנפש :

(This is) *in what manner was bestowed* (the) *kingship on
Aut* (Bayt) *in* (by) *Hhaim* (the living) *and bound* (a) *crown on
it and created with Schabatai* (Saturn) *in the universe and Yom
Rischon* (the day of principle) *Beschinah* (in the transformation) *and Ein Yamin* (right eye) *Benefesch* (in the individual).

IV,6 מ"ו המליך אות ג' וקשר לו כתר וצר בו
צדק בעולם יום שני בשנה ועין שמאל
בנפש :

Bestowed (the) *kingship on Aut Djimel and bound* (a)
crown to it and created with it Tsedeq (Jupiter) *in the universe, Yom Shnei* (day two) *Beschinah* (in the transformation)
and Ein Semol (left eye) *Benefesch* (in the individual).

IV,7-11 מ"ז המליך אות ד' וקשר לו כתר וצר בו
מאדים בעולם ויום ג' בשנה ואוזן ימין
בנפש :
מ"ח המליך אות כ' וקשר לו כתר וצר בו
המה בעולם ויום ד' בשנה ואון שמאל
בנפש :
מ"ט המליך אות פ' וקשר לו כתר וצר בו
נונה בעולם ויום ה' בשנה ונהיר ימין
בנפש :
מ"י המליך אות ר' וקשר לו כתר וצר בו
כוכב בעולם ויום ששי בשנה ונחיר
שמאל בנפש :
מי"א המליך אות ת' וקשר לו כתר וצר
בו לבנה בעולם ויום שבת בשנה
ופה בנפש :

These verses bestow the kingship, successively, on Thalet, Khaf, Phay, Raysh and Thav, binding the crown on them and forming with them Planets, days and openings in the head.

Recapitulatory Table

Vayt (2) forms	day one *Shabatai* (Saturn)	right eye
Djimel (3) forms	day two *Tsedeq* (Jupiter)	left eye
Thalet (4) forms	day three *Meadim* (Mars)	right ear
Khaf (20) forms	day four *Hhamah* (Sun)	left ear
Phay (80) forms	day five *Nogah* (Venus)	right nostril
Raysh (200) forms	day six *Kawkab* (Mercury)	left nostril
Thav (400) forms	day seven *Lvanah* (Moon)	mouth

IV,12

מי"ב שבע כפולות כיצד צרפן . שתי
אבנים בונות שני בתים . שלש
בונות ששה בתים . ארבע בונות ארבעה
ועשרים בתים . חמש בונות מאה ועשרים
בתים . שש בונות שבע מאות ועשרים בתים .
שבע בונות חמשת אלפים וארבעים בתים .
מכאן ואילך צא וחשוב מה שאין הפה יכול
לדבר ואין האוזן יכולה לשמוע . ואלו הן
שבעה כוכבים בעולם חמה נוגה כוכב לבנה
שבתאי צדק מאדים . ואלו הן ז' ימים בשנה
שבעה ימי בראשית . ושבעה שערים בנפש
שתי עינים שתי אזנים ושני נקבי האף והפה.
יבהן נחקקו שבעה רקיעים ושבע ארצות ושבע
שעות לפיכך חבב שביעי לכל חפץ תחת השמים:
סליק פרקא

Seven Doubles. (This is) *in what manner has combined them: two stones build two houses; three stones six houses; four stones twenty-four houses; five stones one hundred and twenty houses; six stones seven hundred and twenty houses; seven stones five thousand and forty houses,* founded (established).

(These are the number of permutations of the objects from 2 to 7. The stones and the "established" houses give a general meaning to these calculations, relating them to everything made in the seven spheres of cognisable space-time.) *Beyond (these seven spheres) of Tsadde-Aleph (of structuration) that which is important (to know) is why the mouth is unable to speak and the ears are incapable of hearing.*

There are seven heavenly bodies in the universe: Hhamah (Sun), *Nogah* (Venus), *Kawkab* (Mercury), *Lvanah* (Moon), *Shabatai* (Saturn), *Tsedeq* (Jupiter), *Meadim* (Mars). *There are seven days Beschinah, seven days of Bereschyith* (Biblical Genesis), *and seven energies moving in the individual's* two eyes, two ears, two nostrils and mouth. *And Hhaqaq* (engraved), *seven spaces, seven lands, seven times and that is why is loved the seventh for everything moves under Schamaim.*

(End of Chapter IV)

The Twelve Simples

V,1

פ״ה מ״א שתים עשרה פשוטות ה״ו ז״ח
ט״י ל״נ ס״ע צ״ק יסודן ראיה,
שמיעה, ריחה, שיחה, לעיטה, תשמיש,
מעשה, הלוך, רונז, שחוק, הרהור, שינה.
מדתן שתים עשרה נבולים באלכסונן . נבול
מזרחית צפונית, נבול מזרחית דרומית, נבול
מזרחית רומית, נבול מזרחית תחתית, נבול
צפונית רומית, נבול צפונית תחתית, נבול
מערבית דרומית, נבול מערבית צפונית,
נבול מערבית רומית, נבול מערבית תחתית,
נבול דרומית רומית, נבול דרומית תחתית .
ומרחיבין והולכין עד עדי עד והם זרועות
עולם :

Twelve Simples: Hay-Waw, Zayn-Hhayt, Tayt-Yod, Lammed-Noun, Sammekh-Ayn, Tsadde-Qof establish, Riyah (sight), Schmiya (hearing), Rihha (smell), Shihhah (speech), Leitah (nutrition), Tashmisch (coition), Meassa (doing), Hilokh (walking), Roqhez (anger), Schhoq (laughter), Hirhour (thought), Schinah (sleep), are measuring twelve diagonals (or

486

oblique lines): *endless East-North, endless East-South, endless East-High, endless East-Low, endless North-High, endless North-Low, endless West-South, endless West-North, endless West-High, endless West-Low, endless South-High, endless South-Low. Are widening out and leading from eternity to eternity: these are the arms of the world.*

V,2

מ״ב שתים עשרה פשוטות ה״ו ז״ח ט״י ל״נ
ס״ע צ״ק חקקן חצבן שקלן צרפן
המירן וצר בהם שנים עשר מזלות בעולם
סימן טש״ת סא״ב מע״ק נד״ד . ואלו הן שנים
עשר חדשים בשנה ניסן אייר סיון תמוז אב
אלול תשרי מרחשון כסלו טבת שבט אדר .
ואלו הן שנים עשר מנהיגין בנפש שתי ידים
ושתי רגלים שתי כליות טחול כבד מרה
המסס קיבה קרקבן [שתי לועזים ושתי עליזים
שתי יועצים ושתי יעוצים שתי טורפין ושתי
ציידים] . עשאן כמין (מדינה) [מריבה] וערכן
כמין מלחמה גם את זה לעומת זה עשה
האלהים :

כיצד צרפן . המליך אות ה׳ וקשר לו כתר וצר בו
טלה בעולם וניסן בשנה ויד ימין בנפש זכר
ונקבה . המליך אות ו׳ וקשר לו כתר וצר בו שור
בעולם ואייר בשנה ויד שמאל בנפש . הכליך אות ז׳
וקשר לו כתר וצר בו תאומים בעולם וסיון בשנה ורגל
ימין בנפש . המליך אות ח׳ וקשר לו כתר וצר בו סרטן
בעולם ותמוז בשנה ורגל שמאל בנפש . המליך אות ט׳
וקשר לו כתר וצר בו אריה בעולם ואב בשנה וכוליא
ימין בנפש . המליך אות י׳ וקשר לו כתר וצר בו
בתולה בעולם ואלול בשנה וכוליא שמאל בנפש .
המליך אות ל׳ וקשר לו כתר וצר בו מאזנים בעולם
ותשרי בשנה וכבד בנפש . המליך אות נ׳ וקשר לו
כתר וצר בו עקרב בעולם ומרחשוון בשנה וטחול
בנפש . המליך אות ס׳ וקשר לו כתר וצר בו קשת
בעולם וכסלו בשנה ומרה בנפש . המליך אות ע׳
וקשר לו כתר וצר בו גדי בעולם וטבת בשנה והמסס
בנפש . המליך אות צ׳ וקשר לו כתר וצר בו דלי
בעולם ושבט בשנה וקיבה בנפש . המליך אות ק׳
וקשר לו כתר וצר בו דגים בעולם ואדר בשנה
וקרקבן בנפש :

Repetition of the Twelve Simples: Hay-Waw, etc. They are *Hhaqaqan, Hhatsavan, Schaqalan, Tsarafan* and *Hamiran* (as seen before) and form the Zodiac whose symbols are given by their initials: Tayt-Sheen-Tav; Samekh-Aleph-Bayt; Mem-Ayn-Qof; Ghimel-Dallet-Dallet. The twelve "form" the months of the Hebrew year: *Nisan, Yaar, Sivan, Tammouz, Av, Eloul, Tishri, Marhhaschon, Kislev, Teveth, Schevath, Adar.* They also "form" two hands, two feet, two kidneys, the spleen, the liver, bile, the stomach, two intestines. In the following passage six pairs of equations play on the permutations of the letters: for example, one pair is Yod-Waw-Ayn-Tsadde—Yod-Ayn-Waw-Tsadde, and so on. It seems useless to transcribe this passage because it means something only if read directly by the code. Reading it in Hebrew is still less interesting than reading the names of bodily organs as given in *The Sepher Yetsira* if it is not taken as an analogy of the structuration of the One energy.

In the last half of this verse, probably an addition to the initial text, the twelve are reconsidered one by one, kingship is conferred on each of them and "forms" a symbol of the Zodiac (this time the symbols are named with all their letters), one month of the Hebrew year and one part of the human body. Here is a general picture of it:

5. *Hay* (East-North) *Toleh* (Aries). Month: *Nisan* — right hand, sight.
6. *Waw* (East-South) *Schaur* (Taurus). Month: *Yaar* — left hand, hearing.
7. *Zayn* (East-High) *Theomim* (Gemini). Month: *Sivan* — right foot, smell.
8. *Hhayt* (East-Low) *Sartann* (Cancer). Month: *Tamouz* — left foot, speech.
9. *Tayt* (North-High) *Arieh* (Leo). Month: *Av* — right kidney, nutrition.
10. *Yod* (North-Low) *Betolah* (Virgo). Month: *Eloul* — left kidney, coition.

30. *Lammed* (West-South) *Moznaim* (Libra). Month: *Tishri* — the liver, doing.
50. *Noun* (West-North) *'Aaqrav* (Scorpio). Month: *Marhashon* — the spleen, walking.
60. *Sammekh* (West-High) *Qaschoth* (Sagittarius). Month: *Kislev* — the bile, anger.
70. *Ayn* (West-Low) *Guedi* (Capricorn). Month: *Teveth* — heat, laughter.
90. *Tsadde* (South-High) *Deli* (Aquarius). Month: *Schevath* — the stomach, thought.
100. *Qof* (South-Low) *Daghim* (Pisces). Month: *Adar* — the intestines, sleep.

When the names of the months are scrutinised, the rhythms of the cosmic energy affecting mankind become clear: sometimes they favour the instituting of something (*e.g.* structures, services), sometimes they destroy them; sometimes they increase the tonus, sometimes they decrease it; sometimes they inspire powerful enterprises (centrifugal), sometimes causing them to backfire. To understand to what extent these variations of energy correspond with historical events — independent of the rhythms of the seasons — requires an elaborate scientific history, based on all the factors in the Qabala relating to the people still living under the influence of this almanac.

By way of example let us consider the month of *Av* (Aleph-Vayt) already mentioned as it is formed by Tayt (9), it is further described by the line North-High, under the sign of *Arieh* (Leo): 1.200.10.5. This sign is the house of *Hhamah*: Hhayt-Mem-Hay (the Sun) where the Sun manifests its two "opposite qualities": a Hhayt (one life) which destroys, and a Hay, which causes proliferation. The name Aleph-Vayt of *Av* is the starting point of a new cycle formed by Tayt (9) archetype of the first cell. The line North-High is the connection between the 10th and 5th Sephira. The 10th, to the left of Adam Qadmon, is the last: it is the conjunction of the end and the beginning by the Name (*Schem-El*). As we have seen, the 5th is YHWH's stamp on the seal of his Name. Hence the two aspects of the double event — destruction-new birth — are the direct result of YHWH.

For further evidence, the East in the cube of space is the future, and the West the past. The Wailing Wall in Jerusalem is therefore rightly called "The West Wall."

The following chapters will be confined to studying how *The Sepher Yetsira* reveals the foundation of astrology.

V,3-4   מ״ג שלש אמות שהם שלשה אבות שמהם
יצא אש ורוח ומים, שלש אמות ושבע
כפולות ושנים עשר פשוטות:
מ״ד אלו עשרים ושתים אותיות שבהם יסד
הקב״ה יה יהוה צבאות אלהים חיים
אלהי ישראל רם ונשא שוכן עד יקדוש שמו
כרים וקדוש הוא.

Three Mothers and from them (issue) *three Fathers, whence are formed Esch and Rouahh and Maim. Three Mothers, Seven Doubles and Twelve Simples.*

Here are (the) *twenty-two Autiot,* (as measured by) *YAH, YHWH Tsebaoth Elohim Hhaim Elohi Israel, Exalted, On High, his eternal dwelling, holy* (is) *his noble Name, holy* (is) *to him.*

(End of Chapter V)

10

A View of the Whole

פ״ן מ״א שלשה אבות ותולדותיהן ושבעה
כוכבים וצבאותיהן ושנים עשר
נבולי אלכסונין וראיה לדבר עדים נאמנין
עולם שנה נפש חק שנים עשר ושבעה
ושלשה ופקידן בתלי ונלגל ולב. שלשה אש
ומים ורוח אש למעלה ומים למטה ורוח חק
מכריע בינתים וסימן לדבר האש נושא את
המים. מ״ם דוממת שי״ן שורקת אל״ף חוק
מכריע בינתים:

*Three Avot (Fathers) and their Toledot (generations) and
seven Kawkabim (heavenly bodies) and their Tsebaot (mass
or constellations) and twelve diametrical boundaries (or di-
agonally) and proof is in the spoken word. Faithful witnesses:
Olam (universe), Schinah (transformation or year), Nefesch
(breath or individual). The boundary: twelve, and seven and
three. And they act quivering (vibrations) and whirling and
"where, how?" (indefiniteness). Three: Esch and Maim and
Rouahh. Esch towards the height, Maim towards the low and
Rouahh limits them (makes rules) kneeling between the two
(as an intermediary) and in the spoken word indicates that
Esch is subject (or object) of Maim: Mem is silent, Sheen (of
Esch) is restless and Aleph (of Rouahh) rules them, kneeling
between the two.*

The first thing to observe in this text is that it lays down
that there are three, and not four elements: Fire, Water, Air.
Earth is not considered to be an element.

1. Note that the symbolic Fathers have a feminine plural
Avot. The word *Toledot* (generations) appears in *Genesis* II,4

where it is said: *Here are the Toledot of Schamaim when they were made, the Yom where Elohim made Eretz and Schamaim.* *Toledot* (generations) is used in the same sense here.

2. The heavenly bodies are *Kawkabim*; the plural of Kawkab, which as has been said, is Mercury, "the messenger."

3. The twelve lateral boundaries are the twelve ridges of the cube of space which determine the frontiers of the consciousness enclosed within them. They define the twelve signs of the Zodiac which affect communities and individuals simultaneously. (This subject will be investigated more deeply later on.)

4. "Proof is in the spoken word": these words define the linguistics of the Qabala as an analogy for the energies involved in the universe.

5. The *Olam* (spatial universe), the *Schinah* (time or the alteration of things) and the *Nefesch* (both "breath" and the individual) are "faithful witnesses." The *Sepher* leaves everyone free to understand "the whatever it may be" of the evidence. The word *Nefesch* appears in *Genesis* II,7 (note that 7 is the number of this verse) when YHWH-Elohim blows the breath of life into *Adam's* nostrils. Then *Adam* "becomes" *Nefesch* (an individual).

6. The twelve, the seven and the three, that is, the twenty-two Autiot, or aspects of cosmic life, are whirling and swirling in "where, how?" (uncertainty). Science is discovering something close to this.

7. The end of the verse reunites, in a single phrase, everything which has been said on all levels about the Mothers. Sheen forms *Esch*, fire; Mem forms *Maim,* water; Aleph forms *Rôuahh,* air. In III,2 we have seen Aleph-Mem-Sheen "very secretly" and "marvellously" creating themselves by an inverted projection of Aleph becoming male and female energy, and forming the *Avot* (Fathers) from which "everything is created." We have seen them uniting between them Sheen and *Maim* to form *Schamaim* (the heavens), Aleph burying itself in *Eretz* (earth), the latter being the solidification of *Maim,* etc. Lastly, in III,4, we have seen them projected into passing

492

time (*Schinah*) where they become heat, cold, and air. It is in these circumstances, in the general context of structuration, that we find them here.

Envisaged in its natural state water can become very cold (ice). Fire, on the other hand, tends to burn things to a cinder and make them disappear. Air absorbs water by evaporation and, by contrast, fans fire. In the biosphere respiration (or breath) regulates the temperature of bodies and the water composing them. Life is possible within the limits of heat and cold controlled by Aleph-air. These things are taken as symbolic projections of less obvious activities.

The text says that *Esch* is the subject (or object) of *Maim*. It has been seen that the 4th Sephira is called *Esch-Memaim*, that is, Fire in Water, which is a good definition of the perfected man structured by the first four Sephirot.

Completing this picture the verse ends with one last analogy, the phonetic: Mem is mute, Sheen vibrates, and Aleph, which is sometimes mute and sometimes a vowel (knelt down: denoting a weak character) is a tie between the two, as has been seen earlier.

VI,2

מ״ב תלי בעולם כמלך על כסאו. גלגל בשנה
כמלך במדינה . לב בנפש כמלך
במלחמה. גם את כל חפץ זה לעומת זה
עשה האלהים . טוב לעומת רע . טוב מטוב
ורע מרע. הטוב מבחין את הרע והרע מבחין
את הטוב . טובה שמורה לטובים ורעה
שמורה לרעים :

Vibration in the universe (space) *is like a king on his throne: whirling in change* (time) *is like a king in his Medina* (city): *"the uncertain heart"* (indetermination) *in the individual is like a king at war*: (and) *also* (from) *Aleph* (to) *Tav* (from beginning to end) *all dies out: this opposing that* (contradiction). (This is) *caused by Elohim. Good opposed to evil. Good with good, evil with evil. Good with* (from) *Aleph* (to) *Tav, the appearance of evil, and evil with* (from) *Aleph* (to) *Tav, the ap-*

493

*pearance of good. The good guardian of goods, the evil
guardian of evils.*

VI,3 מ״ג שלשה כל אחד לבדו עומד . ז' חלוקין
שלשה טול שלשה וחק מכריע בינתים .
שנים עשר עומדין במלחמה שלשה אוהבים
שלשה שונאים שלשה מחיים שלשה ממיתים.
שלשה אוהבים חלב והאזנים והפה . שלשה שונאים
הכבד והמרה והלשון . ואל מלך נאמן מושל
בכולן , אחד על גבי שלשה שלשה על גבי
שבעה שבעה על גבי שנים עשר וכולן
אדוקין זה בזה :

*Three: each keeps itself apart. And 7 separates them three
by three. The twelve in battle array: three friends, three enemies, three with the living, three with the dead. The three
friends are the heart, the ears, the mouth. The three enemies
are the liver, the bile and the tongue. And EL, faithful king
dominates everything. One is above three, three above seven,
seven above twelve, and all communicate with one another.*

The text says no more. Perhaps it wishes the reader to be
left to his own questions. Whatever the reason, just as the
different parts of the body are not scanned, everyone is left to
discover the three living and the three dead.

VI,4 מ״ד וכיון שצפה אברהם אבינו ע״ה והביט
וראה וחקר והבין וחקק וחצב וצרף וצר
ועלתה בידו אז נגלה עליו אדון הכל ב״ה
והושיבהו בחיקו ונשקו על ראשו וקראו
אוהבי וכרת לו ברית ולזרעו והאמין בה'
ויחשבה לו צדקה . וכרת לו ברית בין עשר
אצבעות רגליו והיא ברית המילה , ועשר
אצבעות ידיו והוא הלשון . וקשר לו עשרים
ושתים אותיות בלשונו וגלה לו את יסודן
משכן במים דלקם באש רעשן ברוח בערן
בשבעה נהגם בשנים עשר מזלות:

סליק פרקא, וסליק ספר יצירה.

494

A VIEW OF THE WHOLE

Schetsefa Abraham, our father (may he rest in peace) (when he was set on emitting a flux, on participating in the vital flow), *he looked, he saw, he explored, he articulated, he mapped out, he hewed, he combined, he structurized, he raised his hand and Adon Hakol (blessed be his name) filled him to overflowing, revealed himself to him, received him in his bosom, kissed him on the head, called him my friend and made a covenant with him and his descendents, which he authenticated with Hay* (Abram becoming Abraham) *and meted out justice to him* (gave him an exact measure). *And concluded with a covenant between the ten toes of the feet, and it is the covenant of circumcision, and between the ten fingers of the hands, and it is the covenant of the tongue, and attached to his tongue the twenty-two Autiot, and revealed Yassodan* (their foundation) *and sunk them in water, singed them by Fire, shook them by blowing, consumed them by the Seven and guided them by twelve constellations.*

(End of The Sepher Yetsira)

PART THREE

THE ZODIAC

11

Some Important Explanations of the Text and of Astrology

IN ORDER to write this book in its original version, in French, I needed the help of a few friends whom I acknowledge here with thanks for their contributions. Firstly, Mr. Edrei, who gave me some most valuable information which enabled me to determine the spatial cube and the Menorah. However, he declined to collaborate with me on the astrological section as he was trained in a different tradition. Secondly, Mr. and Mrs. Lance, and Mrs. de Ponthière who were in accord with my views. Mr. Lance drew some excellent charts under my direction. As astrologers they largely confirmed what I had more or less understood.

The French edition (Editions du Mont-Blanc, Geneva, 1968) was well received by the public, but the chapters on astrology were said to be inadequate for students of the subject. I was well aware of this, and for the last six years I have been consulting all the astrologers I know in an attempt to enlarge my understanding.

Fragments of knowledge, from many different schools of traditional astrology failed to fill the gap between my correct reading of the Autiot and their interpretations.

Meanwhile, I became more and more convinced that the so-called knowledge of astrology was merely a tradition and that it lacked any real basis for the origin of the keywords of the Planetary and Zodiacal signs. The modern approach, with all its complex calculations, could not possibly discover the very intimate nature and character of Planets considered as living bodies, such as I know them to be.

If we fail to understand that consciousness is everywhere and in everything, and that everything is related, we will soon belong to past history. Yet scientific research, all over the world, is already far-advanced in the study of consciousness as energy and energy as consciousness.

I implicitly trust qualified astrologers to cast scientific horoscopes based on correct ephemeris. Precious information concerning events can be obtained from them — whether or not the business one is starting will be successful, which is the best date to begin it, whether I will have an accident, an illness, and so on and so forth.

However, a successful business can be psychologically disastrous, and vice versa. Is it the real self that has these experiences? The astrologers answer: You are the Taurus, Gemini, Scorpio type. Yet however these supposed "types" are read, it is irrelevant and extraneous to the inner lives, the souls, of the persons concerned.

There is no such thing as a "Zodiacal sign" type. Those signs describe only containers, or "dwelling houses" and are not, by any means, the persons who happen to fit some calendar at the moment of birth. Moreover, the names of animals, or of Roman deities — Mars, Jupiter, etc. — are misleading. Not only as words do they have nothing in common with what they designate, but they are misleading because, when using them, one is prone to attribute to the Planets the qualities of the mythological personages, or animals, attached to them. Such views are only mental projections, without any reality. You will never find the letters M A R S when seeking to know the inner quality of the Planet, whereas *Meadim,* in code, reveals it clearly.

Gradually I became convinced that the astrology of *The Sepher Yetsira* is an inner exploration of the individual. Whether it also deals with outer events I do not know. Before coming to any conclusion on that matter one will have to learn what there is to learn from *The Sepher Yetsira.*

So we will not deal with learning astrology, but with learning how to read *The Sepher Yetsira*. By this I mean, how to read every Aut, every equation, every inter-relationship, the Autiotic formation of the Planets, the names of the Planets, the formative Autiot of the Zodiacal signs, the names of those signs and, finally, the names of the qualities of the Planets in their own dwellings. This amounts to formulating and solving a complex series of equations with, sometimes, twelve or sixteen variables.

It is not as difficult as it sounds. A trained doctor of medicine, for instance, can, intuitively, immediately diagnose a patient's illness. This same diagnosis, when made analytically, is the resultant of twelve or sixteen data, which include a description of the patient and his symptoms. A cabalist who has a deep cognition of the Autiot can read a horoscope at first sight. I mean that he has an immediate insight into a person's psychology and its orientation.

This last point is important and I hope to explain it when studying the seven double Autiot. We are not static focusses of energy; we are moving focusses, going in one of the two opposite directions of the dual One energy. And the essential thing for every one of us to know is whether we are oriented in the right or wrong direction, with respect to our innermost and strongest natural impulses.

I was experimenting on this during the years that Shambhala Publications was asking for my interpretation of *The Sepher Yetsira*. I said that I was not ready. Tentatively I drew different Zodiacs, hesitating as to the best way to establish where their reading point began, and on many other factors, such as how to write the names of the Planets and of the Zodiacal signs: if they should be written facing the circumference, or, if the author were to envisage himself in the centre, the letters should be in opposite positions. I had a feeling that their places in the Zodiac were important.

Having decided on different Zodiacs I asked some friends to cast a few horoscopes on transparent paper, stipulating that they should be anonymous and very simple: just location of the seven Planets and of their ascendents at birth. I super-imposed them on my Zodiacs and concentrated my attention on them, allowing myself to be guided by a few suppositions on the general reading of the Zodiac which I had been led to formulate. The results were more positive than I had hoped they would be: they gave a vivid picture of the inner drives of the persons concerned, and of what was to be expected from them.

Half a dozen, or so, of these experiences convinced me that a door to astrology can be opened if some astrologers are will-ing to enter through the obligatory ante-chamber of the Autiot. So far the response has been practically nil, and I am not prepared to go any further along that line, or any other diverging from the centre of the Qabala, where my place is. Many more lines are being explored today, in physics, biology, in the most recent developments of para-psychology, psycho-kinetics, and so on. All tend towards the study of consciousness as energy. On this question the ancient, original Qabala has much to say, if we were to know how to put it in modern, scientific terms.

In the following pages I will try to deal as clearly as possible, in the proper sequence, with the data in *The Sepher Yetsira*.

The three "Mother Letters" come first; then the seven "Doubles," and lastly the twelve "Simples." Afterwards I will construct the Zodiac and suggest four different ways of be-ginning to read it.

The Three Mother-Letters

In *The Sepher Yetsira* the three Mother-Letters have noth-ing to do with the Zodiac. If they are primary elements there are three of them, and not four (as I noted above). After much consideration it seems to me that the introduction of "four elements" (fire, air, water, earth) to astrology, and in the study of human types, is only a survival of an ancient classification which is mistaken and irrelevant.

After making lengthy experiments with all the Autiot, I have come to the conclusion that Aleph, Mem and Sheen are correctly called "Mothers," although they are no more than symbols. In plain language, Aleph is maximum energy, Mem is minimum energy, and Sheen is the action of Aleph upon Mem. In III,2 they are said to be the origin of the Fire and the Waters, both male and female, "out of which are born the Fathers, creators of all that is." In III,3 the process is in the reverse order: Aleph forms the atmosphere (*Avir*), Mem the Waters (*Maim*), and Sheen the Fire *(Esch)*. In III,4 the text becomes more complex. However, the general idea is fairly simple: when a maximum energy is postulated as acting upon a minimum we are speaking in the abstract. In manifested existence there is no fire without air and the result of the dual action of the 3 Elements upon each other is: *Schamaim* (wrongly translated as skies) and *Eretz* (meaning, in a limited sense, earth).

Schamaim and *Eretz* express One energy flowing in two opposite directions. I developed this point in previous writings. Here my purpose is to eliminate the four and the three Elements from the Zodiac, and from astrology as a whole.

12

The Seven Doubles

WHEN DEALING with Chapter IV,1, I was faced with a world of complexities: the Hebrew text, phonetic transcriptions in English, verbal symbolism (IV,2), the extremities of space (IV,3), the formation of the Planets (IV,6), the formation, one by one, of the seven Planets, the days of the week and the seven orifices of the face — two eyes, two ears, two nostrils and the mouth (IV,5 to 12) — and lastly a mathematical calculation of the combinations of the numbers one to seven.

I could only follow the text and had no opportunity to check or delete the items which cannot be verified scientifically. These constitute the totality of the text except, perhaps, the reference to the Planets, and even these seemed doubtful.

After having surveyed all the implications of the "Seven Doubles," which I had to do, I was able to go to the roots of the matter and to explain what these 7 are, and why they have dual characteristics. This allowed me to describe the nature of the Planets according to *The Sepher Yetsira* — to be accepted, or not, by astrologers.

The Hebrew text and the code are at the reader's disposal. If he is really interested he will read the analysis of the Sevens' opposite qualities: *Hhaimmot, Shalom-Raa*, etc. At this stage I must assume that it can be understood why *Hhaim* (Hhayt-Yod-Yod-Mem) means, roughly, Life, and so on and so on. For it would be useless to begin the a b c of the code all over again while trying to go further. Here are the Seven Doubles (IV,1) and their opposite qualities, briefly stated in their colloquial meanings, but *not* in their decoded meanings.

THE SEVEN DOUBLES

Vayt is *Hhaim* = alive	*Bayt* is *Mot* = death
Djimel is *Shalom* = peace	*Ghimel* is *Raa* = bad
Thallet is *Hhokmah* = intelligence	*Dallet* is *Olet* = folly
Khaf is *'Osser* = health	*Kaw* is *'Oni* = poverty
Phay is *Hhan* = charm	*Pay* is *Kee'or* = dreamy
Raysh is *Zar'* = seed	*Raysh* is *Shemama* = waste
Thav is *Momshela* = government	*Tav* is *'Abadot* = slavery

The constant factor is that the unpointed seven (soft in sound) are "good" and the pointed (hard) are "bad."

We know that all the Autiot are not only symbols of different states of energy, but are actually those states which they represent. They are not, as it were, snapshots of fixed, congealed states; they are alive and active. Hence, they can react in opposite ways to the cosmic flow of living energy. In that they allow themselves to be penetrated by it, they are "soft;" in that they resist it, they are "hard."

Obviously, then, when these Autiot absorb the cosmic energy (most favourably at night during sleep) my *Vayt* (body) is life, my *Djimel* (organic movement) is completely at peace, my *Thallet* (response to life) is intelligent, my *Khaf* (actions) are rich, my *Phay* (level of unconsciousness) are no longer cramped and complex but graceful and charming, my *Raysh* (projection of the cosmic body) is fruitful, my *Thav* (echo in me of the cosmic response to the flow of life) is in order.

Contrarywise, if the Autiot in me react in daytime (as action) to the flow of life my *Bayt* (body) dies, my *Ghimel* (organic movement) spreads evil and calamities, my *Dallet* (response) is foolish and stupid, my *Kaf* (actions) only lead to poverty and affliction, my *Pay* does not know that it is half awake and half blind, my *Raysh* (cosmic container) is waste and void, my *Tav* (resistance to Aleph) drives me into a state of slavery.

These statements are paradoxical only for the everyday, matter-of-fact state of consciousness. However, we must keep in mind the "Nativot Phayliot" of the 1st verse of *The Sepher*

Yetsira which shows that our sensorial world is the reverse of the Energy that pervades it. Thus understood, these statements are nothing but plain common sense and dispel, once and for all, the clouds of "occult mysteries" that have been wafted around *The Sepher Yetsira* by many generations of erudite illiterates.

IV,2 asks us to re-establish the twofold flow of life in opposite directions. It contradicts the notion of life emanating from a deity in a one-way direction, and is therefore expressed with caution.

IV,3 places the seven in space, taking the Earth as the centre (or observer). In this case the observer is the centre, the inner point where Aleph and Tav (life and its sanctuary) meet. This is my reason for composing a Zodiac to be read from the centre, from an Aleph. The Zodiac will have to be read by rotating it.

IV,4 casts the seven in the skies and opens the way to astrology proper. The emphasis of the number seven and its variations, such as *Shabyi, Shabatot, Shabat,* leads us to *Shabataï* (Saturn) to whom priority is given. It is therefore formed by *Vayt.*

The Planets

Here is the chart of the seven Planets formed by the seven double letters, as re-established by the Zodiac:

Shabataï (Saturn)	formed by	Vayt is *Hhaim* (alive) in *Ghedi* (Capricorn) Bayt is *Mot* (dead) in *Deli* (Aquarius)
Tsedeq (Jupiter)	formed by	Djimel is *Shalom* (peace) in *Daghim* (Pisces) Ghimel is *Raa* (bad) in *Qoshet* (Sagittarius)
Meadim (Mars)	formed by	Thallet is *Hhokmah* (intelligent) in *'Aqarav* (Scorpio) Dallet is *Olet* (folly) in *Toleh* (Aries)

Hhamah (Sun)	formed by	Khaf is *O'sser* (wealth) in *Arieh* (Leo) Kaf is *O'ni* (poverty) in *Arieh* (Leo)
Nogah (Venus)	formed by	Phay is *Hhan* (charm) in *Shaur* (Taurus) Pay is *Kee'or* (dreamy) in *Meoznaim* (Libra)
Kawkab (Mercury)	formed by	Raysh is *Zar'* (seed) in *Betolah* (Virgo) Raysh is *Shemama* (waste) in *Teomaim* (Gemini)
Lvanah (Moon)	formed by	Thav is *Memshalah* (ruler) in *Sartan* (Cancer) Tav is *Abadot* (slavery) in *Sartan* (Cancer)

The next step for the students who wish to establish the position of the sky according to *The Sepher Yetsira* is to imagine themselves as inside the spatial cube, facing East (as described above) and, following the instructions of IV,3, to put *Shabataï* (Saturn) at the top, *Tsedeq* (Jupiter) below, *Meadim* (Mars) in the East, *Hhamah* (The Sun) in the West, *Nogah* (Venus) in the North, *Kawkab* (Mercury) in the South, and *Lvanah* (The Moon) inside.

Then, in accordance with verses I and II, six diagonals should be imagined, each carrying a flow of energy in one single direction, thus:

East-North with Hay forming *Toleh* (Aries)
East-South with Waw forming *Shaur* (Taurus)
East-Top with Zayn forming *Teomaim* (Gemini)
East-Bottom with Hhayt forming *Sartan* (Cancer)
North-Top with Tayt forming *Arieh* (Leo)
North-Bottom with Yod forming *Betolah* (Virgo)
West-South with Lammed forming *Meoznaim* (Libra)

West-North with Noun forming *'Aqarav* (Scorpio)
West-Top with Sammekh forming *Qashot* (Sagittarius)
West-Bottom with Ayn forming *Ghedi* (Capricorn)
South-Top with Tsadde forming *Deli* (Aquarius)
South-Bottom with Qof forming *Daghim* (Pisces)

I do not think that it is necessary to make a drawing of all the zodiacal signs and planets within this elaborate cube. Nor do I know what such a construction would lead to, because, as I pointed out when dealing with it, (see page 85-87) the cube is not a representation of physical space, but a chart symbolising our psychological structures. (And where would be the starting points of infinite directions?)

Therefore, the position of the six planets on the surface of the cube and of the seventh (the Moon) inside it have definite psychological meanings expressed by their names; these meanings and names describe, in order, the values of their innermost energy, by means of the double Autiot which form them, and locate them in different zodiacal signs.

Shabataï (Saturn) is formed by Vayt-Bayt on the upper surface of the cube and thus graces us with the blessing of the Sabbath. It gives us freedom of action through the release of our complete vitality. Its name is Sheen, the cosmic breath, Bayt, our physical body, Tav, the completion of our body as a Tabernacle of universal life-death and, finally the Yod of manifested existence. Thus Shabatai on our head showers us with symbolic fire, that which forms the head: it is Hhaim (alive) by Vayt in Ghedi (Capricorn), and Mot (dead) by Bayt in Deli (Sagittarius).

Tsedeq (Jupiter) formed by Djimel-Ghimel on the bottom surface is the sense of Justice upon which we stand: the sense of our rights and duties. Its name, Tsedeq, is, first of all, the Tsadde of all structures; then the Dallet of the necessary resistance to structures, leading to the cosmic Aleph: Qof. It is Shalom, (in peace) by Djimel, in Daghim (Pisces), and Raa (uncertain) by Ghimel in Qoshet (Sagittarius).

Meadim (Mars) formed by Thallet-Dallet to the East, towards which we look, is always ahead of us. However long we look in that direction we can never completely grasp it. The name Adam is contained in its name, mixed with Mem and Yod, the Autiot of the Waters. We project on Mars the wisdom which we have not yet attained. Our response to that projection is Hhokmah (intelligence) by Thallet in 'Aqarev (Scorpio); our blunt resistance to the future is Olet (folly).

Hhamah (Sun) formed by Khaf-Kaf is behind us (West) as we face the East. We do not see the sun, but only our shadow cast at our feet. We cannot look at it fixedly: it would blind us. We cannot stand the power of its emanations. It provides all energy: it destroys, burns and calcinates by its power. Its elemental Hhayt has to meet the elemental Mem of the Waters, and only then does it give forth its third Aut, Hay (life), and fertilise our actions. Its two formations are both in *Arieh* (Leo). By Khaf Hhameh it is *O'ser* (richness) and by Kaf it is *O'ni* (poverty).

Nogah (Venus) formed by Phay-Pay, is on our left, on the Northern surface. Its name, Nogah, is a pleasant, naive, charming, thoughtless copulation, before sin was invented. The Northern energy, entering the waters of our body through the left hand, has no reason to be other than it is until it meets the psyche. In *Shaur* (Taurus) Nogah is *Hhan* (Hhayt unstructured, Noun final indeterminate). When by Pay, Nogah is in *Meaznim* (Libra) she is *Ki'Or* the mirage in which we have lived and perhaps of the illusions of our dream world. The name, Noun, Waw, Ghimel, Hay, is the picture of an organic life.

Kawkab (Mercury) formed by Raysh unpointed and pointed is South, the flowing out through the right hand of the energy we receive through the left hand. Its name means, traditionally, the messenger of the gods and expresses (Kaf-Waw-Kaf-Bayt) a dual action of self-fertilisation, thus justifying the epithet "messenger": an action towards an action, carrying the message, brought unconsciously by Venus, into conscious activity. By unpointed Raysh, Kawkab is *Zar'* (a seed) in *Betolah* (Virgo) and by pointed Raysh it is *Shememah* (waste) in *Teomaim* (Gemini).

Lvanah, the Moon, alone is inside the cube, at the centre. Therefore it is inside our psyche. It is formed by Thav and Tav, a strange tabernacle of cosmic energy, resisting Aleph to the point of being Aleph itself. Its name, beginning with the Lammed of Al, projects an infinite organic movement into our consciousness and engenders both the Noun of manifested life and the Hay of life — two lives, one manifested, the other essential. The moon is regarded here as the source of our psychic energy. Its two formations by Thav and Tav, are both in *Sartan* (Cancer): *Memshelah* (towards a high evolution) by Thav, and *Abadot* (in slavery) by Tav.

At this point a fundamental question arises. The cube, the planets with their positions, names and formative Autiot, their briefly-described inner nature, all form a consistent picture. But has this picture any relationship at all with the planets, as they exist in our solar system, and with their influence, if any, on our lives and on our physical and psychological bodies?

When preparing the first, French, version of this book my chief concern was to find out if, by putting the names of the planets and of the zodiacal signs face to face, according to the code, I could reach conclusions more or less in agreement with the (absurd) encounter between Venus and a Bull, or Jupiter and the Fishes, and so on. As I have already stated, the results were far better than I could have expected, although I am totally ignorant of astrology.

The horoscopes were cast by qualified astrologers by means of their calculations; the ephemeris and many traditional correspondences between the ascendent signs, the ecliptic, houses, degrees of the Zodiac, and other learned things of which I know nothing. I cannot cast a horoscope, but why can I read one as a psychological projection of the person concerned?

I hardly believe that astrology is the result of physical observations of the sky and, I dare say, many astrologers also have their doubts. Imagine a time when there was no astrology: how could it have begun? Before investigating the cause of an effect, we must have felt the effect. So, to begin with, the influence of the planets on human lives, bodies and psyches must have been observed. Yet, if the system be the result of statistics, how many millions of lives would have had to be followed, day after day, for how many generations? How could such a fantastic number of records have been classified and read? Moreover, we must, *a priori,* grant that the anonymous authors of *The Sepher Yetsira* had serious intentions, and that they were not "joking" when they stated that different parts of the body are "formed" by Autiot corresponding to planets (e.g.: the seven orifices of the face), or that Zodiacal signs and their Autiot establish such functions as sight, hearing, nutrition, etc.

My conclusion is that the originators of astrology were in direct conscious relationship with the life of the seven planets. (Uranus, Neptune and Pluto were discovered only recently, and their qualities are much a matter of speculation, leading to contradictory conclusions).

We feel directly, and partially know, only the Sun and the Moon. Our awareness of the solar system as a whole, our galaxy and all the galaxies, is fragmentary, although we receive their impact.

Many rays are being discovered — cosmic, alpha, magnetic, electric and so on — but we have yet to learn how universal energy has projected us as human beings limited to a physical body and to a personal consciousness. Such things have become known directly and intuitively. We are wanderers on a fossilized world, and thanks to scientific investigations using electronic and other more and more subtle and accurate devices, we can prove and recreate this knowledge.

The very days of the week bear witness to the long-lost knowledge: *Sun*-day; *Moon*-day; in Italian *Marte*-di, the day of Mars for Tuesday; in French, *Mercre*-di, the day of Mercury for Wednesday; *Giove*-di, in Italian, the day of Jupiter (Giove, in Italian) for Thursday; *Vener*-di, the day of Venus

(Venere in Italian) for Friday; *Satur*-day for Saturn, or Sabato in Italian, for Shabatai, the Sabbath. And there are seven planets.

Leaving aside references to the human body, the days of the week, and the months, I now come to a study of the Twelve Simples.

13

The Twelve Simples

VERY LITTLE is said about the Twelve Simples, but there is enough to guide us in our study.

Upon examining them we see that two of them are not really simple, but contain, in embryo, opposition qualities reconciled by their twinship, and together operating in a single vital process. Resistance in them to the cosmic life appearing in the seven Doubles, as death, evil, etc., is put in motion and responds as an outer flow of energy, parallel, and in inverse direction, to the inner.

These two Autiot are Hhayt and Tayt. In its form, shape and dwelling Hhayt contains Cancer (Sartan), the Moon's two opposing qualities. Tayt forms Leo and contains the two opposing qualities of the Sun (see the Zodiac) in its dwelling.

The other ten are simple because they cannot be double. Hay, life, cannot have the quality of its opposite, death. Examined one by one, the same is true for all of them.

If we interpret their description in Verse I, and if we place ourselves again inside the spatial cube we can see them as diagonals. In a flow of endless energy they may be depicted thus:

Hay forms Aries in a flow from Mars to Venus (East-North).
Waw forms Taurus in a flow from Mars to Mercury (East-South).
Zayn forms Gemini in a flow from Mars to Saturn (East-Top).
Hhayt forms Cancer in a flow from Mars to Jupiter (East-Bottom).
Tayt forms Leo in a flow from Venus to Saturn (North-Top).

Yod forms Virgo in a flow from Venus to Jupiter (North-
Bottom).

Lammed forms Libra in a flow from Sun to Mercury (West-
South).

Noun forms Scorpio in a flow from Sun to Venus (West-
North).

Sammekh forms Sagittarius in a flow from Sun to Saturn
(West-North).

Ayn forms Capricorn in a flow from Sun to Jupiter (West-
Bottom).

Tsadde forms Aquarius in a flow from Mercury to Saturn
(South-Top).

Qof forms Pisces in a flow from Mercury to Jupiter (South-
Bottom).

We cannot see these diagonals and we cannot even imagine
them, because they begin and end in the non-beginning and
the non-ending, fathomless, infinite depths of directions. As
currents of energy flowing from one infinite to another, they
completely evade our space-time continuum. But in the case
of the planets this is not so, because the currents flowing East-
West, Top-Bottom, North-South pass through us in our consecrated position inside our cube. Mars-Sun, Saturn-Jupiter
and Venus-Mercury are as threads and we as eyeholes. (By the
way, that is the reason for them appearing to us as being
double: for instance, a current flowing from the East (Mars)
and after passing through us, is still coming from the East, but
when we about-turn we call it West. The same is true of the
West; when we look in front of us we say we are facing East.)
It is difficult to grasp the fact that such one-way currents are
dual psychologically. However, the impact of these three and
the significance of their directions are important factors.

In each of these three binomials the interplay of the two
terms varies with the variations of their respective energies
which can, as in a tug-of-war, sway the result in one direction
or the other. When dealing with any Planet we must always

know whether it is formed by an unpointed or pointed letter, at the time when the horoscope is examined. Its energy must be evaluated accordingly. I have already said that the "contrary" characters must be read according to the code, Aut by Aut, and must not be accepted in their idiomatic meaning. No living body (as are the Planets) ever rejects the cosmic energy. Saturn formed by Bayt (pointed) is said to be dead, and Jupiter formed by Ghimel (pointed) is said to be evil. After many discussions with astrologers I decided that the unpointed Autiot express the inner flow of energy that permeates us most when we are asleep, and that the pointed ones refer to our activity during the day.

The Sepher Yetsira does not specify positions for the Planets in the Zodiac, so I decided to fix them according to the nocturnal and diurnal classifications given them by certain traditional astrologers. I put the unpointed in the nocturnal positions and the pointed in the diurnal, thus . . .

Letter	Planet	Zodiacal Sign	Contraries in terms of energies
Vayt	Saturn	in Capricorn is nocturnal	(inner life)
Bayt	Saturn	in Aquarius is diurnal	(active life)
Djimel	Jupiter	in Pisces is nocturnal	(inner life)
Ghimel	Jupiter	in Sagittarius is diurnal	(outward assertion)
Thallet	Mars	in Scorpio is nocturnal	(wise)
Dallet	Mars	in Aries is diurnal	(uncontrolled)
Khaf	Sun	in Leo is nocturnal	(fertile)
Kaf	Sun	in Leo is diurnal	(burns away)
Phay	Venus	in Taurus is nocturnal	(potentiality)
Pay	Venus	in Libra is diurnal	(mirages)
Raysh	Mercury	in Virgo is nocturnal	(seed)
Raysh	Mercury	in Gemini is diurnal	(selection)

| Thav | Moon | in Cancer is nocturnal | (energy penetrates) |
| Tav | Moon | in Cancer is diurnal | (energy springs forward) |

These qualities, although but roughly described, can be further simplified in relation to the symbolic meanings of the directions in which *The Sepher Yetsira* places the Planets:

binomial
{ Mars: East, future
{ Sun: West, past

binomial
{ Saturn: Top, higher aspirations
{ Jupiter: Bottom, assertion of rights and duties

binomial
{ Venus: North, libido, sensual impulses
{ Mercury: South, outward activity

We can thus see that our future life must be organised so as to take into account what we have been in the past, and, reciprocally, we must carry our past into the future. If either the future or the past resists the other, Mars hardens and thrusts us into absurd adventures that do not correspond with what we are, or the Sun blocks the unresolved conflicts of the past (complexes, etc.) and destroys future possibilities.

The same is true for the other two binomials. If our higher aspirations cause us to neglect our rights and duties, we lose our connection with the world, and if we over-emphasise our rights and duties, we become authoritarian and imperious, claiming high rank in the scale of faked religious values. Moreover, our sensual impulses and outer activities need to fertilise each other.

With a clear, if elementary, view of the energies flowing between the seven Planets we can now reconsider the twelve Zodiacal signs described as diagonals of the cube. (The Moon's inner and outer flows are self-sufficient: they will be examined later.)

Whether we regard our bodies as extending to "the depth

of beginning" and to "the depth of the end" of the six directions, or whether we chose to make a cube limited to our ordinary physical bodies, or if we stop trying to visualise the diagonals, the result will be the same.

I hope I have made it clear for the reader that, when dealing with this astrology, we must follow the spatial cube and the Zodiac, omitting Uranus, Neptune and Pluto, as our purpose is simply to read *The Sepher Yetsira*. (However, here they are: Uranus retrograde in Scorpio, Neptune and Pluto in Gemini. In spite of their importance we will also omit the ascendent and the "Houses," because they are not mentioned in *The Sepher Yetsira*.)

We can now follow in the Zodiac the formative Autiot of the signs, as cast by *The Sepher Yetsira*. It begins with Aut Hay (5), symbol of life, forming a cell *Toleh* (Aries) which initiates an organic movement (Lammed) giving birth to life (Hay). In brief, *Toleh,* is where all life begins.

Following the Zodiac, we now have Waw (6), the second named function of the cell,[1] the symbol of reproduction. It forms *Shaur,* called Taurus, often considered as having a very earthy copulative character. It is far from being so: *Shaur* (Sheen-Waw-Raysh) is the cosmic activity of *Aur* (Light): Aleph-Waw-Raysh, the Sheen being the active agent of Aleph, "The Breath of God." It is the actualisation of the mythical "Cosmic Bridal" of the two energies as one. *Shaur,* as such, is the cosmic androgyn.

Next, Zayn (7) forms an extremely interesting sign, *Teomaim,* in which Tav (400) and Aleph (1) in joint action (having united) fertilise the Waters, Maim, with Waw. Priority is given to Tav (the Aleph disguised as its own sanctuary). It will be emphasised in the next sign.

We now come to Hhayt, unstructured energy, forming *Sartan* (the female) Sammekh facing Raysh; then Tayt, (the

---

[1] See especially "Tree," II, published by Christopher Books, Santa Barbara, Calif., U.S.A., 1971, where I gave some biological notes based on the original Hebrew alphabet.

cell, and Noun in 700 terminal). That sign, the official residence of the double Tav of the Moon is, as is evident, an unsolved equation: we do not know how its formative Hhayt operates, for the clear reason that Hhayt, unstructured as it is, cannot act but must be acted upon.

The life, Hay, that carried us from *Arieh* is no longer operating. Reaching Cancer we are at a dead-end. There is no real contradiction between the position of the Moon inside the spatial cube and its residence in *Sartan*, the diagonal East-Bottom. The Moon, formed by Tav (400-6), cannot be fertile through its 6 before it has realised that its number, 400, is none other than 1, Aleph, where the two currents of energy are in a deadlock.

Likewise, Cancer being the diagonal which directly projects Mars into Jupiter, is always in need of help if the person deeply affected by that sign really wants to reach a higher state of consciousness. Mars is always immature unless it reaches Adam-Qadmon, the state of perfection. It is immature because it is ahead of us. When it falls upon Jupiter it will probably produce a "Jupiterian type," so set in performing its duties and asserting its rights in the concrete, material, everyday world, that such a person will never soar up, so to speak, unless through attachment to an ideal, or, rather, to someone embodying an ideal. In that case, the female Sartan could be of vital help and protection to a man who would otherwise be absorbed in his highest aspirations, to the point of losing connections with the world as it is.

In conclusion, *Sartan* filled with Tav, formative of the Moon, needs a new cell to fertilise it, but Tav can only blend with Aleph: the two opposite poles of energy must meet. So we come to *Arieh*, (Aleph, Raysh, Yod, Hay) meaning that Aleph gives existence (Yod) and life (Hay) to its cosmic container, Raysh. The name of that *Arieh*, meaninglessly called Leo, is, in fact, formed by Tayt, a cell, and is the residence of the purveyor of all earthly energies, the Sun.

So we realise that we have been carried from Toleh to the

threshold of Cancer by an archetype of life Hay, forming
Aries, and not by an actually existing life. We will now read
the Zodiac in two other ways, starting from *Arieh,* in two opposite directions. (The fourth reading will begin with Capricorn.)

To do so we take four steps (1, from Aries to Taurus; 2, to
Gemini; 3, to Cancer; 4, to Leo) and enter the residence of
the Sun. Four more steps in the same direction will take us
to Sagittarius, where we will stop again. This is the itinerary
of physical energy emanated by the Sun. Four last steps from
Sagittarius will lead us back to Aries.

The Sun's name in the Zodiac, *Hhamah* (Hhayt-Mem-Hay),
will carry the physical life given by the Sun. But the unstructured Hhayt will retire to the Hhayt forming *Sartan* and, perhaps, arise as unconscious psychological energy, assuming one
of the two qualities of the Moon. If it remains buried it becomes *Abadot* (slavery); if it rises and springs forth it is *Memshelah* (free, uplifted) and can begin its return journey, first
encountering Gemini where it can make a choice between the
two halves of Teomaim (Tav-Aleph, Waw, Mem, Yod, Mem).
A person can choose to be the projection of the cosmic Tav-
Aleph, pregnant with Waw, or to be *Maim,* the Waters. In the
first case *Shaur* in this itinerary backwards with its many adventures, will be waiting until the soul, after a long and
difficult journey, now backwards, now forwards, finds its rest
in *Meadim* (Aries), where at last the East of future life will
unite with the North of sensual impulses.

The obvious reason for this itinerary backwards is the fact
that the evolution of the psyche comes from the dissolution of
its structures. Physical life, on the contrary, depends upon
maintaining and consolidating its structures.

Thus, accentuating the Tayt forming *Arieh* as a cell, energy
flowing into the next sign, *Betolah* (Virgo) emphasises Yod
forming that sign, symbol of actual existence. The name *Betolah,* so wrongly said to be Virgo the Virgin, is pregnant, and
Kawkab in that residence is *Zar'* (seed).

The following sign, *Meoznaim,* formed by the organic movement of Lammed, is an ambiguous "balance" (Libra) in which the weight of Aleph in the first three letters (Mem, Aleph, Zayn) and the weight of Yod in the last three (Noun, Yod, Mem) creates in Venus, the sensual psyche, whose residence it is, a state where dreams and imagination are mixed up with concrete reality. In that state of Venus, Aleph, the explosive producer of light *(Aur)* is projected into innumerable symbols and images. It is important to note that the Aleph comes from Mem, which can be read as *Ozen* (the ear) in *Maim* (the Waters). These Waters are very fruitful. This sign is the first diagonal (West-South) lit by the Sun. West-North, West-Top and West-Bottom will follow up to Capricorn. Here are ceaseless emanations from the Sun's four flowing currents, which are in diametrical opposition to the four currents flowing from the East (Meadim) in Aries to Cancer.

Continuing our way we come to *'Aqarav* (Scorpio) where the fruitfulness of *Meaznim* reaches its climax, under the formative Noun, archetype of manifested life. This existential culmination is contained in the name *'Aqarav* (Ayn-Qof-Raysh--Vayt), where the Ayn (70) testifies that the process of creation has achieved its cycle. It therefore states that the cosmic Aleph, Qof, has permeated its universal container, Raysh, to the point of penetrating the archetype of all single containers, Vayt. Thus the name *'Aqarav* is formed as a completeness in which Meadim, whose abode it is (Meadim in unpointed Thallet), finds all the elements of wisdom. But beware! *'Aqarav,* that sign of perfection, is one of the most dangerous places to stop in. The dramatic opposition between the diagonals in the psychological part of the Zodiac (seen as the four eastern diagonals) and the physical side (the four western diagonals) can literally murder someone in Scorpio who receives its flow of energy before attaining the psychological ripeness required by *Meadim* (Mars, East).

Such a person would, as Abel (whose real Biblical name is Hevel, meaning vanity), be destroyed by the simple presence of Cain (whose name begins with Qof, the cosmic Aleph). Likewise, 'Aqarav, driving Qof into the body (Vayt) can be suicidal for those whose Meadim is not ready, psychologically, to receive it.

The following sign, *Qoshet*, whose three cosmic letters (Qof-Sheen-Tav) are so impressive, is actually formed by the female sex, Sammekh, and is, almost ironically, *Tsedeq* (Jupiter's) abode. In this sign *Tsedeq* is formed by the pointed Ghimel, indicating that it is resistant to its own residence. This residence also, with its fiery, cosmic Aleph, its active "Breath," Sheen, acting upon Tav, apparently contradicts its formative Sammekh. This sign, although diametrically opposed to Gemini (as seen in the Zodiac), is in conjunction with it. In the two preceding signs we saw the West-South of Libra opposed to the East-North of Aries, and the West-North of Scorpio opposed to the East-South of Taurus. Here in Sagittarius we see West-Top in combination with the East-Top of Gemini flowing towards Saturn. And the next sign, Capricorn, is flowing West-Bottom in alliance with Cancer's East-Bottom, towards Jupiter.

Sagittarius and Gemini have a quality in common: both force a choice. In Sagittarius, *Tsedeq* (Jupiter) with its structurising Tsadde and its resistant Dallet opposing their structures to Qof, paralyses it and does not allow it to carry its impulses through Sheen to Tav. (The inscription of Qoshet and Tsadde in the Zodiac is eloquent.)

An immature Jupiterian type will automatically usurp the power of Qof and introduce it into his female, psychological structures. He will be ambitious to attain the highest possible position comensurate with his capacities. If he can, he will become a king, an emperor, a high priest.

The mature psyche will cross the threshold and enter a new life with Capricorn, where the blessed *Shabatai* is alive.

With this, we re-enter the Zodiac through its fourth door, and in four steps complete the twelve steps around the Zodiac, back to Hay and Toleh.

Superficially, we can accomplish this by reading the formative letters in order: Ayn (70) forming Saturn opens every possibility; Tsadde (90) forming Aquarius destroys and builds structures; Qof (100) forming Pisces gives birth to the perfected man. They can also be read according to their names: *Ghedi* is a symbol of the birth of organic life; its Ghimel (3) originates a movement; its Dallet (4) is the response to it; its Yod (10) is the symbol of existence. Continuing, we see the same process in *Deli,* with its functions in inverted order: Dallet, the response, engenders Lammed (30), the 3 of Ghimel brought into actual existence, and then Yod again. Finally comes *Daghim* (Fishes) signifying proliferation of organic life.

Only adequately evolved psyches can enter these signs because *Shabatai,* living in *Ghedi,* is none other than "sanctification of the Seventh Day," a symbol whose realisation, considering the average state of human consciousness, is very far away. It is a state of endogenous life and action, a focusing of cosmic energy in unity and in its essential duality. We do not meet the living *Shabatai* on this route from the Sun to Sagittarius, but it comes suddenly, as an unseen world of unknown dimensions. Yet, in my experience, it can enter us after our psyches have freed themselves from time, as a one-way current flowing from past to future through the present.

When such freedom occurs, history appears as a gradually unfolding psychological projection, like a story unfolding as we read and turn the pages of a book: the whole story is already there.

Two of the three signs we are considering now must therefore be read along what I call the psychological direction, beyond Aries, to Pisces. Thus Pisces assumes the dimensions of a two-thousand-years-Era, said to have begun with the psychological event called "The Birth of Christ," and to be ending now with the coming of Aquarius. Just as Qof forming Pisces is an appropriate symbol for Jesus, Tsadde, forming Aquarius, is a symbol of perfect womanhood. (Abraham aged one hundred — Qof — and Sarah aged ninety — Tsadde — are the allegorical, fruitful human beings: they give birth to Isaac.)

Tsadde, forming our coming Era, is also, as we have seen, the symbol of all structures. *Deli* diametrically faces *Arieh*, the Sun's residence formed by the diagonal North-Top (Venus-Saturn), whereas its own diagonal is South-Top (Mercury-Saturn). Twelve thousand years of sensorial aspirations towards *Shabatai* to the activity of Mercury, the mythological messenger of the gods. Twelve thousand years of structures will fall to pieces, and with the gradual awakening of womanhood new structures will be allowed to build a new world. With the ending of Pisces the Scriptures are already fulfilled, although most people are unaware of it. Organised religions will have to re-discover the Sacred Fount of Knowledge, or else they will be more and more petrified. Their rituals will be adopted and accommodated more and more to the customs, creeds and superstitions of primitive communities. They will lose all their original significance.

Helped by the consent of Jupiter, the powerful drive of Pisces (diagonal Mercury-Jupiter) will force its way through the dead Saturn of Aquarius. It will be an era of great hopes, but of great strife, destruction and conflicts. The human or, rather, pre-human mass, as a result of proliferation where conditions are at their worst, will be in a state where it will be impossible to live, while the rich, technically highly evolved part of the world will destroy itself in all respects, so that its life also will become impossible.

Aquarius will be an Age of difficult transition before humanity really meets *Shabatai,* living in *Ghedi,* whose diagonal West-Bottom (Sun-Jupiter) will join its diametrical Cancer with its diagonal East-Bottom (Mars-Jupiter). Then, perhaps, the Cosmic Nuptials may be celebrated on Earth: either humanity will be worthy of such a blessing, or be in conditions more or less similar to those of the Deluge, or to some pre-historical glacial Era, with no one to witness it.

★

Readers who have followed my circuit, step by step, around the Yetsira's Zodiac will have realised that the first requirement is a knowledge of the original code of the Autiot. If one is not willing to go into it, heart and soul, *The Sepher Yetsira* and its Zodiac should be left alone. Many people toy with Astrology as an objective scale of references. There are even coin-in-the-slot machines which are supposed to give you your character.

It is essential to realise that this Zodiac deals with our innermost religious relationships to cosmic energy. We can verify it as we are our own best witnesses, by reading our own horoscope. It can be very useful.

Here is mine (12 May 1892) with *Kawkab* and *Tsedeq* in *Toleh*. When I consider seven dots on my photo-copy of the Zodiac — seven planets which happened to receive me at birth — in one all-embracing panorama, I see my whole life, as it was set out and as it completed its programme. I see why I was born and why at that particular place; why I had to wait so long for the unfoldment of an extremely difficult inner purpose. I see that I was able to pass successfully through the many tests that are called Initiations, because I was without fear or apprehension.

None of my Planets were in their residences. The Moon, having deserted its abode for the benefit of *Nogah,* had gone to *'Aqarav,* in exact opposition to the Sun which was occupying *Nogah's* place in Taurus. *Shabatai* in *Betolah* was pointed towards *Tsedeq,* in conjunction with the diametrically situated residence of *Tsedeq* in *Daghim,* while *Meadim* was waiting in *Deli* for the dawning of the new Era.

How could I not announce the second coming of the Rabbi called Jesus; how could I not be in that Coming, inside it, as it is already being enacted? If I am "programmed" to live my 84th year, the cycle will be complete, and I will either die or become "someone else" ($84 = 7 \times 12$) at my 84th birthday.

Thus I have verified the truth of that Zodiac to my satisfaction. Readers could have no better proof of the Zodiac than to let it testify to their own horoscopes. They will understand that it can and must reveal what is inaccessible to every other kind of astrology: the thorough and explicit investigation of a soul, its purpose or vacuity, its conquests or defeats, the meaning of a lifetime.

The reading of the Zodiac cannot be made externally, mechanically. It requires the reader to be qualified, just as a cleric is supposed to be qualified in matters of religion. But the astrologer in the Holy Qabala cannot receive that qualification from anybody. He must always keep in mind the ever-perfect command:

"This, above all; to thine own self be true."

14

Some Exercises in Reading

REPEATEDLY I have stated that the original code of the Autiot, as I have given it, is only an elementary approach to their study. In *The Cipher of Genesis* and *The Song of Songs* there are examples of how to read them, without any claim to have accounted for their total meanings. By now readers know that every Aut in any given equation is a symbol of an energising process that varies in direction and in intensity, according to the context. It comes practically to knowing what one is going to read before reading it.

In the same manner as in the two volumes mentioned above I will give a reading of the Zodiacal signs and Planets in relation to the Autiot which form them. I will then proceed with a reading of the seven Planets compared to the twelve Zodiacal signs, which is a necessary exercise when dealing with the ephemeris.

A SURVEY OF THE TWELVE ZODIACAL SIGNS IN TERMS OF ENERGY.

The First Four Signs, beginning with Aries

1° Hay (5), life, forms *Toleh*: (Aries) Tayt-Lammed-Hay.

From the zero of the Zodiac life, Hay confers on the primordial cell, Tayt (9), the Lammed (30) of the organic movement and life (Hay): *Toleh*. Here *Meadim* (Mars) is seen marked with pointed Dallet (4) which forms it, symbol of resistance, to become *Olet* (translated: madness). This last word, Aleph-Waw-Lammed-Tav indicates that Aleph rises, fertilises

Lammed, the organic movement with Waw, and projects Mars's resistance into the cosmic 400. This fantastic projection destroys all personal resistance to life: enough for anyone to be 'fixated'!

2° Waw (6) forms *Shaur* (Taurus): Sheen-Waw-Raysh.

The process born at the 1st sign is now present and amplified. *Shaur* is a new division: formed by male forces, Waw (6), it reveals the Sheen, or cosmic organic movement, actuated by the same Waw which fecundates the Raysh: that is, the entire cosmic container. The equation Shaur and Aur (light) are almost the same. Here Venus is *Hhan* (8.700), unresolved equation of the undifferentiated and the undetermined (what is "before" and "after" evolution?).

3° Zayn (7) forms *Teomaim* (Gemini)

The 7 of every possibility distinguishes this energy. *Teomaim* is composed of *Teo* with Aleph and of *Maim* (the Waters) with Yod. Here Mercury exercises its power of selection: it is *Shamama,* that is, *Sham* (the Name) with the addition of *Mah* (meaning "What?").

4° Hhayt (8) forms *Sartan* (Cancer):
Sammekh-Raysh-Tayt-Noun.

Biological development re-starts from the undifferentiated Hhayt. Female and feminine fertility, Sammekh (60), draws from the Raysh (cosmic 200) its primordial substance, Tayt (9), and engenders all the cosmic possibilities, Noun final (700) in the name Sartan. In this sign the Moon, *Lvanah* (30.2.50.5) is very alive. It gives rise to two poles of energy, burying itself in the ground and rising.

These first four signs of the Zodiac describe the stages of cosmic fecundation starting from the primitive cell; *Aries*: (Toleh 9.30.5) early organic life, its capacity to break the resistance of crystallisation. This resistance in Aries is personified by Mars, whose letters, *Meadim,* 40.1.4.10.40 express a resistance in which the rise of Aleph is forced to project itself in a repetitive but certainly living existence (10), incapable of evolving. Broken by the thrust of Aleph, Mars is projected into the cosmic-lunar 400. *Olet*, Aleph-Waw-Lammed-Tav (1.6.30. 400), translated "the madness" of Mars, is none other than the triumph of Aleph, fertilising the cosmic 400.

It is important to note that *Shaur*, the name for Taurus, begins with the cosmic 300 (or fecundation). In this house Venus in inert. It is made solely of undifferentiated substance, but its inner state Hhan (8.700), sets the unresolved equation of all forms of evolution, from the undifferentiated to the undetermined.

In Gemini selection comes into being: one current of energy takes the direction of involution towards the undifferentiated. Here we are exactly under the sign of 400 (the initial letter of *Teomaim*) where the previous sign has taken us. Gemini, being under the sign Zayn (7), all possible meanings are here possible, and Mercury in that house can gather up everything with both hands. It is active, being formed here by pointed Raysh.

In the fourth sign, Cancer is formed by Hhayt and is the abode of the Moon, formed by Tav (400). Tav is the sanctuary, the base of operations, for all cosmic energy. Tav, the last letter of the alphabet, is where the end and the beginning meet. Here the burying of energy in matter and its emergence coincide. The feminine is completely fertilised on all levels: the initial letter Sammekh (60) of Saturn (Cancer) proves it.

The Next Four Signs

5° The Tayt (9) forms *Arieh* (Leo): Aleph-Raysh-Yod-Hay.

At 1° we have seen Hay, life, form Tayt (9) with Toleh. Here at the sign 5° (Hay) the Tayt forms the Aleph. The name Arieh shows that the Aleph projected in the universe Raysh exists as Yod. This projection (the fundamental theme of the Qabala) is possible because the primordial cell, Tayt, engenders the Aleph. They are both alive, and hence the Hay and the Hhayt of *Hhamah* (the Sun) whose sign is Arieh. *Hhamah* here causes all the biological and conscious possibilities.

It is here that the primordial female gives birth to the in-temporal, to the principle, to this Aleph that in so many ways is deified. Sign of endogeneity, it is the balance of two lives, Hay and Hhayt, that express the Sun, *Hhamah* (Hhayt-Mem-Hay: 8.40.5). *Hhamah*, our source of energy, is twofold in its "house": it speeds up evolving organic life and also its drying up and destruction.

6° Yod (10) forms *Betolah* (Virgo):
Bayt-Tav-Waw-Lammed-Hay.

Manifestation (existence) of Yod (10) projected under the previous sign forms its container, Bayt. The name *Betolah* indicates that these containers become structurising energy with, as support, the Tav (cosmic) logical development of the previous sign. The container and the contents are both alive, just as Mercury bears witness (*Kawkab*: 20.6.20.2), magnified in its own sign and giving all its fruits here.

The name *Betolah* fully extant expresses parthenogenesis where its resistance becomes organic movement. Here Mercury, *Kawkab* formed by unpointed Raysh, strongly supports this process with its own magnification. Earth (in the Alchemical sense) produces all its grain, 'Zar (7.200.70). All possibilities have flourished. A cycle is completed.

7° Lammed (30) forms *Moznaim* (Libra):
Mem-Aleph-Zayn-Noun-Yod-Mem.

Lammed (30) is the symbol of organic movement. Here its affirmation of everything that exists is expressed by *Moznaim*'s first Aut (40). Following the previous sign this is an entirely living process. *Moznaim* is made of *Maim* (Waters) inside which is *Ozen*, the ear. (The capacity to hear is again submerged in the Primordial Waters.) In this sign *Nogah* (Venus) is active and lively, but consciousness is reflective and not yet an intelligent reflex. It is incapable of selecting which of all possibilities offered has the quality Ki'aur (20.10.70.6.200). Birth of myths: the unconscious has its own life.

8° Noun (30) forms *'Aqarav* (Scorpio): Ayn-Qof-Raysh-Vayt.

The half-awoken consciousness projects innumerable images. Manifested life (Noun) opens the way to all the possibles forming *'Aqarav* (70.100.200.2), Scorpio. This schema projects the image of the cosmic Aleph (Qof) into the manifested world and animates its contents (Bayt). This process actuates Mars which, here, is in its unpointed sign, The "Wisdom" of Mars, is earthly. Its name *Meadim,* when decoded, shows a particular condition of Aleph.

The Last Four

9° Sammekh (60) forms *Qoshet* (Sagittarius): Qof-Sheen-Tav.

The cosmic Aleph, Qof (100), is in this ninth sign, which is formed by the female Sammekh (60). The name *Qoshet* is cosmic and complete: 100 and 400 are connected by 300, the breath, completing the terrestrial female cycle. Here *Tsedeq* (Jupiter) equips a building to contain and represent the cosmic Qof. Does it not have the dual female-male realisations with 90 and 100 (Tsadde-Qof)? From this fact it acquires authority over spirits in the name of the Higher Powers it is thought to represent.

10° Ayn (70) forms *Ghedi* (Capricorn): Ghimel-Dallet-Yod.

The priestly myth of the previous sign has no connection with reality. Here reality resumes its rights through the Ayn (70) which safeguards all living possibilities. Structurising energy sets out again from zero with Ghimel (3) which asserts its living (Yod: 10) authority (Dallet: 4). Hence the name *Ghedi.* This sign *Shabatai* (Sheen-Bayt-Tav-Yod: 300.2.400.10) explains with Sheen and Tav that every kind of "container" (shell, measure or number) comes from the meeting of the cosmic 300 and 400. Here *Schabatai* becomes *Hhaim* (Hhayt-Yod-Yod-Mem: 8.10.10.40). It bears the twofold existence (Yod and Yod) of all organic life (container and germ).

11° Tsadde (90) forms *Deli* (Aquarius):
Dallet-Lammed-Yod-Ayn.

12° Qof (100) forms *Daghim* (Pisces)

Eleven is the number of going beyond oneself. Deli is formed by Tsadde (90), feminine perfection. Twelve is the number of Zodiacal completion: it is formed by the Qof (100). Aquarius, feminine, supports it with the 30 of Lammed (Deli: 4.30.10). Pisces is multiplicity in motion. Saturn dies (Mot) in Aquarius, just as the structures of evolution die one after the other. Jupiter is Shalom (at peace) in Pisces.

A General View of the Twelve Signs

In classical astrology the first six formations are below the horizon and the last six are above. This explains the fact that their formative numbers — Hay, Waw, Zayn, Hhayt, Tayt, Yod (5.6.7.8.9.10) in order — project life (Hay) into existence Yod (10), only at the 6th sign. They are therefore abstracts; no more than archetypes. Yod forms the sign of Virgo. In the habitat of the reflecting consciousness, Mercury's ability to think is the same as the ability of existence to be aware of itself as living on the wrong side of energy, and, therefore, to be aware of the right side: *YHWH*. Proceeding from there, Venus in Libra (which is formed of Lammed, the 30 of organic movement) is the initiator of the second cycle, in which conscious activity develops in the physical world until it is reborn in Ghedi.

At the end, at the 11th and 12th signs, the feminine and the masculine find schematic settings which do not put obstacles in the way of their emotional maturity. There they can fulfil themselves, and energy can resume its flight after passing through the weariness of all levels of human experience.

How the Seven Unpointed and Pointed Work

To re-discover the source of Revelation is to re-discover the source of its language. Semantics and linguistics are to be found there. Like everything living, the development of a language is a process having the same pattern as all structuration. We will now approach this pattern with the formative triad of the first three Planets named by *The Sepher Yetsira*: *Shabatai, Tsedeq, Meadim,* which occupy the upper half of the Zodiac.

It is imperative to think in the abstract here, in pursuance of the fundamental theorem of the Qabala: in so far as every phenomenon is considered as a particular instance of the play of the One living energy and is analogous to every other phenomenon in a similar place of structuration, controlled in a parallel manner.

The Sepher Yetsira places man at the centre of phenomena; it puts the Planets in space; their "contrary qualities" are two opposite directions. One can imagine that for each astrological topic the aspect of the triad *Schabatai-Tsedeq-Meadim* in control of their non-pointed formatives should prescribe the course of the subject in his position in the graph of his evolution.

1st Stage: Vayt-Bayt (2) *form Shabatai,* which in *Ghedi,* marks the beginning of a new formation.

We have seen the reasons: *Ghedi* (in Hebrew, kid: hence, "Capricorn") is formed by Ayn (70), the number of every activated possibility. Here independent life resumes its rights, following the dead-end of the Jupiterian dogmatism of Sagittarius. *Ghedi* is an equation (3.4.10) indicating a birth: it is an archetype of organic movement (3) in an archetype of living (10) resistance (4). Amidst this catalyst unpointed Vayt (2) forms *Shabatai* alive which, as we have seen, shows by 300.2. 400.10 that every formation, however minute it may be, is a cosmic occurrence: every "container" is an impact between 300 and 400. Here *Shabatai* being Hhaim (8.10.10.40), has a dual existence, two Yod, risen from the undifferentiated Hhayt. Hhayt-Yod makes Hhai live. Yod-Mem makes Ym, the sea. In Deli, *Shabatai* formed by the resistant Bayt, blends with the resistant Dallet (4) of *Deli* and dies.

2nd Stage: Djimel (3) forms *Tsedeq*, non-pointed in *Daghim*. In this sign *Tsedeq* is a movement, a proliferation drawing its substance from the Primordial Waters, which begets 40 indefinitely. (*Dag*, fish: *Ym*, the sea; *Daghim* 4.3.10.40). Here the 4 and the 3 are reversed in relation to Ghedi: existence is assured.

Tsedeq (90.4.100), formed by *Djimel* (3) in *Daghim* (4.3. 10.40), which in turn is formed by Qof (100), summarises the abstract conception of a human being, which follows from *Genesis* and *The Sepher Yetsira*.

In fact, the numbers of the name Tsedeq express both feminine and masculine perfection, resulting from the movement of Djimel-Ghimel (3). But does this perfection ever occur? By asserting itself with pointed Ghimel in Sagittarius Jupiter blocks human evolution.

3rd Stage: Thallet-Dallet (4) form Meadim which expresses in its two signs, Scorpio and Aries, man undergoing and realising, or not, his mutation. It is a formation where contradictions existing together must, and can, be caused to coincide. In fact, the name *'Aqarav* (Scorpio: 70.100.200.2) shows the 70 with the cosmic 100 and 200 converging on the 2, the individual "container" (the ego, the "myself" of consciousness), which always tends to prove itself and ascribe the universe to itself ("I am the truth, the life, etc."). Besides, the occupant of this sign is *Meadim* which seizes Aleph and Adam in its equation and holds them between Mem and Mem. A mere nothing separates it from the Jupiterian Sagittarius . . . would not the completed man, the initiated who is fully alive, the Jupiterian destroyer of forms and illusions, know how to take a back seat in *Meadim's* acquired nudity? *Meadim*, from the cell in *Toleh* (Aries) onwards, has never ceased to oppose its resistance to life, with increasing hardness. This "folly",

Olet, projects it into the repository, Tav (400), of universal life. In Scorpio it acquires humble wisdom, *Hhokmah* (8.20.40.5), which consists in knowing things according to their names in the hierarchy of structures.

The particular importance of the triad *Schabatai-Tsedeq-Meadim* for the "man-in-the-cube" is obvious: the flow of energy from top (*Schabatai*) to bottom (*Tsedeq*) passes through his entire body, from head to foot. And I have explained at length the meaning of the East (*Meadim*). Yet the significance of this triad needs to be plumbed, in respect to the general context of the Qabala, and to *Genesis*.

According to the traditional translations the Sun and Moon were created on the fourth "day," Yom Rabi'i. However, we know, as is explained in *The Cipher of Genesis*, that Yom (Yod-Waw-Mem) is the projection of *Aur* (light) into existence (Aleph-Waw-Raysh). Aur, expresses the fertilisation of Raysh, its cosmic container, by Aleph. In other words, the infinite energy of Aleph imparts to our universe the greatest speed of which it is capable; that is, the speed of light. As to the number Rabi'i (200.2.10.70.10), it is a "reply" by two Yod of two sources of energy: the Sun (outer), the Moon (inner) that animates man.

How is it that we cannot remember that *Schabatai* in the 5th Sephira, is blessed with two seals by Yod-Hayt-Waw? How is it that this prodigious energy is not recognised to be monopolising its sign, *Ghedi*, a new life, whose common elements are movement, resistance and existence? Why is the evidence that *Ghedi* is formed by 70 not recognised? Lastly, why is it not seen that *Shabatai* is here Hhaim?

In the coded sacred language everything lends itself to deep and endless meditation. How obvious it is that the names of Roman gods, derived from the Greeks, are inadequate for describing the Planets. This terminology only makes discoveries difficult.

On moving from *Ghedi* to *Deli* the method of formation confirms its viability: from 3.4.10 it becomes 4.30.10. The archetype 3 comes into existence (30) in the structurising force of 4.

The formative number of *Deli* is Tsadde (90), the completion of the feminine. Here *Shabatai* fulfils itself in *Mot* (Mem-Waw-Tav), translated "death." It is Tav's return to maximum powerfulness (400), total resistance to life, the sanctuary and tabernacle of universal life: fertilising death, ambivalent death, life-death of resurrection.

Tsedeq, the second Planet, is complete, finished (*Schalom*) in *Daghim,* the following sign, whose formative number is Qof (100). The name *Tsedeq* 90.4.100, is the very symbol of ambivalence. In Hebrew *Tsedeq* is Justice; in mythological language it is Jupiter. Neither of these two allegories fits with the hermaphrodite who represents the profound purpose of the aim, or the fusion of the sexes.

After the exalted beginning in *Shabatai* and the bottom reached in *Tsedeq, Meadim* (Mem-Aleph-Dallet-Yod-Mem) brings the extraordinary pattern of the whole of human existence. In it the Aleph (of Adam) is seen still immersed in the Waters (between two Mem) which engender him. There Aleph, who now appears in the Zodiac, is held back, blocked, entangled in a thick resistant network in Aries and acquires intelligence and wisdom in Scorpio.

This distressing situation is, as for all the Planets, in two contradictory signs. Here, in fact, the contradiction is none other than *Meadim* itself, because man, Adam is within its Autiot.

The other four planets are allocated thus: a binomial on the level of tens, Khaf and Kaf: 20 form *Hhamah,* the Sun; Phay and Pay (80) form *Nogah,* Venus; a binomial on the level of hundreds, Raysh and Raysh, 200, form *Kawkab,* Mercury; Thav and Tav (400) form *Lvanah,* the Moon. The Sun and the Moon have only one sign each for housing their "contrary qualities." The Sun, *Hhamah,* is, in current Hebrew, *Shemesh.* These two names have the same meaning.

Kawkab and *Lvanah* revive the whole initial theme of the cosmic sphere: the universe's reply to the breath which animates it. *Kawkab* unpointed is Zar' (7.200.70): it produces all seed corn. Let us remember that in its name, 20.6.20.2, two states of being, 20 and 20, fertilise one another.

In a final abstraction this achievement reaches perfection in *Lvanah*, where Thav and Tav are reunited. There the deeply hidden energy and its arising as a result of primordial substance, resumes the fundamental theme of the Qabala. This has given rise to a death and resurrection of a deity, a mythological conception that reflects the idea that life perpetually dies and is re-born. Here, to those "who search, who see, who study thoroughly, who understand, who map out, who group ideas, who carve their way, and who erect with their hands" is shown the endogenous nature of the universe.

The Pointed Seven: A Survey

When they are pointed, each of the seven doubles finishes its own trajectory. There they are not subject to a common structural cycle: they undergo it, being the very elements which sustain the cycle.

1) Pointed Bayt is *Shabatai*'s "death" in *Daghim,* in the sense in which it is said that "If the seed does not die . . . or the shell is broken at the birth of a chick." Of this nature is the fruitful death of *Shabatai.*

2) With pointed Ghimel *Tsedeq* rises in *Qashot* to the highest degree of the hierarchy. Powerful and rich its personal evolution ends here. Of this nature is *Tsedeq*'s arrested movement.

3) Formed by pointed Dallet, *Meadim* in *Toleh* takes leave of its senses from the impact of the magnified solar shock. This "brainstorm" sends it into the cosmic 400. Such is *Meadim*'s return to the cosmos.

4) Pointed Kaf forming *Hhamah* in *Arieh* expresses all human possibilities. Is it necessary to allude to what men make of Kaf, their activity?

5) Formed by pointed Pay, *Nogah* imagining itself to be awake, projects so many vivid myths from its dreams and cannot extricate itself from them. Of such is the imagery where Pay comes to nothing.

6 and 7) In *Teomaim, Kawkab,* formed by pointed Raysh, projects *Shemamah*: the Sheen of the eternal breath in the sub-soil (Mem and Mem) of matter: such must the intellect achieve through Raysh.

In *Sartan, Lvanah,* formed by Tav, hides living energy in the furthest limit of the passive hardening, whose resurrection depends upon man's accomplishment.

In conclusion, let us recall that the twelve signs of the Zodiac are named in threes by their initials, while the twelve simples which form them are named in pairs: Hay-Waw, Zayn-Hhayt, Tayt-Yod, Lammed-Noun, Sammekh-Ayn, Tsadde-Qof. These connect the Zodiac's twelve by pairs.

7 × 12 = 84 Possible Conjunctions

Seven Planets and twelve Zodiacal Signs. We will consider the Planets as sources of impersonal energies and the Zodiacal Signs as their active environment. Then we will compare the name of every planet with the name of every sign, all read according to the code, and we will consider how a given energy can respond to a given dwelling: what, for instance, happens to an energy called Sheen-Bayt-Tav-Yod (*Shabatai*) when happening to be inside a container described as Ghimmel-Dallet-Yod (*Ghedi*). For the sake of readers who are not familiar with the Autiot we will write all their names phonetically. To check our conclusions they would have to be reestablished in their original Hebrew.

1° *Vayt-Bayt form Shabatai*

In *Ghedi Shabatai* is *Hhaim*. The equation *Ghedi* places the elements 3,4,10 in their simple state of life. In this sign *Shabatai* drives the individual to work hard, both internally and externally. Its Sheen (300) and its Tav (400) on either side

537

of Bayt, try to confer a double animation on it (with the two
Yod of Hhaim) by causing *Hhayt* to arise from its unconsciousness.

In *Deli Shabatai* is *Mot*. What is usually translated as "the
death" of *Shabatai* in *Deli* (and *Mot* in general) is the transfer
of physical Mem (40) to cosmic Tav (400). In this sign *Shabatai* opens unknown worlds that attract the individual and tend
to make him lose his balance. By a succession of jumps through
space, going from 40 to 400, the individual dies to himself, or
at least, to the sense of his own reality. By the Dallet (4) of *Deli*
and its organic Lammed (30), the individual can react against
this current, but it requires an extreme effort.

In *Daghim Shabatai* is washed away in the moving waters
(Im), or in the organic movement of Ghimel (3). Following
his "death" in the previous sign, the individual, like Jonah in
the whale, is busy here recording his death.

In *Toleh Shabatai* acts on the Tayt (9) of the living cell,
which offers no resistance, and therefore does not lead it anywhere. Whether this sign is, or is not occupied by its "owner,"
Meadim, Shabatai spreads all its energy in this unpolished,
organic movement.

In *Shaur Shabatai* finds an analogous setting: Sheen for
Sheen, Waw for Bayt, Raysh for Tav. The Bayt of *Shabatai*,
as well as its Tav (2 and 400) give consistency and resistance
to the Waw and to the Raysh of Shaur, stabilising them, so to
say, in a solid container. The conjunction of the two Sheen
afford deep meditation.

In *Teomaim Shabatai* is, as we have seen, in a setting where
Aleph and Yod live together characterised by separate identi-
ties. Aleph comes out of its Tav sanctuary, and its fruitfulness
(Waw) meets Maim, Waters in whose depths is Yod. *Shabatai*,
being precisely the "reply" of Tav and Yod to Sheen, the
breath of Aleph, is here the catalyst. The individual is faced
with having to blend two different directions.

In *Sartan Shabatai* is in a sign which follows from the
separation of two currents of energy. The two first letters of

Sartan, Sammekh-Raysh (60.200) indicate a structuring, fertilised feminine in the cosmic 200. The last two letters, Tayt-Noun final (9.700), restore energy to the level of the cell where all cosmic possibilities are but potentialities, without predetermined solutions. The energy which is completely liberated by *Shabatai* vitalises the course of the two opposite currents and does not divert them. It is known that they lead to "the contrary qualities" of Lvanah, emergence and burial. Here the individual can master the two above-mentioned different directions.

In *Arieh Shabatai* is confronted with the burial, and the emergence of energy which were becoming visible with the previous sign. Here they are fully worked out. Aleph hides in Raysh; Yod-Hay, living existence, emerges. In Hebrew Yah is the divine name. In the sign *Arieh,* Aleph-Raysh-Yod-Hay, *Shabatai* brings a flicker of consciousness because its Sheen (300), identified with Breath, is the very functioning of Aleph. By externalising Yod, *Shabatai* adds the power of Yod-Hay-Yod to the Yod-Hay of *Arieh,* making *Yahi,* which can be translated as "I am."

In *Betolah Shabatai* strengthens and lightens the character of this sign, by doubling the Bayt-Tav elements of its name. By these elements *Betolah* (the "virgin") follows the previous sign: Bayt ("House," the "container," the "I" of condensed consciousness), coming in contact with the cosmic Tav (400), has the sensation of being "a virgin" energy giving birth to its own activity, Waw, Lammed, Hay. By supporting this conception with its Sheen, *Shabatai* can introduce the idea that this very variegated "I" is an immortal soul, a divine spark, etc., and when centred on the personal qualities of Betolah can be a diligent and analytical scholar.

In *Meoznaim Shabatai* is in course of becoming a consciousness which, according to the previous sign, becomes further and further immersed in matter. *Moznaim* means "balance" in Hebrew, and, in fact, in this sign, the individual tends to weigh everything. It includes the Zayn (7) of all possibilities and the Noun (50) of external life, in *Maim,* the Primordial Waters. For it, life is a biological phenomenon. *Shabatai* brings it to a cosmic vision and incites it to leave its mode of thought.

In *'Aqarav Shabatai* intervenes to safeguard the scintillating qualities of this sign. *'Aqarav* means "Scorpio" in Hebrew. Its 'Ayn (70) and its Qof (100) can destroy an individual who is too fixed in his ways and habits. Rav or Reb, with which the name ends, have several meanings in Hebrew. *Shabatai* can confer the name of Reb (Rabbi) on it, by means of its cosmic vitality, and introduce the individual to the intemporal of life-death, without fearing life or death.

In *Qoshet Shabatai,* having gone all round the Zodiac, spreads out the cosmic numbers of this sign marvellously well (100.300.400). (In Hebrew *Qoshet* is rainbow rather than bowman: a light that the individual likes to share.)

In the following pages, as I have already analysed the structure of the Zodiacal signs, I will restrict myself to pointing out concisely   some of the characteristics of their conjunctions with the different Planets.

2° Djimmel-Ghimel form Tsedeq

In *Daghim Tsedeq* is *Shalom.* It destroys the psychological crystallisations maintaining the "Imaginary I" and the conflicts engendered by it.

In *Toleh Tsedeq* offers the prospect of a life that is still very primitive: its virtual perfections look idealistic, without much judgment.

In *Shaur Tsedeq* finds an excellent ground for expanding a successful ambivalence. Sheen fertilising Raysh in *Shaur* acquires a refined sensuality, a relaxed and pleasant femininity.

In *Teomaim Tsedeq* acts upon that contrasting sign with Tsadde and its cosmic Aleph, Qof. It fertilises the Waters (*Maim*) if the Tav does not drown in them (Teomaim is dangerous in that respect.) There can be a transfiguration of the feminine Waters.

In *Sartan Tsedeq* provides this feminine sign with the

awakening it needs in order to develop its undetermined equation: Tayt-Noun final (9.700).

In *Arieh* *Tsedeq* restores their cosmic meaning to the hidden Aleph and the subjective Yah: the ego can be transcended.

In *Betolah* *Tsedeq* introduces into this feminine and analytical sign the cosmic elements which discern its vanity. If the individual yields, *Betolah* can, in a constructive sense, develop its final Lammed-Hay in a material world.

In *Meoznaim* *Tsedeq* can make its stabilising voice audible. Do not let us forget that if *Moznaim* balances, weighs and measures, it is because this sign which is immersed in the Waters listens with attention (Ozen=ear). *Tsedeq* brings to that sign what this consciousness is searching for.

In *'Aqarav* *Tsedeq* is carried away by the scintillating dynamism of this sign, because of their joint Qof (100). Nevertheless, this sign is open, by the first letter of its name, Ayn, to all possibilities, so that *Tsedeq* can show it a feminine side (psychic) which it did not suspect.

In *Qoshet* *Tsedeq* finds the best setting for its material triumph. Its Qof final is extended into the initial Qof of Qoshet, which gives it, through Sheen and Tav, the feeling of having been chosen for a divine mission. Its feminine, blossoming through the Tsadde (90) of *Tsedeq,* is no more than a sumptuous religious display of ceremonies.

In *Ghedi* *Tsedeq,* the Planet of completed maturity, finds itself foreign to this sign of a beginning. Only their Dallet (4), archetype of resistance, common to both, couples them.

In *Deli* *Tsedeq* is found in a sign formed by Tsadde (90), the initial of its own name, symbol of the completed feminine (mould). The effect of *Tsedeq* in *Deli* depends upon the quality, the potentiality and especially the maturity of the individual. Almost always, it goes beyond him and remains unrealised as he loses his balance under the power of his passions. *Tsedeq,* in this sign, can help the individual to find his balance between obsolete crumbling structures and new ones yet to be found.

3° Thallet-Dallet form Meadim

In *'Aqarav Meadim* is Hhokmah; the conditioned man finds his personal realisation in this sign. He is Hhokmah (8.20.40.5), that is to say, his subconscious (8) comes into view, enters fully into existence (20) and tries to resolve all kinds of problems (Mah: what?). In fact, *'Aqarav* opens all possibilities to him (Ayn: 70) and, by Qof (100), permits the Aleph captive in him to have access to the Universal. *Meadim's* awakening, however, does not change its nature, which can be summed up in the one word: resistance. It impounds Raysh and Vayt, the outcome of *'Aqarav,* in a "house." *Meadim* claims to know itself and gains positive confidence.

In *Qoshet Meadim,* for the very reason that its force of resistance holds Aleph and maintains its life, is ready to receive the impact of the cosmic energies of Qoshet (100.300.400) as a personal message. In this conjunction the individual feels that he is chosen, that he has a spiritual mission, that "The Truth" is in him.

In *Ghedi Meadim* brings an echo of the Adamic vocation into the material world.

In *Deli Meadim* dwells in a sign whose formative Tsadde is almost always only a latent potentiality. Here the individual is active but outside the concrete. *Meadim* shows him a glimpse of the difficulty of realising complete manhood.

In *Daghim Meadim* introduces difficulties due to the formative Qof of *Daghim* (100). Human conflicts represented by *Meadim* increase uselessly.

In *Toleh Meadim* is Olet from its hardening that occurs in this sign. It breaths its cosmic resistance into an embryonic consciousness.

In *Shaur Meadim* introduces conflicts where apparently there were none. Remember that *Shaur* is a materialised projection of *Aur,* the light.

In *Teomaim Meadim* introduces increasing difficulties into

542

a sign torn, like itself, between Aleph and the Waters: they are hard to bear without sympathisers.

In *Sartan* Meadim adds to the confusion in this contradictory sign where the passivity of Sammekh collides with the indetermination of Noun final.

In *Arieh* Meadim introduces into the ego which this sign affirms, the essence of the conflict of energies which is the very self.

In *Betolah* Meadim finds, wrongly or rightly, a sense of being parthenogenetic. *Meadim* is an ill-received stranger, judged to be dangerous, whom the individual prefers to ignore for ever.

In *Meoznaim* Meadim finds a sign both very close to it but inconsistent with Zayn-Noun in the position of its Dallet. These two schemas want to fuse, but collide: believing they understand one another, they contradict themselves.

4° Khaf-Kaf form Hhamah

Hhamah the Sun, concentrates and projects the triadic energies constituting man: *Shabatai, Tsedeq, Meadim.*

In *Arieh* Hhamah is both 'Osser and 'Oni. Its dual life (Hhayt, undifferentiated and Hay, evolutionary) express themselves in this sign where the ego establishes itself in every possible way, both in the universal Sheen-Raysh and in the contingent, repetitive Noun-Yod.

In *Betolah* Hhamah vitalises the two opposite energies: Aleph-Zayn-Noun and Maim, where Aleph is detained, increasing the physical Mem in such a way that if the individual does not reach maturity, the Aleph's summons can become the desperate cry of the person interned within.

In *Meoznaim* Hhamah vitalises the two opposed energies: Aleph.Zayn.Noun and Maim, where Aleph is drowning. If the person lacks maturity and emphasises the Mem, the call of Aleph can be a desperate cry for freedom.

In *'Aqarav* Hhamah increases the vitality of this powerful

sign whose schema shows that it retains the 70, the 100 and the 200 in its Vayt, its 2, its individuality. If this stresses its egocentricity, it directs it towards the physical Mem, which makes problems for it.

In *Qoshet Hhamah,* in its physical powerfulness and in its influence over vital spirits, sees proof that a special blessing is granted to it by the three cosmic letters: Qof, Sheen, Tav. A steadfast peace is conferred on it.

In *Ghedi, Deli* and *Daghim, Hhamah* can allow the individual to attain a flourishing physical and psychic vitality, depending on his maturity.

In *Toleh Hhamah* can only throw a light on this sign in which the cell is born and grows.

In *Shaur Hhamah* illuminates both the Sheen and the Raysh, and allows this sign to blossom, unless the Mem of *Hhamah* causes it to drop down into values which are too materialistic.

In *Teomaim Hhamah* particularly vitalises the second half of this sign, for it brings a third Mem, strongly framed by Hhayt and Hay, to *Maim* (the Waters), inciting a liberating, trinitarian movement in the physical world, sometimes too swift for the Aleph of *Teomaim* to know how to behave.

In *Sartan Hhamah* could give meaning to the Noun final (700) whose irresoluteness confuses the Sammekh, the Raysh and especially the Tayt (9) of *Sartan*. The Tayt, checked in front of the 700, can and only wishes to muse on it, but *Hhamah* is able to quicken it and ultimately bring it a revelation.

5° *Phay-Pay form Nogah*

In *Shaur* what can *Nogah* do when its organic life is Hhan (8.700), that is, unconscious, and when it is immersed in the dynamism of *Shaur?* What can a very sensual person do in a world that projects cosmic pleasures upon the human individual?

In *Teomaim Nogah* introduces an organic unity into this

sign, a movement common to *Teo* and *Maim,* a perception uniting and establishing them in a conscious sensitivity.

In *Sartan Nogah* comes upon the feminine Sammekh and Tayt facing the enigma posed by the final Noun (700). From its affinity with its animating feminine and organic movement, it can be a wonderful element of relationship. In such a case, the cosmic meaning of Nature's beauty can be revealed to *Sartan.*

In *Arieh Nogah* is in direct contact with the ego. The latter, which does not stop transforming the Aleph in Yod, transfers its sensuality to the external world, just as it transfers the intemporal to the wizardry of forms.

In *Betolah Nogah* brings a new element: the full life of its Noun (50). Furthermore, its Waw-Ghimel-Hay combines with the Waw-Lammed-Hay of *Betolah.* This intense organic movement allows the sign to attain the revelation foreshadowed in the sign *Sartan.* It is at a deeper level.

In *Meoznaim Nogah* acts, as in all spheres where energy has two aspects, as an organic and physical connecting agent. The scope and depth of this harmony depends upon the individual's degree of maturity.

In *'Aqarav Nogah* is not at the same level of intensity as that sphere. There is no fusion, no synthesis here. At one time, *Nogah* plunges the individual into ordinary sexuality; at another time, *'Aqarav,* detaching itself from the world of sensuality will, almost in spite of itself, find a life in higher worlds.

In *Qoshet Nogah* is not torn about, as in the previous sign, by the egocentric needs of the individual. Although *Nogah* and *Qoshet* are on very different levels, they both are impersonal. On meeting, these two facets of energy should know each other and recognise themselves. In duration *Nogah,* the sensory psyche, has slowly woven the structure of intelligence. By Sheen, *Qoshet* projects, at a stroke, the scintillating Qof into the cosmic tabernacle of Tav. If the faculties of the individual are adequate, this encounter can be stupendous.

In *Ghedi, Deli* and *Daghim, Nogah* has no story of her own.

She puts the emphasis on physical life, not on evolution and consciousness, except perhaps in *Deli*.

In *Toleh Nogah* develops the cell Tayt (9). Its female characteristic becomes busy.

6° Raysh-Raysh form Kawkab

It is important to note that Raysh (200) forms *Kawkab* (20.60.20.2). This repetition of 2 — once in hundreds, twice in tens joined with the copulative Waw, once alone — makes *Kawkab* one of the most significant Planets. This 2, Bayt, on all levels, calls to mind the text of *The Sepher Yetsira*: "Everything with Bayt and Bayt with everything." We have already seen its connections with *YHWH*. (The twelve signs deserve a study of their development which I cannot give here.)

In *Betolah Kawkab* comes upon both the cosmic 400 (Bayt-Tav) and an organic movement (Lammed-Hay). Its intelligent and wholly earthy perception sees its cosmic significance and becomes active.

In *Meoznaim Kawkab* is the very agent of *YHWH*. Khaf-Waw-Khaf is the actualisation of Hay-Waw-Hay. Here the individual, deep within himself, can find his "second birth."

In *'Aqarav Kawkab* having explored everything intelligently, transfers the exalted cosmic energy to its personal profit (everything ends in Bayt).

In *Qoshet Kawkab* finds no quest for personal profit. The cosmic "Wind at large" rests freely upon an unconventional, awoken mind.

In *Ghedi, Deli* and *Daghim, Kawkab* awards these signs the "breath of life," granted to man in *Genesis*.

In *Toleh Kawkab* meets Tayt (9), which should be able to struggle with it, opposing its desire to lead a purely functional existence. But the strongly structured intelligence of *Kawkab* prevents this.

In *Shaur Kawkab* co-ordinates the physical and cerebral activities of this sign and shows, by the deeper penetration of matter by intelligence, that truth is neither metaphysical nor supernatural.

In *Teomaim Kawkab* makes the two facets of this twinned sign very lively: in the very core of *Teomaim* it incites an intense dialogue.

In *Sartan Kawkab* is within a sign that starts from solid data (Sammekh, Raysh) and does not know how to rebind them either by its Tayt or by its Noun final. It extends the horizon, sometimes too far for an individual who is not mature enough for it.

In *Arieh Kawkab* enlivens both the Aleph and the Yod of this sign. Perception of vital current. Vast magnification of "The Cosmic Game," which will make the individual depend upon his own individuality. (Mythologically, Mercury, here, meets the Sun and carries the fiery torch.)

7° *Thav-Tav form Lvanah*

It is interesting to note that Tav, the last letter of the Alphabet, forms the Moon (the whiteness) as the 7th mentioned Planet (resting inside the individual in the spacial cube).

In *Sartan Lvanah* is both *'Abadot* and *Memshelah*.

In this sign (Cancer) we have seen both the burying of cosmic energy in the undifferentiated world and its rising in the undetermined. Here the end is in the beginning and the beginning in the end. Here all the transfigurations of the feminine can begin.

In *Arieh Lvanah* expresses the numbers of its equation, 30.2.50.5. There we see an organic movement (30), secure in its container (2), gifted with a dual life, existential by 50 and archetypal by 5. This feminine "marries" the masculine, *Arieh,* letter by letter: Lammed adds itself to Aleph, Bayt to Raysh, Noun to Yod, and the two Hay build upon an abstract elation that triumphs over everything. This is a remarkable combination.

In *Betolah Lvanah* is found in a sign which by reason of its functional, analytical character, resembles it unduly. It does not find the catalyst which it needs.

In *Meoznaim Lvanah* is in a sign which expresses expectation: it listens (*Ozen*) in the Waters (*Maim*) hoping to catch a revelation. But it only fails to begin moving. *Lvanah* brings it this organic movement.

In *'Aqarav Lvanah* is in a sign we know as the master of 70,100 and 200, which it succeeds in capturing. Master of all possibilities? Master of the fulgurance of cosmic Aleph? Yes, it is powerful enough to be dangerous. The great organic power of *Lvanah* confers on it the maximum strength which it is capable of possessing: life and death are here very close.

In *Qoshet Lvanah* can give this sign the organic movement which will take it to its own great horizons.

In *Ghedi Lvanah* can grant only an increased organic activity to this rudimentary sign, thus supporting its formative letter Ayn (70).

In *Deli Lvanah* supports the formative letter Tsadde (90) in search of new structures.

In *Daghim Lvanah* supports the scintillating formative letter, Qof (100), of this sign, in the way that a searchlight reveals the abundance of underwater life. It is creative.

In *Toleh Lvanah* establishes its connections with this sign as an adult with a child which resembles it. *Lvanah* shapes and directs Toleh, being fully susceptible to its freshness.

In *Shaur Lvanah* is in a sign which expresses, in a simple, direct and total manner, the Sheen (300) bound in the Raysh (200) by the copulative sign Waw (6). In the Gnostic vision these "Marriages" are well known assumptions. But people whose level of evolution does not permit this transposition are sunk into the ground by Shaur. Here the intervention of *Lvanah* gives them the femininity and the sensitivity which they lack.

In *Teomaim Lvanah* gives both parts of this dual sign an organic movement that strongly activates them.

SOME EXERCISES IN READING

Note

It is important to know that the eighty-four conjunctions of Planets and signs have a meaning totally different from that which they have when, in the complete chart of a person, they appear as foreign, unaccepted elements, unintegrated in the ascendant. Tentatively, I wanted to give elementary exercises and not to enforce interpretations. In reading cases one must take account of the formative Autiot of the signs (The Twelve Simples), because the twelve formatives are joined two by two, and when a Planet is not in its sign, which is nearly always the case, one must know how to discern if it is pointed, or non-pointed. The comparison of the Planet-Signs equations is only part of the problem. What is important is to consider the Planets as sources of energies leading sometimes to evolution, sometimes to involution. It is at that moment — in these "contrary qualities" — that a person who understands the subject intelligently is free to intervene.† A Planet can act where the sign happens to be and "solve" it in its setting. The extraordinary creative freedom disclosed to the individual by an intelligent reading of *The Sepher Yetsira* is, in my judgment, a valuable contribution of this book.

> † "There is a tide in the affairs of men
> Which, taken at the flood, leads on to fortune;
> Omitted, all the voyage of their life
> Is bound to shallows and in miseries.
> On such a full sea are we now afloat;
> And we must take the current when it serves,
> Or lose our ventures."
>
> (From Shakespeare's *Julius Caesar*)